Writing in Style

Edited by Laura Longley Babb
Washington Post Writers Group

Distributed by
HOUGHTON MIFFLIN/BOSTON
Atlanta   Dallas   Geneva, Ill.   Hopewell, N.J.   Palo Alto   London

Washington Post Writers Group:
William B. Dickinson Jr., Editorial Director
Laura Longley Babb, Associate Editor/Books

A Big, Big Man by Nicholas von Hoffman. Reprinted by permission of King Features.

Printed in the United States of America.

Library of Congress Catalog Card Number: 75-18547

Washington Post Company ISBN: 0-88475-004-3

Cover design by John Twohey/Photograph by Charles Del Vecchio

Book design by David Legge and John Twohey

A Washington Novel That Buttons It All Down

By Ward Just

At Their Feet

By Sally Quinn

A Circus Star Rises

By Richard L. Coe

Red, White (Collar) and Blue Patriotic Culprits

By Art Buchwald

Capitol Punishment

This is Style.

It's a section of the *Washington Post* that covers people, the arts, leisure, consumer affairs, books, entertainment, fashion, food, home design, gardening, travel, television, social and cultural trends.

To crusty news pros and crusty readers, all that used to be known as "soft news." Anything which wasn't war, crime or natural disaster. But most of those critics have come to realize that even hard news has a human dimension.

That human dimension is the focus of *Writing in Style*.

Because that's been our focus in this book, we've sadly had to leave out some exceptional consumer reportage, travel articles, arts criticism, and other forms from the section. Then, too, there were the realities of budget and paper.

Two notes: First, the copy appears here as it appeared in the paper, although we'll admit to cleaning up several deadline typos.

Second, the reader will find, besides the introduction to the book, brief introductions to the chapters and to several articles. All these were written by Style managing editor Lon Tuck, who edited many of the stories. Those are his initials at the end.

Thanks for time, thought, and generous assistance must go to Tuck and to Tom Kendrick, Style's editor. Also very helpful were the writers and editors of Style, William Dickinson Jr. of the Washington Post Writers Group, and, on the production and design, David Legge and John Twohey.

We are using a casebook approach in *Writing in Style* which will be used in future books in this series. And although we don't mean to set up the *Washington Post* as some kind of paragon, we do feel there's value in casebooks by working journalists, books that deal with the shortcomings as well as the strengths of a large daily newspaper.

Such an approach, we feel, will provide useful reading for students of journalism. This idea has been reviewed and supported by journalism teachers around the country. We would like to also thank these teachers for providing us with helpful suggestions as we prepared *Writing in Style*.

—Laura Longley Babb
June 1975

Contents

Introduction

By Thomas R. Kendrick

Scene: *On the walls, a Wishbone Ash rock poster and Garry Trudeau cartoon panel, Cicely Tyson and Liz Ashley glossies. On the desk, a Congressional Directory, Diplomatic List and Strunk's Elements of Style. A mock Time cover depicting Henry Luce impaled on cross with spears. Centrex phone, IBM Selectric and Sony color TV. Engravers' cuts and proofs of LBJ, Dylan and Midge Decter. A framed print, in blue tones, of a unicorn . . . the office of the Editor of Style.*

Two editors are talking with Emily Ann Fisher, 22, out of Bloomfield Hills, Mich., and Harvard, Phi Beta Kappa. Former editorial chairman of the Harvard Crimson *and now* Washington Post *reporter-intern. (Application said: "No previous newspaper experience. I began writing for the* Crimson *three years ago as film critic and soon branched out to experiment with other forms of journalism, news editorials, features, interviews, 'New Journalism.'") She exits, saying: "I think I see what the problem is. It's using the personal freedom I came here for in a way that's fair to the people I write about. It's just that I'm not sure where the lines are."*

Door closes on the two editors, one with a visible headache and twelve six-ply takes of heavily penciled copy. First: "I keep thinking of that song about riding a diesel rig to New Orleans . . . 'Freedom's just another word for nothin' left to lose.'" Second: "Yeah, Janis Joplin sang it. And she died of an overdose."

Memo to Emily:

Yes. Well, Emily, it was five years ago that Joplin died in that motel room and, some say, closed an era. And it's been more than a dozen since Tom Wolfe, that point man and theorist of the big-N-big-J, says he first opened up a copy of *Esquire,* read a story by Gay Talese called "Joe Louis: The King as a Middle-aged Man" and wondered "what inna namea christ is this" as he recognized the "tone and mood of a short story."

Wolfe says he got it (the new nonfiction) together himself the next year, though some of us know better, when he suffered writer's block on deadline one night and turned in a 49-page memo on California's custom car culture. The editors, with a rare perception that has been damned and envied by their colleagues ever since, moved Wolfe's name to the lead take — and out, unscathed, came the "The Kandy-Kolored Tangerine-Flake Streamline Baby." Vrrroooooom. Instant art?

Maybe. Maybe not. One certainty is that the old feature formula of a grabber lead, a lively if unfocused anecdote or two, direct quotes and a good kicker was abruptly exposed as curiously obsolescent, unable to cope with the cultural change and revival of individualism that was rolling across the country. That tide rose so high and fast in the '60s that daily journalism often foundered in its task of forging patterns from the chaotic data spewing out of newsroom teletypes.

Perhaps instinctively, journalists knew old forms were too rigid, too restrictive to capture such multiplicity and breadth of change. Some joined and many more were swept up in a search for fresh approaches that would let them get in touch with and translate what was *really* happening.

That search began with the adoption of writing techniques previously associated with realistic fiction, quickly moved into explorations of "subjective reality" and, despite sharp protests, expanded to advocacy and participation in events and issues. Both defenders of literary tradition and of journalism's basic tenet—that the reporter is a neutral ("objective") conduit for information readers use to make their own moral judgments—scrambled to the ramparts and braced for the final charge of the Visigoths.

It never came. But the controversy—there never was too much rational discussion—effectively confused those lines that you, Emily, and a lot of your colleagues are still trying to pin down.

The main elements of that controversy remain with us but most of the words on the subject, and there have been reams, are now coming from professors in academe rather than practitioners in the field.

What this means quite simply is that the "New Journalism"—as cause or doctrine—has joined the New Frontier and the New Criticism on, to use Wolfe's phrase, "the garbage barge of history."

So be it. Your demand for perspective becomes both reasonable and timely. And this collection of stories has much to say, in terms of form and subject matter, about the ground Style's editors and writers have explored daily in the past few years: problems encountered, lessons learned, compass points marked for the future.

First, there are no fixed lines; like the rest of our culture, journalism is in flux. Still, this is a less turbulent time than the decade past, one with an emphasis on evolution, on assimilation, on sorting out techniques and approaches that help build credibility from those that damage.

Second, there never was a "New Journalism" in the sense of a phenomenon without literary and journalistic antecedents. There were scores from Daniel Defoe to H. L. Mencken, Ernest Hemingway to John O'Hara. But there definitely was, and is, a "New Journalism" in terms of the numbers of journalists influenced by its various facets, the breadth and intensity of their assault on traditional conventions of "objectivity."

Third, "New Journalism" was a dangerously imprecise term used to yoke two often disparate strains—"literary," to which Style subscribes, and "advocacy," which Style rejects in most forms—under a convenient umbrella that confused public and press alike. The only real link was the *personal* imprint of the writer-reporter.

Wolfe, one may forget, speaks emphatically for the traditional values and rigors of accurate reportage and dispassionate analysis. What's new, he insists, is essentially *technical*. It's the application of literary devices formerly associated with the novel or short story to the recording of facts—literal versus fictional realism. Wolfe found it "weird" to be lumped with a New Left advocacy journalist like Jack Newfield. Ultimately, Newfield returned the compliment, declaring that there was no such thing as "New Journalism," that Wolfe was interested only in "the flow of fashion" and had "the social conscience of an ant."

So let's forget categories and just concede that there were about as many definitions of "new" journalism as there were writers whose personal approaches brought them public recognition.

W̲hat then does Style stand for in its pursuit of *personal* journalism?

Style's focus is squarely on the human dimension, a dimension that somehow got cut wafer-thin in the who-what-when-where-why formula that seemed nearly computer programmed by the early '60s. Now, as these stories document, Style writers are striving to gather facts without excising their human context, freeze-drying their emotional impact. They try to make contact with the private individual behind the public image; to, as Michael Kernan says: "get the snapshot of Jack Benny trying to buy a bow tie in Minneapolis, patiently coping with the salesman's dumb jokes about his stinginess, rather sweetly resigned to living in a world of doubletakes."

And in the same vein, they try to cut through to the reality behind the institutional stereotypes of a Mardi Gras or a Republican Convention; to identify and record changing sex roles or family attitudes in terms of specific people and their experiences.

In its task of chronicling people and social change, Style has sought to draw distinctions within personal journalism. Generally, it encourages stylistic and conceptual freedom for its writers while balking when the line is crossed to advocacy. That is, a writer's individual perception of, and imprint on, a story is accepted, even demanded—unless or until it betrays attitudes or opinions that make it difficult for readers to form their own judgments.

The problem, of course, involves the precise limits of that perception, what the writer selects in—and out. Do the editor and ultimately the reader have enough raw data for a valid evaluation, or are they unwittingly drawing from a stacked deck?

It's not a new problem, even if the critics of personal journalism would have us believe so, and it can't be solved by conventions. Few people argue anymore that "objectivity" was insured by enshrinement in rigid forms. In fact, that rigidity has often reduced rather than enhanced a reader's abilities to understand events, judge people and issues. A false image of neutrality is easily projected with formula use of on-the-one-hand, on-the-other-hand story structure and the use of alternate adversary quotes in equal measure. Conventions like these can be and have been used by biased or just plain lazy editors and reporters to give the illusion of fairness, the appearance of balance, not the reality.

It's obvious that no writer presents a mirror reflection of an event or individual, but refracts what he or she sees and hears through the lens of personal experience. This isn't news either, even if the advocates of a more subjective journalism would have us believe so. Neither is it necessarily justification for pulling a Norman Mailer and telling all about your personal biases and ego hangups to insure the reader has adequate *context* for interpreting your article.

In the end, stories will be only as fair, balanced, honest as their reporters and editors want them to be. Recognizing the problems of depicting people and events impartially is in no sense an excuse for abandoning the effort to do so. That effort continues to define the mainstream of American journalism, acutely dependent on its source of credibility.

Style's writers demonstrate in the following pages a strong interest in sophisticated literary techniques: scene-by-scene story construction, extended dialogue, evocative detail and scores of other devices to achieve a mood and tone that may reveal far more about the quality and character of people and events than a chronicling of statements and actions.

These techniques may be borrowed from realistic fiction and Style writers employ them here creatively, imaginatively. But techniques neither imply nor impose any compromise with fictional license. They are just tools to better depict reality, to convey the experience of being there, to extract the person from the image.

No matter what devices are used, the journalist is forever tethered to verifiable — albeit *selected* — facts, facts that the fiction writer can ignore or transform. Good journalism has always been an arduous selective process and what Style seeks, essentially, is to mesh traditional reporting disciplines of research, accuracy, moral objectivity and clear thinking with a new freedom of literary expression.

Style, and its writers, make no claim to having invented new journalistic forms. What distinguishes Style, in this sense, is not the techniques themselves, but the breadth and intensity with which they have been applied in *daily* print. Daily newspapers are not magazines, the primary source of all previous anthologies of "new" journalism and the forum where most of its prominent exponents have fled, pleading strictures of time and length.

Style writers want to extend the range and impact of daily journalism, to make it more flexible, more innovative. But decisions to experiment carry serious risks, even for talented writers and experienced reporters. Stories included here, fine as they are, provide clues to what can happen under the pressures of newspaper space and deadlines: a blur in focus or loss of context, a tired adjective or strained simile, a rough transition or absent fact, a simple error or slip to bias.

Many of these stories were written and reported in a day, a few were written in less than an hour, portions of several were dictated from notes on deadline. None involved more than a week of reporting, editing, re-write.

They should be evaluated not as literature but as journalism with all its inherent strengths and faults. They carry both the bite of immediacy and deadline warts, the punch of individual perception and flaws exposed by time's perspective. Still, they hold up — proof that risks are worth taking, daily.

Style's Origins

It may be tough now that the turbulence of the '60s has faded to the rim of nostalgia for you, Emily, at 22, to see what the fuss kicked off by the new non-fiction was all about.

But listen to Wolfe in a chapter titled "Seizing the Power" from his combination manifesto and aesthetic, *The New Journalism* (1973):

"The Sixties was one of the most extraordinary decades in American history in terms of manners and morals. Manners and morals *were* the history of the Sixties. A hundred years from now when historians write about the 1960s in America (always assuming, to paraphrase Céline, that the Chinese will still give a damn about American history), they won't write about it as the decade of the war in Vietnam or of space exploration or of political assassinations . . . but as the decade when manners and morals, styles of living, attitudes toward the world changed the country more crucially than any political events . . . all the changes that were labeled, however clumsily, with such tags as 'the generation gap,' 'the counter culture,' 'black consciousness,' 'sexual permissiveness,' 'the death of God,' . . . the abandonment of proprieties, pieties, decorums connoted by 'go-go funds,' 'fast money,' swinger groovy hippie drop-out pop Beatles Andy Baby Jane Bernie Huey Eldridge LSD marathon encounter stone underground rip-off . . . This whole side of American life that gushed forth when postwar American affluence finally blew the lid off . . ."

Now we've learned that Wolfe can get a bit superheated in his prose and views. He certainly gives short shrift to the historical impact of science, war, assassination and racial conflict. Nevertheless, the words fit with those of *American Review* editor Theodore Solotaroff who suggests succinctly that "the Sixties have . . . been the most cataclysmic decade since that of the Civil War."

Conceived in 1968, Style and its writers, their concepts and subject matter, reflect that era's massive assault on established conventions of every sort.

Style's birth meant extinction for a section called "News For and About Women"—a logo that had become as anachronistic as much of what it covered; absorption of several wary arts critics toiling in the back pages of Metro; an infusion of "general assignment" writers. From the beginning, Style staffers sought to forge much more from that volatile merger of disparate elements than old goods in a new package. They went after people, seeking to offer a sort of antidote to news patterns that seemed to be squeezing out humanity in favor of governmental actions. And they used those people to explore the changing role of women, the expansion of leisure time, the exploding interest in arts; to chart the leading edge of a torrent of social change—sexual attitudes and family structure, drug use and rock music, all the challenges implicit in a movement labeled "counter culture."

All that '60s tumult seemed to overload the circuits of traditional fiction writers and journalists alike. Many withdrew, or stood aside and flailed ineffectively. It was this vacuum that made new approaches both necessary and possible. Style did its share of flailing too, and suffered some fallout: staff departures, bitter arguments (there were about as many definitions of what Style "ought to do" as there were staff writers and editors). It was a time of trial and, often, error.

Yes, there was a mighty fuss, and it's only now subsiding.

You will find echoes of that hectic time in the pages ahead. But the origins of personal, literary and realistic journalism go back much further: centuries in English annals to Defoe and James Boswell in the 1700s, William Hazlitt and Mark Twain in the 1800s, Theodore Dreiser, Sinclair Lewis, John Dos Passos, John Hersey, James Agee and many more in recent decades. The point remains: the techniques have been used before, but never so intensively in daily print.

Style's Audience and Techniques

Newspapers are aimed at a mass audience and to a certain extent content does shape style, both upper and lower case. In one of the most recent and best commentaries on the subject, *The Reporter as Artist: A Look at the New Journalism Controversy,* Professor Ronald Weber argues "that what the rise of the New Journalism mostly signifies is the emergence of a new kind of popular literature, and that it's on this level, the level of reflecting new trends in popular culture, that acclaim and denial might best be offered.

"The mass audience it seeks is not the old middlebrow audience but the large and growing liberally-educated population that has been through the required surveys of literature yet holds fast to the national fascination with fact. It's an audience that wants to know what's going on, that feels compelled to Keep Up, but prefers its information — if it has to read to get it — dispatched entertainingly and with familiar literary trimmings. Information plus art . . . an up-to-date factual fiction that leaps over the dreariness of day-to-day journalism yet doesn't fly off in the strange ways of Barth and Borges and Barthelme . . . rather like [a best selling novel] in other words, except that it's *true*, every last detail . . ."

There's truth in what Weber says. But the limits he implies are too restrictive. The techniques used to explore current trends (Jeannette Smyth's "Role Reversal à Go Go") can be extended to pierce old institutions and cliches (as Sally Quinn does with Mardi Gras and the Kentucky Derby and Henry Mitchell does with a Washington dinner party and a Tarawa veterans' reunion); they can be used to make revelatory contact with the obscure and the famous, with trivial and historic events.

An exploration of the literary techniques used by Style writers quickly reveals that they are often — but not always — more effective when woven together. Dialogue and detail are made integral parts of scene construction. Mimesis and rhythm of sentence structure all work together to give a gut sense of being present, of watching and hearing live people. The usual viewpoint, nevertheless, remains third person, which helps to keep a writer "outside," minimizing the connecting role a reporter plays between subject and reader.

Scene-by-scene construction is an alternative to the simple historical narrative and considerably more difficult. It requires the capture of isolated moments that, examined in detail, can yield an expressionistic montage or composite that conveys the mood and feel — the *experience* — of an event. It takes time and perception, and it is highly selective.

Sally Quinn's "diary" of *(more)*'s first convention is only superficially chronological; the diary is really just a device for recording revealing scenes. There is a close analogy to movie photography — closeups, long shots, quick cuts. Jeannette Smyth, in her account of Joe Hirshhorn at the dedication of an art museum bearing his name, literally follows a documentary crew filming the scene. Watching them work, she repeats *"Focus"* four times to the reader and captures the essential Hirshhorn in as many quick takes . . . of print. In his portrait of Sen. Charles Mathias, Michael Kernan uses similar italic snapshots to counterpoint his story and distill a lawmaker's working day.

S tyle writers frequently use dialogue as an alternative to standard quotation because such natural interaction offers spontaneous character revelation. Sometimes the dialogue is solicited, sometimes it is overheard, sometimes (as in Quinn's portraits of Alice Roosevelt Longworth and Rudolf Nureyev) it includes the reporter and sometimes not. Dialogue is a focal point for individual scenes in many stories in this anthology. The analogy this time is to the tape recorder and, again, selectivity is the key. The distillation process is not unlike that used by Hemingway, or more currently, Thomas McGuane, to make a fictional conversation more "real" than any actual transcript.

As for mimesis and prose rhythms, consider the "literary" and "Southern" ambiance invoked by Henry Mitchell, a master of matching style to subject, in his portrait of Eudora Welty at home in Mississippi. Or the mock British control, precise phrasing and clipped upper-class tone he applies so dryly to an Embassy children's show. Manipulation of syntax shows in the military cadence of Henry Allen's record of his return to Parris Island boot camp and the counter-culture language of his visit to Ken Kesey's Oregon farm 10 years after *The Electric Kool-Aid Acid Test.* Quinn, Savannah born, neatly clears the difficult hurdle of dialect in her Alabama interview with Big Ruby. Kernan subtly mimics the "New Journalism" itself before asking former newspaperman Ward Just why he bailed out to write fiction.

The parallels with the militant street tone of San Francisco's slums that Wolfe used in *Mau-Mauing the Flak Catchers* and the precious Park Avenue language of *Radical Chic* are obvious. So are they in Style writers' constant use of evocative detail, a device Wolfe calls "status" detail and feels is both the most important and least understood realistic technique.

"This," he says in *The New Journalism,* "is the recording of everyday gestures, habits, manners, customs, styles of furniture, clothing, decoration, styles of traveling, eating, keeping house, modes of behaving toward children, servants, superiors, inferiors, peers, plus the various looks, glances, poses, styles of walking and other symbolic details that might exist within a scene. Symbolic of what? Symbolic, generally, of people's *status* life, using that term in the broad sense of the entire pattern of behavior and possessions through which people express their position in the world or what they think it is or what they hope it to be. The recording of such details is not mere embroidery in prose. It lies as close to the center of the power of realism as any other device in literature."

That may well be right. And it's not just a matter of recording Adidas sneakers and Gucci loafers, whether the dress is by Halston, Villager or Jonathan Logan, whether the Jack Daniel's label is black or green. Evocative detail isn't limited to those current status symbols and subculture artifacts that most concern Wolfe. It can be used across the board to make old and new institutions, events, people come alive.

Specific details establish live contact between subject and reader in a few short words. They allow readers to plug in the context of their own experiences; they are stimuli evoking larger pictures, computer signals unlocking personal data banks. These concrete particulars can extend journalistic credibility by providing the reader "eyewitness" observation rather than reconstituted pap filtered through police or PR men. They convey the smell, feel, sight and sound of being there.

If the possibilities of literary devices are myriad, so are the pitfalls. Handling these sorts of facts, like statistics, is tricky. They can be mere stereotype labels that jeopardize credibility; they may be vital or irrelevant, building blocks for impartiality or intentional and accidental bias. Given 60 details, which 15 are to be incorporated into the story? What dialogue, what scenes are to be accepted, and deleted? Time or space may be inadequate for the task attempted, research or legwork too scanty.

Then, as Herbert Gold notes, we now are seeing a lot of Wolfean leads that trail off into standard interviews and "description for description's sake, endless Salems and Winstons being smoked, legs continually crossed or uncrossed, glasses pushed up on the forehead. We are reading a lot more about the sky and the trees and the grass without really knowing why . . ." Personal style can become, as the good Wolfe knows, eccentricity without literary or functional merit, just irritating or monotonous. Technique can mean style without substance, more interest in alliteration than accuracy.

The defenses against all this, Emily, rest primarily on the factual selection process and how you—and your editors—define it. That demands care, fairness and restraint: awareness that "creative" distortion exacts payments in credibility; recognition of the ambiguities of reality; willingness to seek fresh perceptions rather than fill in preconceptions; the wisdom to remain detached and resist moral evaluations of right and wrong; acknowledgement that the refracting prism in your head needs constant checking for perceptual warp; acceptance that the "punch of actuality" is enough, that it needs no amplification.

Tough tasks. Unlikely to be accomplished perfectly on daily deadline. But essentially no different from those that reporters and editors have always faced.

And perhaps a bit easier now that the traditional desk-reporter adversary relationship is relaxing. During the chaotic '60s, desks became foxholes with embattled editors often defending the trappings as well as the substance of old formulas. Frustrated reporters fired volleys that often confused style and advocacy. Today, confrontation of a productive sort continues to insure checks and balances. But there is a new openness to fresh approaches and solving problems of time and space.

Both sides have come to realize that the room for literary techniques must be paid for with more short articles if Style is to meet other coverage responsibilities. Emphasis has been placed on the example, the individual, the illustrative phenomenon in broad cultural trends—tacit recognition that Style often lacks the resources to thoroughly explore more than the microcosm. National or regional context may be inserted in personal journalism in digest form. (That data is likely to have been extracted from a government, foundation or university research project; and it may well have been printed earlier in Style, at greater length in a more conventional format.)

Style's coverage has many aspects unrepresented in this book. A critical one is consumer information ranging from the arts to food and fashion, information best offered in spare, lucid prose. Here, literary devices can be irrelevant, counterproductive. Another aspect is individual viewpoint, critical commentary on the arts or political opinion. Style has retained the traditional forms of column and review. Besides preserving valid newspaper functions, such categories help isolate the first person viewpoint and ego factor that many editors and readers regard as a dangerous virus when encountered elsewhere in the paper.

The personal and literary journalism collected in this book comes only from the Style section but the form is practiced with distinction, if less frequently, elsewhere in the *Post*. Scene and people stories are a consistent element of Sports, Metro and National coverage, often providing "sidebar" insight into Page One "hard news" accounts. Meg Greenfield and Colman McCarthy periodically infuse the Editorial Page with a warm humanity. The *Post*'s Sunday magazine, *Potomac*, is a frequent showcase for examples of the genre.

Future Directions

Pressing further experimentation in the literary techniques of social realism, Emily, are the thousands of degree holders like yourself (AB Anglo-American History and Literature) who have poured into a profession that used to be called a trade.

They have been taught to question, to test rules for viability. They've pruned a lot of dead limbs off that journalistic oak, variety *objective observer*, and aerated its roots. But if they've established that a good reporter may or may not be a good writer, they haven't established the reverse. That is, credible journalism demands that excellent writers be excellent reporters, because it binds the two functions to the common denominator of fact. And *that* fact, no matter how some people try to stretch it, forever divides journalism from art.

This isn't to say that there's not a lot of art in the personal style, techniques and structure of the stories in this anthology. It's simply that they must be acknowledged as hybrid. Using art forms to extend journalism is one matter, using facts to make art is another.

Literary interest can lead to shaky ground like "composite characterization," the melding of attributes of several persons into one representative character. Or "interior monologue," the alleged recording of people's thoughts, which Wolfe and Talese believe is feasible with "saturation" reporting. Maybe. This remains territory where Style declines to tread. How do you really do it? We know that people sometimes tell you they are thinking something other than what is really in their minds, that they often have several thoughts concurrently. No, taking a reader inside somebody's head seems to necessarily involve a creative step across a line—the most important line you need to know, Emily—from fact to fiction. And it is precisely there that journalism becomes most vulnerable to attack as both second-rate reportage and second-rate art.

Dwight Macdonald, Wolfe's arch critic, is contemptuous of what he calls "parajournalism," declaring acidly that it is a "bastard form, having it both ways, exploiting the factual authority of journalism and the atmospheric license of fiction. Entertainment is the aim of its producers, and the hope of its consumers."

It can be only that, of course. But like many hybrids, literary journalism can provide new—and quite legitimate—strength and vitality when carefully tended. There is nothing inherently wrong in "exploiting the factual authority of journalism" and no necessity to take license with fact. And there is no reason that much information cannot be conveyed entertainingly; indeed it may have to be if newspapers are to survive.

But more than entertainment is involved when talented writers make real contact with people and cultural phenomena. Their stories fill a need for readers who feel out of touch, isolated in an era that threatens their perception of reality with its pace and scope of change. Print can pin the fleeting TV image, connect it to experience.

There are many routes, as different as those employed by Hunter Thompson and Gay Talese or Style's Tom Donnelly and Sally Quinn.

Wolfe may call to mind pyrotechnics, but those who worked beside him in the *Washington Post* newsroom 15 years ago know he also understands the "tedious . . . tiring . . . humiliating" requirements of reporting. They remember a gifted and modest colleague who valued facts while trying to present them in fresh guise to a blind desk. And they know the Kandy-Kolored Baby was not the product of one night.

One may demur when Jack Newfield calls participation and advocacy the "touchstones" of new journalism, but not when he later decides "the New Journalism does not exist," that it is a "false category" embracing a dozen different styles and that "it all comes down to good writing, and hard work, and clear thinking."

So, Emily, there is no new journalism, just changing journalism with lines that must be constantly realigned as you and Style go along. Rules *do* need testing. And what the best stories in the next pages reflect, in essence, are proven disciplines enclosed in fresh forms—a quest for grace with precision, a search for live contacts with live people.

People, always. Your colleague Michael Kernan, now on sabbatical leave in London, sends along this codicil:

"The strength of Style, I think, is that whatever its shortcomings, it always has clung like a ferret to the one attribute all our heterogeneous readers have in common: they're people. And people will always read about people."

—June 1975

I. Cultural Currents

All the stories in this volume were written for the Post's *Style section during the 1970s. And in most the perspective of the 1970s is crucial; they are stories of our society in the aftermath of the decade when, according to Tom Wolfe, "manners and morals, styles of living, attitudes toward the world changed the country more crucially than any political events."*

This first of five chapters consists of stories that deal specifically with developments new to the '70s. Some events extended the changes of the '60s, as in the first two pieces on journalists in high profile. Others, such as the interview with Ken Kesey as a reclusive farmer and the downbeat look at London after the swinging '60s, show a society pausing for breath after all the turbulence. — Lon Tuck

Next: (more) Convention

"When a personal friend [of a journalist] becomes a public man a predicament soon arrives in which friendships and professional duty are at odds."
— Walter Lippmann, 1936.

In that column, Lippmann was writing about the necessity for political writers to keep their distance from politicians. If that is a "predicament," what about the situation several decades later in which journalists themselves increasingly are public people (both in print and on TV) and thus are the subjects of reports they make on each other?

In that sense, the two-day (more) convention of 1972 was a sort of milestone. Writers, reporters and editors convened the way lawyers or morticians do, and were covered by the media. It was intended as an anti-establishment counter-convention—writer rather than editor oriented—and ended up dominated by "New Journalists," especially those of the advocacy sort.

There were two ways to cover the convention. One was the fragmented hard news approach—"Gore Vidal declared bitingly to Norman Mailer at an acerbic (more) convention seminar last night that . . ." Another was to record the parts as they went along, then review them at the end with the hope that the whole would add up to a perception more important than the sum of its parts.

Sally Quinn sensed that the more significant story there was in the risks to journalistic credibility for the high-profile participants and chose the latter approach. The assignment was particularly difficult because (1) she was writing for and about her peers; (2) she was writing an extended essay on deadline, a much more complex challenge than a hard news story; and (3) she was on the way to being one of those high visibility writers herself.

Faced with Lippmann's "predicament," she was true to her perceptions and wrote an honest, unflattering story. Instead of being the advertised "journalistic Woodstock," it was for many an ego trip that exposed the suppressed exhibitionism of many participants. Some came away more damaged than enlightened and her account did not make her more popular (soon after, Mailer called her "poison Quinn").

This snapshot diary, with its clipped, dispassionate tone and its flexibility in range of subject and mood in limited space, may not be the definitive word on the journalist as star. But it stands as an early warning of the even greater post-Watergate dimensions of the problem. —L. T.

Journalism's New Nation

By Sally Quinn

NEW YORK—For days it had been talked up as the Woodstock of journalism.

Several weeks ago (*more*), the iconoclastic New York City journalism review, sent invitations to thousands of journalists around the country. They read: "Twelve years ago, the late A. J. Liebling, then *The New Yorker*'s press critic, wrote: 'The (American Newspaper Publishers Association) convention reaches here at the same season as the Ringling Brothers and Barnum and Bailey Circus. . . . Like the big show, the convention always bears a certain resemblance to its predecessors. . . .' If you're tired of circuses come to: the A. J. Liebling Counter-Convention."

While the publishers were meeting at the Waldorf-Astoria, the counter-convention was to be on the Far West Side at the Martin Luther King Labor Center, open to the public, free of charge, seated on a first-come, first-served basis—audience participation welcomed at all panels.

"We wanted it to be as proletarian as possible," explained (*more*) publisher William Woodward III.

Saturday

To celebrate the beginning of the convention, a party was planned for 9 p.m. at Nathan's Famous, Times Square, with hot dogs and beer at $3.50 per person and Jimmy Breslin as the speaker.

Unfortunately, Nathan's went on strike—and of course no good Newspaper Guild member would cross the picket lines.

The next thought was the ballroom of the Royal Manhattan Hotel.

But the Irish were picketing there.

Finally, the Sun Luck West Chinese Restaurant down the street was settled on, with its little bridge and trickling pond, tinsel, and paper dragons.

"How come they're having the party in this ritzy place?" asked one guest. "I thought this was supposed to be a convention for the people?"

Gay Talese was there. Studs Terkel, David Halberstam, Murray Kempton. So were several hundred lesser bylines—even Amanda Burden—all of them studiously underdressed. Some hid in red leather booths, but most angled for conspicuous positions in the center of the room when they weren't squeezed in, byline to byline, at the bar fighting for drinks.

Breslin balanced himself uncomfortably on one of the tables to keynote the convention.

"We're right and everyone else stinks," he deadpanned. "While [William] Buckley is over at the Waldorf speaking to all those publishers with money, I'm stuck here B.S.'ing to you." It was a nice, secure feeling.

Sunday

The first session was not to begin until noon, but everyone arrived late. Crowds (nearly 2,000 attended each day's sessions) milled around in the lobby of the labor center trying to get a handle on the situation before it began. Coats and ties returned the inquisitive stares of blue jeans and raggedy jackets. The trouble with bylines is that there are usually no faces to match.

Still, there were many who passed up the chance to get good seats just to remain exposed just a little longer in the lobby. There were few blacks, as Breslin had pointed out the night before, even though many, it seems, had been invited.

"We really tried to do this whole thing in the most unelitist way," said convention co-chairman Nora Ephron. "But no matter what we did, we managed to offend someone."

Some of the counter-conventioneers were exhausted and rumpled by long road trips from California, Arizona, Colorado, Canada; one even came from Hawaii. There were hundreds of journalism students and scattered emissaries from small-town Midwestern newspapers who had come to see the media celebrities in their New York ego center and if what they aspired to was really all that hot. Some had brought their babies, their tape recorders, their suitcases, their lunch pails, their clips.

The first panel was the big draw—Gay Talese, Gail Sheehy, Tom Wolfe, Calvin Trillin, Pauline Kael, Renata Adler, and Benjamin DeMott—all gathered to talk about themselves and "the new journalism."

That's where it was at, anyway. Deny it as they might, the new (personal) journalism was the only reason this whole thing ever took place. Could you see a convention taking place among the "old (objective) journalists?" New journalism had created celebrities out of writers and put them on the Dick Cavett Show and made covering personalities as important as covering issues. "We had to read all your articles for our journalism class, Mr. Wolfe," said a young man from the audience.

All the women new journalists wore skirts and the men new journalists wore coats and ties and most of them denied being new journalists, and talked seriously about their own work and each other's, not always in complimentary terms. A couple of people mentioned how Tolstoy was a new journalist and Tom Wolfe was comparing his works, *Electric Kool-Aid Acid Test; Kandy-Kolored Tangerine Flake Streamline Baby; Radical*

3

Chic (Mau-Mauing the Flak Catchers) to Balzac and Dickens when a colorfully dressed, long-haired, underground press group marched up to the stage, passed out flyers to the panelists and the audience, complaining "F----- again" and demanded seats on the panels.

The floor was then open to questions, which turned out to be mostly rhetorical statements from people who had never had an audience or a microphone before in their lives. This problem persisted throughout the convention. The star of the questioners was a consumer woman named Fran Lee who is famous for her tireless crusade against dog excrement. "You're all pimps and prostitutes up there on that stage," she declared.

During this time there was another panel going on entitled "Democracy in the Newsroom." That's what the discussion was about and as one distinguished reporter noted afterward, "If that's what's going to be running my newsroom, I'll settle for the editors I've got."

During lunch the counter-conventioneers patronized the continuously open bar, socialized, re-uned, made contacts, looked for jobs, talked to publishers soliciting authors, discussed the declining number of literary outlets.

The afternoon saw "Covering the Campaign: The Wayward Press Bus," with a panel of established political reporters and the newly added Tom Forcade, projects coordinator of the Underground Press Syndicate.

While the panelists, including Dan Rather, Martin Nolan, and Jeff Greenfield, tried to talk about how to cover a campaign honestly, Forcade, in halting, indistinguishable phrases, lost his audience and his anti-establishment credibility in a feeble, tedious boast that he had been barred from the White House.

Sunday night was the panel everyone had been waiting for. Charlotte Curtis of the *New York Times* was to moderate six famous people telling "How They Cover Me."

"This is the only panel where we didn't offend anyone," said Nora Ephron. "Every famous person in the world was asked to be on this panel and refused."

They were: Joey Gallo. "He was supposed to be our surprise mystery guest," said Nora. "Marta Orbach, who arranged it, made us promise not to tell a soul because they might come here and shoot him." Hugh Hefner was asked, Henry Kissinger, Tom Seaver, Dalton Trumbo, Alger Hiss, Henry Fonda, Shirley MacLaine, Dick Gregory, John Lennon, Bob Dylan, Melina Mercouri, and Daniel Ellsberg.

The final panel was Gore Vidal, Abbie Hoffman, Otto Preminger, Marvin Miller, who represented the baseball players in their recent strike, Rep. Bella Abzug and actor Tony Randall.

Each one began with a statement, then answered questions.

TV cameras and lights were blindingly bright and the room was so crowded people were sitting on the stage, the floor and each other.

It started with Otto Preminger who, in a deep, gutteral accent, told the audience, "I don't want to sound like Agnew but the trouble with most movie critics is that they hate movies."

Bella thought it was good to get together in a "counter-establishment meeting like this." She also felt less charismatic people should get more play.

Gore Vidal had a few testy words about the *New York Times* and reporting in general. "There is a trivialization in our press and everything is personalities. The only publications worth reading are the *New York Review of Books* and *Screw* magazine."

Abbie Hoffman was the only one on the panel who spoke directly to the subject. He read a story he had compiled from errors in clips on him collected over a year. "Six-feet two-inch, blue-eyed blond, millionaire Hoffman . . ." read the short, dark-haired Hoffman. He then passed out copies of his income tax returns proving he was not a millionaire, and named off the respected journals who had contributed to his list of errors.

Jerry Rubin, in a blue net shirt, and Tom Forcade, in his white suit and panama hat, ascended the stage and announced, in the name of the Zippie Party ("Z comes after Y as in Yippie, this is the natural progression") their support for George McGovern.

In less than two minutes.

There were shouts of applause and cries of despair from the largely pro-McGovern audience.

Monday

Surprisingly, the crowd was as large as it was Sunday. The bar was doing a steady business, the Tom Wicker lunch was sold out.

In a panel entitled "Why Journalists Leave Daily Newspapers," David Halberstam, after two hours, finally answered the question.

"I wanted more pay, a longer time to work on stories, respect for my copy and better editors."

The questioners got insulting. "We don't give a s--- if you guys left the newspapers or not," said one brave soul.

"Yes, we do," said another. "The only reason we're all here is that one day we want to be on that panel up there."

*New York Times*man Tom Wicker was the main luncheon speaker. After a picnic lunch of cold chicken and potato salad, he told his colleagues in a very few words what was needed in journalism reform.

"What our work needs is to let its vitality and honesty and ability come through," he said. "We must let a hundred flowers bloom . . . We must be set free to do our best work."

Wicker went on to say that all styles of journalism could be effective in the pursuit of truth and that journalists should be given the "freedom" to employ whichever they felt suited them best, without being suffocated by restrictive conventions, old or new.

He wisely refrained from having a question-answer period.

After lunch the panel "Racism, Sexism, Elitism and Journalism" was predictable. Racism and sexism dominated.

"Should There Be a Women's Page?" was orderly, if a bit dull.

The highlight of the "Alternative Media" panel was when somebody got squirted with a water pistol.

At 8 p.m. the first A. J. Liebling Award was made to I. F. Stone. In a loud blue-and-white striped shirt and red polka dot tie, the tireless muckraker roused his admiring audience, telling them: "By God, the establishment is so full of crap it really deserves to be treated disrespectfully.

"We must help ourselves to understand the power of institutions over men. The path to a better society is the destruction of institutions. Hating the men in those institutions will not get us very far."

"Can the Muckraking Tradition Be Revived?"

This was the title of the final panel, which included Stone. It barely got off the ground before members of the audience, in their last chance to get some attention, brought the whole thing down.

"Shut up and let's get to the questions," began the first hopeful. Some shouted back, the floor was open and that was that. Members of the panel were attacked; other members began taking up for them. Fran Lee started screaming. The anti-war group demanded to know why there was no panel on Vietnam and the press. An angry woman wanted to know why there were no women on the panel, no blacks. A man from Doubleday stood to suggest that books were the one way to spread the truth. Another man mentioned his firm at 999 Madison Ave. Somebody screamed about publishers, another about the reform meeting downstairs. The bar was closing, the crowd was shuffling out . . . people were squaring off at each other and Hal Koppersmith, who was running for Congress, stood up to make a campaign speech.

Woodstock had become Altamont.

"The counter-convention was a success in that it was a forum for discussions of issues but it was too big to be able to come up with solutions," said William Woodward, (*more*)'s publisher, yesterday.

Critics saw the convention as too crowded, too full of rhetoric and superstars for meaningful discussion. To others the talk was interesting if rarely profound.

But like Woodstock, it was not what was said that mattered so much as the "coming together."

6

As Tom Wicker pointed out, the number of people there was the "proof of the vitality, the courage and the validity of what we do."

What some of those people forgot and others were reminded of only too well were the writings of Joe Liebling for whom the convention was named: "There is a healthy American newspaper tradition of not taking yourself seriously. It is the story you must take that way."

—April 26, 1972

Next: Ward Just

"In a time when so much of narrative art has yielded itself to reportage, you have sustained a vital tradition of [fiction writing] . . ."—from a citation for Saul Bellow at Yale commencement ceremonies, June 1972.

With this quote Tom Wolfe introduces his 1973 manifesto of the "New Journalism," a gung-ho proclamation of journalism as the literary wave of the future. And it is on this point too that Michael Kernan picks up Wolfe's gauntlet and launches a response.

First, Kernan accosts Wolfe's position frontally—mocking his verbal pyrotechnics. Then he characterizes him memorably ("Like Joyce, a composer exploring the frontier between language and music"). Then Kernan, the reporter, comes to an issue that complicates the hard-core Wolfe's clean vision of "havoc in the literary world," as an overwhelming wave of novelists and potential novelists discard fiction and flock to journalism (including Bellow himself, temporarily, when he covered the Mideast war of 1967).

Kernan's point is that there is and has been over the years a continuing movement in the opposite direction. His subject is Ward Just, a respected journalist who gave it up for fiction. And Kernan's introductory response to Wolfe serves as a stage-setter for Just's discussion of the flexibility and range that the fiction writer forsakes when he assumes the constraints of reportage. Kernan's ultimate point is not so much to put Wolfe down (in fact, he probably agrees with much of Wolfe's essay); it is to demonstrate that the straight line that some profess to see between the techniques and subject ranges of fiction and nonfiction just isn't there.

Note: The story was written and moved on deadline in less than two hours.

—L. T.

What Is Ward Just Doing Writing These Tales When We All Know Nobody Reads Them Anymore, and Other Stories

By Michael Kernan

So if fiction is dead, why are all these top-line journalists writing novels? The tradition is as old as Hemingway, of course, probably older, and even in the '60s we had the likes of Drew Pearson and old-Washington-hands Drury, Knebel and Bailey writing fiction.

But today, in the era of New Journalism, when everybody, but everybody, is doing these 150-word sentences lubricated by adjectives and commas, and even established novelists like Mailer and Capote and Bellow and Styron are into nonfiction, and when nobody, but nobody, admits to having read a novel since college, whatever could possess reporters of the caliber of David Halberstam, Tom Wicker, Jimmy Breslin, Gay Talese and Ward Just to write for the hammock-and-lemonade trade?

The simplest explanation — suspiciously simple — is that New Journalism had muddied the line between fiction and nonfiction, never all that clear anyway. We will now be expected to define New Journalism.

It is said to have started when Tom Wolfe, a graduate of the sewer commission beat at the *Washington Post,* was doing a piece for *Esquire* on Junior Johnson, the stock car racer. Wolfe was running dangerously close to deadline, hadn't written a word he liked, was suffering a classic case of writer's block. So in something like desperation (intending it as a memo, he later insisted, for some other writer to turn into a finished *Esquire* piece) he started putting it down just as it came out of his id, with strings of expletives, words that balloooooooooooned across the page, and similes that would have startled Swinburne. It was what straight journalists used to call the gee-whiz style, except that it out-gee-whizzed anything ever seen on earth before.

The piece was a sensation, needless to say — nothing exceeds like excess — and pretty soon Wolfe became trapped by his own style, doomed to a career of forever out-Wolfeing Wolfe. Eventually he was driven to write a lead sentence that contained the word "hernia" repeated 57 times.

There were imitators; there still are. There were also complaints from whole barsful of newspapermen, hacks and craftsmen alike, that this was the way they had been trying to write all along, only to be shot down by their desks. Scholars got into the act: The first New Journalist was James Joyce; no, it was Walt Whitman; no, it was Alfred Jingle in *Pickwick Papers*. So far, nobody has detected New Journalism in *Piers Plowman*.

Yet for all its excesses, the glory and despair of New Journalism, what distinguishes it forever from fiction, is its allegiance to fact. When Wolfe writes "hernia" 57 times he is not tripping out, he is describing a machine noise (being, like Joyce, basically a composer exploring the frontier between language and music); when he rhapsodizes on the La Honda, Calif., lair of Ken Kesey's Pranksters with its lifesize dummy lynched from an oak in the front yard or the psychedelic trip bus with more colors than Joseph's coat, he is stating ice-cold fact. The fantasy lies in the world he depicts, not in his style.

Coming at a time when fiction-reading was considered dowdy, New Journalism seemed to offer the best of both worlds. Novelists high and low got into the act: It was fashionable and the pay was good. Its influence soon showed up even in popular novels, which sought verisimilitude if not truth by hitching their formula plots to factual events as in *The Day of the Jackal* and *The Godfather* and a lot of others.

The characters might still be cardboard, but you knew you were getting the real look of the Pentagon or Berchtesgaden or whatever down to the last chipped flagstone. It was a good way to justify travel expenses.

So, with all this, why does a perfectly good newspaperman like Ward Just — 37-year-old veteran of *Newsweek* in Washington and London, of *Reporter* magazine, of the *New Statesman* and the *Washington Post* national staff and editorial board, author of two nonfiction books, a Vietnam correspondent complete with wound — chuck it all to write novels? Really chuck it, that is, not merely take a leave to get a book out of his system.

Holed up at the Cleveland Park home of John Newhouse, himself a new author, Just descended from his study with its seven dictionaries (including Latin and slang) and literally reams of legal-length typescript, brewed himself some instant coffee and tried to get across how it was.

"I started writing fiction early," he added, "but journalism has such neat people, and I didn't have the confidence to strike out on my own. There's no way in hell I could work on the paper in the daytime and do fiction at night. The die was cast for me in 1969 when I went to the *Post* editorial page. I found I had no more respect for facts after my Vietnam experience. Here I was trying to make some sense of facts on the edit page, and I was thinking that facts don't lead you very far, facts don't lead you to the truth, they just lead to more facts."

Already he had done an abortive book of stories while on leave from *Newsweek* in Spain in 1964 ("they were bad") and had taken another leave in '69 to do *A Soldier of the Revolution* about a doomed fictional revolt in Latin America, based on his coverage of the Santo Domingo upheaval in 1965. He also had in his desk a long unpublished novel about his native Midwest.

Soldier was published. It set him up more than he realized, for when he returned to the *Post* he found he was hooked on fiction. He finished the Midwest epic. It was terrible, never published, he said.

"Then in about two days I wrote three stories about Washington," Just added, "and the *Atlantic* accepted them, and I was a goner."

Those stories and others came out this month in book form as *The Congressman Who Loved Flaubert*. A two-part novella will appear in *Potomac* magazine soon. Just has sold the *New Republic* its first fiction in years ("Man, if this works, if we get the newspapers printing stories, what a market") and his new war novel *Stringer* will appear next spring. At the moment he is 10,000 words into a rewrite of his Midwestern book.

A prefatory note in *Congressman* makes the point that the Washington stories are not "à clef" and adds that "the author is obliged to state this clearly, in view of the tendency of the New Journalism to blend fact and fiction."

"I think that journalism, however brilliant, is limited," Just explained. "Why do novelists go into it? Well, part of it's got to be the dough. It's the publishers who don't know who is buying books. They say people have no time for fiction. I wonder. Look at Pynchon: There's a serious fiction audience out there somewhere. Part of it's arrogance. I remember when Bellow decided he would cover the Arab-Israeli war of '67 and Dave Halberstam saw him and asked him why in hell he'd gone to all that trouble to do something any journalist could have done better. Bellow was pissed. But there are special skills a good journalist develops, and you don't just pick them up overnight even if you are Saul Bellow."

Novelists also believe the newly uninhibited journalism can capture the drama of reality, he noted — "but I don't believe that. It takes time: You can't write the great '50s or '60s novel now, but it will come. There can be more truth in fiction than you'll ever get out of nonfiction, because it's so limited. By the facts. You can read nonfiction about the South for years, but for knowing what the South is all about, you read Faulkner — and that's all you need.

"Think of all the stuff published on Vietnam, there's some really first-rate stuff. But my hunch is the real book on it is going to be a novel. Written by a madman," he chuckled. "And someday a novelist will tell the truth about Washington, and it won't be a roman à clef, either."

Good books about Washington are hard to find, he admitted. Gore Vidal's *Washington D.C.,* maybe. "But the difficulty is we bring so much luggage to a book like that, we're always trying to identify this senator or that majority leader. So it can't be directly about the corridors of power, it's got to be on the fringes."

Washington seems to be Just's natural subject. His buttoned-down stories, lean and ironic, have the bite of truth. He could be one of his own characters: the traveled correspondent, son of a newspaper publisher, living with his second wife and their five children in a rambling Cleveland Park house full of books on politics and Proust, getting ready to take off for the Vermont woods to write, a little world-weary, subdued, tense, almost painfully intelligent.

It may be that in turning from war stories to Washington's poison-ring dinner party scene, Ward Just has turned another important corner: freeing himself from Ernest Hemingway, that prototype of the journalist-gone-novelist, whose life so parallels his that his friends have been known to address him as "Ernie."

Hemingway was born in Illinois, not Indiana; he got his war-correspondent wound in Italy, not Vietnam; his early works were set in Spain, not Santo Domingo. But it's close.

"My friends say, 'Just's got this Hemingway thing, death wish and all,' " he laughed. "It started when I spent that leave in Spain writing that first book of stories."

In a Hemingway appreciation, Just gives us a glimpse of himself in those days: "a 25-year-old romantic who is wandering around a mountain with a shotgun and good Spanish friends (not the rich kind but the ordinary kind from the campo), drinking red wine and eating sausage . . . and watching the sun go down somewhere in the vicinity of Cadiz and thinking about the book you are going to write. . . ."

Just said he doesn't like to think of himself as a Hemingway acolyte ("he's so square now"), but he still gets a rush from the last 12 pages of *A Farewell to Arms.* He also turns out a wicked Hemingway parody. His *Post* piece on covering an Oregon election begins with an italic passage: "Near the summit of Mt. Hood in Western Oregon there lies the dried and frozen carcass of a politician. No one has ever explained what the politician was seeking at that altitude." And the article itself begins: "In the late spring and summer the election was still there, but we didn't go to it any more. . . . We would listen to the advance men, and then we would consult the schedules and go into the bar and drink a Bloody Mary. That was a very good year for Bloody Marys."

And this, from his new book clearly haunted by Hemingway:

"She stopped crying after a minute, and I went into the kitchen and made tea. She was sitting quietly in the middle of the sofa, a bleak look on her face, her hands in her lap, listening to Bunk Johnson. . . .

" 'Do you want to talk?'

"She shook her head.

" 'Drink your tea,' I said.

"She held the cup in both hands, sipping the tea.

"'Trouble,' she said.

"'A man?'

"She nodded, yes."

If a writer must be influenced, and a writer must, he could do a lot worse than Hemingway.

Journalism is still close to Just's heart—"A lot of literary establishment snobs think if you're a journalist you're some kind of moral cretin. Goddammit, one thing that journalism gives you is that professional sense, you go to work every day, you're not afraid of the typewriter. Discipline. You don't wait around for the muse"—but he knows there's no going back.

"You've really got to make choices when you get to be a certain age," he said. "You can't carry water on both shoulders."   —June 20, 1973

Next: The New Yorker

"There was The New Yorker, though. They have the idea it's the writers who should make some money from the magazine. They pay well; yes, even when they know they could get a story for less. . . ."—Eudora Welty, 1972, from a portrait that appears elsewhere in this book.

What one of the magazine's most distinguished authors observed has been true both in fiction and nonfiction. In coming to terms with this "happiest blend" in American periodicals on its 50th birthday, Phil Casey, an inveterate (strike that, compulsive) New Yorker reader moves into his subject fast (with a sort of simile lead that works rarely, and only in a case like this where its implications are no exaggeration). Then he cuts fast through The New Yorker's extraordinary chronicle of literary triumphs, aiming toward the real object of the story—the how and why of the special attitude toward rewarding good writers for good writing.

His technique is contrast of setting (the offices look, "with some restraint, awful") with mood ("serene"), and then he chooses the latter as his point of departure on which to pile quotes, background, anecdote, observation and extended quotes about the special nature of the place.

The piece's core is a two-hour interview with the elusive William Shawn ("the number of interviews he gave can be counted on one hand," says a colleague), who succeeded Harold Ross, the founding editor.

—L. T.

A Little Weekly Magazine After All, After 50 Years

By Phil Casey

Once upon a time, there was a unique and splendid magazine, beautifully written, edited and produced, a little weekly work of art, perhaps the happiest blend of fact and fiction, reminiscence, humor, journalism, commentary and criticism there ever was.

Lucky for us, that time is now, and has been for most of our century. *The New Yorker* will observe its 50th anniversary February 21st.

It would be nice to say *The New Yorker* will celebrate this wondrous event, but that's not the way it does things, It will merely observe. But the chances are good that the magazine's members will celebrate in their separate and various ways, with a lot of drinking, singing and crying.

The New Yorker's beginning was far from auspicious, and there were those, an overwhelming majority, who figured it would never meet a payroll. But it came to be that it flourished, after a few uncertain years.

The roster of writers, poets, artists, essayists, humorists, journalists, critics and editors seems too much. They go from then to now, and they include (how awful not to name them all) Robert Benchley, Peter Arno, E. B. White, George Price, James Thurber, Donald Barthelme, Woody Allen, Ann Beattie, J. D. Salinger, John Updike, Truman Capote, Charles Martin, Edmund Wilson, Arthur Getz, S. J. Perelman, Richard Harris, Joseph Mitchell, A. J. Liebling, Frank O'Connor, Eudora Welty, Wolcott Gibbs, John McNulty, John O'Hara, John Lardner, and where do we stop?

And many of the *New Yorker* people, despite their great talents and skills, remain relatively unknown. The magazine was never for mass circulation and probably never will be. The circulation now is only 485,000, the most it ever has been, and this seems to be okay with *New Yorker* people.

Once, many years ago, when the late Harold Ross, the founding editor, learned that his magazine was selling more than 300,000 copies a week, he is alleged to have muttered, "We must be doing something wrong."

Ross didn't want an empire. He wanted a great magazine, and so does William Shawn, who has been editor for 23 years and with the magazine for more than 40 years.

Ross inspired and conceived *The New Yorker* in 1924, with financial backing from the late Raoul Fleischmann. The first issue, Feb. 21, 1925, came out with a cover drawing of a dandified fop peering through a monocle at a butterfly. He came to be named Eustace Tilley. What that cover means and what it has to do with the work *The New Yorker* has produced is unknown. But that cover graces every anniversary issue. It's a crazy, meaningless cover, but for those who love the magazine, it has become a comforting sight.

The magazine, week by week, is a comforting sight to Shawn, who loves it and works endlessly for it. About the only thing he doesn't like about the job is the temptation it gives to magazine and newspaper writers to interview him. Shawn, submitting to an interview, is courteous, cautious and dubious, much like a man being seated in a dentist's chair. He is 67, soft-spoken and courtly. He came to *The New Yorker* when he was 25, and he plainly wants never to leave it.

The New Yorker occupies several upper floors of a building at 25 West 43d Street in Manhattan, and its offices and corridors are, to put it with some restraint, awful. They look as though they were designed by *New Yorker* cartoonist George Price, a man who can make life look more ramshackle than it really is. But, no matter, at least to Shawn. There's apparently nothing about the place that he doesn't like. But nevertheless, he's not celebrating the big anniversary.

"I don't understand anniversaries and birthdays," he said, seated behind his long desk in his large, comfortable and nondescript office. "I don't even understand them journalistically. But I have to give in to your interest. It is an occasion to say, perhaps, that *The New Yorker* is here. Naturally, I'm happy, and I can't quite believe it.

"The odds were against it. We went our own way, and by going our own course, we were in greater jeopardy than we might have been. I hope it continues to work out. We're not certain about the future. It's surprising and pleasing that the magazine is still going.

"Each issue has to be as good as we can make it. We can't depend on what we did 20 or 30 years ago. I worry about each issue, to make it as good as we can. I read every word in the magazine, at least twice."

Shawn thinks that, despite the hard times now upon us, "humor is beginning to flow more readily, even in our own office. But humor is hard to come by at any time. Funny people are rare."

He wonders about some future time and "how people will look back at *The New Yorker* someday." He recited a list of names of *New Yorker* writers and artists, dead and living. "I'm dazzled by them," he said. "I am. What a brilliant group, what very distinguished people. We've been faithful to ourselves and our readers. It's insulting to the reader to do anything less than that. We take delight in what we are doing."

14

Shawn is short, brown-haired and blue-eyed and seems far younger than his years. He dresses unobtrusively. He wore a dark blue suit and vest, a pale blue shirt, an olive green tie, black socks and black shoes. Near one end of his desk is a framed photograph of his mentor and friend, Harold Ross. Ross wasn't the most photogenic or handsome of men, but Shawn found a photograph in which Ross looks great.

Shawn was born in Chicago and his name was Chon. He is of Polish-Jewish descent. The name is believed to have been invented by grandparents. Shawn felt the name was "meaningless and confusing," so he changed it long ago.

He went to the University of Michigan and dropped out after two years. He apparently had the wanderlust, or something. He looked at a map and found a town named Las Vegas, N.M. "I thought I'd like the climate," said Shawn, "and I just arbitrarily went there."

It turned out that the *Las Vegas Optic* needed a reporter, and Shawn got a job, for about $30 or $35 a week. He's not sure. "I stayed there only about half a year," he said, and got a job as a photo editor for a news service in Chicago. He married a newspaperwoman, Cecille Lyon, (to whom he is still married, with three grown children) and they went off to Europe. There, in Paris and other cities, living on little money, he tried to write and to compose music, mostly ballet music.

"But it wasn't any good," he said. "I was an uneducated musician. My work was primitive. We stayed there about half a year."

Shawn plays the piano and loves the old standards of popular music — the Gershwins, Cole Porter, Rodgers and Hart. He doesn't do it well, he said.

He and Cecille came back and settled in New York, and he landed a job of sorts with *The New Yorker*. He did pieces for The Talk of the Town, the lead section of the magazine, which includes interviews, commentary and scene stories.

"I was paid $2 an inch, when the pieces appeared," he said. "I'd work two or three weeks on a story. I don't know how much I made. It was practically starvation. But everybody was in that situation. It was the worst part of the Depression. After a while, they let me come into the office and work."

But, only a couple of years later, Ross hired him as an editor, an "idea" man. That was 1935 and Shawn was in his late 20s. Four years later, he became managing editor. He was managing editor until Ross died in 1951. Shawn became editor officially in January 1952.

Shawn first read *The New Yorker* in New Mexico. He was having a good young time and "I was falling in love with the magazine."

He apparently got along with Ross from the start, and his spoken memories of Ross are not like anything else you will hear or read. Ross, in the anecdotes and memoirs of *New Yorker* writers, comes across as an extremely complex man, ignorant, profane, boorish and bigoted, yet somehow able to inspire and direct the most thoughtful and subtle magazine our times have had.

Indeed, Ross could be a bother about things that shouldn't have been bothersome. Peter Arno drew a cartoon about a man drowning in a shower stall. Ross said the situation was impossible. The man should turn off the faucets, he said. The drain in the floor would let the water out, he said. If all else failed, water would be bound to leak out around edges of the shower door. Moreover, there is open space at the top of shower doors, so no man is in danger of drowning in a shower stall. Arno's drawing finally got published and became one of his most famous.

Shawn saw something in Ross that others on *The New Yorker* seemed to have missed. Ross was a high school dropout and had a strange and mixed newspaper and magazine career. He was in his early 30s when he founded *The New Yorker*, which was his idea and love.

"Harold Ross was an editorial genius," said Shawn. "He was extraordinarily intelligent. I think it must have been helpful for him not to have a lot of formal education getting in his way. He was freer to respond to things. More intellectual people are apt to react conventionally. He had a direct, free response. I was very fond of him, and there was no trouble between us. He was considerate and kind. Ross gave me a great deal of freedom to direct . . . I was educated by Ross, and I learned from him. I learned to see many things his way in many respects."

Shawn was much younger than Ross, by about 17 years, and they didn't mix socially, but their professional life together is something that Shawn obviously cherishes, although he's not about to dwell on that. What Shawn doesn't say in an interview would fill volumes. But what he does say, in his eloquent and cautious way, is that *The New Yorker* wouldn't have been born without Ross and that Ross' intention is Shawn's: to encourage talented people to do their very best and then see what happens out in the marketplace. It's been a perilous journey, but it has worked so far.

Although *The New Yorker* isn't celebrating its 50th anniversary with anything like the joy it should, there are little celebrations going on. One is *New Yorker* writer Brendan Gill's book, *Here at The New Yorker,* being published on the anniversary date. In this book, right at the end, is Shawn on Ross, with a description and explanation and defense in several thousand words. Too much to quote, of course, but impossible not to quote some of it:

"'Harold Ross presented himself to the world as a raucous, clumsy, primitive, somewhat comic figure. He said extremely funny things spontaneously and intentionally. . . . He lent himself to anecdote. Because of this, and because his personal qualities were large in scale and included a formidable charm and magnetism, the serious and inspired work that he did as an editor tended at times to be lost sight of . . . Ross founded *The New Yorker*, but he did far more. He gave it its character, he shaped it . . .

"Mrs. Thurber was charming but mad. 'That Brendan Gill is no friend of Thurber's,' she said."

and he edited it in its every detail for 27 years . . . If those of us now who are loosely bound together in this common enterprise manage every once in a while to bring out an entire issue that might be called a work of art, it is because Ross, who thought he scorned works of art, prepared the way. . . . at the source, abounding in promise, was Ross.'"

Gill has this to say at the end of his book: "Shawn on Ross, yes, but one perceives that it is Shawn on Shawn as well."

Gill, a novelist, short story writer and *New Yorker* reporter, is the magazine's theater critic and is much admired, but not by Mrs. James Thurber; at least not lately. Mrs. Thurber lives at the Algonquin Hotel much of the time, near *The New Yorker* offices.

She was encountered at the hotel the other day and asked about her reactions to Gill's book. The book is marvelous reading, particularly for anyone who has ever cared about *The New Yorker,* but it contains a certain amount of malice. We apparently can't expect a bunch of talented people to sit around working and liking each other. It must get to be too much for them. Anyway, Gill has a lot to say about Thurber as a person. Thurber comes out of this book with all of his talent, but that's about it. Gill starts one sentence with, "Thurber, that malicious man . . ."

Mrs. Thurber was charming but mad. "That Brendan Gill is no friend of Thurber's," she said. She said a lot more, but that's another story.

The New Yorker, over the years, and particularly in the past 20 years, has done some magnificent journalism. It was always a delight with its humor and short stories and poems and drawings and criticism, but more and more it has become a magazine of political and social comment as well. John Hersey's *Hiroshima* was first published in the magazine, an entire issue being devoted to that book. Rachel Carson's *Silent Spring* and Truman Capote's *In Cold Blood* first appeared there.

The list of these achievements goes on and on, too many to mention, but they include pieces on oil supertankers, Robert Moses, Vietnam defoliation, the Justice Department, the Mylai massacre, the problem of nuclear energy, the American Medical Association.

Gill says in his book: " . . . better than any other editor of our time, he (Shawn) has been able to measure the distance of our national fall from grace; better than any other, he measures today the difficulty of regaining that grace. . . . For more than 20 years it has been Shawn's fate to edit a humorous magazine that, holding up a mirror to life, everywhere reflects the darkest shadows and yet manages to make us laugh."

The New Yorker's content has been such that about 700 books have been published containing articles, essays, short stories and drawings which appeared originally in the magazine.

Yet, so many of these writers and artists are known only to other writers and artists.

We talked about Joseph Mitchell, who has been with the magazine for about 35 years and is greatly admired by people who care for English sentences. Mitchell has five books, four of them compiled from the fine pieces he did for *The New Yorker*; yet, he is far from known, even to many people who would delight in his work, if only they had heard of him.

Of Mitchell, who is a former newspaperman now in his 60s, and one of the most unprolific artists extant, Gill has this to say:

"In the opinion of many (which is by no means a modest way of saying 'in my opinion'), the finest writer on *The New Yorker* is Joseph Mitchell ... a Mitchell sentence, to say nothing of a Mitchell paragraph, is as unmistakable as a sentence by Twain or Hemingway."

One of Mitchell's books is titled *Old Mr. Flood*, compiled from three stories he wrote for *The New Yorker*. Mr. Flood is part fact and part fiction, drawn from several old men Mitchell met and knew around Fulton Fish Market in New York. Mitchell's prose is simple, lucid and poetic. This is his first page on Mr. Flood:

"A tough Scotch-Irishman I know, Mr. Hugh G. Flood, a retired house-wrecking contractor, aged ninety-three, often tells people that he is dead set and determined to live until the afternoon of July 27, 1965, when he will be a hundred and fifteen years old. 'I don't ask much here below,' he says. 'I just want to hit a hundred and fifteen. That'll hold me.' Mr. Flood is small and wizened. His eyes are watchful and icy-blue, and his face is red, bony and clean-shaven. He is old fashioned in appearance. As a rule, he wears a high-stiff collar, a candy-striped shirt, a serge suit, and a derby. A silver watch chain hangs across his vest. He keeps a flower in his lapel. When I am in the Fulton Fish Market neighborhood, I always drop into the Hartford House, a drowsy waterfront hotel at 309 Pearl .Street, where he has a room, to see if he is still alive."

It is clear from the books of Gill and Thurber and others that despite all the ego they must have, the writers and artists have chosen to work for what is, truly, a "little" magazine. Fame was not their goal.

One of *The New Yorker* artists, a veteran of 35 or so years, is Charles E. Martin, who signs his work with the initials "CEM." He has done more than 160 covers for the magazine, and hundreds of cartoons. He remembers with great fondness something a fellow artist told him many years ago: "Charlie, working for *The New Yorker* is like playing for the Yankees."

If *The New Yorker* won't celebrate officially, there are events besides Gill's book to do the job. There's a biography of Thurber coming out, and there's a new art gallery devoted solely to exhibits of *New Yorker* covers and cartoons. It's the Nicholls Art Gallery, on Madison Avenue, run by Barbara Nicholls, a young woman who worked for the *New Yorker* art department before she opened the gallery.

And across the street from *The New Yorker,* in the Algonquin Hotel, with Thurber drawings on the walls and people who are fond, there were memories. There's a waiter there who remembers Thurber drunk and breaking chairs in the dining room, and there was a visitor, Bernie Lefkowitz, a former newspaperman and magazine writer who is lecturing at Duke University now.

Lefkowitz worked for *The New Yorker* in the late 1950s and he remembers being detailed to meet Thurber, who was almost totally blind then, at Grand Central Station. He met him, but then lost contact.

"I went back to the office saying I had lost James Thurber! It was awful," he said.

But, in Shawn's offices, things are serene, except when he's submitting to an interview. He had agreed to an hour or so of being questioned, and the thing had gone on for two hours.

Shawn had borne it all with grace and charm, and he rose and asked, "Could I walk you to the elevator?" Then, at the elevator, he asked, "Could I shake your hand? I'm afraid my hands are cold. I was so nervous."

We told him we had been nervous, too, and that we'd had a couple of martinis to quiet all that.

Shawn, who barely drinks at all, nodded approvingly. "I should have done that," he said.

—February 16, 1975

Next: Three Visionaries

"Wherever a man goes, men will pursue him and paw him with their dirty institutions, and, if they can, constrain him to belong to their desperate odd-fellow society." — Henry David Thoreau, "The Village."

Thus one of the 19th century's anti-establishment visionaries (he proclaimed to an increasingly complicated and intimidating society, "Simplify, simplify") explained the forces that drove him into solitary isolation. The kindred, free-spirited loners of this century who brought the same message during the rise of the counter-culture, beginning in the '60s, ran into the same problems as Thoreau, but magnified enormously. The media — television, the printed press, big-time book publishing and a $2 billion record industry — made them into celebrities, and Thoreau's answer (isolation) became not just an act of will, but a knotty problem of logistics. Where does the celebrity-visionary find a Walden Pond and how does he protect it? This is the common theme of the following pieces, each with a different viewpoint.

Bill Woods looks at Dylan in the perspective of years; the singer-composer as the point man of a generation emerges from seclusion in 1974 for a series of long-since sold-out appearances at the country's leading entertainment palaces. Woods' rhetoric is self-consciously massive, and Dylan is one of the few subjects for whom it could be suitable.

With contrasting irony and understatement, Henry Allen characterizes the Ken Kesey of 1974, secluded on a remote farm in Oregon. He is fleeing the image of "the dope-and-giggle champion of the '60s" that came with instant fame, on the publication in 1968 of a book about Kesey that became more famous than any book by Kesey — Tom Wolfe's Electric Kool-Aid Acid Test.

On the other hand, Robert Pirsig is a latecomer. But the nervous instinct that publication of his philosophical work, Zen and the Art of Motorcycle Maintenance, *would subject him to a barrage of frustrating publicity was sound. He had three follow-up volumes to complete, and fled to the Montana mountains in a camper, leaving his family behind. Tom Zito tracked him down there, catching him in town for repairs to the camper, and got a strenuous (for Zito) exclusive interview.*

A technical note: Zito realized that Pirsig's work was unlikely to be familiar to a majority of readers. Thus he calculatingly juxtaposes quotes from Zen . . . *with quotes from the interview. It is a concise technique that works well, at least when material from the subject as author and the subject as person do not suffer by comparison; and even then, in some cases, it could have its sneaky uses.*
                                                                    — L. T.

By William Crawford Woods

On Tuesday, Jan. 15, Bob Dylan and The Band will open the Washington portion of their national tour with a concert at the Capital Centre, to be followed by a second Wednesday night. The tour, which reportedly has drawn about 5 million requests for less than 660,000 available tickets, marks the singer's return to the road after an eight-year absence.

"Look yet again, the little lower layer . . ."   — *Moby Dick*

Knock on Dylan's door; a ghost, a shadow answers. It speaks to an interviewer: "There is no Bobby Dylan." To an audience: "I've got my Bob Dylan mask on tonight." Through an old friend: "Dylan was constantly inventing himself." In the musings of a biographer: "(He) built a new identity . . . in order to escape identity."

Just so. Our lies about our histories tell the truth about our souls.

And—from the changing of his name (an act itself explained by contradicting stories), through the mutations of his music and the shiftings of

Illustration by Terry Dale

21

his voice, to the rapid adoption and dismissal of serial personae as much at odds with each other as they were in opposition to the penultimate assumptions about them—Dylan's primary defensive mission has been to render every judgment made about him invalid or irrelevant before the utterance is complete. An artist must protect himself; his self being what protects his art.

Dylan got what he wanted—St. Teresa warns us of the risks in answered prayers! What he wanted was to make myths one size larger than himself at each stage of his career and fill them full to overflowing at the next.

His luck with that gamble is a convenience for the historian, for his past is littered with phases as conveniently marked as Picasso's: the adolescent years in Minnesota which he organized toward the conquest of New York; the quick victory over the Village with his folk invasion; the strategic move to protest songs; the explosion into Rimbaud, rainbow rock; the retreat into country music; the retrenchment into visionary art. It is a life's list compressed into a decade, but then the '60s were a very speedy time . . .

This is the stuff of genuine myth: the increasingly invisible creator whose fame owes a bow to his obscurity, whose fixed star glows alone and sets no standard. We have had a problem pigeonholing the man from the beginning.

Shy of prophets and wary of secular saints, we have painted him "genius," and complained when he fell short. What foolishness. Genius is readily available. It's very small praise to apply to Dylan, whose intuitive project has been to educate the consciousness of a generation with his vision and then curb its excesses with his authority. Such activity stems from nothing smaller than apostolic force. But such a view may make his current tour hard to account for.

For Bob Dylan is on the road again, apparently with the wish that his audience can once more match his metamorphosis, this time from easygoing exile to pop star, and turn themselves from followers into fans. "I hate debt," he's said somewhere, "especially moral debt." Which suggests that the widespread speculation that his new move (to the tour, new songs, a new record, a new record company) has been made only to redouble his winnings is not so much cynical as simply ignorant.

For years we've publicly fondled the idea that Dylan owes us something more because he's given us so much already. That's prophet-guilt: Since we forgot to stone him, he has to sing again.

And so he does. The old songs, mostly, leaking out a few of the new at each whistle-stop as part-payment of our voracious need to be reborn. It is, at any rate, a need felt by that part of the audience sparked to a social conscience and then to surrealistic dreams by Dylan a decade ago. But if the rare, recent interviews with the singer are a reliable guide, he has no intention of locking the clock. Forced once to be a demigod, he is determined now to become an entertainer, and the generally warm response to his Chicago opening indicates his audience is happy with the new approach. On the other hand, the younger members came to hear the songs that raised their older siblings' consciousness, and it is the repetition of those early visionary songs that pleases them.

What the hell. Old Hemingway said, "What you win in Boston, you lose in Chicago," and there are provocative resemblances in their careers. Both men came from the Midwest. Both went early into exile. Both adopted rebel styles. Each stayed a jump ahead of his audience. Neither pleased critics who demanded that his art bow to politics. Either might have gone for the money — each made the money come to him. And, like Hemingway, Dylan has provided no ground rules for his critics. On the contrary , he has opened himself to them with deliberate contempt, employing a series of ragged interviews over the last several years to forge a new image of himself as just another good ole boy with a geetar, eyes wide for *Cashbox* and closed to the sorrows of the age.

Another mask, of course.

"The stage was arrayed with a couch, a lamp, and candles," John Rockwell reported from the Chicago opening for the *New York Times*. This is the stuff of a seance, Dylan announcing with his props that he was offering his audience a fundamentally Proustian venture. Those of the crowd of his generation probably were able to take their cue and do some time-traveling, but Tom Zito has quoted in this paper the reservations of a friend as to how the singer may weather the demands of a new assembly:

"'Going out on the road for him is a very traumatic thing. It's really laying his career on the line. And you can bet that if he starts singing some simple country songs and the kids in the first 10 rows are all zonked out on Quaaludes and start screaming, "Boogie," Bob Dylan's gonna think twice about doing any more tours.'"

That fear — if it really is Dylan's — may help him place himself in his own history, which is a fairly large project for a man of 32. Nor is it insignificant, because conceptually this tour has to be less "about" Dylan's relation to his audience than that audience's fresh response to his music. But it is in a way irrelevant because it questions the serene authority that derives from the singer's prophetic legacy. Seen in that aspect, the idea of a "comeback" becomes a vulgarity used by an audience to disguise from itself the fact that they are the ones who've been away (Dylan's encore in Chicago posed that point in lyric code); and most of the questions by which this tour may be dissected become no more sensible than the assaults that hit Dylan in 1965 when he plugged himself into the AC current and showed some of us the scary furniture of our own minds.

Which is to say: What's he supposed to do, go back to protest with ballads about Watergate and energy? Those things are in his songs of 10 years gone. Listen again. And this tour says: Listen again.

I am, of course, being deliberately naive — that's one of the requirements of faith. Objections to Dylan are littered all over the countryside, growing fiercer as the early claims for his gifts are stripped of their most desperate pretensions. Through his whole career, his instrumental dexterity has been no more than adequate and his voice no better than untutored. His melodic imagination has been at best work-a-day and at worst purloined. The claims of his lyrics to be poetry mostly evaporate when his words are put upon the page and his biographers have no difficulty finding cast-off, armed, and armored enemies who will testify to a career built with cynical precision on the generosity of neglected friends.

So what. None of these things expresses a significant truth about Bob Dylan's stature and all of them together fail to add up to his achievement. To posit them is to seek misguided refuge from the terror any offer of salvation inspires. I say "salvation" partly because it's an idea that crops up continually in his songs and a word that appears occasionally in his interviews, sometimes prefaced by a homely diminutive that gives a key to his new direction —

> Nat Hentoff: What do you have to look forward to?
> Dylan: Salvation, just plain salvation.

— but mostly because it's impossible to make sense out of his accomplishment without liberating our view from secular attitudes. He wants his own salvation and has learned that salvation is never complicated, and because he has a special gift that transcends genius, he finds it linked in part to his attempt to break some psychic logjams for his audience with his art. If he doesn't do it now the way he did 10 years ago, it's because our needs are different, and they include the fact that he's become one of our needs by having become a part of our history.

The songs he did it with remain. Their repetition establishes them as liturgy, and their survival patents them as something beyond pop: art. They're real art. "Pop art" doesn't mean a thing and never did, though "pop" means something, but it doesn't mean Dylan and never did, not even when he brought it from London to Newport in 1965 by surrendering his denims to the Edwardian velvet that meant the best of a bad time.

It was a move that would have been hard to predict when Dylan headed east as the Eisenhower era lost its benign deathgrip on the culture. Later he would say he went from Hank Williams and Little Richard (childhood heroes his manhood would reclaim) into folk music and protest songs as a calculated risk. But unfeigned deep devotion to Woody Guthrie, and the fervor with which his disciples elevated "Blowin' in the Wind" to the status of civil rights anthem, suggest that the man, whose boyhood had been freed from stasis by his fictions about it, was importing some defensive disclaimers into his past. No matter. The fanfare of the '60s flushed

"Where the style of Dylan's music used to contain his protest, the sound alone now carries the load."

several idols from hiding, and Dylan was about the right size for a scarecrow suit. The folkies just pure worshipped him, and CBS wanted him for Holden Caulfield in a TV version of *Catcher in the Rye.*

It was not to be. The folky embolisms of his first two albums were set adrift in the next two by hints that he was probing more personal themes in increasingly impressionistic language. But nothing prepared us for the impossible majesty of the two that followed, "Bringing It All Back Home" and "Highway 61 Revisited," albums that minted a genuinely new music from the foliage of folk and rock and from a dreamy private monologue of vengeance, grief, and unchained melodies. This was the music that made fellow singer Phil Ochs proclaim in awe, "He's really done it . . . he's in his own world now."

He was. Though it was inspired by Dylan's exhilaration over a Byrds version of his "Mr. Tambourine Man," and by the electrifying experience of a tour of an England in thrall to the Beatles, this was no daily ration of pop. It was the work of an artist fully engaged in an artist's work of creating a world more real than the real one.

There are more than a few of us now who, 10 years later, still find in songs like "Desolation Row" a satisfying pre-R. Crumb guide to the infernal regions, and in "Like a Rolling Stone" the awful answer to what was blowing in the wind. And there were more than a few, 10 years ago, who saw in Dylan's breakout something like betrayal, a fulfillment of their nightmare on that satanic day in '65 when he went electric at the Newport Folk Festival.

These were mostly the limited, decent people, the folk-and-protest holdouts, who failed to see what Dylan had sensed, that the '60s were going to be a decade too beautiful and terrible to be captured in the split circle of a peace symbol. They wrote, mostly in the pages of earnest movement magazines like "Sing Out," impassioned "open letters" to Bob, begging him to forget the poison flowers in his skull and come back to the fold.

Time has shown their criticisms merely served to testify to his power, but to read their pleas and curses today is to be astonished at the frenzy of anger and fear Dylan's new music provoked in the souls of those who perhaps had loved him best; and to whom his immediate response was, as it had to be, "Blonde on Blonde," a tough two-record set, arguably the finest album of rock 'n' roll ever recorded.

His eventual response was a deal more mellow. After the cryptic theodicy of "John Wesley Harding," his muse led him to peaceful sunlit fields that troubled many of his new fans as deeply as his quantum leap into rock had outraged an earlier following. Obviously a few people hadn't been listening or didn't want to hear Dylan when he said *in 1961*, "I sing a lot of old jazz songs, sentimental cowboy songs, Top-40 hit parade stuff."

Well, sure.

The irony is that much of Dylan's recent music — *Nashville Skyline et passim* — has represented an involvement in proletarian life far more genuine than the sanitized idolatry of the "folk" of the early '60s, a largely collegiate enthusiasm underwritten by singers of moonshine who'd probably have s--t if they'd ever seen a still. If explicit political comment was now absent from his songs, that absence was itself political. Was "With God on Our Side" a more significant statement than the act of singing a duet with Johnny Cash, effecting the symbolic union of blue collar and freak?

Where the style of Dylan's music used to contain his protest, the sound alone now carries the load. *Rolling Stone* may scoff — but all the albums since "Skyline," uneven as they've been, have had a healing touch no less potent than the epic rage that made the early music great.

It is perhaps the final irony that, 50 or 100 years from now, what best survives of Dylan may be the gentle manners of his most recent songs rather than the boiling cathedrals of his middle youth.*

We may not quit this meditation without trying to resolve the contradiction at its core. It has been observed that no single part of Dylan's work rises much above a modest standard (though he's always attracted backup men of the highest excellence), yet suggested that its totality achieves our best contemporary sacrament. The appeal to faith falls flat in an age of reason, but it is there that our synthesis must take place.

Critics throughout Dylan's career have toyed nervously with this sizable idea. Ellen Willis early on suggested that when we call Dylan a poet, we mean a visionary. Vision is a mode of inquiry that gets short rations from serious folk these days; it has built neither napalm nor high-rise, it has invoked the moon but been unable to walk there. So to say that we find — in the long lines of Bob Dylan's public dreaming, the pith of his affectionate verse, or the final total image of his career thus far — the fullest metaphor for the experience of the generation that survived the '60s with him, that walked the picket lines to the wail of his folksongs, lazed in

---

*This judgment was made before the release of *Planet Waves, Before the Flood,* and *Blood on the Tracks.* Much of this new music, not to mention the 'new voice,' tends to dispute it and to suggest that Dylan's pastoral period was, to some extent, an aberration. — W.C.W.

acid splendor to the beat of his wicked rock 'n' roll, or died under mortar fire with the growl of his voice filtered through some jungle-rotted cassette recorder—to make this claim is to say a truth that the ordinary march of conventional criticism cannot capture.

"This," writes critic Steven Goldberg, "is why Dylan merits our most serious attention. For he stands at the vortex: When the philosophical, psychological, and scientific lines of thought are followed through to the point where each becomes a cul-de-sac, as logic without faith eventually must, Dylan is there to sing his songs."

He sings them much as Blake sang his, from the unique authority of a vision that partakes of the divine. That notion, far from being extravagant, is economical in the extreme, because it is the only way to account in full for Dylan's protean dimensions. When systematic analysis has exhausted his components, joy remains to explicate his whole.

Doubtless there are quotidian sensibilities, already irritable at the idolization of a "pop star" who will be incensed at his elevation to something like sainthood. No reply can be made but the one we began with: Listen and listen again.

It's all there still—the music with which Dylan made his self-renewing advances against the walls of the cowed culture that was the target of the countervailing culture of the past decade. Just as Mick Jagger of the Rolling Stones and Jim Morrison of the Doors infused new health into the scene through their recovery of the shaman's role, and the Beatles puffed it full of lively grace and color, so Dylan—whether he liked it or not, and he mostly didn't seem to like it very much—became the point man in the march toward something like a new world. Neither he nor we ever really found it, though he healed some heads along the way. But the swamp is rising again, the bad gases brewing—perhaps Bob is back with nothing more than reminiscences. Kierkegaard—whose distinction between a genius and an apostle lies a layer below this essay—says that, between them, the individual and his generation always bring each other to a standstill.

No doubt we're stuck again. But Bob *is* back. If you can get a ticket, why not go and see him, just to say thank you and hello?

—January 13, 1974

A '60s Superhero
After the Acid Test

By Henry Allen

SPRINGFIELD, Ore. — Ah, yes, feeding the cows. Ken Kesey, at 38, all genial and hulking in his dungaree jacket, his big, tough Buddha face goofy under an earflapped green-and-yellow knit cap, strides out through the pasture mud to feed his 26 beef cows, a bale of hay sagging from each hand.

Kesey is back on the land. There's an old veteran feeling about it. Kesey, the hero college wrestler who became the hero novelist (*One Flew Over the Cuckoo's Nest, Sometimes a Great Notion*), who became the superhero field marshal of the acid heyday's Merry Pranksters, has moved out like Cincinnatus to 60 acres of farm outside his home town, living in a barn he converted to house himself, his wife Faye, and their three kids. And the hungry cattle are shouldering their way through the rain toward him.

The sky boils gray over the valley in the chronic drizzle that is weather in Oregon half of the year. It's near sunset. The decision to feed the cows has seized Kesey the way a lot of routine decisions seem to, as if it were a blast of inspiration: "Hey! Let's feed the cows!"

So, flanked by Ken Babbs, his tall, fast-talking, neon-eyed first lieutenant from the old Acid Test days, back when Kesey and the Merry Pranksters were a day-glo guerrilla squad for the LSD revolution in California, Kesey has rushed into the gloom to feed the cows, Babbs loping alongside him, singing "Every cloud in the sky . . ." with the stagy brio of a silent movie burglar whistling past a cop.

Lotsa laughs. For one thing, it's been a terrible winter, even for Oregon, where the epic winter rains make suicide a meteorological phenomenon. So the first signs of spring have inspired a certain giddiness. And the first edition of Kesey's new literary magazine, *Spit in the Ocean,* is just out. And Mike Hagen, another of the Pranksters who followed Kesey back to Oregon in 1960 after Kesey's five-month jail term in California for possession of marijuana, has organized a beer-and-boogie blowout in an exhibition hall at Lane County Fairgrounds, across the Willamette River in Eugene. And Kesey has a huge project lumbering down the runway,

Photo by Barry Lopez

called the Bend In The River conference, for which he and a committee have scored a $12,000 planning grant.

The conference, scheduled for July 5 in Bend, Ore., is to bring in big-name experts for televised debates on Oregon ecology, Oregon tax use, and so on. The next day Oregonians are to vote on the issues on ballots printed in local newspapers. It's the biggest Kesey/Prankster turn-on since they drove around California 10 years ago in Further, the most famous psychedelic bus of them all, rewiring the citizenry with LSD-spiked Kool-Aid. (Hence the title of Tom Wolfe's book about Kesey, *The Electric Kool-Aid Acid Test*.)

And Babbs showed up an hour ago to rescue Kesey from a long, rainy afternoon interview, and Kesey twisted up a few cigarettes to be passed around and . . . it's time to feed the cows, and Kesey and Babbs walk out past the dome, past Further. . . .

Further is backed up next to a wire fence in the barnyard now, the seats torn out, a pool of water on the floor, the mind-blitzing super-swirl day-glo paint job fading under the corrosion of these Oregon winters. Further was "the bus" of the great Prankster dictum: "You're either on the bus or off the bus." Next to Further is the weather-grayed frame of a geodesic dome attempt Kesey and friends made five or six years ago, like myriad New Age explorers after the cosmic-salesman/psychedelic-bus thing withered out of relevance. There's a lot of counter-culture history sitting here on this property, plus Kesey himself, the superhero of the '60s the way Bob Dylan was the poet laureate.

Still singing "Every cloud in the sky . . ." Babbs heads for the far end of the pasture while Kesey takes the closer, the weight of the two hay bales causing no visible hitch in his stride, which is boyish—big chin up, big chest out. The cows sway through the mud toward him. Kesey looks brisk and pleased as a waiter delivering a birthday cake.

The mud, he explains, is the legacy of the terrible winter.

"It just lashed out," he says in a high, soft voice, the voice of a modest, confident high-school football captain. "The ground froze, hard, and the rains came after, harder than I've ever seen it rain. It leached out all the topsoil. It's a disaster for the farmers in this valley.

"I think we were smitten by the Lord for the way we voted. You can't vote for Nixon and what he stands for and get away with it. And we all have to pay."

The rain has been slanting down in the fine spit that Oregonians ignore, or maybe accept as the next best thing to sunshine. But for a moment, now, the clouds veer apart to release a glow of near-sunshine, not outright beams, but better than anything else all day. Kesey stops. He looks up, still holding the bales. His face knits into one of those combination frowns and tight smiles that herald the discovery of one of Nature's truths. Kesey says, "You see? No matter how bad it gets, sometime during every day the sun always comes out, even if it's just for a little while."

Blithe as ever, he strides on, busting up the bales and spreading the hay around until a persistent birdcall catches his ear. He stands and listens. He shouts across the pasture: "You hear that bird? Folks up here say that what it's singing is: (and here Kesey sings) 'Oregon's a pretty little state!' Hear it?"

Earlier that afternoon, inside the barnboard snugness of the house, the rain rattling against a floor-length window behind his worktable in a corner of the big ground-floor room, Kesey frowns in thought, pursing his lips — a fatigued, baronial look, especially now that his face has fattened out from its old wrestler's leanness. But his blue eyes, tucked deep behind the northern European slant of his eyelids, are cool and clear, despite his epic 15-year diet of marijuana, LSD, mescaline, peyote, DMT, psilocybin, dexedrine, benzedrine, methodrine, hashish, cocaine, nitrous oxide, all washed down with generous draughts of beer, wine and whiskey.

He is worried, he says, about the youth of America.

"I was down at Stanford for a reading, and I was sitting around talking with a bunch of buys about the way things are going, the food supply, population explosion, pollution and so on. Now, these are the guys who can save us, the cream of the crop, smarter than I ever dreamed of being. One of them is one of these big, tall, gangly guys, you know, with his glasses taped together in the middle? He's kind of hanging there in the doorway listening to us." And Kesey stands up to illustrate the gangling droop of an overgrown boy scientific genius.

"I knew he had a bombshell, I could see he was just waiting for his chance. So I looked over, and he says: 'You know, in 20 years, 91 percent of Africa and 84 percent of India will be dead. It's simple arithmetic. There's no way around it.'

"Nobody said anything, just sat there. I said, 'Wait a second. Don't you guys realize the future is open, that we can do anything we want if we just put our minds to it?' They all shook their heads. All that incredible education is teaching them there's no way out. I could get them talking, get them excited about an idea for a few minutes, then they'd lose it. These kids have given up. They just want to smoke dope and giggle."

This is very ironic, seeing that Kesey was the dope-and-giggle champion of the '60s. If adolescence had become the lifestyle model for America, Kesey, operating with mind-blowing insouciance, raised it to cosmic significance, to a religion, nearly, taking the wonderfully doomed "we few" feeling of every high-school cadre and making it permanent — fun forever, costumes and face paints, pranking Mr. and Mrs. Front Porch USA into blinking astonishment. And pioneering their way not through college and marriage, because they'd already done that, but into . . . the Beyond, the leaping, leering zoo of LSD's other side.

Muscular, V-bod, soft-but-oftspoken Kesey became Captain Marvel, flying through all kinds of impossibilities, Dimensions X, fame, busts, stoned suspicions that he just might be God, friendship with Hell's Angels. The Pranksters became not so much followers as spin-offs from the Kesey energy: brash Mountain Girl, Hagen the lothario, Page Browning lighting up Prankster faces with his paintbox, Neal Cassady spieling out his speed-fraught jumble of minute details, the sort of details that had fleshed out Kesey's novels; though Cassady was more teacher than spin-off, having won his spurs in the late '40s with Kerouac, Ginsberg and the Beat generation.

Arthur Miller has written that Kesey "voyaged into his own arteries fueled by drugs, sailed away from history and the lockjaw of political intercourse, kicked dust into the eyes of Power, and laid himself down in the middle of the road of Progress and cried out, "F... work."

Now, at 38, a member of the PTA, coach of wrestling at the junior high school, Kesey worries about American youth. Then again, Kesey himself never lapsed into drugs to beat a case of terminal suburban malaise. He believed in acid, the same way he had believed in that holy grail known as the Great American Novel.

Acid promised "that the millenium was here, that courses would be taught in the use of it, for consciousness expansion, that with LSD we could do anything with mental power. I believed that," Kesey says now, sitting at the table. Radio station KZEL FM plays rock at a Muzak volume. Rain pocks the tiny pond you see through the window. A boat lies in the weeds up the bank from the pond, a semi-cabined fishing skiff that must take up nearly half the pond when launched. The relic of some Prankster fantasy? Kesey plays with his gold wedding ring. He has big fingers. He has big arms, big shoulders, big chin, big nose, big bald head with pale rusty curls piling out over his ears just a bit like the wig that Clarabelle the clown used to wear.

He had believed in the big novel, opening *Sometimes a Great Notion* with a high magnificence that had vanished with the idealism of the '30s: "Along the western slopes of the Oregon Coastal Range . . . come look: the hysterical crashing of tributaries as they merge into the Wakonda Auga River . . ."

He believed in it, not only as art, but as reality.

Writing about his boyhood in *The Last Supplement to the Whole Earth Catalog,* which he co-edited, Kesey slips seamlessly into one of the finest cliches of the Great American Novel genre: "When I'd hear that whistle, lying there blinking out at my mysterious futures, I'd think, 'Someday I'll go someplace on that train. . . .'"

His only book since *Notion,* in 1964, has been *Garage Sale,* in 1973, an anthology of underground press interviews with Kesey, a mock screenplay built largely on Prankster in-jokes, and Kesey's thoughts on everything from ginseng to Bible reading. But he's writing fiction again, after swearing off it during his heavy acid days. He's working on one novel based on his prison notebooks and another about the whole Kesey family, with himself appearing as Devlin Deboree, a character who shows up in *Garage Sale* as the codgerly "Old Man" Deboree.

The old man personifies, perhaps, the feeling of a lot of experienced dopers that despite their still-sound minds and bodies, they are somehow very, very old, a notion which inspires the Walter Brennan routine you'll hear from a porch-load of hippies, groaning that "Yep, a man can't get a good ounce of grass for less than $15 nowadays, and it's a damned shame, too."

Anyhow, writing: "It's a difficult yoga," Kesey says. "Very difficult. You become what you write about. Sitting in lotus position and doing breathing exercises would be a lot easier." Ultimately, of course, Kesey is a writer. He is probably no more a farmer or community politician or mystic seeker than Hemingway was a bullfighter (despite his efforts) or Fitzgerald was rich. But Kesey believes fervently in brighter tomorrows, in the dream of progress. So when it comes down to the bedrock of his main work as a man, it's not surprising that his voice quiets to vexed despondency. "The thing about writing is that writers never seem to get any better than their first work. This bothers me. This bothers me a lot. You look back and their last work is no improvement on the first. I feel I have an obligation to improve, and I worry that I won't. I talked with Norman Mailer about it, I talked with Arthur Miller, and they agreed, they worry about it too. I've got a lot of writing left to do. I wrote about fear in *Cuckoo's Nest* and despair in *Notion*. The jail novel is about anger. There are two more I want to write, one about vanity, and then one about attachment. But I wonder to myself, 'Is *Cuckoo's Nest* the best I'll ever be?'"

By prolonging adolescence with the Merry Pranksters, Kesey had held tight to the promise of growth. The finalities of American adulthood could be forestalled forever, it seemed. He still hasn't closed the door on acid. "I'm not through with my work on acid, and nobody I know is, either."

So it's understandable that Kesey's hope and fascination, now, is the mystique of the land, the stations of nature, farming for awareness, not money.

"If you're not connected to the yearly protein resurrection, the calves being born, the plants pushing up through the ground after the long winter, you have a hard time having any real hope for anything. I watched my cows staring at a newborn calf, and I felt I knew what it meant to them, I saw it in their eyes, that it was proof of renewal, that it was going to get sunny again. I'll stay on this piece of land as long as I can. When I work out there I know that land is what it's all based on. I know the sky, know when it's going to rain. You want to be in touch with something like this, you see.

"I am asked what happened to the revolution. I say: 'Food stamps.' They put you outside the whole natural cycle of things. Living off food stamps is like being in exile."

All this high seriousness has made Kesey fidgety, drumming his heavy fingers on the tabletop. It ends the minute Ken Babbs strides in the door, spinning off news and gossip laced with his big Babbs laugh, which goes "Hwawh! Hwawh!"

Babbs has been Kesey's Number One sidekick since the beginning of Kesey's career as an arbiter of realities, back at graduate school in creative writing at Stanford. He is also an alter ego, one suspects, rangy next to Kesey's bulky compactness, sarcastic next to Kesey's conspicuous sincerity. And his eyes: Babbs' luminous eyes have the focusless—or superfocused—glare you see in other Pranksters' eyes, after all that acid. Kesey's face, for all his tripping, shows none of the subliminal dysplasia you sense in the features of old acidheads. Babbs' face, on the other hand, shows the wear of the journey in a peculiar blend of adolescent rosy cheeks and the bony angularity of a man pushing 60. He is 39, and lives nearby with his wife, Gretchen, known on the 1964 bus trip as Gretchen Fetchin the Slime Queen. Babbs looks intelligent, charming and crazy.

Kesey brings a shoebox out of hiding and dips into it to roll up something to smoke.

"Hagen's got a final cut, now, of the movie," Babbs says. He's referring to a film Hagen will show at the fairgrounds party the next night. The film will show a party of a year ago, when the Grateful Dead came up to play a benefit for the Springfield Creamery, owned by Kesey's brother Chuck. When you're Kesey, you can get the Grateful Dead to play benefits for you. Cut into the film is footage from the legendary 30 hours the Pranksters shot, years ago, the 30 hours of Acid Tests and pranking that has defied editing into a coherent record of the Prankster days, maybe appropriately.

"It's a premiere," Kesey says.

"Right, right," Babbs says.

"Yeah, we should do it up . . .," Kesey says, lifting whaddyathink eyebrows.

"People driving up in limousines!" says Babbs.

"A spotlight!" Kesey says, getting into the fantasy.

"We ought to have a spotlight," Babbs says, and sweeps a long arm through the air, spotlight-wise.

"Hey, we'll do it," Kesey says with conspiratorial vigor. "We'll do it and we won't tell Hagen. Let him. . . ."

"Let him show up and there's this great big spotlight, oh man. . . ."

"I'll make a call," Kesey says, murmuring that Nnnn-Nnnn-Nnnn of his laugh, and runs to the phone, awesomely inspired.

At this point, Faye and the kids come home: Shannon, 13, Zane, 13, and Jed, 10. Faye, married to Kesey since their freshman year at the University of Oregon, has the patient but long-suffering look of a woman resigned to living in a maelstrom. Shannon is pale and blonde, and full of a 13-year-old girl's suspicions that the grown-ups are up to their usual childishness. She sits as the table, ignoring everybody.

"There's a cold front comin' in, Shannon," says Babbs, apropos of nothing, which is her response.

Shannon worries over a pair of eyeglasses.

"The pin came out," she says, pointing to the joint between the frame and the right earpiece. Babbs lifts them away from her with a know-how air, explaining in an exaggerated explanatory lilt that "this is always the problem, Shannon. Those things are always coming out of glasses, a constant problem."

Meanwhile, Jed, gentle and shy-faced, is showing his mother a shoebox filled with moss, a project for a school fair.

"Ken," she says, when he gets off the phone, having failed, apparently, to find a spotlight to blow Hagen's mind with.

Kesey frowns into the shoebox while Jed watches his face.

"That's really fine, Jed. Hey, look at what Jed made for the fair," Kesey says, crackling with enthusiasm, with 100 percent attention. "Okay, now. What if you moved this over there, and there's something out in the garage, just the thing you could use to . . . help him out with it," Kesey says, looking up at Faye, who stands there saying nothing while Jed says "Sure," and Kesey totes the shoebox off toward the garage, Jed trailing behind, and . . . you begin to see the incredible fierce energy of the man, the charisma that turns on like a health-club sun-room, the famous aura. But more than aura. It's a quickness of gesture, too, immediate as a baby's, totally doubtless, and the fascination ringing in his face. When he disappears through the door, you suspect you're missing something out there in the garage. You understand now, given Ken Kesey on the bus, the power of the old Prankster dictum: "You're either on the bus or off the bus." It's the sort of charisma that makes almost anything forgivable, at least for a while.

Kesey and Jed tramp back into the house, the father satisfied and proud, the son satisfied if somewhat resigned to puzzlement.

"The way we moved it over to the side, there," Kesey is saying, "it brings out what you were doing. . ."

Shannon hunches over a sewing machine. Faye, back from her day of studying organic chemistry at Lane County Community College ("Now she'll be able to make speed for me," Kesey likes to say), fusses around the sink with the air of a woman getting her kitchen straight after a weekend of guests. There's a moment of silence, in the late afternoon gloom.

"Hey, let's feed the cows!" Kesey says.

Babbs pulls a jacket off the crowd hung on pegs by the door. Kesey tugs on his onion-spire, ear-flapped Tibetan-style green-and-yellow knit cap, and they rush out into the rain.

—June 9, 1974

The Art of Metaphysical Maintenance:
On the Road in Montana With Robert Pirsig

By Tom Zito

"I am a pioneer now, looking onto a promised land."
— Zen and the Art of Motorcycle Maintenance.

BOZEMAN, Mont. (elevation 4,461) — The snow on the peaks ahead is melting now, gouging a fast-flowing and forceful artery beside the red dirt road. The sound of the surging stream masks the groans of the pickup camper Robert Pirsig is plowing further into the Hyalite mountains.

Silent, with eyes straining and transfixed somewhere beyond, Pirsig seems pushing to leave Bozeman and all else behind, gazing ahead to the Alpine-flowered slopes, perhaps caught once again in the reality that had surrounded him six years ago as he headed west on a motorcycle, *the fear that comes from knowing there is nowhere you can possibly run.*

Earlier in the day a clerk at Phillips Book Shop on Main Street had taken Pirsig's first and only work, *Zen and the Art of Motorcycle Maintenance,* out of the display window. Never mind that critics in London's *Times Literary Supplement, The New Yorker, Newsweek, The New York Review of Books* and virtually every other low-, middle- and high-brow publication were hailing Pirsig as one of the most profoundly reflective thinkers to stimulate the popular consciousness since (pick one) Jack Kerouac, Aristotle, Charles Reich, Hermann Hesse or Buddah himself. Never mind that Bantam had bought the paperback rights for $370,000 after the book stunned even its publisher by selling almost 50,000 copies in its first two months. Never mind that Pirsig was *invited* to apply for a Guggenheim fellowship — which he received — as a result of *Zen.* . . . Never mind that professors at Princeton were clamoring in annoyance because the university book shop was sold out of it, that rock musicians and doctors and bank officials and street vendors were talking avidly about this travelogue of mental inquiry, that the Book-Of-The-Month Club had decided, after once rejecting it, to choose *Zen* . . . as its Septem-

Photo by M. A. Feldstein

ber alternate, that traditionally macho *True* magazine had excerpted the first five chapters in its July issue.

"No, I haven't the slightest idea what a book with a title like this is about at all," the clerk had said. "But some of our customers complained that it wasn't very kind to Bozeman."

Again, in the camper, a sense of the demon that haunts Pirsig: the night before the author had had a nightmare. It was April 15, Publication Day. The Soviet Union launched a nuclear attack on the United States. He had labored four years to yield this compulsive mind map of a book and milliseconds of torrential energy had reduced it to cosmic dust.

A motorcycle functions entirely in accordance with the laws of reason, and a study of the art of motorcycle maintenance is really a miniature study of the art of rationality itself.

It is summer, 1968. Robert Pirsig, 39, and his 11-year-old son, Chris, straddle a 305cc red Honda Superhawk and leave their home town of St. Paul, Minn., for a two-month motorcycle adventure.

Pirsig, who holds a BA in philosophy and an MA in journalism from the University of Minnesota—where his second-generation German father is dean of the law school and his wife a public relations official—is taking time off from his technical writer's job at Northern Ordinance, a large manufacturer of naval equipment. The two Pirsigs are traveling with John and Sylvia Sutherland, friends of the family.

You see things vacationing on a motorcycle in a way that is completely different from any other. In a car you're always in a compartment, and because you're used to it you don't realize that everything you see is just more TV. You're a passive observer and it is all moving by you boringly in a frame.

On a cycle the frame is gone. You're completely in contact with it all. You're in the scene, not just watching it anymore, and the sense of presence is overwhelming. That concrete whizzing by four inches below your foot is the real thing, the same stuff you walk on, it's right there, so blurred you can't focus on it, yet you can put your foot down and touch it anytime, and the whole thing, the whole experience, is never removed from immediate consciousness.

The motorcycle trip was the genesis of an immense mental journey. It was a return to Bozeman, where in the late '50s and early '60s Pirsig had taught English at what students call "Moo-Yoo—The Udder University," to distinguish Montana State here from the more prestigious University of Montana; where, he recalls, "You'd ask a student why his face was all bloodied up and he'd reply, 'This guy said a Chevy's better than a Ford . . .'"; where he had encountered the dilemma of determining whether Quality—the central concern of his book—is subjective or objective; where his obsessive anxiety over the problem would seed a mental collapse that eventually hospitalized Pirsig for a series of shock treatments:

"The book was offered to 122 publishers...Only Morrow accepted."

Approximately 800 mills of amperage at durations of 0.5 to 1.5 seconds had been applied on 28 consecutive occasions, in a process known technologically as "Annihilation ECS." A whole personality had been liquidated without a trace in a technologically faultless act. . . .

The strain still shows. Now 45, Pirsig's hair is gray and the stress lines around his eyes are set too deep to be relieved by sleep or vacation. He's back in Bozeman, up in the mountains in his camper, the same camper he parked on the north shore of Lake Superior to write the last five chapters of *Zen . . .*, again seeking the wilderness for work on a second book.

He dresses sloppily: every day a green Army fatigue shirt over a white T-shirt, black slacks and socks and a pair of tennis shoes. He drinks a lot: perhaps a martini before breakfast, another at lunch, a pitcher of beer in the afternoon, a martini before dinner and a Scotch after. He carries anthropology books and a clipboard around with him and is constantly making notes to himself: call home, take a bath, buy oil for engine. His favorite expression is "real good," which he uses as a greeting, a farewell and a general exclamation. He'll say "Wanna take a ride," get in the pickup and drive without further talking across several hundred miles of two-lane Montana roads, looking off at the solid masses of mountains miles in the distance.

Writing *Zen . . .* took Pirsig 600,000 words and four and a half years, "four years if you don't count typing the third manuscript," he says. It was completed in June 1972, with the last five chapters written in the camper.

"I would go to bed at 6 p.m., get up at 2 a.m. and write until I went to work at 8," Pirsig says. "I did that for two years, first at home but then my wife threw me out. I expected the kids to shut up at six so I could sleep and she didn't think that was fair. So I got a $12-a-week room at a flophouse. My boss let me come into the office and write early in the morning and I'd show up for breakfast at my own house each day. Writing this book was a compulsive act, and whoever stood in the way of it was going to get hurt."

The book was offered to 122 publishers, by mail and in person, none of it through an agent. Only Morrow accepted.

Zen . . . is Pirsig's attempt to synthesize his past and present as well as the subject/object dichotomy that has fascinated philosophers from Socrates on. It's a quest for a reassertion of maligned classical values, an attempt to reconcile philosophy, science and humanism, all done within the context of the trip: events on the road spawn cognitive acts. John's distaste for "creeping technology," his lack of interest in maintaining his motorcycle for instance, prompts Pirsig *to see if in that strange separation of what man is from what man does we may have some clues as to what the hell has gone wrong in this 20th century.*

Pirsig develops a classic/romantic dialectic, a separation of the worlds of form and appearance. For him, *the motorcycle is a system of concepts worked out in steel.* He analyzes 2,000 years of epistemological arguments — the Sophists, Plato, Aristotle, Hume, Kant:

In the high country of the mind one has to become adjusted to the thinner air of uncertainty, and to the enormous magnitude of questions asked, and to the answers proposed to these questions . . . What is the truth and how do you know it when you have it? . . . How do you really know anything? Is there an "I," a "soul" which knows or is this soul merely cells coordinating senses? . . . Is reality basically changing, or is it fixed and permanent? . . . When it's said that something means something, what's meant by that?

These are the things Pirsig concentrates on: the questions professors traditionally tell students are the *raisons d'être* of college; the problems men study for 13 years in hopes of becoming Jesuits; the paradoxes mystics in Tibet contemplate their entire lives. They're timeless concerns, unusual only in the way *Zen . . .* has turned them into a salable phenomenon of concern in an age of unconcern.

"Certainly we were surprised when the book took off," says 32-year-old Jim Landis, the Morrow senior editor who bought the book. "A hit of this level is something you don't count on. Obviously it was a good book; it had rhythm. Now it's a cultural artifact; it lives by itself."

Singer/songwriter Dory Previn, who's read the book, says simply, "The logic of the man's mind is astounding."

Marc Jaffe, the Bantam senior vice president largely responsible for buying the paperback rights, says, "The combination of Pirsig's personal story and the way one has to live in America is an intellectual, inspirational message. We expect to sell millions of copies after the paperback comes out next May, especially because this book is going to be around for a long time. It's not a nine-day wonder."

John Matthews, a co-owner of Record & Tape Ltd. in Washington's Connecticut Avenue shopping area, says he stayed up all night reading *Zen. . . .*

"It was like going out in the country and looking at the stars," he says. "It makes you ask yourself a lot of personal questions that can get very scary."

Pirsig frames the reaction to the book in an image of crystallization.

"There was a supersaturation condition in the country — all the problems everybody is feeling, what direction our whole national culture is going in, a general feeling of unhappiness about the quality of American

" 'Type, type, type until the typewriter wears out, it's your . . .nirvana.' "

life: everything from Watergate to the price of bread at the local grocery. I think the book is acting as a seed crystal to solidify ideas about what's going on.

"But it can get troubling. People are calling it another Bible and I don't want that."

In fact, it was Pirsig's dislike for publicity that brought him back to Bozeman.

"What got to me was one day I was walking to the post office and some woman came up to me and asked, 'Aren't you Robert Pirsig?' That really bothered me. Then the mail started getting heavy — a lot of it from people with mental problems. People are calling on the phone: 'What motorcycle should I buy?' 'You wrote a great book.' In St. Paul I had never had to learn the privacy routine. Some guy calls and I answer the phone and talk. Now I've got to learn all these privacy things. How much of the public person can be real? If it's all real you get killed. I didn't want to be a phony.

"So one morning I just woke up at three. I told my wife, 'I just have to get out of here.' We had the camper packed in half an hour and I was on the road. Trying to adjust to the sudden shift of personal situation is probably the worst part of success — certainly it is for me. Maybe everybody *is* talking about the book. That's a good reason to be in Bozeman. Here I have my anonymity."

Pirsig came here in June, to escape the demands mounting in St. Paul so he could seriously work on his second book. He's been avoiding impediments, particularly interviews — consenting to this meeting only because the brake shoes on his pickup and the propane heater in the camper back needed replacement. That meant wasting some time down in Bozeman, away from the mountain quiet he likes for work. His call to agree to an interview was revealing:

"I'm standing here in a phone booth," he had said. "My wife just told me Bantam bought the paperback rights for $370,000 and there's just no one here in Bozeman I can tell that to and have it mean anything."

Up in the mountains, Pirsig's camper becomes a mobile study. He works with a large card file, scratching ideas on individual index cards and then arranging the book by shifting the order of the cards. He types drafts of chapters on an old black Royal portable that was his wife's high-school graduation present. Pirsig stretches out on a mattress in the camper, the typewriter on his lap, card catalog to his right, half-frame eyeglasses balanced on his nose. Sometimes he says he'll sit for a week and do nothing, just trying to clear his mind.

When a photographer asked to make a picture in the camper, Pirsig assumed his usual working posture, slipped a piece of paper in the machine and began typing: "Now that the pictures are being taken there's no way of escaping the problems that come up. Up in the mountains it's very cool now, but the thing you want to learn may not be so cool. Type, type, type until the typewriter wears out, it is your real source of nirvana."

The second book Pirsig is working on is called *Them Pesky Redskins.*

"I'm trying to examine the interface between cultures," he says. "If *Zen* . . . was a prolegomenon to any future metaphysics, this book tries to apply the metaphysics of Quality worked out in *Zen* . . . to anthropology. It's going to be very scholarly. The only people who'll be disappointed will be people who want to be entertained. I mean, this is going to be a real dull son of a bitch.

"Let me explain. I want to look at the places where Indian and white cultures butt up against each other. American Indians are involved not in a refusal to accept the American way of life. They're interested in a separate reality. Anthropology will open up a lot of new ways for looking at this. Out of 162 definitions of culture made since 1948, one deals with common values. Before that it was common language and artifacts. What determines a culture is a consensus on value. And the fallout from that consensus can be seen in terms of artifacts and values. If you get a red culture and a white culture you're getting a consensus of realities on both sides but along the interface there's no overlapping—no one is seeing anything the same way. I want to look at some new ways of seeing cultural problems, like busing. It forces the confrontation between values. For Northern liberals to say blacks are the same as whites is the most serious form of racism. I made my kids go to a black school and they got the s--- beat out of them. Now, there's got to be a reason.

"A lot of my interest in Indians was prompted by the work of Verne Dusenberry. The high point was when he took me to a Cheyenne peyote ceremony in 1958. Generally I don't approve of the use of drugs, but the way the Indians did it was all very carefully controlled. They had guards posted around to make sure no one would get hurt. Anyway, I came back from that with a feeling I had crossed cultural lines. Dusenberry was a prophet without honor. He couldn't get a Ph.D. in this country. He was told that his experiences with the Indians were too subjective. He went to the University of Stockholm and they accepted his thesis.

"All the things the Zen Buddhists say you should do but don't, the Indians do without even talking about it. I have an intuition that they're all after the same thing, but the Indians are on such a higher level."

The One in India has got to be the same as the One in Greece. If it's not, you've got two.

"It's like Quality. For you Quality may be Kant. For me it's hamburgers. Regardless, we both want Quality.

42

"That's really all I tried to do in *Zen*. . . . At first I thought of writing a few essays. I'm a Zen Buddhist and I had gotten interested in motorcycles after I was turned down for a pilot's license in 1964 because of my mental problem. It's all 'Catch 22.' I'm a tech writer because I can't be a teacher because a teacher can't be nuts. Anyway, the motorcycle took on a special meaning to me because it was a way of overcoming the hangups of the hospitalization. So after the trip I started writing these essays and I found I had to cross a lot of thought paths I'd already been over. I started to see cracker-barrel conversation potential. They sounded pontifical, so I decided to put it in the mouth of a narrator who's vulnerable.

"I wrote 600,000 words. I cut the final manuscript to 200,000 and at my publisher's suggestion I cut if further. They wanted more trimmed but agreed to publish 130,000 (412 pages) at $7.95 if I'd take a cut in royalties. Which was fine, because I wanted the book out there.

"I'm trying to make the classic concepts more relevant today, helping people lead more imaginative, productive lives. The problem today is that one has to succeed in some terrible chain of values. The book just says, 'Be true to your own interests in terms of Quality.' If you can go in your own basement and fix your motorcycle that's fine.

"My third book I've tentatively titled *Heresy and Insanity*. It'll be a comparison of activity among the people who pressed the Inquisition and psychiatrists. I think that psychiatric authority is a form of social control, necessary in the sense that cops are necessary. They're not there to help you; they're there to keep you in order. Their duty is to society, not to the individual. That was true of the Inquisition.

"Maybe after that, one called *The Dialectics of Quality,* working out on a scholarly basis things posed in *Zen*. . . . Where were the weak spots, the logical problems, things you can spin off in your head? A kind of workbook. Maybe to do it as *Leftovers From 'Zen and the Art of Motorcycle Maintenance.'* Print the original 600,000 words on one side of the book, with commentary on the opposite pages."

He glances out the window of the camper. "At my point in life it's all giving," he says. "I can live comfortably on $8,000 a year. So now it makes no difference to me when some guy comes up and says, 'Here's $3,000 for an essay.' I don't have to think about money or fame. All I can do now is give. I hear it's said that it's better to have all this attention happen after you're 40. You're already set in your ways."

He removes his eyeglasses, sets the typewriter down and walks out into the lush mountain meadow. In the distance a stream is rolling down off the peaks and today Robert Pirsig has decided to search for the source.

All italicized quotations from Zen and the Art of Motorcycle Maintenance, *published by William Morrow & Company, Inc.*

—August 5, 1974

Next: Trends and Fads

These are two stories about swingers — and pop culture. Both appeal to what Michael Kernan calls a "goggling world" in his report on the mid-'70s letdown that followed the exciting '60s in London.

A problem for the editor in such cases is to try to separate the trends, with lasting effects, from the momentary phenomenon or "fad" that represents it. That is not to say that one subject is less newsworthy than the other. The object is never to sell short what is a trend, with worldwide repercussions, as in the change in attitudes (particularly sexual) as exemplified by the London of the '60s, and to keep in context what is merely an example. This is the category to which probably belong the go-go boys who drew adoring female crowds in the suburban Washington of the '70s.

Kernan's story focuses on London in the years after it was the center of the action, *describing a counter-reaction and its main characteristics: "the truculence toward outsiders and the need to conjure up yesterday's glories." But Kernan knows that London is there to stay and has gone through similar down periods and has always revived with what designer Mary Quant calls its "phoenix quality."*

By contrast with Kernan's "Quant revolution" (though he is well aware that the vibrations of '60s London reach far beyond Mary Quant and her miniskirts), Jeannette Smyth acknowledges that her go-go boys in Camp Springs, Md., are just "a fad that won't alter the course of civilization as much as, say, Volkswagens." But she knows, also, that the fad is a manifestation of something deeper. The sexual role reversal element is the point: the man as the sex object counterbalances female toplessness. And who is really to say that changes in sex roles aren't now changing the course of civilization? —L. T.

London's Mood: Looking Back

By Michael Kernan

L ONDON — If you had to describe in just eight words what has happened to London in the last decade, all you'd have to say is: Mary
Quant has gone into the wine business.

Because Mary Quant, more than any other single person, appears to
have invented that whole giddy era of Swinging London. If Courreges
pioneered the short skirt, it was Mary Quant who immortalized the mini
and exposed to a goggling world more thigh in one season than a funhouse
operator used to see in a lifetime. If Balenciaga first experimented with
wild-colored tights, it was Mary Quant who brought them out of the
closet and onto the legs of young women. As for hot pants, they were
Quant's all the way — mad colors, imaginative fabrics, a design that intelligently celebrated the body's proportions and also stimulated the male
libido in a most knowing way.

Even before the Beatles made London the hub of the pop universe,
there was Mary Quant, and one could argue that the Early Beatle little-
boy bangs and prep school jackets were a direct steal from her.

Today Mary Quant Limited is an international octopus dealing in
cosmetics, clothing accessories, coordinated sheets, pillowcases and
curtains, underwear, fabrics, children's books, dolls — and now wine.

"The clothes go tottering on," said Mary's husband, partner, mentor
and friend Alexander Plunket Greene, "but the cosmetics are by far our
biggest international line. We've just started on the wine and we hope to
make it a major part of the business. It's a mail-order thing, which means
we can sell decent French wines at 25 percent or more below the regular
market."

The point of Mary Quant, who began in 1955 with the presciently
named Bazaar on Kings Road, soon to become one dazzling rosary of
boutiques, is that she introduced high style to the low budget: her clothes
were good but cheap. Perhaps it was a byproduct of the early stirrings of
women's liberation, for Britain was full of young women who refused to
slip passively from parental nest to school to husband; they took jobs and
shared apartments and sometimes didn't get married at all. They had

money, but not much. They aspired, thanks to the fall of empire and the rise of television, that great leveler, to at least the look of wealth and position — that is, chic. And when The Pill freed them to indulge their sexual imaginations they turned, as in the '20s, to the naughty-girl look.

Quant had rivals, hordes of them. A 25-year-old Polish genius named Barbara Hulanicki started a mail-order dress business from her Kensington flat, got 7,000 orders in one day, moved into a store, then a bigger one, then a bigger one. She did dresses in four sizes — 8, 10, 12, and 14 — turned out six basic designs and thousands of permutations of fabric and color, restocking the shop completely every two or three days and, most important, creating an atmosphere, a fever, that made shopping a way of life. She named her boutique after herself: Biba.

(1966: a visit to Biba on Kensington High Street. Through the art-nouveau swirls painted on the windows one gets an impression of chaos. Inside, the impression is instantly confirmed. A tape blares "Sunshine Superman" into a dark clutter of potted palms, full length mirrors, Victorian coatracks festooned with skirts, shifts, blouses, hats, coats, evening dresses, beads and boas, an old-fashioned counter backed by a wallful of cupboards jangling with underwear in electric colors and flanked by velvet window seats covered with cushions (orange, pink, chartreuse, violet, yellow, ochre and scarlet) and customers' mums. Through the gloom drift the girls, shrugging hat angles in the mirrors, rehearsing blouses beneath their stretched necks, dancing out of the dressing room in unzipped minis, trading clothes, fingering through a haystack of baubles, bracelets and Ubangi earrings, skeptically expanding with their hands the patterned bras and panties apparently designed for a Barbie doll, posturing in boas and high-domed fedoras colored mauve, ultra-marine or coral, and chattering, chattering, chattering. The Sandpipers break into "Guantanamera.")

There was Hung On You, a man's boutique where the Beatles shopped and where Lord Snowdon bought a wildly violet suit which he wore to a shooting party at Balmoral Castle. Fortunately, he is one of the best shots in England. There was the incredibly scruffy secondhand stall called I Was Lord Kitchener's Valet on incredibly scruffy Portobello Road, selling colorful old uniforms for about $3: dramatic capes, scarlet tunics with gold braid and epaulets, black tunics with red collars, ruffled shirts, cloth-of-gold admiral suits, three-cornered hats, firemen's hats, burnouses, topis and so on.

There were more places than you could visit in a week, each more outrageous than the last. It was, as one 26-year-old entrepreneur yawned, "a bit of a giggle."

Recently the London Museum featured an exhibit titled "Mary Quant's London." A first-rate show, it contained full-scale dioramas of British living rooms before and after the Quant revolution. There was a blowup of the map of Chelsea that accompanied *Time* magazine's famous piece

"There is a slightly grim air about London, an air of discouragement."

on what it dubbed Swinging London. Display windows paraded Quant's deceptively innocent-looking clothes, the kind of thing a little girl would wear, you think, and then you look again and see it is not a little girl model at all, but a droop-lidded Lolita.

The miniskirt in a museum. . . . What has happened to London anyway?

In the pop culture, the changes are obvious. Boutiques have joined the commercial mainstream, Quant proliferating into a kind of glorified design consulting service, Biba consolidating into a giant department store (formerly staid Derry and Tom's in Kensington) with an awesome roof garden graced by flamingos, brooks and 20-foot trees; a period restaurant straight out of "Gatsby;" Art Deco trimmings and stock that seems generally overpriced and a bit dated; Hung On You is gone; Lord Kitchener's Valet is a Piccadilly Circus souvenir shop. Most of the new boutiques are, as Plunket Greene put it, "run by big Seventh Avenue companies pretending to be amateurs." It's just another business.

Whether a cause or an effect, the British interest in clothes has dulled. One wonders where all the birds have gone, who expressed not only their personalities but their moods by what they wore. Today the young wear ankle-length dirndls, shawls, denim jackets, frightful clubfooted platform shoes and jeans, jeans, jeans. Minis have retreated to the provinces.

"It's the very-rich-peasant look," commented Mary Quant, who confided to an interviewer that she loves jeans for their sexy but sturdy appearance. The sewed-on patch, which in middle-class America has reached the final stages of rococo, never caught on here, where poverty is all too real.

"Of course we couldn't have gone on forever with the '60s look," said Quant. "Fashion anticipates the time; hemlines went down long before the stock market, and the classical look came in before the recession. Today people just buy accessories, not the whole thing. In any recession, women buy cosmetics and underwear and things that will cheer them up. Today it's the country look: the rich all have taken up their country places, and the others copy that rough, outdoors appearance."

It's not only the clothes that look dull. There is a slightly grim air about London, an air of discouragement. On the street, eye contact is rare.

Though an Islington churchyard placard urges "Hats off to the Past, Coats off to the Future," the impression is that people are sick to death of being exhorted.

Forced to acknowledge they they no longer dominate the world, Britons seem to be reverting to insularity. More and more, as foreigners crowd in among them, they act like an island people. Kensington is awash with Americans, even in winter. They rent the swankest flats, eat at the haughtiest restaurants, insouciantly buy everything in sight at any price. Even the American students, poor as many are, are generally better off than $50-a-week working class people. (A white Cadillac with Texas plates parks illegally in front of the august Hyde Park Hotel, and out steps a man with a belly and a 10-gallon hat. Resentment radiates from the passersby.)

American influences are infinitely more visible than they were 10 years ago. Ginger beer is hard to find, but American ginger ale is everywhere, as are American soft drink brands, junk foods and pop records. TV newscasts follow the American formula even to the logo lettering, doom music, talking heads and gimmicky weather reports. The *Times* has embarked on that oldest of journalistic cliches, the search for the perfect hamburger.

Americans aren't the only foreigners to arouse British hackles. The Italian has always been a figure of ridicule here, but the other night a TV newscast of France's President Giscard d'Estaing was accompanied, unbelievably, by an insulting kazoo version of the Marseillaise.

TV interviewer to football star named Jones: "Are you Welsh?" Fervent reply, "Oh no no, I'm English through and through!"

As the foreign rich are resented, so are the foreign poor. Rush hour incident in Hackney, a Cockney stronghold now flooded with West Indians, Africans and Cypriots: A loaded double-decker bus pulls up at a crowded stop. The conductor can allow only five people on, leaving frustrated a group that has been waiting 15 minutes or more. A tough Anglo youth climbs onto the boarding platform right in front of the conductor.

"Didn't you hear me?" shouts the conductor, a slight, swarthy Cypriot. "No more!" The youth swears viciously at him. They make fury-faces at each other like Japanese wrestlers. The bus begins to move, with the youth hanging on, but the conductor signals, and the big vehicle halts in the middle of the street. In a few seconds the other riders will join the conductor in impatient wrath. Cars begin to honk. The youth steps off; the bus starts forward. Then he spits in the conductor's face.

Incidents like this certainly occurred in the '60s and possibly even during the Blitz. The spitting is new.

(Many young Third World immigrants, by the way, reject the low-paid jobs that their parents have accepted, as conductors or janitors. Result: jobs go begging even as unemployment rises, and London Transport service gets even spottier.)

48

"A museum exhibit of miniskirts is nothing. Would you believe a nostalgic musical about the Beatles?"

It doesn't take an economic analyst to find a reason for the glum faces here. A successful National Health physician may earn $10,000 a year which he plumps out with occasional private practice; but other salaries run much, much lower. Food prices are on a par with those in major American cities. Rents are right up there with New York's: $500 a month might get you a small house in dowdy Hackney five miles from the heart of town, $100 might get you a dingy two-room bed-sitter "near" Swiss Cottage where the artists are supposed to live. Or it might not, for recent London legislation against evictions has frightened landlords, creating a desperate shortage of rentals.

Yet there is more to it than high prices and low salaries. There is more to it than the usual modern city troubles, rising crime, the new hostility toward and from police, breakdowns in municipal services, food shortage scares, the generally harried, ungracious atmosphere—they have even curbed the buskers, or street musicians. There is more to it than the tensions produced by pub bombings that now seem to occur every few days. The thing that is special about London's mood is an obsession with the past.

A museum exhibit of miniskirts is nothing. Would you believe a nostalgic musical about the Beatles? And what a musical: played by four men who have the not-quite-right, or Madame Tussaud, resemblance to those symbols of a joyful past, this show is shockingly bad. Literally, one has seen better high school plays. But don't tell the Londoners; they love it. Find it delightful. Weep over it. Roar at the tiresome routines, spurious dramatics and bearded jokes. Two American visitors, perfervid Beatles fans, walked out. (These particular visitors have walked out of several other London productions that were being complacently hailed by local critics. The great British theater tradition is surviving on sheer memory and a handful of competent performances.)

The usually-exciting Hampstead Theater Club has been featuring a ponderous burlesque of Bulldog Drummond, a James Bond forerunner, and followed it with a play about World War I. A 26-part TV series on that war is being rerun, as is another series on War II, not to mention a multi-part review of Britain's role in the rise of Europe and a situation comedy about the '40s Home Guard. And almost every weekend one can watch yet another special recalling the heroic days of the Blitz, or Churchill's coming to power, or a soap opera about Churchill's mother — Lee Remick, radiant in one of her best parts.

Other current plays include Barrie's "What Every Woman Knows" (or, what every high school student had to read in 1938) as well as "Peter Pan," plus "Treasure Island," a homage to Cole Porter, a John Osborne revival, a Wedekind, an Agatha Christie or two, a handful of Shakespeare standards and a musical about Jack the Ripper. Along with these period pieces there are, to be sure, a few new plays.

Galleries feature British painters, British portraits, British photographs, British views of Italy or the Arctic, and the music of Elgar is played to distraction, like Strauss in Vienna. Sadlers Wells has settled down to a four-month wallow in Gilbert and Sullivan.

Chauvinism ramps through the newspapers, from the letters anathemizing the Common Market to the Sunday-supplement reminiscences about the Finest Hour, or Nelson, or Waterloo, or the Briton who broke the German code and thus won World War I, closely followed by a piece on another Briton who broke another German code and thus won World War II.

One supposes that both these London symptoms, the truculence toward outsiders and the need to conjure up yesterday's glories, indicate a massive loss of self-confidence.

At an elegant dinner party in Chelsea, one's table partner turned out to be a member of the ancient family of Percy, a name as aristocratic as, say, Bolingbroke or Plantagenet. The thing was, she felt she had to work it into the conversation, to drop her own name. Considering the magnificent, languorous, cold-staring arrogance of the traditional English aristocrat (the lady was charming, one hastens to add), this slip argues a loss of class self-confidence that is hard to believe.

———————

In spite of it all, London remains for many the world's greatest city, the most livable, the most civilized. The parks are still thriving, superb even in winter. The transport system is still quite possibly the best in any metropolis. There is an air of authenticity about the place: A man seen wearing a fez is not a Shriner pretending to be a Turk; he is a Turk. An ad for a Tudor house does not mean a house built in Tudor style; it means a house actually dating to the 15th-century Tudor era. An unremarkable and unremarked Islington pub, the Pied Bull, is the same inn (rebuilt, to be sure) where Sir Walter Raleigh once lived, and open-air Chapel Market next door, where he perhaps bought apples and cobnuts, still bustles daily.

Most of all, despite the bombings, despite the violence at football games (after one stadium stabbing police detained the entire audience and somewhat literal-mindedly took down 5,000 names), the celebrated British sense of justice still survives. A recent news item illustrates, maybe rather too neatly, both the punctilio and the insistence on fair play that lie behind this rare concern.

A prosperous young Egyptian factory owner visiting London had $500 in an American bank here, in the name of his American wife. But she had lent a camera to a friend going abroad, and her passport was in the case. Unable to withdraw the money, the Egyptian had stolen $12 worth of cheese, ham, apples and other food to stay alive. The city magistrate not only absolved him but lent him $65 from the court poorbox to tide the couple over. Not to make too much of this, three things do seem to stand out: the rigidity of the banking regulations, the alacrity with which the young foreigner turned to crime in his despair amid a relatively hostile environment, and most of all the judge's direct and human actions to relieve a ridiculous legal situation.

First and last, London is a city of individuals. You can see personality in the very graffiti, from the printed sign on a forbidding apartment tower, indignant and mysterious, announcing that "This building is not Rawleigh Phipps," to the gigantic spray-painted scrawl that blazes across the length of a wall near Euston station: "The Tygers of Wrath are Wiser than the Horses of Instruction."

William Blake . . . street poet.

"London has a phoenix quality," said Mary Quant. "It's a generating city. Something will start happening."

—December 29, 1974

Role Reversal à GoGo

By Jeannette Smyth

On Ladies' Night the Hangar Club out near Andrews Air Force Base in Maryland is full of women clapping in time to the loud rock band. All evening, the Camp Springs ladies have been getting up one by one to thread their way past tables full of women, up to the white Formica platform where the go-go boys dance, women walking up in front of all their friends and slipping, stuffing, dropping, wadding dollar bills into the go-go boys' peach satin, baby blue, black rhinestone-studded, faux Pucci bikini briefs. Sometimes they stroke a dancer's chest or bottom. Sometimes the men give them a kiss.

Over in the corner, a secretary sits with six friends from work. She is fingering a dollar bill. "Is it customary," she asks carefully, "to tip go-go girls?"

Since everybody around her is a woman, and none of them knows much about go-go girls, or strippers, or nearly naked people in public, no one can give her an answer.

Instead, the friend sitting next to her says, "We're paying the men back now for all those years of burlesque. I'm not interested in [touching him] when I go up there to put money in his pants. I'm just happy we're liberated."

The secretary gets up from her table. Bravado overcomes taboos against sharing the limelight with a performer, touching him; against a woman's paying a man. "I like his hairy chest," she explains. She walks up to the Formica platform and puts the dollar bill into her favorite dancer's pants. He kisses her.

She returns giving the thumbs-up sign. The women at her table cheer. She sits down. "He's sweating," she says, a little surprised. She wipes her face with a paper cocktail napkin.

Another patron, 25-year-old secretary Diane Wright, came to see the go-go boys with her mother, her sister and her Kodak movie camera. She films her favorites as they dance. "I'm going to show the film to my husband," she says. "He wants to know what it is about all this that turns me on." She visits the Hangar Club once a week. Her mother is there for the first time. "I love it," her mother says. "I don't think it's embarrassing."

After the women-only part of the evening is over, Diane Wright's favorite dancer comes to sit and talk with her. They dance.

"It really started as a joke," says Hangar Club manager Nick Simonetta. Last summer, women who came to the 5-year-old bar for "the regular night club discotheque scene started saying, 'Hey Nick, you have go-go girls for the men. Why don't you have something for us?'" So four and a half months ago, Simonetta advertised for what he calls "go-go guys." He hired three men to dance on Tuesdays and banned male customers.

"Women don't want any guys in here," he explains, "boyfriends peering over their shoulders from the bar, a husband waiting outside in the car. They come in groups. There's a sorority-type atmosphere."

Since the dancing started, business has increased 35 percent, Simonetta says. Ladies' Night has gone from one night a week to four, 11 more dancers have been hired, and the Hangar Club, which holds 185 people, is booked three weeks ahead of time with reservations. Simonetta won't say what the dancers' salaries are or what the dollar volume increase in business has been. He does say he had to drop the old 90-cents-a-drink policy. "Some of these girls would sit there for two hours and drink Cokes," Simonetta says. "I'm a businessman after all."

That doesn't mean that total nudity will come to the Hangar Club. Simonetta thinks the go-go boys are a suburban phenomenon—because women are afraid to go downtown after dark—and that involves "certain values."

"I think these women and the community would consider [total nudity] vulgar," says Simonetta, "and be totally opposed to it."

Most of the women who come to the Hangar Club are around 30, dressed up in pantsuits and hair spray. Some are housewives and some are secretaries. Most are reluctant to have their names published even though they show no reticence toward the dancers. They drink beer or mixed drinks or something pink, in goblets, called a "Red Baron." There's a Safeway down the street. Sometimes men fight in the parking lot. Inside the club, embossed vinyl brocade tablecloths and patio candles encased in plastic net grace the tables.

Last Friday, the Baltimore County Liquor Board ruled that male go-go dancers in a Dundalk bar had to cover their breasts, could not allow customers to stuff money into their briefs, and that the bar's management would not turn away male customers during Ladies' Night.

Simonetta, who supplied the dancers for Merritt House, the bar involved, says that despite the ruling 250 enthusiastic women showed up Sunday. The men's pasties kept falling off; customers, though warned by Simonetta they were subject to arrest, stuffed money into the men's briefs anyway.

What *is* all this? Is it good clean fun or is there something grotesque going on? Here are all these suburbanites out in Camp Springs, Md.—men and women who could hardly be called revolutionaries — making a burlesque of the sex roles heavy thinkers are making dialectic of. Who's liberated? Who's crazy? Who knows?

Here you have women stuffing money into men's briefs: a graphic, if not gross, symbol of changing sex roles. The gesture elicits strong but deeply ambivalent reactions. Some people laugh; some people are repulsed; some people blush and look anyway; most people are fascinated or at least curious. Whether it is the sex part or the role part that interests people, the go-go boys are certainly the most colorful characters to come out of the "women's liberation" movement recently.

They generate a powerful amount of confusion. If a woman's place is no longer in the home, then man's place is on the go-go platform, right? Is that amusing or degrading? Healthy sensuality or exploitation?

Is the role reversal revolutionary or is it the same old sexism, unbecoming to the fair sex? Are these "new women" liberated from sexual passivity and general ignorance of male nudity? Or are they belatedly going through a rite of passage that most men traditionally have performed during adolescence?

The Hangar Club doesn't have any answers. A sociological watershed it is not. And while the spectacle of go-go boys dancing in a bar is a fad that won't alter the course of civilization as much as say, Volkswagens, these exotics, and the ambivalence of reaction to them, give a limited, but sharp, focus on feminism in the suburbs.

Between their 15-minute dance gigs, the go-go boys stand around in the kitchen. Offstage, they wear shirts over their bikini briefs, as go-go girls cover up with blouses.

The men are mostly in their late 20s. Most have jobs during the day — there's an Army staff sergeant, a truck driver, an out-of-work actor, a salesclerk, a computer analyst and a painter.

The painter and the sergeant are the only ones with previous experience — it's not exactly a big business. The painter says he was a stripper in Mexico. The sergeant says he did sex shows in Germany. They have a stage presence that goes over — they are the most popular dancers this evening in terms of applause and pin money.

Jim Stanzak, the sergeant, is doing push-ups next to the steam table to limber up. Jeremiah Shastid, the actor, went skiing earlier in the day and is flexing his sore legs. He is trying out tonight, dancing for the first time, nervous and ambivalent.

"I had funny reactions from men when I told them I was going to do this," Shastid says. "A cab driver said to me he thought all the guys who danced there were gay. Another guy, a doctor, said to me, 'All you are doing is prostituting yourself.'"

Nobody admits to being a homosexual, but truck driver Marvin Hall says, "There's a few I don't know about." He offers no evidence.

As for the idea that they are peddling their flesh, the men offer the same matter-of-fact rationalizations that female exotics do: "Dancing is art; go-go is show biz; it's flattering; it's fun; I needed the money."

The painter calls himself Pazen. He has show business aspirations—he's putting together a rock band. He was a gymnast and a dancer at Wheaton High School.

"This is men's lib too," he says. "It shows role reversal." The switch doesn't bother him. He likes being a sex-object-performer; he doesn't feel degraded and he doesn't hate women. What does it feel like when a woman old enough to be your grandmother sticks a dollar bill in your waistband?

"I love it," says Pazen, "because I'm really getting something across. It's entertainment. I'm transmitting energy."

When they mingle with the customers after an evening's dancing, Pazen says, the men are sometimes propositioned. "They say they like the way you dance. They tell you what they like about your legs or your hair or your chest. Sometimes they ask if they can spend the night with you, if they can take you home. There are guys, including myself, who will go home with a girl. Do I get paid for that? No. I've never put myself in that category." There are limits.

Computer analyst Wayne Mackert says, "I was astounded at first by the older women, how they reacted—yelling and screaming and jumping around. Now it's a job. You gotta let 'em do it. You gotta satisfy the public."

Mackert says he started dancing because the money was good. He adds, "A lot of it has to do with a sense of adventure." He races motorcycles; truck driver Hall took the job on a $120 bet with a group of women who dared him to.

There is the exhibitionism. "It's nice to get some recognition," says Mackert. "You get a pretty steady diet of it here."

Sex always gets a lot of media attention. Jim Stanzak—who explains that the Army lets him pursue his moonlighting career because "rank has its privileges"—has a rap for the radio, TV and newspaper people about liberation.

"A man just can't go home any more and ask his wife what's for dinner," he says. "He's got to give her some kissing and loving because he knows he's got some competition now."

Whether or not the sweaty allure of the go-go boys will make the husbands of Prince George's County change their ways is a moot (if intriguing) point. The point is that the allure is there for many people. That men should enjoy being sex objects, and that women should enjoy being fanny-pinching sexists, may prove that the "revolution" is just going around in circles after all.

Pazen has taken to painting his heterosexual fingernails with glittery nail polish. "I'm a dancer," he says. "I try to attract attention to other parts of my body. It doesn't work." —February 25, 1975

Next: The Fading Past

Both of these stories "evoke a place, a time, an atmosphere," as Jean White writes in her account of auctioning the furnishings of one of the "last of the private mansions the House of Morgan built." On the surface the subjects could hardly be more disparate. The first is the passing of the Long Island North Shore's way of life, "very rich, comfortable and secure with no need for ostentatious show." The second is the "withering" of Boley, Okla., an all-black community that grew in Indian Territory as a refuge from Jim Crow repressiveness and terror in the turn-of-the-century South.

Both declining Boley and the abandoned Morgan mansion, however, are fading relics of social needs that no longer exist. Jean White writes of the "sadness" of the infirm Louise Converse Morgan's possessions, from her "very private" world, going up for public auction. And an undertone of sadness exists in an 83-year-old Boleyite's statement to Hollie West: "Boley's been a good town to me." In Boley, though, there is an added twist, for with the town's decline it has assumed an unexpectedly idyllic character.

Both stories rest heavily upon individual recollection of the past. It was a striking example of reporter's luck when, at the Morgan auction, Jean White happened upon a couple who years before had been taken in as strangers at the mansion after their rowboat swamped in a squall on Long Island Sound. The remoteness of their recollections smoothly suits the story's elegiac mood. In West's Boley profile, the recollections are more numerous, vivid and specific. And they are further bolstered by the author's own family roots in the town. —*L. T.*

A Rich, Very Rich, Lifestyle at Auction

By Jean M. White

With packed lunches, Thermos bottles and the in-laws, Harry and Joy Neuman had rented a rowboat with a dropline and were spending a day fishing on Long Island Sound.

"Suddenly a storm moved in and the other boats started back," Joy Neuman recalls. "But we were catching fish and who leaves? Then came this fierce rain, and we started swamping and headed for shore and I saw this building that looked like the New York Public Library. We got ashore, and a butler was clearing off tables on the terrace. For years, I thought the only way to get here was by rowboat."

That was 32 years ago, and last week Joy and Harry Neuman, of Merrick, L.I., came back to Salutation, the Louise C. Morgan estate on West Island, Glen Cove, L.I. Partly it was nostalgia, but there was also the hope that they could make a bid on some small item to take home with them.

Nostalgia and the name Morgan also played a part in the estate auction that produced sales to pleasantly astound Sotheby Parke Bernet, who handled the exhibition and on-the-premises sale. The four-day auction ended late Saturday afternoon with sales of $1,211,535 — more than double the estimates of the auctioneers. A set of well-used placemats went for $10, the cheapest buy of Morganiana, and six kerosene lanterns tagged at $10/$20 brought $500 in the bidding.

"I guess people wanted to say they had bought something from a Morgan estate. It's a name that has an atmosphere," a spokesman for Sotheby Parke Bernet explained.

Morgan and the north shore of Long Island in the Boom '20s — Gatsby-land — are names that evoke a place, a time, an atmosphere. It was a time when the very rich were rich together, as F. Scott Fitzgerald has described it; a time of private mansions, private polo fields, private railroad cars, private art collections, private yachts; a time of long summer afternoons, long drinks on terraces while watching triangular sails on the Sound. There were the Long Island palaces of the Morgans, the Whitneys, F. W. Woolworth, the Theodore Roosevelts at Oyster Bay, the original "Hillwood" of Marjorie Merriweather Post at Roslyn.

Newport might have been the queen of watering places and Southampton the social dean of Long Island resorts, but the North Shore was rich, very rich. The J.P. Morgan estate on East Island was one of the places where the dashing Prince of Wales was entertained on his visit to the United States in 1924. He was taken for a spin on the Sound in a speedboat capable of 42 mph.

So the Sotheby Parke Bernet auction of "the collection of Louise C. Morgan" — the furnishings of Salutation, among the last of the private mansions the House of Morgan built — was more than an auction of silver, porcelain, rugs, kitchen utensils, works of arts, books, furniture. It was an auction of an era, a past, a lifestyle that has passed into legend and social history.

And along with the Neumans, hundreds of people came to wander through Salutation during three days of public exhibition before the auction. *New York* magazine had listed it as a "best bet" to spend a holiday weekend. There were dealers in silver and porcelains, but they were far outnumbered by those who "always wondered how those people lived."

Sotheby Parke Bernet sold 9,000 catalogs at $8 each, a ticket of admission for two persons. They came in tennis shorts, carrying Pekinese dogs; they tested the beds, sank in the softness of the huge couches, looked at a 330-piece dinner service spread out on a makeshift table in the basement, used the mounted binoculars in one of the guest rooms for a sweeping view of the Sound, and ate hot dogs and roast beef sandwiches from a concession set up on the grounds.

"It's sort of sad when you think how much Mrs. Morgan loved this place," said Roy Rogers, the superintendent whose family has been living alone in the 35-to-50-room mansion (do you count wine cellars?) for over

"Salutation. . .reflects the life of a family that . . . could surround itself with beauty and quiet elegance."

two years. It was clear that it was also sad for Rogers, who first came to Salutation 13 years ago as a dog trainer when there was a staff of 14 or 15 servants. He kept busy doing chores in the basement as the hundreds of visitors tramped through the mansion.

Louise Converse Morgan, now 79 and infirm, had lived in Salutation for more than 40 years before she left in November 1971 to enter a nursing home. She was married to the late Junius S. Morgan, grandson of J. Pierpont Morgan (founder of the House of Morgan) and the son of J.P. Morgan Jr., who consolidated the fortune and was *the* J.P. Morgan of the '20s.

Salutation, completed in 1929 just before the Wall Street crash, is a lovely, graceful mansion of gray fieldstone, imposing without being distinguished architecturally. It is termed "English classic" for want of a style. Situated on a tip of West Island, it is near the old J.P. Morgan estate on East Island. (Fitzgerald writes of West and East Egg in *The Great Gatsby*.) The J.P. Morgan estate now is the summer home of the Russian United Nations delegation, and other neighboring million-dollar mansions, with the passing of fortunes and lifestyles and the encroachment of suburbs, have been sold to foundations, religious orders and national organizations.

Salutation is being sold separately by the Morgan Guaranty Trust. A spokesman said the asking price was $760,000 for the mansion and 22 acres of land. Although there have been some inquiries, no definite offer has been made. "There are not too many private individuals who want such an estate and can afford the upkeep," he explained.

Along with taxes of $30,000 a year, there is a $60,000 annual assessment for membership in the West Island Association. There are six other families beside the Morgans who own land on the 48-acre island and are members of the association. They pay the $60,000 a year to maintain the common grounds and the causeway that leads to the island and to have the convenant right to veto any potential buyer. No one says so directly, but the feeling is the members would veto any foundation or religious order that might bid up the price on the mansion.

The Morgans, with the protective insulation that the very rich and the very celebrated need if they are to keep any part of their lives to themselves, are a very private family. Sotheby Parke Bernet said the only information they were given was Louise C. Morgan was the granddaughter-in-law of J. Pierpont Morgan and lived at Salutation from the time it was built in 1929. Her husband, Junius S. Morgan, had died in 1960.

But the lives of the archmillionaires in the early 1900s were followed and chronicled in the press as minutely as those of today's rock stars.

When Louise Converse, of Boston, married Junius Spencer Morgan at high noon on June 15, 1915, the *New York Times* noted that the bridegroom's grandmother, with other members of the family, sailed to the Boston wedding from New York on the yacht Corsair. Junius was to enter the firm of Morgan and sail for San Francisco with his bride on a honeymoon trip in mid-July, the paper also faithfully reported. But, on July 3, 1915, the news of the young couple moved to the front page and an eight-column banner headline. The couple, coming to the East Island estate of J.P. Morgan for a dinner party in their honor, is stopped by armed guards at the lodgehouse at the causeway entrance. J.P. Morgan has been shot (not mortally) by an intruder. The servants are talking about the ill omen of 13 guests invited for the dinner.

There are later notes in the press when Junius launched his yacht, Windward, in 1929 shortly after the couple moved into Salutation, when he put his one-fourth seat on the Stock Exchange for sale, of Mrs. Morgan's activities with a society ladies' committee while her husband was in Navy service during World War II.

Salutation, open for the exhibition-auction much as Mrs. Morgan left it two years earlier after more than four decades in residence, reflects the life of a family that could afford what it enjoyed and could surround itself with beauty and quiet elegance.

They were the genuine rich, comfortable and secure with no need for ostentatious show and frenetic partying to prove their wealth and worth as the Gatsbys of the world felt they needed. They bought what they liked and didn't care whether it was antique or rare. Louise Morgan could raise 75 black labradors (the portable kennels were up for auction); her husband could collect four-foot high ships' models of fully-rigged vessels of the reign of James II (one brought $22,000 at the auction) and display them in a huge hallway running the length of his home.

There were very fine pieces of furniture, indeed, but not the priceless antiques some had expected. Books were stacked haphazardly on the sills by the window seats, from *Bulldog Drummond Strikes Back* to the *Endowment Funds of Harvard University*. On the bookshelves lining rooms and hallways were richly bound collections of classics, volumes of first editions of *Punch* from 1840, children's books like *Freddy Plays Football* and *Hans Brinker or the Silver Skates,* records of the Zodiac Club, an exclusive men's dining club of 12 members in which J.P. Morgan succeeded his father, J. Pierpont, to the sign of Libra after the elder Morgan's death in 1913.

"A glazed pottery figure from the Ming dynasty sold for $23,000..."

In the toy room, there still are boxing gloves and quoits and clay models. Stacked dangerously on one shelf is piano sheet music, including "Love Walked In" from the Goldwyn Follies, "introducing Edgar Bergen and Charlie McCarthy" to the movies. The name Marie Converse was scrawled on the music to "He's a Rag Picker" by Irving Berlin. In a large third-floor room, brightened by a skylight, the painting brushes and sculpting tools once used by Mrs. Morgan, an amateur artist, were still on an artist's workbench.

Salutation is a mansion of views, and every one invites contemplation with no ugliness to intrude on quiet beauty. Guests could choose bedrooms overlooking the Sound, with its changing skies, or the garden, with its octagonal pool and corridor of copper beeches and weeping beeches. Nearby was a tennis court and two pools, with a choice of fresh or salt water.

The Morgans could afford to collect what they prized for beauty — silver, Chinese porcelains, Oriental rugs, Audubon prints, Wedgwood & Bentley black basal circular wall plaques, Coromandel screens. At the auction, the silver and porcelain attracted the professional dealers. Among the items were a rare William III inkstand (London, c. 1700), a Louis XV chocolate pot, a German silvergilt canister (Leipzig, c. 1660) and 18th-century pieces by Huguenot silversmiths. As it turned out, the highest bid — $44,000 — came for a painting of shipping and small vessels ascribed to artist Samuel Scott and cautiously given an estimated value range of $550/ $6,500 by Sotheby Parke Bernet. A glazed pottery figure from the Ming Dynasty sold for $23,000, and two large dinner services of more than 300 pieces each (one with 123 dinner plates) brought $25,000.

"Mrs. Morgan never liked to give very large dinner parties. She enjoyed small groups of people whom she liked," Rogers, the superintendent who lives on the third floor of mansion with his family, recalled. "She loved to paint, until she developed cataracts. She loved her dogs, which she showed both on the bench and in field trials. When they put in the salt-water pool, she put on boots and worked in the muck with the workmen."

Mrs. Morgan's children have their own lives and homes. John P. Morgan II is a vice president for Morgan Guaranty Trust. One daughter, Louise, is Mrs. Charles R. Hook Jr., who lives in Gates Mill, Ohio. Another daughter, Anne Simoneau, lives at Stowe, Vt.

"Mr. Morgan (the son) has built his own house on the island and Mrs. Hook has just built a place in Mexico," Rogers said.

For the auction, a bright yellow-and-white canopy was erected on the terrace overlooking the Sound, much larger than the one that Mrs. Morgan had for her dinner parties on the terrace. It was such a dinner party that the storm interrupted when Harry and Joy Neuman's rowboat was swamped and they came ashore at Salutation in 1942.

"The butler told us that we couldn't stay because 'the people are here,'" Joy Neuman recalls. "Then this lovely woman came out and invited us into the anteroom to get out of the rain. I remember the Chinese figures in the wall niches and peeking down the long hall lined with ship models — just as today.

"Then Mrs. Morgan sent a guest — I think he was a British admiral — down to help us bail out the rowboat, and we used the cup off the Thermos bottles."

— June 3, 1974

Once a Town of Hope, Now a Fading Dream

By Hollie I. West

Say, have you heard the story,
Of a little colored town,
Way over in the Nation
On such lovely sloping ground?
With as pretty little houses
As you ever chanced to meet,
With not a thing but colored folks
A standing in the streets?
Oh, tis a pretty country
And the Negroes own it, too,
With not a single white man here
To tell us what to do—In Boley.

BOLEY, Okla.—That's how E.J. (Uncle Jesse) Pinkett sang the praises of Boley as its town poet more than 60 years ago. Today, a traveler speeding east along U.S. Highway 62 through rolling slopes of Oklahoma sandstone and shale could whisk by here without ever knowing this "little colored town" still stands.

Only McCormick's gasoline station, cafe and motel face the highway. The community, a mile square, sits on a hill screened by briar bushes and catalpa trees. The first, and only, advance notice of the town is a simple road marker, "Boley—5."

Boley is a dream that faded. Its thriving farming base withered, the town today is made up largely of the middle-aged and elderly. Pecan Street, known by most as Main Street and built wide, once bustled with mule-drawn wagons laden with bales of cotton. Today it moves at a drowsy pace except on Saturday nights when the few remaining bars and cafes throb with jukebox soul music, the click of pool cues hitting balls, the thump of dominoes on a wooden table, and the dancing feet of the town's dwindling youth. But on a Monday noon, chickens walk leisurely across Main Street, stopping traffic.

Abandoned buildings, brick, frame and sandstone, that once housed flourishing businesses are rapidly crumbling. Only one business new to Boley, according to Mayor T. R. McCormick, has opened on Main Street in the last 30 years. Boley has no shoe repair shop, bank, automobile dealer, motion picture theater, health clinic, hospital or lawyers.

The time was, however, when Boley couldn't be missed for the filling stations and cafes dotting the highway, trucks and horse-drawn wagons entering and exiting the town. Boley was a mecca in the early part of the century for hundreds of blacks fleeing the racial persecution and terrorism of the post-Reconstruction Deep South.

Boley is still an all-black town, one of several score in the nation and one of about 15 in Oklahoma. It was founded in 1904 by blacks, for blacks. The town symbolized the black separatist idea, the separate-but-equal racial thinking of that time, espoused by Booker T. Washington and converted into legal doctrine by the U.S. Supreme Court in 1896 in the Plessy v. Ferguson decision.

Like many of the black towns in Oklahoma, Boley emerged in the aftermath of an attempt by blacks in the 1890s to persuade the federal government to carve an all-black state out of the Twin Territories, Oklahoma and Indian (which later became the state of Oklahoma). Failing the objective, territorial blacks established all-black towns that constituted bastions of black nationalism.

In the beginning, Boley had a magnetic appeal pulling in blacks attracted, in part, by the clarion call of the local newspaper: "All Men Up— Not Some Down." Boley boomed in its early years, swelling to more than 2,500 persons. But cotton failed as a cash crop for the region's small farmers in the '30s and the depression hit the town with a force from which it never recorded. By 1940 its population had plunged to 942. Today the town has only 500 citizens.

L.L. Dolphin, 88, his eyes atwinkle with a glow found in younger men and still an avid reader of history, came here from Alabama in 1907 (the year Oklahoma became a state) as advance man for his father's family. He sums up the principal reasons blacks made the trek: "The Negroes were being mistreated everywhere. But they located here and nobody came in and tried to tell them what they could do and what they couldn't do."

J.L. McCormick Sr., 83, leans back in his frayed easy chair, draws a long puff on his stubby cigar and recalls his family in flight from racial terror in Alabama in 1891 for the security of Indian Territory:

"My father looked down the road one morning and saw a bunch of white people leading a Negro boy tied to a buggy. He was the son of a man accused of molesting a white woman. Dad saw his family doctor driving the buggy. He was a white fellow. And my father respected him— thought he was quite a man. But they lynched this colored boy. So my

" 'If the government took welfare away, Boley would collapse in a day.' "

father said, 'Wife, I'm going to gather this crop and leave this doggone place.' And he did."

Wearing his usual khakis and 10-gallon hat, McCormick at 6-feet-2, still cuts a striking figure. He retired in 1966 after being county deputy sheriff and Boley town marshal for 40 years. Probably the most colorful storyteller in town, he continues:

"I remember my dad—Joe McCormick was his name—saying that when he decided to leave Alabama, people told him: 'Joe, don't go out there. Those Indians will eat up your children.' We never had no trouble with Indians and not too much with white people. Boley's been a good town for me."

The McCormicks settled in Boley in 1906 after living in other parts of the territory. The elder McCormick farmed and operated a general store.

The saga of the McCormicks and Dolphins represents what only two of the families did in making the exodus from the South to the West. For them, like the white migrants, the move westward signified a chance at a fresh start in life, a new stake with cheap land. But for blacks it was more. The lure of the West for them was the dream of freedom from racial discrimination.

That same yearning is voiced today by much younger people who remained in Boley after growing up there. Sam Wilcots, 42, mayor here between 1962 and 1972, says: "I always felt I was free here. Nobody, no white man, could come in and order me around. That's why I stayed."

Boley is also a place where a black person like T.R. McCormick, 62, decendant of the first settlers here, can create with ingenuity and hard work, a network of businesses. A tireless worker, McCormick is known in town as the man who never sleeps. He owns the town's only motel, one of two gasoline stations here, a cleaning and pressing shop, cafe (he's the cook) and, with his wife, a mortuary.

Acting as his own architect and contractor, McCormick is building a city hall himself, a construction role he assumed in putting up his funeral home. Says he: "If I hadn't done most of the blueprint work and my own building, I couldn't have done it. If you want to own something, you just have to sacrifice."

Boley's transition to quiet backwater means a lot of its citizens are on welfare, either old age assistance or aid to dependent children. Says one observer: "If the government took away welfare from this town, it would collapse in a day."

Like many small towns, Boley possesses a tranquillity and friendly atmosphere that its citizens enjoy. Velma Dolphin Ashley, daughter of the pioneers here and a teacher in the Boley school system for 42 years, says: "There's a certain type of freedom that the people in Boley have and that we don't find elsewhere. We [she and her husband, who is school superintendent] never lock that front door as long as we're at school."

Precise and articulate, Mrs. Ashley continues: "I enjoy that freedom. I've been told that because of my health, I should walk. I walk two miles a day. And I don't mind walking in any direction from my house without fear of being molested. I can walk all across town."

That serenity has lured back Gene and Henrietta Hicks (he's 42, she's 39) from lucrative jobs and comfortable living in Los Angeles. Both left Boley in the '50s, he in 1950 and she in 1957. He became an engineer for Capitol Records, received three gold records in recognition of his studio work on behalf of three separate million-selling Steve Miller Band records. She coordinated an educational program for adults in eight hospitals for the Los Angeles School District.

They decided to leave L.A.'s hustle and bustle for the calm of Boley. In truth, they returned for several reasons, according to Mrs. Hicks: to take care of the Hicks family farm after her husband's father died, and to find a less polluted atmosphere for their 6-year-old son, Gregory, who suffered from asthma. But says Mrs. Hicks: "Gene's main thing was peace, quiet and comfortability. I had to get myself ready for it because I knew I was going to miss L.A. I was thinking: How am I going to like it? Where am I going to shop? How many groceries am I going to need to buy for two weeks?"

The Hickses have joined many other Boley citizens who commute 60 miles each day to jobs in Oklahoma City. He's now an audio specialist for the Oklahoma City School Board and she's a job development counselor for the Oklahoma City Urban League office.

Does the commuting bother them? He answers: "We enjoy it. We did it in California — only there it was longer time, shorter distance. And here we use just one car."

Their three-bedroom house is a showplace in Boley. A local carpenter says it may be worth $100,000. That estimate might well be high, but the house looks as if it would surely be valued at $80,000 to $90,000 in Washington. The Hickses' master bathroom (one of three) is as large as some bedrooms. Their den is larger than many living rooms.

Do they miss going out in Los Angeles? Says Hicks: "If we want to go someplace, the highways are good and the cars are good. So if we want to go to a movie or to dinner, we can go into Oklahoma City or Tulsa. In an hour's time we can be in either place."

Neither expresses any fear that their son will miss any cultural advantages he might have had in Los Angeles. Travel, they say, will make up for what he might miss.

"Many people want to come back, but some of them have invested so much that they don't want to give it up." Henrietta Hicks says, "They just can't afford to. I wish we could encourage more young people to return to Boley. I don't want to give you the impression that Boley is the best place in the world to be, but I'm beginning to wonder what other town is better."

The Hickses' idea of Boley as a town of success, security and neighborliness for blacks goes back to the origins of the town. It has held many citizens who were asked to try their luck elsewhere.

J.L. McCormick says he never considered moving his family. "I live here," he says. "My family was here. I bought a home here. And I bought a few acres of land. I always liked Boley, and I always got along with everybody in surrounding towns."

Get on the Fort Smith and Western
The train will bring you here.
Take any of the coaches
You have no cause for fear.
Here a Negro makes your dresses
And a Negro makes your pants
And hands your mail out
If you'll give him half a chance —
In Boley.
— E.J. (Uncle Jesse) Pinkett

With so many people in the territory and cotton enjoying quick cash status, the Fort Smith and Western Railroad began to build from the Territory-Arkansas border to the territorial capital at Guthrie. The plan was to encourage settlements every six miles, and not more than 12 miles apart.

Velma Dolphin Ashley, who wrote her master's thesis at Kansas State College of Pittsburg, Kan., on Boley's development up to 1940, says, "They [the railroad] got six miles from Okemah to Castle, then the next six miles they were in the middle of the Creek Freedman area, which means Negroes. So the question came up: Shall we put a town here? Blacks can't control themselves. They'd need a white man over them."

But, according to a generally accepted story, two railroad officials maintained that blacks could govern themselves and plans for the town went ahead. It took the name of one of the white officials, W.H. Boley (the first thought was to name the town Barnett after the Creek Freedman on whose land the hamlet was built, but there was already a Barnett, Indian Territory).

Newspapers, black and white, all over the South carried articles proclaiming the advantages of life in Boley. Ads appeared appealing for blacks to move to Boley. The exodus was on.

Nothing like her ever happened before. Nothing like her will ever happen again. The birth of this town reads like a fairy story. . . . The whole of Boley in which but a few short months ago almost the only fire scent was that raised from the Indian teepee or hunting camp, is now curling from hundreds of chimneys of the residents, and the busy hours of business mark the onward march of civilization.
—From the first issue of the *Boley Progress,* March 9, 1905.

Boley was founded in 1904 in the part of the Indian Territory that was the old Creek Nation. At that time, and several years earlier, the territory was the last easily accessible frontier in the United States. Although the land legally belonged to the Indians of the "five civilized tribes"—Cherokees, Seminoles, Creeks, Choctaws and Chickasaws—which had been driven out of the South before and after the Civil War, white migration into the territory was widespread.

According to anthropologist William E. Bittle and sociologist Gilbert Geis, there were 108,000 whites out of a total population of 175,000 in 1889. Many blacks also settled in the territory. Estimates show that between 4,000 and 5,000 were brought in as slaves by the Indians.

Many people are unaware that Indians owned plantations and slaves in the South. A primary difference between Indian and white slave owners was that the former regarded blacks more as workers than chattel. This attitude carried over to Indian Territory, particularly among the Creeks, who allowed their slaves to run most of their own affairs.

Boley grew quickly. Lulu Mixon, 91, says: "People were coming in so fast there was no place for them to sleep."

J.L. McCormick Sr., who was 15 when he arrived in Boley in 1906, says: "There were quite a few people here then. They were living in tents. But there were also some houses and a few stores."

Booker T. Washington, whose many roles included heading the National Negro Business League, visited Boley in 1905 and said afterward that the black town movement represented "a dawning race consciousness . . . which shall demonstrate the right of the Negro . . . to have a worthy and permanent place in the civilization that the American people are creating."

Meanwhile, another movement was developing—in Oklahoma—this one back to Africa. Chief Alfred Charles Sam, who claimed to be of royal African blood, began recruiting blacks from back-country cotton farms in eastern Oklahoma in 1913 and by August 1914, he and 60 passengers steamed off into the Gulf of Mexico bound for the Gold Coast (now Ghana).

"Today Boley stands at the crossroads . Will it slip further and eventually out of sight?"

Some say this movement helped destroy Boley because of the unrest it created. Although many blacks didn't make the trip to Africa, they sold their land and were homeless, deflating the inspiration black towns once kindled. Recalls 88-year-old L.L. Dolphin: "Boley started declining during that back-to-Africa movement of Chief Sam. Boley never got over it. Entirely too many people left. A bunch of them went to a camp down at Weleetka and just got bogged down. They never recovered the land they'd sold. It was a mess.

"People flocked to Chief Sam because they were getting upset over the Jim Crow policies the Oklahoma legislature was passing. Many blacks were not in favor of statehood in the first place because they didn't expect to be treated well, and they were right. It got to be so bad that the districts in this county (Okfuskee) were carved up so much that our vote in Boley didn't mean a hill of beans in the county elections. So people became bitter and started listening to Chief Sam."

.If the back-to-Africa movement dealt a damaging blow to Boley, the depression in the '30s almost did it in. Cotton fell in price from 40 cents to two cents a pound. And the Fort Smith and Western pulled out the rail line in 1938.

Between 1911 and 1940 Boley had three cotton gins, all doing prosperous business. But they started closing as the economy slumped. By the end of World War II the bottom had fallen out in the state, county, and Boley. Today there is only one gin in what was once cotton-rich Okfuskee County. Pecans, peanuts, corn and wheat are staple crops, but the region around Boley is not the farming area it used to be.

While the depression floored most people in the '30s it inspired a tumultuous rash of bank robberies in the Southwest and Midwest. Oklahoma was one of the primary areas hit. Hold-ups were taking place almost weekly.

At attempted robbery of the Farmers State Bank in Boley in 1932 is still the subject of much discussion. Three men were gunned down — D.J. Turner, the bank president and a Boley pioneer, George (Handyman) Birdwell, a white henchman of Pretty Boy Floyd, and Charlie Glass, a black accomplice.

69

J.L. McCormick, who took part in the shootout, recalls: "The boys here kind of expected that thing to happen here. A lot of these people here had rifles. Several burglar alarms in stores on Main Street connected to the bank.

"I remember I was walking down the street. It was about 10 o'clock in the morning. And somebody ran up to me and said, 'The bank's being robbed, the bank's being robbed.' Well, I went over to the American Legion hall and got some rifles and took off down the alley, jumping over fences. And by the time I got there, the shooting was on.

"I won't say I got one, but I kept them [the robbers] busy. My brother, H.C. McCormick, killed Birdwell after Birdwell shot Turner. After all the smoke cleared, somebody wanted to kill Patterson, but I said, 'Don't kill this man.' He was laying there on the sidewalk. And somebody said, 'You heard the marshal. Don't harm this man.' My wife, Annie, asked if I was all right, and I said yes. Then she said, 'Let this man live. He might reform and do something for Jesus.'"

The attempted bank robbery shook the town, but economic decline was rapidly ensuring Boley's sleepy present. Today Boley stands at a crossroads. Will it slip further and eventually out of sight? Or will it manage to stay afloat and perhaps experience resurrection?

There are still nine churches in Boley, one for about every 55 residents. But it has no industry. The plant it had, the M.W. Lee Manufacturing Co., turned out barbecue cookers in an abandoned hotel on Main Street. It went bankrupt. Another part of the Lee plant made wooden shipping crates. It closed its doors last year when the federal government failed to renew a contract fast enough. As a result, Boley residents lost 80 jobs.

The meaning was clear. Says owner M.W. Lee Jr.: "Those 80 jobs represented employment for about 40 families. Out of those 40 families, we have about 10 left in Boley. The others went to Tulsa, Oklahoma City and other places. And they were younger people with children in school."

Boley's economy is precarious and now commuter-oriented. Its businesses are strictly of the small, mom-and-pop variety, some generations old. Mrs. N.E. Tieule has operated a women's clothing store on Main Street for more than 60 years, and she says she keeps it going so "I'll have something to do everyday." But like most businesses here, it is a store out of the past: dimly lighted, old fashioned wooden and glass counters and goods scattered about in disarray.

To many people, Boley is an anachronism hopelessly swimming against the tide of racial and economic interdependence. It's not that Boleyites are opposed to whites. A white woman, Mary Harshbarger, heads the local chamber of commerce. A social worker at the nearby state reform school for boys, Harshbarger, a native Oklahoman who doesn't like to be called white but rather "human," is the only white person living alone in Boley (there are two mixed couples in town).

Why does she live there? "I came here to get rid of my racism," she answers. "People accept me on my own. I'm a Boleyite. There's no color thing."

Velma Dolphin Ashley says: "Mary Harshbarger didn't come in here to look down on people. She came to help the town, and she's one of the most faithful civic workers we have."

Although there are technically no barriers against whites, there has been almost no success in attracting industry of any kind. Says school superintendent L.G. Ashley: "Boley was built on the idea that farming would last indefinitely as an economic base. That was a mistake. And we're stuck with it."

The result of the economic malaise in Boley, naturally, has been a youth migration to urban centers nearby like Oklahoma City and Tulsa or to distant places like California. Says Mrs. Ashley: "I'm going to be honest with you. I don't know what we're going to do if we can't hold our young people. I don't know what can be done [about the economy] in view of the limitations for the chances of getting money, federal or otherwise. Manufacturing is what we need. But how do we get it?"

The writer of this article, Hollie I. West, was born and reared in Wewoka, Okla., a racially mixed town about 35 miles southwest of Boley. West's mother was born and reared in Boley and he visited the town frequently over the past four decades. His maternal grandmother was a member of the McCormick family, among Boley's earliest settlers. J.L. McCormick Sr. is his great uncle and the town's mayor, T.R. McCormick, is a cousin.

—February 9, 1975

II. Portraits

"Characters who have motives . . . are the very thing that journalism can never deliver, because there's no way a reporter can see into a man's heart." — Ward Just, the Washington Post, *March 1975.*

The rigidity with which Just's observation can be applied varies according to the elusiveness of the subject and the skill of the journalist. But certainly there always comes a point beyond which the reporter, and sometimes the subject too, cannot articulate or perceive what is in the subject's own psyche. This, we learn from an earlier story in the book, is what drove Just from daily journalism to fiction. Yet the remaining possibilities that can be brought to journalistic portraits are broad enough that fiction writers themselves have flocked to the medium. The best portraits here show how the writer, using a wide range of literary and reporting devices, can go far beyond the recorded statements of an interview to probe personality and lifestyle.

Some in this section, because they epitomize these possibilities in the complexity with which they employ different devices, will be discussed in detail. Others, using similar techniques to shed light on the subjects, will be left to explain themselves: the grim Kernan piece on Elie Wiesel, written in 40 minutes against deadline; Tom Shales' profile of Dustin Hoffman as the dedicated theater professional; Jeannette Smyth on Joe Hirshhorn (dictated by phone on deadline from notes); Gene Meyer on Mr. L. G. Broadmoore; Myra MacPherson's Dreiser-like profile of a returned Vietnam POW at loose ends; and Sally Quinn's delicious encounter with Rudolf Nureyev, which is, by implication, a kind of essay on what charisma is all about.

Next: A Writer of Fiction

Eudora Welty. About a third of the way into the story, the writer of this memorable profile of the prominent Mississippi author (a Southerner himself and a personal friend of hers) quite precisely characterizes her prose style: "The speech of the narrative, the plainness and elegance of the language, the stripped quality of the action . . ." But by contrast, nowhere in this profile does he balance out those words with specific characterization of the author herself. Instead, just as Welty would do in developing a fictional character, Mitchell draws from a full range of literary devices that implicitly portray the unassuming, mellow, proud and acute Eudora Welty.

The piece is one of this book's most complex exercises in the devices of literary journalism. Most important, perhaps, is the unmistakably Southern, plain tone of the prose—established emphatically in the lead and sustained throughout the narrative. Mitchell picks up the sound of Welty's quotes and, beyond that, of her writing. (As a result, the reader has a rare feeling of intimacy with the subject)(sometimes Mitchell refers to her, simply, as "Eudora").

Then there is the seemingly rambling structure; though Mitchell says this is an account of two days he spent with Welty, chronology is thrown out the window and the reader gets no clue as to the sequence of events. This frees Mitchell to move the narrative from the substance of the interview into exposition on her writings and back again any time a reference to her work sheds light on a point in the interview.

All this is held together by ingenious, almost devious, bridges (the Welty profile is one of the few stories in this volume which hasn't a single break). One moment we are in her garden and then the next sentence is: "Her characters in her stories are like roses—some make it, some don't." And what a bold use of evocative detail that is, as well. All sorts of allusions abound ("The idea of a reckless Eudora Welty is something to make a dog laugh"). And though the tone stays cheerful and leisurely (like Welty herself), Mitchell lets some of the darker aspects show through in passing— her mother's death, her inability until recently to make ends meet off writing alone.

Most profiles of the famous focus primarily either on the person's work or on the personality; the Welty profile is an unusual case where the two elements are in roughly even, and complementary, balance. This story, by the way, drew a laudatory note from its subject that would be the envy of almost anyone who aspires to fine writing.

—*L.T.*

Eudora Welty:
Storyteller of the South

By Henry Mitchell

JACKSON, Miss.—Some say Eudora Welty writes best of all, in all Hinds County, but she has never taken to prideful airs. Others say she's the best in all central Mississippi or all America.

"Shoot!" she says, or "Foot!" when the paid or, as you might say, store-bought critics start up their steady songs of praise.

"Now Eudora," a friend once said to her, "how come you read those reviews. Lots of writers don't read reviews at all."

"I know a lot of writers that don't," she said, "but I do. I've got too much curiosity not to."

Which is, as the Lord knows, true. Miss Welty has more curiosity than a tiger cat. Besides, though she won't exactly say so, it's fairly nice to pick up a paper or magazine and see them having consistent and urgent fits about both your last two books. She writes them for hours off and on in her bedroom right here in Jackson and they are, as some would say, a wonder to behold.

One fellow in the *Washington Post* (writer Reynolds Price) just flung up his arms in print and said there's no point comparing *Losing Battles* (1970) to other American novels. He suggested, for starters, you might compare it with "The Tempest" by the late W. Shakespeare, and then just took it on from there.

"Yes, I know he did," said Miss Welty when I had the pleasure of her company and her cooking for two days recently, "and I am really going to speak to him about it. Shakespeare is a bit much."

He was the worst, the *Post* reviewer, for making a decent person blush. The paper down in Houston just said the book was a "gigantic achievement" and at the *New York Times* they only spoke of their "general rejoicing" though they did add Miss Welty has the surest comic sense of any American writer alive. In Philadelphia where the cautious restraining Quaker influence is still felt they modestly called it a masterpiece and let it go at that.

"I do like to read blurbs," said Miss Welty. "And when I go through a book I look unconsciously for good ones."

"Ain't she kind of a recluse?" asked the cab driver that eventually showed up to carry me to the Welty house in the first place. He pronounced it "reckless." (The idea of a reckless Eudora Welty is something to make a dog laugh.) Reckless she is not. But then recluse she is not, either. It would irk the fire out of her if she knew that cab driver thought she was that.

It's a rare day she doesn't meet a friend (and when you're born and live 60 years in Mississippi and went to school and are still in the same not-very-big town, you have enough friends to get by on) for a small toddy or lunch or supper. Usually it's at home—theirs or hers—because Southern people are not much for wandering about in strange restaurants except in New Orleans where their origins are different.

Miss Welty's family had no Deep South background though she is famous for her Southern characters. Her father came to Jackson from Ohio and her mother from West Virginia. But Miss Welty has lived all her life in Jackson; she won a holiday from school once for learning to spell all 82 counties of Mississippi along with the county seats, and some of them are tricky—Oktibbeha, for instance. It is also known with certainty she used to purchase penny Tootsie Rolls and with equal certainty that even then she had a care with her writing and delighted classmates.

She still lives in the new Welty brick house (built scarcely 50 years ago), with spacious 1920-generous halls. Some of the walls have cracked—Miss Welty says Jackson is built on marl over shifting sands. It is somewhat like a time-lapse earthquake: You resign yourself to repairing cracked walls.

Miss Welty was pitched right out of a Jackson restaurant recently, though, which shows among other things she is no recluse. It was all because she was hostess to two young men with Jesus haircuts, and long hair is something the restaurant owner has a real thing about.

"But maybe you were mistaken—maybe you misunderstood the waitress," somebody asked Miss Welty since, after all, a restaurant is no more likely to throw Miss Welty out in Jackson than Alice Roosevelt at the Rive Gauche, it being an honor in both cases.

"I did not misunderstand the waitress," said Eudora, with just a slight rise of tone, as if to say she did not go around misunderstanding anything humans are likely to do. "She said very plainly, 'You all will have to go.'" But she did say not to feel bad about it—they pitched customers out all the time for having long hair and the wonder of it is they have any customers left, barber styles being what they are.

The humor was not lost, even at the time, on Miss Welty, but there are times to express anger so she fired off a letter to the *Clarion Ledger* about it. The young guests weren't drunk or disorderly or doing anything but sitting there like unshorn lambs hoping for a shrimp cocktail. Eudora won't go back.

She stated her position right there in the letter. She acted and now need not dwell on it further. She has no grudges. Or if she has, it's not about restaurant owners but grand and immortal enemies like death, yellow leaves or nematodes:

"You wouldn't know it," she said, "but this garden was once beautiful. My mother really kept after it." Both mother and daughter were fine gardeners — the ones that really know, as distinct from the ones that just have masses of color. They used to read V. Sackville-West in the *Observer* and Elizabeth Lawrence and so on. And from those excellent rungs they went right on up, to a garden that really meant something.

The year the nematodes came things mainly died. Mrs. Welty was ill — she died in recent years — and Miss Welty was writing *Losing Battles* at home with her and two nurses and laughing a great deal (the book is beyond grief and funny as owls in heaven) and the nurses did not approve of anything.

And right in the middle of it the nematodes did in the roses, which had been packed in that garden tight as a trunk, but nothing that could be tried availed at all. Miss Welty planted a crabapple at the beginning rose-bed to keep her mother from being too much aware of disasters in the main planting.

Ordinarily an attack on her roses would have brought Mrs. Welty right out of the kitchen, as they say, but she was past those battles then. Many treasures went. The old "Gloire de Dijon" and "Fortune's Yellow Climbers" succumbed, and so did even the great "Mermaid." But "Safrano," the old tea rose, is blooming yet, and "Silver Moon" pulled through and so did "Lady Banks."

Her characters in her stories are like the roses — some make it, some don't. Her first story, "Death of a Traveling Salesman" (1936, when Miss Welty was 24), is about a man whose vehicle doesn't work, who sees nothing the way it really is and who dies without having made much sense of himself or anything else in the world.

Her last novel, *The Optimist's Daughter,* is also about people who are trying to figure out who they are (and who are commonly confused and mistaken) and one point of the story is that there is little difference among classes once the accents, the intonations and the other superficial marks of caste are allowed for.

That is why, probably, the story of Phoenix Jackson (in *The Green Curtain* decades ago) is still admired, though few of its readers have any direct experience with the heroine, a very old black woman walking to and from the doctor's to get medicine for her grandson who swallowed lye.

Some of her readers think *Losing Battles* is her most typical and best book, though critics seem to keep hinting it's a tour de force.

It is the story of a white farming family in that part of Mississippi near the Tennessee-Alabama-Mississippi border. The time is the 1930s, the characters are of the poorest sort, but proud and self-reliant and highly conscious of the claims and bonds of family.

The author thinks nobody would believe it, if the setting were the present, and that is why it is set 40 years ago. "I wanted the characters to be down to bedrock — no money, no education, no nothing, except themselves — the rest being all cleared away to begin with."

Even so, the characters are complicated, and most of them misunderstand their roles. *Losing Battles* is partly about the battles they lose, and the title is partly ironic, about the battles they win, sometimes without knowing it.

The hero is named Jack, scion of the family, who has been sent to Parchman Prison for no good reason and who returns in time for the annual family reunion.

If a comparison to Shakespeare seems extravagant, and it does, one man who objected to that extravagance found himself comparing it to "The Iliad" and *Don Quixote.*

"It reminds me of 'The Iliad' he said."

"Everything reminds *me* of 'The Iliad,'" Miss Welty replied.

The speech of the narrative, the plainess and elegance of the language, the stripped quality of the action, the intense quality of the personal relationships and the occasional heightening of the dialogue for emotional effect — even to the extent of introducing an archaic note — all reflect the general method of Homer more than Shakespeare.

The comic element of this and many other stories is more like Damon Runyan or Cervantes than Mark Twain.

But just as one critic risked seeming like a fool by comparing it to Shakespeare's "Tempest," many readers seem a trifle foolish recalling (as they read it) Cervantes and Homer. Just as the reviewers seemed generally to think in large terms and high precedents, so readers often seem to react as if Miss Welty were an oracle or a priestess rather than a good storyteller.

"I got a letter last week from a man in Taiwan," she said, "who for reasons best known to himself wanted me to be 'the grandmother' for his children. It's a warm nice letter, but how do you answer anything like that? I don't want to be anybody's damn grandmother.

"And here's a letter from a nun — I think nuns write letters a good bit — complaining some story I wrote is unfair to Campfire Girls or Girl Scouts. I don't know how to answer that. Here's another one, from a nun in India who has fallen in love with a priest and wants my advice. How would I know? I do so wish these people well, but I have no idea how to write them or even how to begin."

Another letter recently came from a nice person who wanted to know why her stories had not dealt with the Jews in the Mississippi ghettos.

"We have Jews in Mississippi as you know, but they don't live in ghettos. They are more likely to be mayor of the town. When I get letters

" 'Words almost don't mean anything anymore...anything can be a lie.' "

that bewilder me—well, I'm thinking of getting some letter paper that says 'You Just Can't Get There From Here.' "

But what many of the letters have in common is an unspoken assumption that Miss Welty understands all there is to understand about virtually any human relationship.

Her last two novels, like all her work, began as short stories. *Losing Battles* was meant to end when Jack returned from prison to join the family reunion, but Miss Welty had fallen hopelessly in love with him by the time he made his first appearance on page 71, too many characters had already built him up as a hero.

So she allowed herself a few more pages to deal with Jack—436 pages, to be exact—and the result is her novel that she still thinks of in terms of a story rather than a grand panorama of the world.

Her last novel, issued this spring, *The Optimist's Daughter,* also began as a short story that wouldn't stop.

"It's the first thing I've ever done that has direct autobiographical information in it. I'm not sure that was right—the mother is based on my mother. The boys are her brothers—I think I may have added an extra one—and the West Virginia part is set in her own country."

The most notable thing in the book is a prolonged and lyrical coda (". . . His white shirt would shine for a long time almost without moving in her sight, like Venus in the sky of Mount Salus, while grandmother, mother and little girl sat outlasting the light, waiting for him to climb home. . .").

Few things are riskier than "fine writing," but Miss Welty has never been afraid to risk it. She spoke once in conversation of plant explorers who go to Nepal and Sikkim, risking their lives to introduce alpine flowers to gardens.

"Now that's something—discovering new primroses—that's worth taking trouble with, worth risking something for," she said.

She seemed to set the plant explorers bringing garden treasures from the Himalayas over against the ordinary world we all live in everyday: "Words almost don't mean anything anymore. The meanings, anything can be a lie now. It doesn't make any difference whether something is fair or makes sense."

The decline of personal courtesy, the increasing power of pressure and loudness, the reliance on shadowy image rather than substantial reality, all disturb her.

But nothing, apparently, disturbs her comic sense, even when she alludes to politics, and she goes no farther than an allusion: "All these people, come to think of it, so many politicians, people like Napoleon, are not much taller than short."

It was pointed out you couldn't say Lyndon Johnson was short.

"No," she said. "I guess you'd have to say he was not much taller than tall."

As a now-celebrated writer, Miss Welty tries to give herself time to think and feel—she has cut out lecturing since she no longer has to do it to earn money, and she does not usually see reporters, not out of snobbery, but because she is never sure what to say to them and because there is only so much time in life.

But if a reporter does get a chance to see her, she will talk for 12 hours and cook supper as well. She is fairly sure in the back of her mind that a visitor would rather eat a hamburger in the local Horror Room than dine at ease at home with Eudora Welty, but once she is persuaded that her visitor will make do with Eudora Welty's food as readily as the local hash house, she spreads a feast of cold consomme with avocado puree and sour cream it it and roast beef and other sliced meats and fine cheeses and a salad and tomatoes dead ripe and red as an Indian Cling (the peach of Southern childhood memories) and strong fresh coffee.

It tasted great—no danger of confusing it with something out of a vending machine.

Not only does she like to cook, and to cook without any interference or "help," she also likes to talk and refuses to let anybody help her with the dishes.

In her own reading, apart from garden books, cookbooks and virtually any other kind of book, she has a special enthusiasm for mystery novels or whodunits and for dictionaries. She has the great Oxford English Dictionary and wastes many delectable hours with it just for fun.

She likes poetry, especially Yeats, Donne and Marvell, but says, "I'm really afraid I'm not on the right wavelength for modern poetry. I'm a thoroughly visual person. I have to have a sensuous—is that right, sensuous?—yes, I always have to think—a sensuous image."

The fondness for visual images is constant throughout her stories. She compares such visual, if unlikely, things as fading red roses to the color of a bird dog's tongue and the locust's evening song to the sound of seed being poured into a tin bucket.

But always her taste for comedy breaks through. Apropos of nothing (except the American belief in signs) she mentioned her favorite sign, once seen in a train station: "No laughing or loud talking while train is in station."

And in spite of the intense admiration of many readers—the ones that ask her advice about falling in love with a priest, for instance—she sees no sign of becoming a "cult" writer with her own set of worshipers.

" 'Until my last two books I never could live on just my writing.' "

"I'd hate to be a sort of cult figure, and I've never seen any signs of it. It would be dreadful. First you'd begin to believe it, then you'd get absurd and stupid. I've never been a big seller, not really a popular writer, and most people never heard of me."

It's true that only in the last two years has she been able to support herself—in her 60s—by writing. Her famous short stories at first were turned down endlessly and then published cheap. Her collection *The Green Curtain,* with such famous stories as "The Worn Path," "Why I Live at the P.O." and "The Petrified Man," has been in print since the early '40s but has sold only 6,700 copies in its first three decades and first two editions.

As Miss Welty's agent, Diarmuid Russell of New York, observed in *Shenandoah,* the literary quarterly, that is "not riches for author or publisher," or, for that matter, agent.

"I couldn't live without Diarmuid," said Miss Welty. (The name is pronounced Dermott.) He became her agent in 1940 and she's never had another. Russell is son of the writer A. E., and, incidentally, is an authority on American wild flowers.

"When he offered to be my agent, I didn't even know there *were* agents. I just sent my stories off to magazines and when they came back, I sent them off somewhere else. It's still the best way. It's how everybody gets started. But now with legal things—permission to reprint and overseas rights—I could never keep up with all that.

"Until my last two books I never could live on just my writing. I was very lucky, I was able to lecture, and schools were good at getting me to come, sometimes for a one-shot lecture, sometimes longer. So I was always able to manage, but I never made any money. There was *The New Yorker,* though. They have the idea it's the writers who should make some money from the magazine. They pay well; yes, even when they know they could get a story for less. But of course the trouble is, you never know if you can write a story. . . .

"You can't time that kind of work to fit in with when you need the money."

From one *New Yorker* story Miss Welty bought two Fords, one for a niece and one for herself.

Somebody once suggested that if she drove about in an amazing automobile and issued epigrams on television once a month she'd soon be thought an oracle.

"Oh, no, I've already tested that in a way. I had a 16-year-old Ford. It ran fine, I still don't know why I turned it in. But anyway, even when I had it, nobody thought I was an oracle."

When she sees her books newly issued she feels uneasy — "I'm never prepared for the reviews. I'm never prepared for anything, I mean I have no idea what people will think of the book. When I see my book for sale, I realize here's something I've been doing privately in Jackson, and now suddenly people anywhere can see it, what only I've seen. I feel very vulnerable."

Her own favorite author is Jane Austen, a writer she returns to again and again. Unlike many Southern writers she has no special taste for Milton; she took a course in Milton years ago and has barely read him since.

"Are you trying to say you're not a Puritan?" she was asked.

"No, I'm a Puritan, all right. But I am saying if you substitute Jane Austen instead of Milton, you'll come closer. Sorry."

No sketch of a Southern writer in the past century has ever been written, so far as I know, without the writer adoring Milton. It was suggested that maybe Milton's influence is so pervasive that she has absorbed by osmosis.

"Sorry. Jane Austen."

But then writers often are not aware of major influences, as we all know.

"And I've never read one word of James Fenimore Cooper. Yes, he's having a revival. I think that's sad. As if he had to be revived. I know a literary reputation is a fragile thing. Somebody told me once, watch out when a woman writer passes 50, they all turn on you. Sometimes I think they decide, 'Oh, we're so damned tired of saying she writes well.' "

She grinned and rose from her chair to fetch a private literary treasure somebody sent her — a student's essay question on Shakespeare. The allusion to critics made her think of Shakespeare and her somewhat saucy humor made her think not of some great scene in a play but of a Georgia boy's essay. It was clear the youth did not know Shakespeare from a sack of vanilla beans but he did understand he was supposed to say something grand, so he wound up:

"Some say William was a moment without a tomb, star of the poet, swan of the lake."

Miss Welty, reading it, laughed almost to limpness.

"Moment without a tomb — now there's a title for you," she said between gasps. (Henry Miller once said he loved her stories but not her titles.) She is a connoisseur of titles and names. Naming her characters is very difficult for her.

"There are some marvelous names right here in Mississippi. I used to take a lot of the state newspapers and in the old days I loved to read the *Oxford Eagle*. There was one woman whose name kept turning up there, but I always felt any name around Oxford was automatically the property of Mr. Faulkner. He had such perfect names. I don't know if this is true, but somebody once told me they mentioned a name to Mr. Faulkner and he said, 'Yes, I know the name well. Can hardly wait for her to die' so he could use it."

Miss Welty now is thinking of publishing a book of lectures, but is not sure—would there really be anything fresh and fine, would there really be any point to it?

"Well, with two sensationally received novels in a row in two years, had you ever thought of writing a flop just for a change of pace?" somebody asked her.

"What would really bother me was if I wrote a flop and it was praised —just out of habit. And I think things like that can happen."

Milton, of course, would have thought so, too.

—August 13, 1972

A Survivor

By Michael Kernan

"I saw him at the railway station, watching us leave on the train. He got smaller and smaller, and he just stood there looking rather nostalgic, as if he was sorry to see us go, sorry that the job was done now. . . ."

The statement sounds unexceptional, until one learns that the train was full of Hungarian Jews headed for Auschwitz. And that the man at the station was Adolf Eichmann.

The boy on the train, now remembering as a man, was Elie Wiesel, a survivor of the Holocaust, who has become a legend through the novels in which he tries to distill the experience, to tell the untellable and somehow to pass it on.

Wiesel, 41, is in town to lecture and to promote his ninth book, *A Beggar in Jerusalem,* already a prize-winning best seller in Europe. At the time he saw Eichmann he didn't know who the man was, or that this was Eichmann's final job, the extermination of 600,000 Hungarians in six weeks, and that the Germans wanted it to be a masterpiece of efficiency.

"I saw him again at the trial," said Wiesel. "I didn't want to be a witness, but I wanted to see him. I wanted to know if this man was normal. I hoped the witnesses and the guards and the others would tell me he was abnormal. They did not."

The writer's fingers jabbed at the air as though nailing up the words one by one: "He was a human being."

This fact Wiesel calls the greatest discovery of the war: that Adolf Eichmann was cultured, read deeply and intelligently, played the violin, had sensibility and humor, defended himself with consummate skill, never once broke down at the trial — and still could be what he was.

"The Eichmann trial changed a basic attitude of the Israelis," Wiesel said, "and the Six-Day War changed it even more. It became a different country. The Holocaust became a unifying factor — you had Yemeni tribesmen who never had heard of Auschwitz shouting, 'No more Auschwitz!' "

The rebellions, the vocal and often violent protests of today's youth, he added, are a phenomenon that is a generation late. It is the protest that the victims of the Holocaust should have made before it was too late.

"Even the terminology today is the same. The police are called Gestapo pigs; you hear talk of the ghetto and genocide — the whole vocabulary of the Holocaust. This is a generation determined to do what we have not done."

Wiesel was 13 when he and his parents and three sisters were taken from their home in Sighet, in the Transylvanian highlands of Hungary.

Taken first to Auschwitz, then to two other camps and finally to Buchenwald, he became separated from his two older sisters and presumed them dead. His younger sister and his parents died early, at Auschwitz. When Buchenwald was liberated he was one of some 400 children who refused to be sent back to their homelands.

"I saw the lists of the known survivors," he said matter-of-factly, "and I didn't see my sisters' names on them, so I had no reason to want to go home. I wanted to try Palestine, but the British weren't letting us in."

Packed into a train bound for Brussels, they were diverted into France on orders of General de Gaulle. The children were told that all those who wanted to be French citizens should raise their hands.

"A lot of them did," he said. "They thought they were going to get bread or something; they would reach out for anything. I didn't, so I remained stateless."

Taken to Normandy, his group was eventually interviewed and photographed by journalists, and shortly after his picture had been published he was called into the camp director's office.

"He was talking on the phone," Wiesel smiled, "and I heard my name mentioned. When he hung up I said, 'Who was that?' He said, 'Your sister.' I didn't believe it. How would she know I was alive and in France? How could she have found me in this place?

"So the next day I went to Paris to meet her, sure it was a mistake. But it was my sister. She had seen the article and picture, of course."

Later, Wiesel, who now lives in New York, an American citizen, found his other sister, who migrated to Canada, but he insisted that this experience is commonplace today among Jewish survivors of the Holocaust. It has happened hundreds of times, and Israel is full of people with stories that could make sentimental novels were it not for the horror on which they are based.

One instance: A little girl, whose parents in desperation literally pushed her out between the slats of a boxcar that was taking them to their death, survived and came years later to Israel. One day a man heard her singing a song from her childhood. He wanted to know where she came from. He was her father. . . .

"I don't talk about the camps," said Wiesel. "None of us do. I had a friend from my home town; we studied together till the last day. I see him today, but we don't talk about it. For one thing, there is the fear of not being believed, but mostly there is the fear that the experience will be reduced, made into something acceptable, perhaps forgotten."

—February 6, 1970

Not Only Is He Beautiful, But He Can Dance Too

By Sally Quinn

Rudolf Nureyev seems so much smaller in real life than he is on the ballet stage. Everybody says so. He is about 5 feet, 8 inches and weighs 150 pounds. But he is beautiful.

He has those high Tartar cheekbones, the slightly slanting eyes, the full cruel mouth slashed by an old scar, the taut muscular body, strong but gentle hands, tousled brown hair, and a provocative half-mischievous, half-soulful look in his eyes. And, of course, there is his behind. He has a fabulous behind. Women follow him around and stare at his fanny as blatantly as some men would stare at a woman's bosom.

There is no doubt that at 36 Rudolf Nureyev understands the full extent of his animal magnetism. If pressed, he will admit to an interviewer, with a half smile and a teasing sincerity, "I know I am beautiful."

He strides with a sense of confidence, a confidence he has gained with the years. He has shed his legendary arrogance, an arrogance he developed, probably, out of a sense of insecurity and perhaps fear. What may seem like arrogance now could be a sort of reverence he has for his own body, which is, after all, the instrument of his craft.

At a Kennedy Center rehearsal, upon entering the room, he walks to the mirror and looks at himself. He falls instantly into a posture of shyness, almost as if he were a teen-ager meeting someone for the first time who he thought was terribly attractive. It is not offensive. He seems objective about his own subjectivity. He is straightforward about himself. He has a good sense of humor, though somewhat childlike in its simplicity, possibly a holdover from his peasant childhood in Siberia.

There is a strange regal quality about Nureyev, especially considering his lowly origins, though he says he is not a Russian peasant but a Tartar. The dictionary defines Tartar as an "unexpectedly formidable person." One is reminded by this regal simplicity of the king in "The King and I." Indeed, when he first defected he wanted badly to dance for Balanchine. But Balanchine wouldn't have him and reportedly said, "Rudolf, when you are tired of playing the prince, come to me."

He is playful and he can laugh at himself. Talking to him one has the feeling of playing with a lion cub: you don't want to go too far for fear of making him angry or annoying him. He does, as everyone who has followed him knows, have quite a reputation for an erratic temperament.

In 1964 at the Spoleto festival, Nureyev arrived for a dinner at composer Gian Carlo Menotti's and reportedly ordered one of the guests to get him a plate. Told everyone was to serve himself, the dancer allowed as how, "Nureyev never serves himself. He is served." And he smashed his glass on the floor and stomped out.

Later, when a photographer was trying to take his picture he announced, "I give you three minutes, photographer, and I start counting now." He wouldn't stand next to Margot Fonteyn or lean toward her. "Everyone leans toward Nureyev."

One morning earlier this week the press was invited to watch a Royal Ballet rehearsal by Rudolf Nureyev and Merle Park. Television cameras, reporters and photographers gathered in rehearsal hall four and waited for the Big Star to appear.

Suddenly the door creaked open and a small face peeked around the corner, the head covered in a heavy wool ski cap, the body swathed in thick hand-knitted peasant sweaters, the feet wrapped in knit stockings and peasant clogs. The person smiled a bit reticently, then unprepossessingly entered the room, shook hands with everybody, answered a few questions politely, then went over to Merle Park to prepare for the rehearsal.

As they began to dance, cameras clicked and cameramen and reporters hovered over the two, making noise, shooting pictures, and staring, until they couldn't concentrate any longer. Shortly afterward he quietly asked to be left to dance privately and he smiled as everyone cleared out of the room.

"Are you sure that was Nureyev?" one reporter asked outside.

In 1964 during Lyndon Johnson's inaugural, when Rudolf Nureyev was in Washington with Margot Fonteyn to dance for the inaugural, he was approached by a reporter. "Get away from me," he ordered. "I never talk to the press."

One night last week, after his opening performance, Nureyev was to appear afterward at a black-tie function in the Kennedy Center Atrium. He was quite late getting there. Finally arriving, he was besieged by women asking for his autograph, gushing over him, staring at him, firmly nudging each other aside for a good head-to-toe look, grasping his arm to get his attention. He smiled, answered their questions politely, signed autographs, and got himself an omelette. He was friendly and warm and correct for more than an hour.

"Are you sure that was Nureyev?" one woman asked another.

Nevertheless, Nureyev did not want to be interviewed. And when he finally agreed several days later, he asked a PR woman and several others to come along. "I wanted her as a witness," he said in his soft Russian accent. "She is supposed to interrupt, to barge in there and protect me from difficult questions. There are always questions I don't want to answer."

It was midnight and the lights were dim at the Watergate Terrace. A small party arrived shortly before closing to precede Nureyev, who was changing after his performance of "La Fille Mal Gardee."

"We will want," said the PR person from the Royal Ballet, "one thick rare steak, done on both sides for two minutes and warm inside. So please take it out of the fridge now."

"Madam," said the maitre d'hotel, "we never keep our steaks in the fridge."

A few minutes later, out of the shadows of the room, appeared Nureyev, in a dark wool Yves St. Laurent jacket. He was shivering.

He sits down, puts on a fur Dutch cap, and hugs himself. "This air-conditioning," he says, "I hate it. I like the cold but not air-conditioning. All you Americans love it. I have to wear sweaters all the time to keep warm."

The waiter comes over to take the order. "OK, five minutes if you want anything to eat," he barks.

"I think," says Nureyev. "I will have a soup."

"Onion?" says the waiter. "No." "Gazpacho?" "No." "Vichyssoise?" "No. I will have turtle."

"We don't have turtle."

Then he reiterates the first order.

"I will have a steak, *bleu,* cooked two minutes on each side. And not cold inside."

"Well, what do you expect, it'll be cold if you want it that rare," said the maitre d'hotel. He obviously doesn't know who Nureyev is. Nureyev doesn't care. He shrugs and pours himself some wine. It is California wine. Too sweet. He asks for imported wine. They bring it.

"I should have eaten in my room," he says. "I have my driver who cooks."

A question is asked that he doesn't like. He laughs and answers, "You are on a wild-goose chase." He seems pleased with that expression. He says it again. And again. "You are chasing wild gooses." He smiles triumphantly.

"...his accent is...just heavy enough to make him seem mysterious..."

He makes no attempt to carry on a conversation and will answer questions politely if succinctly, constantly on his guard. His English is fluent, his accent is not heavy, just heavy enough to make him seem mysterious. He doesn't mind long silences.

Nureyev talks first of his life in Russia. Of being a peasant child with nothing to eat. The scar on his lip, he explains, he got when he was 13. "We were only allowed a ration of so many grams of bread a day. I gave mine to my dog. When I leaned down to hug him, he tore my mouth open."

He ran away from home when still young and went to Leningrad where he quickly became the star of the Kirov Ballet. But on a tour of the West in 1961 he defected, one of the first of numerous Russian artists to do so.

"I don't see my friends from Russia very much when they come to the West," he says. "We have grown apart. We have nothing really to talk about. Everything is so different. Because I am not involved in politics. I don't care about American politics or Russian politics. You cannot be a dancer and care about it and I devote myself to my art. I think it can be dangerous. Like in Russia. If you are not involved you are out of it."

Nureyev admits to having less training and to starting later than most dancers. But, without modesty, he will admit that he has something special that "nature gave me. I had a talent, a gift. I was talented, I knew I would be a dancer from the beginning . . . but, you know, everyone in any field who becomes great has to overcome something, a major defect or flaw."

What was Nureyev's major defect?

"Secret," he says solemnly. Then breaks out in a grin. "I will never tell you. Nobody will ever know."

But once one overcomes the major defect, the flaw, and one has achieved success, that's the worst part, according to Nureyev. "It is terrible to be a success," he says. "I mean that. Because once you become a success you have to maintain your excellence. You don't compete with anybody else anymore. You compete with yourself. It is exhausting. You are tired all the time because the hardest thing is maintenance. And there are always people coming up behind you. People who are good and who want to be as good as you. So you must be as good as you were. Not the same. But a lot of young people don't understand that it is a long way from the rehearsal hall to the stage. For me it was a short way. Because I had the strongest driving ambition. Dance is everything for me. I knew what I wanted."

Nureyev knew, too, that what he wanted would be hard. "Ballet is a very hard life. But it is a good one too."

He rewards himself for his energies with a Mercedes, a villa in the south of France, an enormous record collection, a wardrobe designed for him by Yves St. Laurent, and the company of people like Jackie Onassis and Lee Radziwill. But ask him what kind of people he likes to hang out with, who are his friends, and he stiffens, then laughs defensively.

"What do you want me to say," he asks warily. "You are closing in for the kill. I know. You are not interested in the dance. You are interested in the man."

The answer, carefully reflected upon, is "people who are involved in the arts."

Nureyev seems shocked at a distinction between art and entertainment. He does not consider what he is or his personality or his mass popularity as anything like "show biz."

"I don't bring ballet to their level or tastes, they come to mine. If it is because I have the personality or the character to attract people then that is good. It happened in Russia, it happened in London and it happened in America. If I made ballet popular then that is good for other dancers too because they will come and see them. If it's me, that is good for me, but if it hadn't been me, it would have been somebody else."

In the early years of his career, Nureyev tended to be temperamental. But now, a new Rudolf (he hates to be called Rudy) has emerged. Now, everyone seems to agree that he has changed, mellowed, calmed down. He is nicer to deal with and delightful to work with, though members of the company say they have no idea where he lives or what he does. They say they know nothing about him at all. He is remote.

"Having a temperament is part of the ballet," says Nureyev. "It is part of being a star. To sign autographs, have your picture taken, accept compliments, that all takes time. Before I never had the patience. It bored me and I didn't like it. I used to be difficult, rude and temperamental. But I have found now that it is easier than not to be polite. It takes not so much time as I thought. I am older. I learn by time and experience."

He is on his third glass of wine and he is beginning to giggle.

He begins to talk about the movies. He left immediately after a performance the other night to catch a flick downtown. He is a movie freak. He says he goes to more movies in New York than ballets. "Paul Newman is my favorite movie star," he says.

Some people think Nureyev looks like Warren Beatty. He's not too crazy about that. "He's a nice boy," Nureyev says and dismisses that subject with a shrug.

Nureyev stays up until 3:30 or 4 a.m. when he's in New York, watching the late and the late-late shows. "I saw 'Anchors Aweigh' with Gene

"Some people think Nureyev looks like Warren Beatty. He's not too crazy about that. . ."

Kelly and Frank Sinatra last night," he says. "I love to watch Gene Kelly dance but Sinatra is my favorite."

He turns to the waiter and asks for a cup of tea.

"I think I am getting drunk. I want to be able to think straight. This interview is so acid it's good we didn't have vinegar with the salad." He laughs.

"I want to be sober when you drop the bomb question, when you do a Hiroshima on me," he giggles again.

Well, then, Mr. Nureyev, how's your sex life?

"I knew it, you see, there it is," and he clasps his hands and throws his head back and laughs with Slavic glee.

"Sporadic," he announces.

Well, tell us more. The ladies will be disappointed with that little morsel and nothing else.

"The ladies will just have to remain tense," he says sadistically.

He leans back smugly, ponders his own words, then leans forward and asks with real earnestness: "This is a city of politicians. How am I doing in this interview? Am I as good as the politicians?"

When told he has revealed absolutely nothing of himself, that he is still a complete mystery, that he is impenetrable as an interviewee, he beams like a Boy Scout receiving a medal.

"Now we must go," he says, his success complete. "We will pay the bill, then you will feel guilty and your conscience will make you write nice things."

And he gets up from the table and stalks triumphantly out of the restaurant, as though he is taking bows for a magnificent performance.

—June 1, 1974

Dustin Hoffman:
A New Direction for
a Compulsive Perfectionist

By Tom Shales

NEW YORK—The Graduate has graduated. Dustin Hoffman, 37, is no longer just an internationally known movie star, widely respected actor, and reluctant identity figure to members of more than one generation. He is now a director, too.

Yes, a director.

Yes, 37.

Hoffman's Broadway directorial debut, with Murray Schisgal's new social comedy "All Over Town," is now in rehearsal here. It begins a three-week run at Washington's National Theatre Saturday and then goes back to Manhattan and the Barrymore Theater for its crucial test.

Not that movies have been forsaken. Hoffman's new film, "Lenny," just opened in New York with a bigger first-day gross at the Cinema I Theater than "The Exorcist" had, and critics have applauded the performance.

For Hoffman, the directing job is a risky, demanding, and professionally unnecessary challenge, and one he is taking, as he takes most things, very seriously. He is spending so much time on his friend Schisgal's play that he has had to cut down his sessions with an analyst from five to two per week.

"He's very nervous about this," says someone close to the play. Hoffman admits it. In person, he seems like the guy who's always knotted up anyway, only now the knots are tighter. But this is the sort of agony on which fast-metabolizing, high-energy types like Hoffman seem to thrive— exquisite, self-generated torture that can produce work of pure integrity. Hoffman is a worker, and Hoffman is driven.

"I've always liked directing more than acting, and I enjoy it more," he says over a big fat breakfast. "It's not easier; there's probably even more pressure, but it's not the same kind of pressure for me. Even after the film and some success, when I look back at the most enjoyable time I ever had, it was directing. In terms of enjoyment."

This was nonprofessional theater, not Broadway or even Off-Braodway. "I couldn't get work acting years ago—that's why I directed. At that time I felt I would become a director just because I couldn't get work as an actor. I directed at the Boy's Club, in Harlem, at New Jersey Community Theater, North Dakota Community Theater. The only professional directing was as assistant director of an Off-Broadway production of Arthur Miller's play 'A View From the Bridge,' which starred Jon Voight. I started getting acting jobs Off-Broadway right after that."

"Overnight success" in "The Graduate" followed a long, hard decade in which Hoffman perfected his craft in small Off-Broadway theaters. He proved his versatility by playing parts of almost every shape and size. He was a cockney plumber in "Eh?" He was an aged Russian clerk in "Journey of the Fifth Horse" (a role he won an Off-Broadway "Obie" for and repeated in a public television production). And he was a homosexual Nazi hunchback in "Harry, Noon and Night." Then he made his first movie—Mike Nichols' "The Graduate," and after years of work as an actor, he found himself a movie star.

"I had just turned 30, and that was really hard for me. I felt it in my stomach. I had just finished 'The Graduate' but it hadn't come out yet. I was collecting unemployment. Literally. Because I turned 30 in August and I had finished shooting in July, and I went right back on unemployment for about three, four months until the picture came out.

"I remember that very bad feeling about turning 30. For the first time, I emotionally felt that the game was limited. We've always heard intellectually that life moves so fast and all that, but it hit me in the stomach: 'You're not immortal, it's about half over.'"

———

"All Over Town" has been rehearsing in space above a slightly seamy 42nd Street movie house. It used to be the New Amsterdam Theater, and the rundown loft Hoffman and company are using was once the scene of Florenz Ziegfield's gala midnight revues. Now, its festivity eroded, its balcony declared unsafe, the theater is merely a wreck.

Onstage, Hoffman is playing a record for his 16 actors—Aaron Lebedeff, an old Jewish-Roumanian singer (who died in 1960) singing "Roumania, Roumania." The music builds in rhythm and few of the actors can avoid jiggling to it. Hoffman does a kind of dance, too—a hesitant, quirky little trot. In his gray sweater, jeans and tennies, he does not look much like the brooding Benjamin of "The Graduate," the ravaged Ratso of "Midnight Cowboy," the ancient Indian of "Little Big Man" or the blue-humored Bruce of "Lenny." That short, concentrated body, that modest shuffle of a walk, that emphatic sloping nose, somehow give the impression of an arrow pointing down. Yet he has the capacity to fill a room with tension all by himself.

The record ends. "That's the celebration of life!" Hoffman exclaims to his actors.

Author Schisgal, bald and bearded and sitting in a front row seat, tells star Cleavon Little, "Cleavon, this is what the play's about."

"Oh," says Cleavon. "This is?"

Later, Hoffman says of the song, "I don't even know what it means. It just has this tremendous energy, it just goes on and on and accelerates; it's a celebration of life. I hope the play will have that."

"All Over Town" is about a well-off Manhattan psychiatrist, Hoffman says, who feels frustrated by his attempts to improve the mental health of only a few people at a time. "He figures, the amount of disturbed people is quadruple that on the outside, so you're helping people to go outside into a madhouse." He decides to try remodelling one lowly human being into a concerned citizen of the '70s, and from the welfare rolls he picks Louie Lucas, who has lived alternately with five women and has produced nine illegitimate children by them.

As the play opens, a black delivery man (Little) appears at the psychiatrist's home and is mistaken for Lucas because the family assumes that only a black man would have led such a life (they are wrong). The man goes along with the mistaken identity, dispatching family members on various errands they consider noblesse oblige liberalism.

"By the way," the psychiatrist asks him in the nearly deserted house, "where is everyone?"

"All over town," Little answers.

At the third run-through of the play's first act, the unshaven Hoffman sits with a stenographer in the audience, leaning forward nervously as he listens and every few seconds leaning back to whisper dictation like "she should be more" this and "he should be much more" that. Hoffman is going at this directing bit in a big way; he spent three months just casting the play — much longer than is usual — and talked with more than 1,500 actors in New York, Los Angeles and San Francisco. He is determined to get what he wants.

"But there's just not enough time," Hoffman complains. "The unions kill you, whether it's the actors' union or the stagehands' union or whatever. That's one of the reasons the theater is in the shape it's in. Now this year Broadway is enjoying a phenomenal season, but that's primarily because of the plays coming in from England — 'National Health,' 'Equus,' 'Absurd Person Singular,' 'Sherlock' — there're nine or ten plays that have proved themselves before they even get here, so the competition in a sense is stuff that was worked out for a long period of time.

"Now we go into rehearsals, we have 24, 25, maybe 26 days, which is not a lot of time, before the actors must get a performance salary. The producer says once they get a performance salary we have to have an audience coming in; those salaries could go from $265 a week for rehearsal to $1,500 a week for some actors. So. There you are—you get barely three weeks of rehearsals out of them. What I would like is to double that, which is not a lot of time, either."

He stares dejectedly off. "They say Washington is 'out of town' but it isn't. Reviewers come in there from other places, even the Washington press are respected and read, and if you're hurt here that influences a whole block of theater party investors in New York and you get no advance. There's over a quarter of a million dollars invested in this show. So what do you do? You work your show the best you can every day and whatever shape you're in, you just open. Even if you're only half way there. I don't know what to do; we'll just do what we can and open. We're a 100-to-one shot. One hundred-to one."

Isn't this kind of pressure part of the adventure of doing live theater? "It shouldn't be. It should be just to do good work. There's so little good American theater around. And money—Jules Feiffer's been trying to finance a play for the last three years. And the same thing that cripples plays cripples movies and it finally eats into itself until what you wind up with is a tremendous amount of bad stuff. People wonder why it's so bad. It's because there isn't any time."

———

This is not Hoffman's first association with author Schisgal. For one thing, they and their wives and the Joseph ("Catch 22") Hellers hang around together and laugh a lot. For another, Hoffman starred in Schisgal's "Jimmy Shine" in 1968. The play tried out in Baltimore and its opening night became show-biz legend: Hoffman cut his hand severely onstage at the beginning of the second act and, bleeding generously, finished the play nevertheless.

"Oooh, that was nightmare," he says, running his hand through his ramshackle hair. "I remember thinking, 'I should walk off the stage,' but I thought, 'if I walk off, that means we have to have another opening night,' and I couldn't bear that. It wasn't noble that I stayed on, I just didn't want to go through all that again.'

"During the show, I was onstage all the time, so the other actors kept bringing me Band Aids. Later they took me to Johns Hopkins Hospital. I was sitting there with the hand half covered. We didn't know if the tendon had been severed—if it is, you're screwed. And in comes a nurse and asks for my autograph and I said, 'I can't, I'm right-handed,' and she takes a pencil and, like this (he puts a fork in his hand) she guides my hand. She said, 'I gotta get it now, honey, 'cause I'm going off duty.' And I, like a schmuck, just sat there. I'll never forget that."

He laughs. As he talks, Hoffman's hands have been very busy—constantly in motion, fingers pointing sometimes up, sometimes down, sometimes at each other. Somebody watching him speak might even think he was using the sign language of the deaf.

Lots of people in the arts, often self-aggrandizingly, call themselves perfectionists. Often this is used as justification for being obnoxious. Hoffman doesn't mention the word in describing himself, but it becomes apparent that he is a perfectionist — an organic, compulsive and cursed one.

"As an actor, I've always loved rehearsals but when it comes time to go onstage or on film, to perform, I've never felt that it was ready," he says. "And it isn't. That's why there's so much crap around, whether its theater or movies. To me, the fun is in the research, the perfection and preparation, and even with the time to do it, I feel very uncomfortable, I feel very inadequate in the sense that I don't feel fully prepared."

Hoffman spent eight months just researching Lenny Bruce before actual filming of "Lenny" began. Some critics jumped through hoops over his performance. Hoffman is not much impressed by that.

"I'm never happy with any film I've ever done. I enjoy them more after a few years than when they first come out. The first time I saw 'Graduate' or 'Midnight Cowboy' or 'Lenny' or anything else I had tremendous reservations about it. It's like a writer — Herb Gardner — once said to me, that it's like, when a writer gets an idea, the whole idea is right in front of you, all there, and then you walk 10 feet to the typewriter and 50 percent of the idea has already gone somewhere, and then you hit the keys and when it comes out, you wind up with 20 percent of what was there less than a minute ago. So on a movie, you start out with a character in a screenplay — you start out with a masterpiece, you think, and then you get into it and hope it'll be just a good film and halfway through it you hope it won't be a bad film and three-quarters of the way through it, you just hope you'll get a film done.

"Now when you talk about 'Lenny,' I never want to go through anything like that again, that's all I know — to do somebody that really existed, has been dead so short a time [since 1966], whose mother, daughter and ex-wife are still living, that the public remembers. Who needs it? Better to do fiction; then at least you don't feel the pressure of misrepresenting somebody."

To young people of overlapping generations, Hoffman, through the character of Benjamin in "The Graduate," is a cool hero figure with which they associate themselves—youth put-upon by a corrupt adult establishment. Hoffman does not see himself that way. Benjamin was just another character, one whom he may actually resemble no more than he does that homosexual Nazi hunchback.

"I don't identify with any generation. I don't. I think I feel a part of my time, more than of a generation, or of a decade like the '50s or '60s. I was never part of that flower thing or drug thing or even the social protest thing. I was going to acting class. I don't fit the times in the sense that I don't want to. I'd rather watch it go by."

That he needs an analyst's help for this is something for which Hoffman would apparently never dream of apologizing. He is very casual about the subject.

"Same doctor. Same sickness. Same neurosis," he says, smiling. "A cure? Well there is none. I think we'll all get to a point where we don't think analysis is for crazy people, for sick people. It's like going to college and taking a course on yourself.

"To me, it's very important to acknowledge 'what is the truth' and then do what you want. We don't face the truth very often. Usually I think we plead to the lesser crime. We say, 'Oh, I'm such a whatever,' when it's really something worse. Like Nixon, you know—you throw the John Mitchells off yourself, protecting the 'office.' I think that's true, that we'd be much healthier as a society if we were healthier individually. As it is now . . . there's no such thing as happiness. At least, I haven't met anyone who I considered to be happy."

One may feel compelled at this point to say, "Relax, Dustin," "Take it easy, Dustin" or "What are you trying to prove, kid?"—forgetting that you are talking to a 37-year-old man.

But your own instant, quack analysis tells you Hoffman is one of those people who will never quite know how to take it easy and never really want to. That is probably the energy source that kept him going long before everybody knew his name and the flat, dry sound of his nasal voice.

Discouragement might have been abundant in those early acting days, but things were seen through—partly through the financial and moral support of Hoffman's older brother, Ronald, now a practicing economist who lives in Northwest Washington. Then, Dustin's mother had doubts about her younger son's ability to make a respectable success of himself. Many movies and plays later, she has no more reason to wonder.

Is she proud of you, Dustin? "Uhhh, yeah," he says, slipping on sunglasses. "Of both of us." Hoffman shrugs, smiles, picks a loose thread off your coat and rushes off to another rehearsal.

—November 17, 1974

Next: The Lawmaker

Sen. Charles McC. Mathias Jr. "Politicians are bad subjects for profiles because they are boring," argues one member of the Style staff whose name is better left omitted. It is true that many Washington lawmakers are such workaholics that their personal lives are severely restricted and tend to be carbon copies of one another. It is also true that, when faced with an interviewer's questions, they have to be particularly careful in the answers not to offend the electorate.

Michael Kernan ran into the problem in trying to profile Mac Mathias, one of the Senate's most widely respected members. His first step was to spend a working day with the lawmaker on Capitol Hill. The activity Kernan observed was routine and dull. What would all that paper shuffling and phone answering tell the reader about a reflective, genteel legislator whose roots in Maryland and in public affairs go back more than three centuries—an aristocrat, deny it though he may?

An anecdote Mathias told about meeting President Coolidge suggested to Kernan that a truer insight into Mathias might come from reporting the forces that shaped him—the generations of ancestors in Frederick, Md., their values, their homes, their artifacts, their friends and associates. With that, Kernan went to Mathias' family home town, and the portrait fell into place. As he writes, "You have to see that big old house in Frederick to understand Mac Mathias" and what the Senator calls his family's "thread of responsibility."

Note: This is the book's most intricate example of film-influenced, fast cut-in-cut-out narrative in which the italicized present (that day on Capitol Hill—deliberately written in clipped, sterile prose) mixes with the body of the story, set in normal Roman type, in which the rich background of the Senator and the ambiance of Frederick is described in leisurely, frequently lyrical style.   *—L. T.*

Mac Mathias: Following His 'Thread of Responsibity'

By Michael Kernan

Early in 1929, when he was 6 years old, Charles McCurdy Mathias Jr. was taken by his father to the White House to pay a farewell call on outgoing President Coolidge.

"One did things like that in those days," said the senior senator from Maryland. "I remember it was a springlike day, and I asked my father if the moving men would be around."

No, his father told him, when a President moves out, all he takes is his wardrobe.

"Well, I had a picture in my mind of a huge mahogany wardrobe—I was raised in one of those big old houses that had such things—and that's all I remember of Coolidge. Except his voice as we left: 'Please go out the othah doah.'"

You have to see that big old house in Frederick to understand Mac Mathias. You have to get the feel of it, with its high ceilings and ponderously ticking grandfather clocks, its ancestor portaits going all the way back to the 1603 brass rubbing of Richard Brooke, whose son Robert brought his family to America a few years later—and along with them the first English foxhounds to reach the new continent.

And then you have to stand outside the massive cream-and-black brick townhouse built in 1816 on Council Street and look across Courthouse Square, where Mac used to play hide-and-seek with his younger brother and sister and the closeknit gang of children who lived in the genteel heart of old Frederick.

You can see the hiding place under the courthouse steps where Mac hit himself a crack on the forehead one summer because he had suddenly grown too tall for it. And the diagonal sidewalks where the studious, pudgy youngster once ran his homemade car, a wagon with a Maytag washer motor that drove all the lawyers and realtors absolutely bananas in their offices around the square.

8:42 a.m.—Sen. Mathias, in a lightweight gray suit, crisp blue shirt and dark tie with the Maryland crest, arrives at his office and establishes his bleary-eyed 14-year-old Chesapeake Bay retriever, Shammy, by the fire-

place. The 3x5 card with the day's appointments comes out of the breast pocket. On it, the interviewer's name is misspelled, and the senator duly mispronounces it. Within the hour, through some staff osmosis, he has it right.

The thing that people always want to know about Mac Mathias: How can anyone with political roots in Frederick County get away with being so liberal?

Mathias himself denies he's liberal, of course. "I'm not all that liberal, in fact in some aspects I'm conservative," he said. "A while ago I introduced a bill preserving the guarantees of the Bill of Rights by prohibiting warrantless wiretaps. I suppose they'll say it's another liberal effort. But it's as conservative as you can get. It's conserving the Constitution."

Nevertheless, the fact is that Mathias rated tops among Republican senators last year with the Americans for Democratic Action, voting their side on 20 key issues 90 percent of the time. He was one of 20 senators given a perfect score by the League of Women Voters, hardly as militant as the ADA but definitely liberal.

9:10 a.m. — An assistant brings in a sheaf of letters. "Why do people always say too much in letters?" he muses, and picks up his pen. For minutes the only sounds are the scratch of the pen and Shammy's soft snoring. Often during the day Mathias will surround himself with this particular silence, contemplative and magisterial. On Capitol Hill it takes a certain force of character to achieve such silences, and it shows in the determined firmness and deliberation of his movements. "He doesn't like to be rushed," an aide says.

Not only has Mathias often broken party ranks, notably on the Cambodia invasion, the Carswell Supreme Court appointment and Kent State, but as early as December 1971 he publicly urged President Nixon to campaign on "the high road" and abandon a strategy "which now seems destined, unnecessarily, to polarize Americans even more."

That was before the Watergate break-in. After it, when the White House and most Republicans were still denying or minimizing the issue, he endorsed the Kennedy investigation into alleged GOP espionage and told the Senate: "The pursuit of truth is the only direction in which we can go in search of the way to preserve our loyalty to the Constitution and the laws."

For years reports circulated that the administration would be gunning for Mathias when he came up for reelection this year, and columnists Evans and Novak wrote that not since New York liberal Republican Charles Goodell "was defeated with White House connivance has any Republican so outraged Mr. Nixon and his senior staff . . ."

The situation has changed today, and the Marylander's Mr. Clean image makes him look better with every new jolt to political bombshelters in Washington and Annapolis. But consider now: Mathias was city attorney of Frederick (1954-58) following a brief term as state assistant attorney general, and in 1958 he was elected to the General Assembly of Maryland, moving up to Congress two years later, and in 1968 to the Senate, defeating his old roomie at the University of Maryland law school, Daniel Brewster. Frederick County and the Sixth Congressional District aren't what you would call rock-ribbed, but they contain plenty of Nixon voters, plenty of people ready to lash out at any Republican who so much as whispered "I told you so."

9:29 a.m. — Press aide Alan Dessoff brings in a tape recorder, and Mathias reads a statement into it, pulling on his left ear. "Handicapped and retarded children face many problems . . ." he says, then stops. "Take two," he begins calmly. On the fourth take he is satisfied. Before heading over to the Capitol for two subcommittee meetings, he sets up staff conferences about busing and commencement speeches, phones his wife at home (she will attend a Pioneeer Women's luncheon for him that noon) and checks another letter: "What the hell? Congratulations Miss Frederick County, but she lives on Route 8 in Hagerstown?" Ponders a moment. "Well, that's right. . . ."

Around Courthouse Square the opinions are remarkably consistent.

"I knew Mac in Frederick High School," said Reese Shoemaker, who followed the senator as city attorney. "In fact we were in the same grade, but we were never close. He was always a bit of a loner, not in sports at all. He was kind of pudgy in those days. Never held class office, but that was a popularity contest, you know. He wasn't extroverted at all.

"There was a coolness. A reserve. It went both ways. I mean, his family had been leaders in the community for generations and Mac was the heir apparent. People feel he underwent some sort of metamorphosis down there[in Washington], but he's still a local boy. They vote for him and respect him, and he goes his own way. That's how it is."

Auctioneer Emmert R. Bowlus, an alderman when Mathias was city attorney, said the liberal views didn't come to light until he went down to Annapolis. "His stand on Nixon hasn't hurt him," Bowlus said. "He hasn't forced any issues. I'd say he was above jealousy."

Charles Sanner, insurance and real estate, a former Chamber president, wears his white hair in a crewcut, has Rotary plaques in his office and calls himself a "middle-of-the-roader."

"I grew up in this community," he said. "How the area feels today is different from two years ago, pre-Watergate, when there was quite a bit of disaffection [because of Mathias' early opposition to the cover-up]. People didn't like to feel they'd been wrong voting for Nixon. But you have to give the man [Mathias] credit. First of all, he's an idealist. As a senator he couldn't vote a provincial line. He keeps his perspective. And he's matured so very much. Above all, he doesn't fear to stand alone."

Sanner, who serves with Mathias on the board of nearby Hood College, recalled a commencement speech by the senator that spring. "He talked about Lincoln, showed how his words apply today, and he charged the class with the challenge of the post-Watergate era. He related the past and the future. One thing that strikes you: the absolute honesty."

11:41 a.m. — The Senate floor. Present: Buckley, Muskie and Mathias. Legislative aide at his side, Mathias proposes an amendment to the Clean Air Act designed to appeal to Maryland commuters, agrees to withdraw it on Muskie's pledge to consider certain changes.

What we have here is the American aristocrat. It is something you don't talk about when you're in politics. Like a prison record. But let's face it: There is a tradition in some venerable families, the Roosevelts, the Saltonstalls, the Bradfords, the Adamses, the Lees and so on, the sort of people who were born to an attitude toward self and society that others, like the Kennedys, had to achieve. It is the tradition of public service, of noblesse oblige if you must, the tradition of Cincinnatus, who left his plow to win a war for Rome and then quietly returned to his fields.

In the same tradition, Charles Mathias denies the whole thing. True, his office is full of the Maryland history which is his hobby. True, there is a window in St. Anne's Church in Annapolis to John Hammond, Major General of the Western Shore, an ancestor, and a whole row of windows at All Saints Episcopal in Frederick to various family members. True, another ancestor, C.E. Trail, served under Washington, and two Mathias great-grandfathers were in Maryland politics, and a grandfather was a Bull Mooser, and Mathias' father, though never in office, was always active in public affairs, a friend of Presidents.

"Maybe you get a little perspective after generations in politics," Mathias commented. "In small communities with strong families there's a kind of thread of responsibility. And I guess if you practice law in Frederick and you're a farmer there, too, you've got one foot in the courthouse and one on the farm, and you just have to have some political sense."

But he rejected the word "squire." Too elitist, he said uncomfortably.

Before he moved his family to Chevy Chase he lived on a 4-acre farm outside Frederick, and there is a larger spread just over the West Virginia border, willed him by a grandmother, where he has beef cattle, sheep and peacocks.

"A farmer is what he is," said his mother, "a real farmer. It's his salvation. He's got a green thumb."

(Sometimes, walking on the Hill, he picks up horse chestnuts, plants them in his yard, and they grow. This spring he had squash and pumpkins thriving on his office windowsill until the frost killed them.)

In Frederick you're never far from the country. Mathias kept his pony in a stable behind the house; now the stable is a law office, with a library in the hayloft, where he practiced with his father after finishing law school in 1949. In the same loft he once put on plays, written, directed by and starring himself — he even printed the programs — and featuring his brother Trail, today a Baltimore attorney, and his sister Michelle, four years younger, who remembers him as a perfect older brother.

12:04 p.m. — Pictures on the Capitol steps with 50 children from Avidon School in Oxon Hill. "How many of you know what the statue on top of

---

" 'He trims a lot in his statements,
you might say he fudges, but it
hardly ever affects his votes...' "

---

*the dome is?" Nobody knows. "It represents freedom," he says. "Think of it,
Abraham Lincoln stood right in this street and watched them hoist it into
place. They did it by hand in those days, with ropes." He promises to send
autographs, gives the thumbshake to several small boys.*

"His first day home from grade school, he tried to teach me what he'd
learned," his sister said. "Our father believed we should go to the local
schools because we would be living with these same people all our lives."

However, like many another brood of children from many another "big
old house" in American small towns, the young Mathiases lived in a special
world: Saturday mornings with their aunts in the gaunt Trail mansion (now
a funeral home) where they could read folio Shakespeares and see newspapers in seven languages; visits to the poor with baskets at Christmas; being pulled out of the Saturday movies by their mother via the usher, while
their less carefully supervised friends saw the picture around and around;
being read aloud to; being spanked; young Mac's being sent to Haverford
College because his father disapproved of fraternities, admired the Quak-
ers — and was a friend of the college's president.

"I think the liberal conscience, if you want to call it that, was instilled in
us early," said Michelle, married to a Frederick banker. "I remember how
we'd see the blacks in the balcony at the movies and would feel uncomfortable . . ."

*12:28 p.m. — A Senate corridor. He greets colleague Glenn Beall, peers
into the room where he will say hello to the Carroll County Chamber of
Commerce luncheon. No one there. He phones a constituent on the spot,
reading the number of a slip just handed to him by Dessoff. "Our goal is a
24-hour response to all mail," he remarks. "We get over 1,000 communications a day." With his home state just a 25-cent phone call away, he faces
demands on his time that would appall a pleasantly remote Western senator. On to the Tuesday Republican policy lunch.*

Living in another cool, darkish old mansion on the square in Frederick
is Col. Philip Winebrenner, a first cousin once removed who was born in
the same house as Mathias and who follows his career with interest.

"He's not affluent," said Winebrenner, "though I suppose there's some
family money. He could dress better. He doesn't seem to care. Now, this
$100 limit on contributions. That could hurt him if he got into a real fight
for re-election. I sent him $100 a year ago, and then when he opened

his campaign I sent another $100. He sent it back. [This has happened to other supporters in town, to their amazement.] Why, a lot of people around here think he's too liberal. But they seem to vote for him. The thing is, he's decent. He's got class."

Today, however, he is regarded by many as the state's top vote-getter next to Gov. Marvin Mandel. Last year some private polls indicated that Mathias would lose if he ran for governor — but that Mandel would lose if he ran for senator. Word is that former Sen. Joseph Tydings, a Democrat, is passing up this year's election in order to have another go at Sen. Glenn Beall Jr., regarded in some quarters as rather less invulnerable. However, Federal Maritime Commissioner Helen Delich Bentley is widely expected to challenge Mathias for the GOP nomination and, with Maryland Republican primary voters generally small in number and conservative in nature, she could give him some real problems.

1:46 p.m. — The Capitol steps again, now with the Chamber group. He seems to have all the time in the world. Striding back to the office, he mutters, "I hope Bowie Kuhn isn't so busy he can't wait. But those were constituents." During the afternoon he will have five office interviews. Administrative aide William Kendall unobtrusively keeps traffic flowing. At 4 the schedule will be interrupted for a floor vote.

"He tries to avoid being abrasive," one former aide said. "He trims a lot in his statements, you might say he fudges, but it hardly ever affects his votes. He picks his spots for a fight. There are times when he can be absolutely fearless."

They talk about his anguish over running against his old friend Dan Brewster, his understanding of what had happened to Brewster, whose career fizzled out in a crackle of indictments, aggravated by alcohol. Mathias drinks little, and never during a campaign.

"He's not a snob," said an associate. "He assumes he can talk to anyone. He's fearless in that sense. He doesn't duck many meetings. He's not combative, but patient."

Sometimes he "turtles," escapes from his life on the Hill, takes Shammy for a walk or gets a haircut or even hides out on the Senate floor. It's almost the only time of day he has to himself.

"To be very honest," he said, "there isn't much left at the end of a day. I hate to have my sons just see me disappear in the morning and reappear at night. My wife feels it; her childhood [as daughter of Massachusetts Gov. Robert Bradford] was the same thing. It was a family decision to run again. The boys — Charles is 14½ and Robert's nearly 13 — designed a bumper sticker and pin for the campaign. If they get involved in it, they understand it better, I think. But the campaign is a hard life for my wife. She's a very bright person, but this life makes many demands on her. She has to fill in with the children for many things I can't do during the campaign. As far as home goes, I'm a nonperson then."

8:14 p.m. — Mathias shows up at Mt. Vernon College for a panel discussion before some Vassar alumnae. The senator has already been to three receptions, stopping for a sandwich along the way. He talks about Tonkin Gulf, the Bill of Rights, warrantless wiretaps, handicapped children, and backs off from giving opinions on Watergate because as a senator he may have to sit in judgment on the matter. He will answer questions for more than two hours. He has been going since 6:45 a.m. His collar is wilted.

Coming in from the vegetable garden behind the pleasant colonial house in Chevy Chase, Ann Bradford Mathias wouldn't quite admit to having a green thumb like her husband.

"I'm sort of the pruner around here," she said. She puts up tomato pickles and Elk Ridge tomatoes (which she calls tomahtoes like any good New Englander).

A campaigner from the age of 3, she has been pitching in as usual this time, and the other night, faced by an antibusing picketer at a meeting where she hadn't even known she was to speak, she ended up by inviting the man to the house to talk with the senator.

"I came to Washington to get away from politics," she laughed. But the family decision to have Mathias run again was easy, despite the terrible drain on family amity. "I think we all recognize where Mac belongs," she said. "He an extraordinary legislator, a man of tremendous depth and judgment. God knows, you have to have people like that in government."

The Mathiases met at a birthday party here in 1952, when she was working for the CIA. Years later they met at another party, and this time it took: They talked politics the whole time. Three weeks later he phoned. They married in 1958.

Every summer the family goes to her childhood vacation place on a remote Maine island. It's part of an agreement: If she would learn to drive a tractor, he'd go to the island every year. "It's not easy for him either," she added. "Imagine — a politician without a phone. The way we learned about Agnew in '68 was someone left a note scribbled on some brown paper on our dock: 'Your governor was named for vice president.' Mac was frantic."

During the conversation Mathias drifted into the house, having returned to dress for a lawyers' association dinner. Quietly at his ease, he showed visitors some Indian miniatures and assorted Orientalia around the room. He had shucked the austerity of the office as easily as he had removed his jacket, and as he strolled about the garden while pictures were being taken, his quiet humor flickered pleasantly, like a coin glimpsed in the grass.

Pointing to an apple tree that had been cut back to within an inch of its life, he muttered, "You can see what we mean about the pruning." And winked.

—June 2, 1974

Next: The Perfect Master and the Wrestler

Balyogeshwar Shri Sant Ji Maharaj and Haystacks Calhoun. "A wise scepticism is the first attribute of a good critic." —James Russell Lowell, "Among My Books, Shakespeare Once More."

The common problem facing the writers of these two stories was that much of what their subjects were saying and doing struck them as flagrant put-ons, but there was no way either could be sure. Thus, each had to communicate skepticism to the reader without passing judgment.

Henry Allen's subject was a pubescent 13-year-old guru representing himself as the Perfect Master and Lord of the Universe. He already claimed 3 million Indian followers; he has since packed them in around the United States and become a talk-show celebrity (his mother, back in New Delhi, recently "removed" him from his post because of his "despicable" descent into hedonism). Allen's account of his first encounter with the Perfect Master and the elaborate buildup that preceded it begins in the solemn tone suited to religion and ritual. Then, as telltale incongruities in the setting and the audience come to his attention, Allen's prose assumes an ironic mock solemnity. At one point in the narrative, Allen shouts to the reader (I guess it's to the reader) a tongue-in-cheek aside in response to a particularly far-out quote from a Divine Light follower about there being no need for reasons in the faith: "No reason, oh Perfect Master?" The effect is almost Biblical.

Judy Bachrach similarly manipulates tone to characterize the flamboyant and harmlessly hokey Haystacks Calhoun, a 600-pound professional wrestler. Calhoun makes a vulnerable claim ("'You could call me an international dresser, I guess'"). Responds Bachrach, to the reader, "You could. *But it would be inappropriate.*" Typically, when overstatement might be expected of her, she surprises the reader with understatement ("*Wrestling is not one of your gentler pastimes*").

In fact, many writers might have told both of these stories in strident hyperbole. Allen and Bachrach shrewdly went the opposite way. There are certain subjects better illuminated by the stroke of a feather than the sweep of a baseball bat. —*L.T.*

'Pretty Far-Out Little Dude'

By Henry Allen

Balyogeshwar Shri Sant Ji Maharaj is a 13-year-old Indian guru-saint with 3 million disciples, a dime-store Frankenstein mask, the certainty he can put you face to face with God, a fondness for zapping people with a water pistol, a boundless love for all mankind and automobiles, except for one disciple's van in Los Angeles that had sheepskins on the seats, a stack of telegrams and letters addressed to Supreme Commander and Sweet Lord With Salutations at His Lotus Feet and so on, plus a set of walkie-talkies, one of which Sharon Kelly, a schoolteacher disciple, carries as she runs out of the house in Northwest Washington, screaming with laughter as she communicates with the Perfect Master in some zany routine about President Nixon.

The Perfect Master is broadcasting from the sanctuary of the second floor, having minutes ago entered the house to a panic of prostrations in the living room. This is no commune or ashram or crash pad, though. It's a suburban middle-class living room with wall-to-wall shag carpet, African figurines, and a baby grand piano with Schumann on the music stand. It's owned by the parents of one of the disciples, Joan Apter, 23.

But today, Sept. 8, the guru is upstairs, on the last of his five-day stay, during which he spoke at All Souls Unitarian Church. It is not known if the guru will descend, or a visitor will ascend, or neither, for a meeting.

Downstairs, the visitor is recovering from the clamor of bad vibrations that went off like a burglar alarm when it looked like he might plunk his tushie in, my God, the guru's favorite overstuffed chair.

The guru spoke last year from a giant throne at India Gate, in New Delhi, to a reputed crowd of 1 million. He needs 1,000 apostles, called mahatmas, to lead and recruit his vast spiritual army. He's the son of a guru from Rishikesh, a region that has spawned holy men the way Appalachia has spawned stock car racers.

According to Dava Lurie, 19, who says the guru told it to her himself, he was sitting alone, weeping, the day his father died in 1966, when suddenly a great light filled the room and a voice said to him: "You are the one to take the message to the whole world."

He'd been getting in shape for years. At 18 months, according to leaflets, the little guru would "wake up his father's disciples at 4 o'clock in the morning and tell them to meditate." At 3 he discoursed to thousands on union with God. At 6 he could do it in English, along with his native Hindi.

Now, the disciples are gathering across the rug towards the newcomer (who elected to sit on the floor) to pass along the word of the Wordless Word. Their bodies tend to scrawniness, youth, and hair. Their eyes range from glitter to dream.

"This is our last trip," says Arthur Brigham, 21, of Denver. He ran into the guru during a year-and-a-half in India, and helped organize the American tour now in progress. "He has given us his knowledge. We are in our last reincarnations. When we die, we will be liberated, become one with God. It will be like a drop of water that falls in the ocean. Can you take that same drop out again?"

The "knowledge" is given in an initiation, in which aspirants are taught to "perceive the soul with all the senses, with total attachment," Brigham says. "It's the inner vibration that's in everything, the word of God."

But the Word "cannot be pronounced, cannot be conceived by the mind. Only by the heart."

It took most of the disciples in the living room at least three days of intense devotion to get ready to hear the Word.

Learning the moral and ethical obligations of the Divine Light Mission, as the disciples call themselves, took no time at all. There aren't any. No commandments, no Laws of the Church, no vegetarian diet, no mantras or yoga postures; thou shalt have no commandments. One doesn't need them, one understands, when one has the Knowledge. One will grow away from wrongdoing by meditating on the Unsayable Word.

In the initiation, however, which consists mostly of pep talk and explanation, the aspirants are asked to promise not to reveal the basic techniques

"...he looks like the kind of little kid about whom adults say: 'He should act like a little kid more.' "

for meditating on the Word. And to meditate every day, and attend the sat-sangs, or lectures.

("Don't use my name," says the woman who describes the initiation and promises. "I've only been in this a couple of days and I don't know if you're supposed to tell about the promises or not.")

The proposition that someone with the Knowledge might believe it his sacred duty to murder someone draws patient smiles from the crowd in the living room. The safeguard of doubt is not necessary with the Knowledge.

"I believe in it absolutely and completely," says Brigham, who has moved to the inside of the circle after correcting a few other disciples' minor errors. "When you see dawn you don't question it, do you? I believe that, spiritually, I am at the dawn."

The Divine Light Mission meets the textbook qualifications for most basic religions: its experience is ineffable, its truth is self-evident, its secrets are reserved to initiates, and its leader, the guru, bears the total tidings of God.

"The guru is such a high," exclaims Lurie with soft wonder. "Actually, the first time I saw him he just looked like a little kid to me. But I went down to L.A. to the ashram. The first day, I hated it. I wanted to go back to Big Sur. Everybody said stick around for another day, and then I started to see it. He left for Boulder [Colo.] and one day I fell apart, crying, weeping, praying to . . . I don't know what I prayed to. Then his spirit came into me and it was such a rush. . . ."

Dan Toomey, 21, of Wilmington, Del., was in Berkeley, Calif., "Looking for a spiritual master" and getting ready "to split for L.A. when some guy, for no reason at all, gave me this poster about the Guru Maharaj Ji coming to Berkeley."

No reason, oh Perfect Master?

The only thing they can't tell you about him, it seems, is whether he will make any more of an appearance this afternoon than a walkie-talkie broadcast.

A large, pimply girl announces the guru has been notified he has a visitor, but he has replied only "okay."

Someone says the guru needs only seven more hours flying time to get his pilot's license. "The first landing he ever made was perfect."

"I should hope so," says the woman who travels with Toomey.

They talk about the 1,000 American followers the guru has garnered; about the guru's large toy collection; about the time in India he watched a magician entertain a crowd and laughed and laughed, meanwhile giving away the tricks; about his penchant not only for water pistols but for dumping buckets of water over people's heads; about the way he builds many of his satsangs around the subject of automobiles.

Various apocrypha are debated: whether the guru was reading a Spider-man comic book the other day or a Captain America; and whether he actually believes the Indian legend that money is sometimes found under snakes' corpses to settle debts from previous incarnations.

The girl messenger re-enters the living room. She brings word from upstairs. "You may go up and knock on his door," she tells the visitor. "He may answer it. He may not." The burglar alarm vibes go off again.

With the grace of cattle panicking in a thunderstorm, electrified disciples stampede up the shag-rugged stairs with the infidel visitor. They swirl around a locus of panic when somebody sees, my God, the visitor's sandals. A sizzle of whispers orders them removed. Everybody piles into a tiny study and readies tape recorders and obeisances.

A mahatma, one whose job is to transmit the Knowledge ("If the guru did it himself it would blow your mind," says Brigham), leans his shaved head through the door and says to the multitude:

"He's in the bathroom. When he is finished he will come here."

Ears perk for the sound of water rushing down a drain, perhaps. Then the door opens.

Balyogeshwar (meaning "born Lord of the Yogis") Shri Sant Ji Maharaj walks in on patent-leather-booted lotus feet. Brigham scrambles to kiss them. Foreheads zoom toward the floor. The ignorant visitor stands up. The guru sits down in an overstuffed chair.

He's a little kid. Smiling but grave at the same time, he looks like the kind of little kid about whom adults say: "He should act like a little kid more."

He wears white trousers and a white, shortsleeved shirt over a sleeveless undershirt. He has a round, brown, confident face. His black hair is parted on the right.

He looks like a young, possibly bored Orson Welles. He wears an enormous underwater-type red and blue watch on his left wrist.

He listens to questions and answers in the quick, high-pitched tones one links with both Indians and prepubescent boys. His hands dart and float like a classical pianist's.

Why, for instance, does he preach no rules or commandments? (Forgetting about those initiation promises.)

"You do not want to just polish the car, the outside. You want to work on the inside," he says.

Does he fear his antics with Frankenstein masks and water pistols might cause people to take him lightly?

"Those people who tell you those things do not see the real me. They are like those who stand in an automobile showroom and look only at the mirrors on the walls, not at the automobiles themselves."

This interest in automobiles?

"Automobiles are one of the best things of man. They are the best examples to use in satsangs. I am very interested in technical things. Pollution? Do you know the lotus flower? The lotus flower grows in filthy water, yet it is pure. Man can use technical things yet stay away from them, stay pure."

He spiels aphorisms and parables with the ease of somebody who's been doing it since he started waking those disciples up at 18 months:

"The shopowner is one, the shopkeepers are many.

"Where the magnet is, iron comes.

"Our duty is what we do. D and D. Duty and Do. We know our duty from our consciousness. If you stole this tape recorder, your face would be red when you ran out of this house, because your consciousness would know it was wrong. If you do good, your consciousness knows this too, and you would feel bright and happy.

"Soon, everyone will have the same knowledge I give. Quite soon. I will not say when. I do not prophesy. But the age of kali yuga (darkness) will change to the age of kali satya (light) soon."

He laughs a lot and looks out the window and keeps checking that huge watch. He says he's teaching nothing new, merely what the great prophets of the past have taught. But there is a pause before his answer when he is asked if anyone else today teaches what he is teaching.

The answer is sure, however; as sure as that of any human whom 3 million people believe to be God's greatest messenger.

"Nobody else."

He stands up. The audience is over. Foreheads fight for floor space again, and he exits, a chubby 13-year-old boy who looks like he just might be tall for his age.

"Pretty far-out little dude," says a bearded boy.

Then the house fragments into a panic of suitcases and shouting, disciples sprinting across the lawn, up and down stairs, even though the guru's flight leaves National Airport for New York at 6:30 and it's only 4 now.

By 4:15 the breathless madness has gelled into a crowd that watches the front door to do obeisance the moment he's satisfied it's all in proper order, which he does, and they do (obeisance) as he strolls down the cement front walk and slides into the front seat of a shiny, bronze four-door Ford LTD ("We always try to find a car he'll like," says Sharon Kelly) and slumps down a little, staring, with that look somewhere between a smile and a sulk. A word is given,. The LTD pulls out from the curb, nearly sideswipes a honking, swerving Chevy. It leaves behind a crowd deflating like curtains in a windy room, when you close the door.

—September 14, 1971

111

Portrait of the Artist at 600 Pounds

By Judy Bachrach

Six hundred pounds of Haystacks Calhoun rises to its full height of 6 feet 4 inches, lumbers outside his hotel on downtown H Street and blocks out the afternoon sun.

"You could call me an international dresser, Ah guess," says Haystacks Calhoun.

You could. But it would be inappropriate. In his custom-made overalls (from Oshkosh, Wis.) his 12 EEEEE shoes (Columbus, Ohio) and his (hidden) underwear, allegedly from Raleigh, N.C., Calhoun looks less like the wrestler who defeated Killer Kowalski at Capital Centre Monday night than the fat farm boy from Morgan's Corner, Ark., which is what he was in the beginning.

Bouncing off the folds of his tremulous belly is a long chain terminating in a large horseshoe. "Given to me by mah daddy," says Haystacks, who removes the chain only in the ring, where he drapes it over the ropes. "Mah daddy, he was a farmer, and he said Ah could be anythin' Ah wanted 'long as I stayed outta trouble. Yeah, Ah stayed outta trouble pretty good. Well, he didn't spare the rod none, either."

Haystacks Calhoun laughs, but it is no ordinary laugh. When Haystacks Calhoun laughs, his stomach trembles, his long round column of an arm pounds the seat cushion, and his throat releases a hearty "Haw Haw Haw."

In wrestling circles Calhoun is known as "a baby face," or the good guy. "In fact," says Joe Jares, an associate editor of *Sports Illustrated,* who is about to publish a book on wrestling, "Haystacks is one of a whole series of fatties." Jares points to the heavyweight antics of the late '40s, the heyday of Martin Levy ("The Blimp"), who later found employment in a traveling freak show. And today there is a substantial female wrestler called "Heather Feather," who wears a lollipop in her hair.

It is, in other words, an entertainment sport. But Jares, whose father ("Brother Frank") was a pro wrestler, says that's the way it's always been. He has talked to Verne Gagne, one of today's great pros, and was told that if you add up all the small TV stations across the nation that broadcast wrestling (like D.C.'s Channel 20-WDCA, which does so Saturday nights), the ratings would outdraw the Super Bowl.

"Wrestling is bigger than ever," says Jares. "That's what people I trust in the business say. And I believe them."

And Haystacks?

"Haystacks is draw," Jares says with great finality. "But probably not much talent."

And here is Haystacks Calhoun at 39, a man who says he grosses about $100,000 a year, which puts him in the upper brackets of wrestling ("but that ain't counting expenses, honey").

His daddy didn't name him Haystacks. His daddy named him William, but when this is inadvertently leaked, Haystacks stops cackling. "Shoot, don't tell her that. Ah'd be starvin' at the box office with that name."

As it is, he is not exactly going hungry. Every morning Haystacks Calhoun wakes up, and if he's at home in McKinney, Tex., his wife (140 pounds) cooks him a dozen eggs with maybe a three-pound steak thrown in, and if he's on the road in his custom-built Travel-All, he does it himself "cause there ain't nuthin' to it."

"Diet?!" The features peeping through the flesh twist in horror. "Honey, Ah been on a diet most of mah life. They tell me when Ah was 14 Ah was gonna die 'cause Ah was so fat. And when Ah was 21, the doctah says, 'You can't make it 'nother couple of years.' An' when Ah was 23, I visit this heart specialist and he tells me, 'Son. You can't live 'nother 6 months.' So mah interpretation is that the doctahs are doin' just what their license tells 'em: *practicing* medicine, haw haw haw."

He became "a wrastler" because he discovered he was far far better at that in high school than, say, "that dad-gummed English literatoor. And then Ah leaves high school and every one wants to know if Ah got experience. So Ah became a farm boy until Ah was 21 and old enough to wrastle. Mah first match was in Kansas City."

Where he won. He came east in '58, worked up and down the coast three and a half years. "That's where Ah sorta hit mah stride. Ah've never been pinned, but about everythin' else happens to me: chains, bottles, yeah, salt in mah eye. . . ."

Wrestling is not one of your gentler pastimes. Monday night for instance, the dread Killer Kowalski bit Calhoun on the nose, and pulled his hair. Not kosher, ruled the ref in repeated histrionic protest.

Haystacks says, "Honey, I never seen anythin' in mah life Ah was afraid of."

Well maybe that's because wrestling is more entertainment than sport.

"Yeah?" Two brows shoot skyward. "Who says that?"

Well, sportwriters often say that.

"Yeah?" The brows lower. "Well honey, you send those gentlemen to me and Ah'll get them in a few holds and they'll tell you if it's a sport or not."

As in most other sports there are wrestling groupies, a subject that instantly pulls Calhoun out of an ominous mood.

"Naw they don't bother me none. Let's face it, honey, when you're mah size no girl can take advantage of you. If they do, it's strictly with mah help. Haw haw. Yeah, Ah get all kinds of fan mail, and some of it comes from the gay society. Why Ah got this one letter from a guy, wanted a pair of mah sweaty overalls. An' he was from the State Department. Haw haw haw."

Because he is generally pitted against the menacing bad boys of the business—like Killer Kowalski—Haystacks' arrival in the ring is accompanied by huge roars of approval and cries of outrage when he is whonked by the opponent.

But life, alas, does not always imitate sport, and Haystacks Calhoun's first wife (now divorced) still sends him little *billets doux.*

"She wrote me a letter, said her husband's a Hell's Angel and in the pen for armed robbery, an' he was gonna get me, soon's he's outta jail."

Well, that seems like a rough number, "getting" Haystacks Calhoun.

"Wa-a-al, let me put it this way, honey. Ah'm too big to hide. 'N too fat to run. So Ah only got one chance. To stand and fight."

At Capital Centre, Haystacks stood. Some of the time. The rest of the time, he was busy fending off Killer Kowalski, a slimmer wrestler in purple tights who had slicked down hair and the face of a disgruntled robot.

It was rumored by two junior high school kids from Lanham who were celebrating this return of wrestling to Washington after a three-year absence, that Killer once "accidentally" ripped off the ear of his opponent.

By contrast, therefore, Haystacks in his Oshkosh overalls and his fat bare feet was a perfect charmer—even when he bounced up and down on Killer's back.

Killer growled. Killer snarled. Killer picked up Haystack's horseshoe chain from the ropes and began to swing it at his face. The unavoidable fact that the horseshoe never made contact did not prevent Calhoun from groaning with pain or the crowd from angry invective or the referee from going bananas over Killer's boorish behavior.

A gong rang. An announcer in snappy attire raised Haystacks Calhoun's broad arm and pronounced him the winner by default. Killer walked off threatening to punch Haystacks in the snoot, gnashing his teeth.

It was a terrific performance.

"Amazing isn't it," said a man who guards the doors of Capital Centre, "what people will pay good money for."

—June 12, 1974

115

Next: The Samurai

Hiroo Onoda. On the surface, this Japanese World War II heir of the samurai who, by his own account, held out 30 years after the war, isolated in enemy territory upholding his "sense of mission" until formally ordered to surrender, would appear to be an intriguing interview.

The primary question is why? Was he a hero or a fool?

But there was no way Henry Mitchell could effectively talk to him about it because they share no language. Also, the interview's setting, a bagel and lox meal in a New York suburb, seemed at first all wrong. Furthermore, reading Onoda's book on the 30 years provided Mitchell with few clues. As Mitchell writes, "It occurs to you that you are not going to find out, in four hours or so . . ." So Mitchell goes about the problem from another direction.

The key is his variation of prose style within the story to suit the changing mood. He begins with a charming anecdote that demonstrates the hopeless incongruity of Onoda and his suburban setting; you think maybe this is going to be a light story. Then he goes on in a relatively straight account of his abortive quest for an answer to the central question. And, suddenly, following a paraphrase of the end of Onoda's book, Mitchell interrupts the narrative with a lurch: "Just here, as the story ends (and the book ends), the real questions begin."

He then launches into a stirring, self-searching, speculative essay, exploring from a lofty perspective and in the most resonant rhetoric just what the implications of the "real questions" may be. "What happens to a man who after so many years goes back home to a popular hero's welcome, and then feels lost . . . ?" He goes on, crossing cultures from the code of the samurai to Don Quixote to the Bible. And Mitchell ends up convincing you that even Onoda himself (who has deserted Japan for South America) has no way of knowing if he is hero or fool and that there is something universal about this problem that transcends a single, confused 52-year-old former Japanese lieutenant.

— L. T.

Samurai's Surrender

By Henry Mitchell

H ASTINGS-ON-HUDSON, N.Y.—The Japanese lieutenant who
required 30 years to achieve surrender and stop fighting World War II
in the Philippines took one look at the lox and bagel on his plate and indicated to his honorable hostess here in suburban New York that he was not
all that hungry.

In his self-appointed guerrilla years, Hiroo Onoda lived decades without
a square meal, without a sound sleep, without a good bath. He almost
fainted from joy when the Japanese youth who finally got to him in his
island hideout gave him a can of beans.

"For the first time in 30 years," he said afterward, "I was eating something fit for human consumption."

But lox and bagel—well. There are limits.

You might assume from his 30-year war that Onoda is not the most
flexible or adaptable fellow in the world. He may smile at strangers, especially if it's his duty (as author making a tour for his book sales) to do so,
and he will even gaze at the Super Bowl on television, though it can hardly
mean anything to him, his first day of a brief trip through America. But
Onoda is a man of great caution—he lasted 30 years in enemy territory
without getting shot—and not a man of snap decisions.

His book is called *No Surrender,* though he did, in fact, surrender last
February. But something like "NEVER" is central to his character, and
whether this quality has ever made him happy or ever will is something he
does not discuss in the book.

He was terribly surprised that Japan surrendered. He had supposed the
Japanese would die to the last man before that happened. When he himself
surrendered, they gave him back his sword, as a nice gesture of respect for
his 30 years of faithfulness to duty as he saw it. He said that when he saw
that respect for what he had believed in, he felt for a second "the pride of
the samurai."

The facts are plain enough, at least from Onoda's version of them, and
it's hard to understand any human without beginning with the facts as
he sees them.

First, he was an intelligence officer, not an infantryman. He was isolated
on a small sparsely populated island of no consequence and when it was
said the war was over, he had no reason to believe it. The enemy was al-

ways telling lies to demoralize you. He was left with two companions, both of them later shot by natives — hostile, because Onoda and his buddies kept stealing rice and burning barns and killing cows and occasionally killing the men, because they thought of themselves as still being at war.

That sounds reasonable enough, at the beginning of peacetime. But for 30 years?

Well, it is true that in those 30 years Onoda did think the war was going on awfully long, and he did, of course, hear rumors of peace. The Japanese government spent a fortune trying to get the message to him, dropping leaflets from planes, sending special missions to fetch him back. Twice, members of Onoda's family were sent to the island and he heard them at a distance, on their loudspeakers, begging him to return because the war was over.

But if a man doesn't want to believe something (and no samurai wishes to believe his nation has been defeated) then it is almost impossible to produce evidence he will find convincing. No matter what anybody did or said, Onoda found some reason to believe otherwise. He thought the news-papers had been censored just to entrap him, and he thought the radio broadcasts (which indicated peace had returned to Japan) were merely propaganda to make him betray his mission.

It is hard to believe that, but it helps to remember that Onoda was isolated. When you live a certain life for year after year in the forest, you do not see things the same way you do if you live in town and go to work every day. One cardinal element was always missing, Onoda says:

If the war was really over, and if he really was supposed to surrender and go home, then why had he not received any direct orders from his superiors? All they had to do was order him to surrender. But they never did, not until last February. The minute he got those orders, he followed them, he says, and surrendered and went home.

One attractive irony was that what the Japanese government failed to do in its large effort to get through to him was accomplished by a young college dropout named Suzuki, who simply took it into his head one day to go find Onoda. He did. He found out Onoda was not going to budge with-out orders. He went back to Japan. Explained that. The orders came promptly. What the state failed at, the dropout accomplished, that is, the end of Onoda's long war.

Just here, as the story ends (and the book ends), the real questions begin. Even if you assume Onoda interpreted events exactly as he said he did (and it is the simplest explanation, for any other explanation is even less be-lievable), and even if you assume that thanks to his military indoctrination, due to his samurai sense of mission (and the kamikaze pilots were under-standable only on the basis that they believed in their duty, just as they said they did), and even if you make allowances for a certain mental cast, if not mental disorder, from living so isolated a life, you are still left with an over-whelming question:

What happens to a man whose whole world has crumbled, whose sufferings of 30 years appear to have been useless, or ludicrous, or wasted? What happens when a faith that the nation would die, rather than surrender, proves false? What happens when you tear yourself to pieces in order to achieve the discipline that allows you to continue your guerrilla mission for 30 years—giving up home and sex and luxury and comfort—only to wonder if it was worth it, and only to see some people grin?

What does a man do who fought a mortal enemy for 30 years, only to find himself presented with lox and bagels in the very citadel of the enemy nation, in a room full of photographers and reporters looking as if they thought maybe you were some sort of rare specimen, if not a certified psychotic jackass?

And what happens to a man who after so many years goes back home to a popular hero's welcome, and then feels lost, and feels increasingly that his own people—for whom he suffered all those years—have become materialistic, grubby, cynical, a bit blind to honor, a bit indifferent to sacrifice?

In Onoda's case, he took one look at Japan and headed off to Brazil for a new life as a farmer and cattle raiser. His favorite brother moved to Brazil after the war, so they'll be there together. But Brazil can never be home, as Japan was.

One thing you can do—one thing people have always done—is tell your story. Hence the book. It is published, interestingly enough, by Kodansha, the one publishing house that seems to have figured out that Onoda was still fighting the war because his superiors never ordered him to stop. Other publishers are said to have offered him more money, but if you've spent most of your life on a cause, you like to believe that even a publisher can understand it.

Onoda got through the brunch Sunday attended by affluent suburban folk interested one way or another in Japan, and friends of the American representative of the Kodansha publishers (who lives in this suburban village an hour out of New York). He seemed to be enjoying it and chatted with reporters through his interpreter, Charles S. Terry, who translated his book into English (it will be published the end of this month).

At one pause in the brunch, Onoda reached for his black leather purse and pulled out a cigarette. He notes in his book, by the way, that the first cigarette he had in the tropical forest in years and years was a Marlboro, which may be the samurai brand, not that Onoda says so. To the brunch he wore an ashes of roses turtleneck shirt, and a natty brown suede jacket. His hair is still jet black, his teeth look great, he eats extremely little, and, as his hostess said, he will probably live forever, having had no additives, no sugar, no artificial sweeteners and no cholesterol.

It occurs to you that you are not going to find out, in four hours or so, whether Onoda is a hero. If you ask him what's that strange ring on his middle finger, he'll tell you an American gave it to him when he surrendered, and sure enough it says "United States Air Force" in gold around its oval stone.

Suddenly it dawns on you that it's not your business whether Onoda is a hero. His story is fascinating, his survival is incredible, his book is absorbing, but it's more than that, that keeps you looking at him:

If he is a samurai, a man of noble and decent sacrifice, then why did not samurai angels save him, or at least grant him a samurai's death in battle, instead of leaving him alone and at loose ends at 52 in a world that half fears what may be his nobility, and half recoils from what may be his sickness?

It's not that you want to judge. It's that you want to know what is real.

And Onoda must be asking the same thing, also: What is reality? Is there any such thing as allegiance, or duty, or is it all just a farce, or a myth, that a man must be faithful all the way to death? Do orders mean anything, or can a soldier make up his own? Can he break his orders the first night of his watch, or the third, or the fiftieth, or can he break them after a year, or 10 years or 30 years?

Onoda says — and it is easier than any other explanation to believe, incredible though it is — he thought his orders were forever, unless and until those orders were changed by new orders from his qualified superior.

Does this amount to allegiance of a high sort, or does it amount to stupidity? To what extent does a man rightly believe in the law (military orders, in this case) and how often or how soon or on what grounds may he break that law and still have respect for himself?

You do not read Onoda's book or talk to him at all without thinking of Quixote, the Spanish gentleman of quite moderate means who perceived windmills to be evil giants, and who damned near killed himself in fighting them. And they were only windmills, after all.

Is duty, is an oath of allegiance, a windmill, too? Is suffering nonsense? Something any sane man avoids?

Onoda is bent on a new life in Brazil. The past is done. Right or wrong. If it leaves him a little baffled, well, reality has a way of doing that.

His friends — if he had any left after 30 years in a forest — could possibly explain to him that his disillusionment is all his fault. He should have done this, should have known that, should have believed the other. One way or another, he brought all those years on himself. That's what friends are for, to show you you're in a jam for your own faults.

There was another baffled fellow, once, whose world was all screwy and he was invited to admit it was all his fault, and invited to spit at every faith he had ever believed in, and he was tempted to, but (according to an excellent translator of some centuries ago) he sort of held on.

"Though he slay me," he said of his faith, "yet will I trust in him. With mine own eyes shall I see God."

Somewhere between the wasted years and the vision that makes it all worthwhile is where Onoda appears to be now.   — January 14, 1975

Next: A Suicide

Christine Chubbuck. When fiction writer Ward Just said that journalism is limited because there's no way a reporter can see into a person's heart, it was stories like this one—testing the limits of reporting—he must have had in mind.

Its genesis was the widely reported suicide before thousands of Sarasota, Fla., TV viewers of Christine Chubbuck, a local television news reporter. Her death was a macabre, unique act. No one had ever done that before, and Sally Quinn was consumed with curiosity about why it happened. She went to Sarasota on a particularly difficult reporting assignment: to interview everybody (Chubbuck's family, friends, professional associates) who might shed light on the singular deed.

Quinn found many of the classic symptoms of suicide. As Chubbuck's mother said, there were "no close friends, no romantic attachments or prospects of any." Chubbuck was deeply depressed over this and over her job. Her family background was riddled with emotional instability. She had threatened suicide so often, before so many people, that they no longer took her seriously, particularly those in the family with psychological problems of their own.

Quinn assembled all the facts there were to be gotten and wrote (in the simplest, most direct prose style) the anatomy of a suicide, which also unfolds as a grim tale of man's inhumanity to man (both by Chubbuck and against her).

As to the ultimate question, why she chose to "bring death into other people's homes," the facts produce no sure answer. Quinn's story carefully respects the ambiguities that make up reality, rather than warping the facts in a way that would produce a clear but faulty verdict. As the minister said in his eulogy for Christine Chubbuck: ". . . we are hurt by her choice of isolation and we are confused by her message."
                                                                    —L. T.

Christine Chubbuck: 29, Good-Looking, Educated. A Television Personality. Dead. Live and in Color.

By Sally Quinn

SARASOTA, Fla.—Christine Chubbuck flicked her long dark hair back away from her face, swallowed, twitched her lips only slightly and reached with her left hand to turn the next page of her script. Looking down on the anchor desk she began to read: "In keeping with Channel 40's policy of bringing you the latest in"—she looked up from the script, directly into the camera and smiled a tentative smile. Her voice took on a sarcastic tone as she emphasized "blood and guts . . . and in living color." She looked back down at her script, her left hand shook almost unnoticeably.

Her right arm stiffened. "We bring you another first." Her voice was steady. She looked up again into the camera. Her eyes were dark, direct and challenging. "An attempted suicide." Her right hand came up from under the anchor desk. In it was a .38 caliber revolver. She pointed it at the lower back of her head and pulled the trigger. A loud crack was heard. A puff of smoke blew out from the gun and her hair flew up around her face as though a sudden gust of wind had caught it. Her face took on a fierce, contorted look, her mouth wrenched downward, her head shook. Then her body fell forward with a resounding thud against the anchor desk and slowly slipped out of sight.

Hours later at the hospital, shortly before Christine Chubbuck died, her mother was interviewed by a local reporter.

"She was terribly, terribly, terribly depressed. She had a job that she loved. She said constantly that if it ended tomorrow she would still be glad she had had it. But she had nothing else in her social life.

"No close friends, no romantic attachments or prospects of any. She was a spinster at 29 and it bothered her. She couldn't register with people. That's the main thing. She was very sensitive and she tried and she would reach out, you know, 'Hi, how are you, won't you come have a cup of coffee with me,' and you say 'no,' but you don't say 'Won't you come have a cup of coffee with me,' that sort of thing, in her personal people relationships, and it really got to her. She'd been very depressed. She'd been seeing a psychiatrist who really didn't feel that she was that serious about not wanting to live. She felt if you've tried as hard as you can, you've prepared yourself, you work hard, you reach your hand out to people and nobody takes it, then there's something wrong with your drumbeat, and she really felt she couldn't register with anyone except her family. And at 29, that's sad."

Monday, July 15, was just another day at Channel 40. Chris Chubbuck arrived about a half hour before the 9:30 morning talk show, "Suncoast Digest." She had had a quick cup of coffee with her mother at their house on nearby Siesta Key, asked her mother to leave her chocolate poodle, "Perspicacity," out because she'd be back at 10:45, jumped in her yellow Volkswagen convertible, "The Lemon," and dashed off to the studio. She looked particularly good that morning. She had a tan, her waist-length black hair was clean and shiny and her black and white print dress complemented her long slim figure. She was in extraordinarily good spirits. Her guest arrived and she showed him and his wife into the studio, then excused herself to write her script for the newscast. This was a departure and it puzzled the technical director Linford Rickard, and the two camerawomen. Chris normally opened her show in her interview area and conducted a rather informal half hour. Only occasionally on weekends had she ever anchored the news and never once had she opened her show with a newscast.

But Chris was so reliable and so professional that everyone figured she knew what she was doing. She sat down at her typewriter, quickly wrote her 10-minute news script, told the control room that she wanted to use film of a shootout that weekend, and took her place at the anchor desk, across the room from her interview area.

She placed under the anchor desk a large bag of puppets she had made, which she occasionally brought with her to use on her broadcast or to give a puppet show at a local hospital for mentally retarded children. Hidden in the bag was the .38 caliber pistol.

She told the two camerawomen that she would open with a short segment of news, then move over to her interview area.

She began with three items of national news, then led into a film piece about a local shooting at a restaurant the night before. When she finished the lead-in she waited for the film to come up, but nothing happened.

"I looked up and said to her, 'Chris, the film's not going to roll,'" said Jean Reed, the camerawoman, "and she just looked at me very levelly and said, 'It isn't going to roll.' Then she just smiled as though she were terribly amused. Normally she would have been furious and said, 'Oh, this damn, two-bit outfit.' But she just sat there calmly.

"Then, when she went into that blood and guts thing I thought what sick humor. And after she shot herself I was furious and ran over to the anchor desk, fully expecting to see her lying on the floor doubled up with laughter. But I saw her stretched out, blood running out of her nose and mouth and her whole body twitching. I said, 'My god, she's done it. She's shot herself.'"

On the desk, after Chris had been rushed to the hospital, a blood soaked news story was found. It was the story of her own suicide attempt, written in long hand. It described the attempt, how she was taken to Sarasota Memorial Hospital, and it listed her in critical condition.

Hours after the shooting, the story was on network radio, television and on front pages of newspapers all over the world. "TV Star Kills Self," "TV Personality Takes Own Life On Air," "On Camera Suicide," read headlines of tabloids from Tokyo to London to Australia to the *New York Daily News*. People were stunned. Lee Harvey Oswald, George Wallace, a Viet Cong prisoner had all been shot before viewers' eyes and it riveted the world. But never in history had anyone deliberately killed herself on live television. It was a first. And it was Christine Chubbuck's story.

She left no suicide note. A week before she died, she mentioned to Rob Smith, 22, the night news editor, that she had purchased a gun.

"What for?" asked Rob.

"Well, I thought it would be a nifty idea if I went on the air live and just blew myself away," she answered, and then laughed her funny cackle.

"I just changed the subject," said Rob. "That was just too sick a joke for me."

Several weeks before she died, she told Mike Simmons, 26, the news director, that she wanted to do a film piece on suicide. He gave her the go-ahead. She called the local police department and discussed methods of suicide with one of the officers. She was told that to kill oneself with a gun, the "best" method was to use a .38 caliber pistol. And to be absolutely sure of success, a wadcutter, a slug that disintegrates into tiny pieces in the body, should be used.

She was also told that the gun should be pointed not at the temple, which wouldn't necessarily kill, but at the lower back of the head. It is there that the heart and lungs, the life functions, are sustained.

When Chris Chubbuck killed herself, she followed those instructions. There seemed to be no doubt that she had every intention of killing herself. There were some who were confused by the word "attempted" suicide in her script. But those who worked with her had a ready explanation. Chris was too good a newswoman to write suicide when it might have failed.

She was too precise. And even her mother thought it not unusual. "Chris was hedging her bets," she said.

So once it had been established that she fully intended to die, obviously the question became why. And of course, why did she choose to do it the way she did?

When somebody commits suicide, especially violently and publicly, once the initial shock dies away and people can absorb what has happened, they can begin to speculate on why. This is what was happening in Sarasota one week after the death of "TV Star Chris Chubbuck." Everyone had his or her own idea of why it happened.

• Everyone agrees that her sexual status was a manifestation of the problems she had in relating to people. Chris would have been 30 on Aug. 24 and she was still a virgin. She made no secret of it to her family, her friends, and her co-workers. But to say that she killed herself for this reason would be extremely simplistic.

• She had worked for nearly a year with a young man named George Peter Ryan, a tall, handsome, blond stockbroker who read the stock reports on the local news show. George ("Gorgeous George" to some of his friends) was divorced and had had personal problems himself. He was heavily involved in transactional analysis. Chris developed a crush on him. In fact, she confided to one of her friends that she had decided George was the perfect person to help her solve her problems. She went to George on his 30th birthday in late June with a cake. And later at a press party, she made it clear to him in a subtle way that she was available. He rejected her.

• Chris' closest friend, if she had one, was Andrea Kirby. Andrea, 32, was the sports reporter for Channel 40. She was Southern, petite, divorced and had a way with men. Andrea was also tough and ambitious.

Andrea had recently been hired by a Baltimore TV station and was leaving Sarasota in a few days. That depressed Chris somewhat because she saw her friend leaving and going on to bigger and better things while she was left behind. It was Andrea to whom Chris confided her plan to proposition George. Andrea had no patience with Chris' tendency to feel sorry for herself. Occasionally she would say, "That's right, Chris. Just kick yourself in the ass." What she didn't say was that she and George were already seeing each other. "When Chris found out that George and I were going out, that depressed her," Andrea said.

• The owner of station WXLT-TV is Robert Nelson. He had owned radio stations in the area and three years ago had started this new channel, an ABC affiliate. The station was getting off to a slow start. Their equipment was old, their staff was small, very young and inexperienced. Everybody did everything. They concentrated on the more sensational news in the area, violence, crime, accidents, "blood and guts," as Chris

" 'She'd walk into a room and every head would turn . . . yet nobody ever ...asked for her phone number.' "

would often put it. Channel 40, sometimes referred to as "Funny Forty," estimates its highest viewing audience at 10,000 sets. In season.

Chris' program had ratings of 500 homes. In season maybe 1,000. She was not by any means a "big TV star." She wanted to be. She wanted to be recognized, she was hard working, diligent and competent.

Her friends and family say she hated Nelson because she thought he seemed unconcerned with the quality of the station. She complained often about what she saw as the number of tasteless and violent stories on the air, about the station pandering, in her opinion, to its advertisers, about the lack of pay. When she died she was making little more than $5,000 a year. That was for putting on a morning talk show, doing sometimes four or five stories a day and occasionally working on weekends, anchoring the evening news. She was bitter about the fact that Nelson seemed to want only those who would work for the least amount of money, not those who were the most talented.

Chris' suicide put station WXLT-TV on the map. Nelson proudly showed his collections of clipping about it to a visitor. "We got the whole front page of the *Daily News*," he boasted.

• On the Friday night before Chris killed herself, she had a terrible fight with Mike Simmons, the news director, about her story being cut, in favor of a shootout.

"She was very emotional, would get unusually upset about these things," said Simmons. "She would, well, throw tantrums a lot."

A week earlier she had thrown a terrible tantrum when the director placed a bouquet of plastic flowers on her interview table. In front of her guest, a state politician, she had flung the flowers across the studio, screaming, "I won't have these damned things in my studio." Everyone was a little unnerved by that scene.

• She had had very few dates in the past months. When she had invited men, several times, to have dinner, they had accepted, then not even bothered to show up or call. "I don't think Chris has had more than 25 dates in the last 10 years," her mother said.

• Last summer she had had an ovary removed. The doctors told her then that if she didn't have children within the next two or three years she probably never would. And, of course, there were no prospects.

She had no real friends. She was a strange combination of someone who at once wanted, needed desperately, the support and friendship of others and in another way rejected others out of a sense of defensive pride. Her initial image was one of a self-confident, totally contained, together young woman. She would seem haughty, distant, standoffish really. Yet when people began to know her she evidenced such a crying need for a completely committed relationship that it drove them away for fear they couldn't give her what she wanted.

"There was a haunting melody in Chris," said Mrs. Chubbuck. "She gave so many presents, spent so much money, not to buy their friend-ship . . . but because she wanted to. It's almost like her life was a little out of gear with other people. She was the only person I ever knew who would walk into a room and every head would turn . . . yet nobody ever came over and asked for her phone number. It's been like that since she was 13."

.

Chris Chubbuck lived at home with her mother and her older brother, Timothy, 32, an interior decorator. But it wasn't the usual situation of a 29-year-old "spinster" living at home. She had left a small town in Ohio several years ago and moved into her family's summer home on Siesta Key. Two years later, her parents were divorced and her mother moved down. Her younger brother Greg, 28, later came down and began to work in contracting. And last year, Timothy developed mononucleosis and moved down from Boston to live in the guest cottage, replacing Greg who had become engaged.

"It's sort of like an adult commune," said Mrs. Chubbuck. "Everybody thinks it's a little odd, we know that, but it's a nice arrangement for us. We all have our own privacy."

Mrs. Chubbuck was 53 last week. She has long, shoulder-length gray hair and a round, open, friendly face, carefully made up over her tan. She describes herself as a "53-year-old hippie who's with it." Her conduct throughout the whole suicide episode had been exemplary. Too exem-plary, some thought.

"That's a tough cookie," people would remark.

"Peg" Chubbuck had not shown any emotion in public, and some peo-ple thought perhaps her coldness might have had something to do with her daughter's reasons for killing herself.

She talked to a visitor about Chris and herself and their family exactly one week after her daughter died. She seemed composed, she could laugh and talk calmly. Yet once, when she was asked about her composure in the face of such a horrible event, her eyes filled with tears and she said, "I know what people are saying. But we're very private people. We grieve pri-vately. Chris threw us into a public position. She knew we could handle our sorrow. But we refused to wear our hearts on our sleeves. Those who think I haven't cried should see my swollen tear ducts."

Chris' brother Timothy is artistic and creative and it was Timothy who decorated the house they live in, all very tasteful and House-and-Garden in pinks and greens. He helped Chris with her bedroom, a yellow and white checked room with a small single bed in a corner with ruffled curtains around the bed posts. It looked more like the room of a young girl than the room of a 30-year-old, 5-foot-9 woman.

Greg, more an all-American boy, described himself as Chris' second best friend. Her mother was "her best friend who just happened to be her mother."

On the Saturday before Chris Chubbuck killed herself, Greg and his fiancée visited her house to use the washing machine. She told him that she was terribly depressed and that she didn't think she was going to be able to cope with life any more. "I'm thinking about killing myself and I'm not exactly sure what I'm going to do," she told him.

"Do you want to talk about it?" Greg asked her.

"No," she said, "let's not. We can talk about it tomorrow."

"I would have discounted it if she had said it to me," said her brother Tim. "She'd said it before."

"We'd all heard it," said her mother. "I think it was always serious. I've always known it might happen."

"But she always said it in an offhand way," said Tim.

"But everything she said was offhand," said her mother.

"I always thought," said Greg, "in my own mind, that she was intelligent and would find a way to carry herself through. In the course of the last two or three years I'd had that conversation with her many times. I didn't think of it as an active thing. I thought of it as something she wanted to talk out.

"Besides, her mood seemed up Saturday and Sunday," he said. "She baked a cake. She improved her tan."

"I guess she was putting her house in order," said her mother. "You know, she's always talked about it. 'If life gets too tough, I'll get out. If I can't handle it, I'll leave.' It was her decision and she decided that it was all just too much for her, whether anybody else thought it wasn't, well, it was."

"It was a recurrent conversation," said Tim. "In times of real downness it seemed to her a real solution for escape. We gave it credence."

"We thought it possible because there wasn't anything in her life," said her mother. "If someone asked me a few weeks ago if it was possible, I would have said yes. For her it was the only way out."

"I don't think any intelligent person hasn't viewed it as an alternative," said Greg. "But in her case it always became a serious alternative."

"We didn't ignore it," said her mother.

"It was kind of interfamily therapy in a way," said Tim. "Suicide had been discussed a lot from everyone's point of view."

Chris' family is a well-to-do, upper-middle-class family from Hudson, Ohio, where her father, now remarried, is a businessman. All of the children had been sent to private schools. After Laurel School for Girls, Chris had gone to Ohio State University and graduated from Boston University in broadcasting and film. Since college she had had many TV jobs with small stations, but never on-camera work until she arrived at Channel 40 last August. It was shortly after that, because the station wanted a public affairs program to fulfill FCC regulations, that she was given the morning talk show.

Even in high school, according to her mother, she had formed the "Dateless Wonder" club for girls who didn't have dates on Saturday night.

"She often referred to herself as someone who still believed in wine and roses, being sent flowers and called up for a date. But she would go through periods of two or three years where nobody would even ask her out for a hot dog. You've got to learn to crawl before you walk and Chris never even had a crawling relationship with anybody. She never had more than two dates with anyone in her life. She really wanted to find someone to love and get married. It was much more important to her than her job. She used to say that even a bad relationship is better than none. Her 30th birthday would have been Aug. 24 and she would have been officially an old maid. It bothered her like hell.

"If you look at it on paper," said her mother, "her suicide was simply because her personal life was not enough."

When George Peter Ryan first heard about Chris' suicide he was not surprised. But he felt angry. Angry that she had discounted his friendship. "I was suicidal two years ago and I got into transactional analysis, a form of group therapy," he said. (In fact he brought his "T.A." group leader to the second interview to analyze his reactions to the questions.) "I tried to get Chris interested in that. I tried to talk to her. I wanted to tell her how important it was to be able to talk to someone from the standpoint of honesty. But she didn't believe anyone wanted to be her friend. But I was made aware that she had a crush on me. On my birthday, I think Chris had set out to plan to take control of her life and she was going to do it her way.

"She never said she wanted to be my friend. I only know what people tell me. She never told me anything. I just know that I didn't want to get involved that way. I had the feeling that she demanded more than I could give. I didn't know until after she shot herself that she was a virgin."

Six months ago, Ryan, admittedly, was a mess and Chris hated him. He thought she was "a liberated woman, a pain in the ass, not very attractive, almost manly. She was doing a man's job, only doing it better than a man. She was precise and efficient. There was nothing feminine about her."

But once he started "T.A.," he improved and so did his opinion of Chris and hers of him. "She was two different people, really. Sometimes she was really together, her posture and carriage and just the way she said hello, were different. She was a methodical and efficient career girl, a Germaine Greer, a Gloria Steinem. There was an 'I can handle it . . . but not really' air about her. Other times her posture was rotten, she made no effort to look attractive, she would put herself down, she had this poor-little-me, kick-me attitude."

It was only on the Thursday before she died that Ryan found Chris totally changed. "I went into the studio and she was flirting and, well, smug, really, almost patronizing. And she was never patronizing. She came and sat on my lap and we joked about my being horny. She was really, really together. I couldn't believe it was the same person, especially after our encounter a few weeks before. The next night I wanted to ask her out but her attitude was 'don't touch me.' I couldn't understand. I told her then, 'I really like you, I want you to know you're okay,' but she just brushed me off. I felt discounted. I felt badly about it. Now I realize that she'd already made her decision to die. Her decision had been made. She'd found the answer and she didn't need to feel afraid of me any more."

To Andrea Kirby, Chris was a woman who had a lot going for her but couldn't get it together. "In the last few weeks before she died, she had turned into a 'yes, but' person," said Andrea. "She became a sniveling, self-pitying creature at the end and I really lost patience with her. I thought that if I got mad at her she would be able to pull herself out of it.

"She discounted me as a friend so many times and other people, too. But I had the feeling that if she had friends she wouldn't have been able to say she wasn't a success. Every time she'd be hurt by someone she could chalk another one up. If you didn't call her or do something positive with her, she'd think you didn't like her. I think she killed herself to say, 'Hey, look at me,' to get attention, to be recognized. And I think she wanted marriage and children more than anything else. She said to me once, "I would like to have, just for one week, somebody I really loved, who really loved me.' Her only trouble was that she came on so heavy, so intense. Her way of covering up her insecurities was to be physically confident. That was just her manner."

Andrea and Chris were dining out the night Chris told Andrea her plan to get George. "She was so excited about her great plan. George had, before the last six months, been too aggressive for her and she couldn't stand him. But as he changed, so did her opinion of him. And she wasn't cool about it. I don't think she could have handled an affair with George. She would have held anyone she had an affair with responsible. And I think men sensed that."

Jean Reed, 54, the camerawoman who was working the morning Chris committed suicide, has mixed feelings about her. They were friendly and occasionally would have dinner together. It was at those dinners that Chris confided many of her problems. "She told me," said Jean, "that she had tried to kill herself four years ago with pills. She said she'd had a hard life. In my view she was very self-centered. Hers were the only important problems. She was constantly aware of how people reacted to her, immediately read things into what they said to her, but it was not a two-way street. She talked about her suicide attempt a lot. She was threatened by everyone. I once tried to do an interview and she got furious. And they let Shay Taylor, the other camerawoman, do one and Chris hit the roof. She even thought Miss Florida was going to take over her job when somebody suggested she do the weather.

"She needed encouragement or support and we all tried to compliment her on what she was doing. She dearly loved a kind word but she could put other people down without flashing an eye."

Jean Reed describes Chris as an elegant dresser, as someone with talent and someone you could have a good time with, a good laugh with. "She had a great sense of the absurd, almost a macabre sense of humor. And of course, she adored to laugh about Nelson. She did not like the unexpected. She insisted on being well prepared at all times. She had begun, toward the end, however, to make nasty remarks about her guests. She said to me, 'I'm getting sick of these people. They're all using me. The only thing they want out of me is to be on my show and I resent it.' The funny thing about that was, she was using them, too, because they were good guests. But she would never think of things that way."

Shay Taylor, the 24-year-old camerawoman, felt that Chris displayed her insecurity by being standoffish, masculine, and occasionally, using crude language in front of her male guests, apparently to turn them off deliberately.

"If she met an attractive man or had a good-looking male guest that I knew she was interested in," said Shay, "she'd always tell them that they ought to take me out."

"I make it a policy of not maintaining a close social relationship with any of my employees," said Robert Nelson, the owner of station WXLT-TV. "But the spring when Chris invited us to an open house at her mother's, we went. I was amazed at the number of VIPs there. Everything seemed to be going perfectly and Chris was the center of attention. But quite frankly, people who live on the beach, on Siesta Key, are just different from the rest of us. They're more bohemian. They have a different lifestyle from us who are more urbanized. Chris fit into that category."

Nelson, a small man with dark skin, a round face and thin lips, had some bones to pick with Chris.

"She wasn't as interested in hard news as she was in features and didn't distinguish as she should between them. She had her own system of priorities. I asked her once to interview a prominent businessman, a restaurateur who was getting an award. She didn't do it and I got a little uptight and asked the news director why. He said Chris felt her program should not be a vehicle for every commercial enterprise in the community. I explained that he was an interesting man, but frankly, I own and operate this business and I didn't have to explain to her."

Bob Keehn, the anchor man for the evening news, was along with the Nelsons during this conversation over dinner. Keehn and his wife own an advertising agency, "Ad Infinitem," representing retail clients, banks, department stores and automobile dealers in the community.

Keehn liked Chris Chubbuck. "She had a protective coloration," he said, "what might appear to some to be no need for friends. I felt she was someone with very deep feelings. Someone who seemed more involved with her job and with her emotions than most people seem to be. She had a little more depth than most people.

"What seemed to concern her was her involvement with the human condition. She would express a negative reaction to people and the way they treated each other. One thing about her, though, she was always self-deprecating. Always. She seemed so hangdog that I'd always compliment her purposefully. And she'd always put down the compliment."

Though virtually no one seemed shocked by the fact that Christine Chubbuck decided to take her own life, there were many who were stunned by the method she used to take it. Including her mother.

"I would have thought she would have swum out in the ocean as far as she could go. She was an extraordinarily strong swimmer. She could have gone three or four miles. The water was her friend. It could easily have been her final resting place."

But Chris didn't swim out as far as she could go. She committed a grossly public act, one that, in its way, reverberated around the world and left those behind to deal with the reason why.

"I think," said her mother, "she was saying, 'Look, world, I've been here all along. How about a date Saturday night?' But her last act was the most selfish thing she ever did. She brought her death into other people's homes.

"I think she did it because she felt the station was a showcase for blood and guts, and a last statement, if you will, that "I have been here.'"

"I think she expected the film of her death to be shown on the networks," said Tim.

"I think she did, too," said Greg. "To draw attention to her life. But I can think of nothing more grotesque than seeing a beautiful young woman blow her brains out on TV."

Mike Simmons, the news director, felt Chris did it because she wanted the film to be aired internationally. "I think it was a last cry for recognition to all the people she had helped, reached out to and who hadn't reached back out. She was saying, 'I was here, not just Sarasota, but I was here, world.' If you do it on TV, nobody's ever done it before. And Chris, being the professional newswoman that she was, always wanted us to have the story first. We weren't even on the map before this happened. Now they know we're here. Perhaps it was her way of trying to help us along."

Bob Keehn sees it differently. "I think she was saying, "Is this what you want folks, this blood and guts? Well, here it is. See how stupid and horrible it is. Is this what you really want?'"

Rob Smith, the 22-year-old night news editor, was closest to Chris at the station. He liked her a great deal and she would confide in him. He thought she was bright and talented and professional, but he was horrified by the way she killed herself and found it very uncharacteristic.

"It was a really bad thing she did," he said. "If you want to kill yourself you shouldn't drag others down. I guess she just was going to do it all at one time. Everybody was going to know her and she was going to be a household word. It wasn't worth it to her to put in all those years to get where she wanted to get and put up with her private life. This way she got there and ended all her problems. Chris and I talked once about the fact that Andy Warhol said that everyone will be famous for 15 minutes in their lives. This was her 15 minutes."

When Chris was 15, she wrote her autobiography. In it she said: ". . . I hope to be able to become a lady with a little spice, a housewife, mother and good friend to all of my acquaintances. . . .

". . . But whatever I endeavor I shall try to make a go of it. Because, if there is anything that leaves a sour taste in my mouth it's failure."

"We suffer at our sense of loss, we are frightened by her rage, we are guilty in the face of her rejection, we are hurt by her choice of isolation and we are confused by her message."
— R. Thomas Beason, from his elegy at Christine Chubbuck's funeral.

— August 4, 1974

134

Next: Two Musicians

Leopold Stokowski and Aaron Copland. "Though age from folly could not give me freedom, it does from childishness." — Cleopatra in Shakespeare's "Antony and Cleopatra," Act 1, Scene 3.

Acting on the assumption stated here by Cleopatra, two writers set out, each to profile one of America's musicians emeritus. We expected that the Aaron Copland of 73 years, America's preeminent classical composer, and Leopold Stokowski at 89, a major conductor since the turn of the century, would turn out similarly. We assumed that both would have lost by now any animosities of the past and would view their decades of musical activity in mellow perspective, their reputations safely secure. This is exactly what Alan M. Kriegsman found with Copland. But in Michael Kernan's encounter with Leopold Stokowski we couldn't have been more wrong. And incidentally, it made hash of Cleopatra on the subject of age and childishness.

The only way Stokowski, who has a long record of grudges against the press, could have been more uncooperative would have been to refuse the interview outright. First, he set an unrealistically short time limit. Then he consumed most of that time in negotiation on the subject range of the questions. Then, in the few remaining minutes, he was condescending to the interviewer. What we ended up with was an extended vignette of a dyspeptic, paranoid old man. It was all the more surprising to Kernan, because earlier he had watched Stokowski rehearsing, and was struck by the warm, mesmerizing quality he exuded from the podium.

The only way Kernan could reconcile the conflicting impressions was with a device that should be used sparingly: paired articles — one on the interview and one on the rehearsal.

Note: Contrary to most portraits in this volume, the structure of Kriegsman's Copland profile deliberately emphasizes what he has accomplished more than his personality, engaging as he is. Kriegsman's intuition was that his subject, unlike most, was a man whose work may well be as familiar in 200 years as it is today, conceivably even more so, and that this, and the reasons for it, should be the central focus of the profile. But Copland's rational bent of mind and easy manner emerge from the quotes that liberally punctuate the story.

— L. T.

The Enfant Terrible of Music: Stokowski in Repose

By Michael Kernan

NEW YORK — Painted like a sunburst on a wall of Leopold Stokowski's penthouse living room overlooking Central Park is a giant one-handed clock, designed by a man who understands time better than most of us: Stokowski himself.

At 89, he appreciates the value of time, not only in music but in his life. He had decreed that the interview was to be 30 minutes long. A tape recorder was to be used. No reference was to be made to his family or his personal habits. He was to be shown the piece in advance.

It was on the last stipulation, predictably, that discussion centered.

Stokowski: "Will your questions be on tape? Will they be question answer, question answer? How will you use what we do?"

Response: Some direct quotes would be used, and sometimes a precis or paraphrase would be used for space reasons.

Stokowski: "Who will decide whether you make a precis or not? Sometimes by leaving out just one word the whole meaning can be changed."

He asked if he would have the right to change things in an advance proof of the piece.

Response: "On the facts, yes. And on the others we have to make our own judgments."

Stokowski, icily: "So do I." He then called in his secretary, Natalie Bender, to be a witness. He said: "We shall now talk to each other. You will write your ideas of what we say here and will leave out what you wish to leave out and you may slightly change some language?"

Response: "Right."

Stokowski: "I don't agree with that."

Stalemate. Eventually it was decided that the interview would be held but that both parties would have veto power on a given wording if negotiation failed. Seventeen minutes of the 30 were left.

The interviewer wanted insights into the details, the nuances that make Stokowski's work uniquely his. In a recent rehearsal the conductor had stopped in the middle of Moussorgsky's "Pictures at an Exhibition" and asked the bass drummer for more rapid tremolo with less volume. The drummer tried it. Not right. He tried again. Stokowski called for a different pair of drumsticks, and this time he was satisfied. The question was: Why?

In a soft, patient voice Stokowski explained that the bass drum has two skins or heads, that it is hard to find good skins large enough for it, that it produces a low-frequency sound.

"We use these two ways," he said. "One is called a sudden — what we call a sforzando, a single beat. Or a roll that can be soft, so that it lies deep below the rest of the orchestra and then can gradually rise. We say low frequency when we really mean slow frequency. There was something wrong with it that day, one of the heads was too loose. It was too loud."

The acuteness that could pick this sound out of a massive Moussorgsky crescendo is not easy to imagine. "I do everything by my ears," the conductor shrugged.

The career that began in 1908 with the Cincinnati Symphony brought Stokowski world fame in his 24 years with the Philadelphia Orchestra. Later he was to create or help create three new orchestras.

That was not all he created. Restlessly searching for innovation, he pioneered in recording music and improved recording techniques; he introduced new instruments, the new sound of jazz, new works from Mahler's Eighth Symphony (in 1916) and Stravinsky's "The Rite of Spring" (first American performances) to Schoenberg, Varese and John Cage, and in a notable attempt to widen Hollywood's musical horizons he not only helped plan Disney's "Fantasia" but broke new ground in animation technique when he shook the gloved hand of Mickey Mouse.

In a sense the "Fantasia" episode summed up all the things that some people didn't like about Stokowski: the showmanship they found so upsetting and the changes — oh, those changes — in hallowed musical scores. A generation ago friends would cut each other dead at parties over his transcriptions of Bach organ music.

There were subtler changes in scores ("You must realize that Beethoven and Brahms did not understand instruments," he is quoted by critic Harold Schonberg), perhaps not detected by the public but certainly spotted by most musicians and infuriating to some.

"Yes, it's true I made changes," he told the interviewer. "A great composer gives his whole life to composing. To understand all the instruments in the orchestra takes a whole lifetime of study. The composer must either compose or study the instruments, because all the instruments in the orchestra have different characteristics. That is what a conductor should do, though it takes all his life.

"Sometimes the composer writes something which the instrument can't play. Then the instrument and the player, they argue."

He cited a place in the Franck D Minor Symphony where the bassoon (fagott) is given a low B flat, pianissimo.

"The fagott can't play that low B flat; it's against his nature. The conductor says, 'Softer please,' so the fagott says to the player, 'Don't ask me to do it.'" A note that low, he added, requires lip muscles so relaxed that a pianissimo is physically impossible.

Another time, according to a Philadelphia Orchestra member, he was unhappy with a certain F sharp that logically belonged to the violins in a Tchaikowsky symphony but had been given to the bassoons because the violin's lowest note is G. Stokowski simply had all 36 violinists retune their G strings a note lower at the right moment, even as they played.

"There is a conflict between the player, the instrument, the conductor and the composer. That is why it is very important for the conductor to make judgments, in my opinion. It is very important to use judgment, to say, 'Here is a place where all the brass are playing fortissimo (as marked by the printer) and all the strings fortissimo, so you won't hear the strings at all, they'll be drowned, so to speak, in sound.' I think the conductor should use his judgment, but many people say no, that is wrong."

Through the conversation he sat, fingertips touching, in a tall-backed chair that faced the waning light of a winter afternoon. He took pains with his words, frequently spelling them. Once he felt it necessary to explain what a musical bar was: "It's what we call a bar, not like a bar where you drink but is a bar—you know what a bar is?" The interviewer, a violinist for 12 years and a lifelong student of music, nodded.

One question strayed from the subject of music: As an early devotee of health foods, how did he feel about today's food fad? He put up both hands and shook his head with a small smile.

"Music," he said, "is all I am."

Stokowski in Rehearsal

S huffling onstage at Kennedy Center where the National Symphony Orchestra musicians were taking their places for rehearsal, Leopold Stokowski leaned on his rubber-tipped cane. As he started into a narrow file between rows of music desks, he saw that someone else was coming toward him and stepped aside with that patient prudence the old use in the face of headlong youth. (He had been a hurdles runner and a boxer once, in his Oxford days, but that was 70 years ago.)

The famous white mane—he used to have it spotlighted at concerts—was thinner than one remembered, and ruffled. The light-gray suit and dark-blue shirt looked just a little baggy on the spare frame, somewhat shrunken from the 6 feet 2 of his prime.

But he moved to the podium with deliberation, his fine hawk nose jutting and his hair blown back as though facing into a wind. He muttered a few words to the concertmaster, then stepped up carefully, set the cane aside and clapped his hands once without force. The sound was all but lost in the rich marmalade of musical tootlings and scrapings, whining arpeggios, aimless oompahs, scales and phrases that are an orchestra tuning up.

He clapped again. The oboe sang the pure A that everyone else tuned by. At last, silence.

"In the Mozart, at Number 4," he said, his head down over the score. The famous hands went up, the music started. Four bars later he clapped, and the musicians stopped raggedly.

"Bow separately, violins," he said. "Use your judgment. Think freely. When you bow together you can hear it, it makes an accent."

(For generations conductors have insisted on all the bows moving together; this is one of Stokowski's most celebrated departures from tradition. Another: the violins were massed at the left and woodwinds on the right, tending, some critics said, to sacrifice sharpness of definition for powerful effect. The seating arrangements changed at almost every concert. Once at Philadelphia he put a piccolo player in the concertmaster's seat.)

Playing only a few measures each time, he took the group through the trouble spots of the previous two sessions. Mostly he wanted changes in volume. Asking the woodwinds for a certain effect, he was told it was not possible.

"Not possible?" he said softly. The whole orchestra sat there with a guilty smile, rebuked.

Again he clapped, the little dry-handed clap that by now commanded instant attention. It was time to work on the slow movement of Beethoven's Seventh Symphony, one of the most beautiful dirges ever written. One could see the logic of his seating now, for the melody and its counterpoint moved visibly from one string section to the next, a stately cortege.

And suddenly Stokowski was a different man. Thirty years dropped away. His arms carved the air with great legato sweeps, his glance flashed from one section to another, his whole body radiated energy. He pulled the players together, concentrated them at their very best to produce work of tremendous power, marvelously articulated and clear, speaking a grief beyond pathos. They played the whole movement without interruption. When it was over the conductor's shoulders slumped a little, the mouth sagged into its accustomed dewlapped petulance.

It was time for a rest period, and Stokowski leaned on the tall stool and sipped orange juice while the world bustled around him.

He was an authentic prodigy, playing Mozart, Beethoven, Chopin and Debussy at 7 on violin and piano. At 10, attracted by Bach's organ music, he learned the organ at a neighborhood church in his native London. Studying in England, France and Germany, he learned all the instruments, a vital part of the conductor's art, which must make an entire orchestra into a single instrument.

When he came to America at 18, he became a church organist in New York and a few years later took over the Cincinnati symphony.

It was not until his long association with Philadelphia, however, that his flair for publicity blossomed: the angry remarks addressed to noisy audiences (once he retaliated by having some of his musicians straggle in, coughing and shuffling, after he had started), the furious radio station scuffle in 1955 over his birthdate—his entry in *Who's Who* still carries the 1887 date he insisted on in the face of birth records—the movies he made, and the constant uproar over his musical innovations, his tinkering with instruments, seating, acoustics, amplifiers and the very notes of the masters, his Bach transcriptions, his refusal to use a baton, even his time-saving insistence that orchestras use scores from his personal library, marked in his own interpretation.

The National Symphony had such scores. They turned to the Moussorgsky now, brought to life by the handclap. Halfway through, jarringly, the whole section of first violins came in one bar too soon. All of them.

It was so shocking a sound that everything stopped. All eyes turned to Stokowski. He leaned toward the second violins and murmured conspiratorially, "What shall we do to them?" Everyone laughed.

For another hour he worked steadily, sharpening, tightening, clarifying. At the end, he called for a little Scriabin piece he had orchestrated, a special favorite ever since he had heard the great pianist in Paris when a child. Toward the end the harpist added a cadenza which Stokowski had requested. It seemed a bit elaborate. He clapped his hands.

"I asked for a cadenza," he said drily, "not a recital." Laughter.

They tried the passage again and finished. The musicians started to leave. His shoulders sank. He stepped off the podium, carefully.

—March 12, 1972

140

Aaron Copland:
If America Ever Had
a Composer Laureate...

By Alan M. Kriegsman

C omposer Aaron Copland, looking decades younger than his 72 years, sat some weeks ago in the studio of his retreat near Croton, N.Y., overlooking the legendary heights and mists of the Hudson valley. Obliging a photographer by posing at the piano, he let his hands wander idly over the keys picking out sounds at random, until they alighted upon a startling, craggy chord. It was an altogether typical Copland sonority—brazen, acrid, broadly spaced out over the keyboard, suggesting the strength and sharp outline of a steel girder.

Copland leaned back with a quizzical smile and exclaimed: "Why is it one always gets one's best chords when people are around—and then later, you can't find them!"

It was just a quip, of course, but a revealing one. Here in a flash were Copland's geniality, his delight in discovery, his boyish self-mockery.

America has never had a composer laureate, but if it ever did there could hardly be an argument over who'd most deserve the honor. By almost every measure imaginable, Copland is Number One.

To the concert world at large, Copland and the lean, astringent sound of "American" music go hand in hand. As a composer, pianist, conductor, teacher, author and advocate of musical causes, he has been active on the international scene now for more than 50 years. And among his countrymen, his influence has been so pervasive that one can scarcely put on a record, go to the movies or turn on the television set without hearing unmistakable traces of the Copland idiom. (CBS, in fact, used a tune from "Appalachian Spring" for years as theme music for a TV news show.)

No one man, of course, can be fairly said to embody the whole spectrum and achievement of American music, and Copland, the author of "Lincoln Portrait," "Billy the Kid," "Appalachian Spring," the film score for "Our Town," the opera "The Tender Land," and "Fanfare for the Common

Man," is no exception. Copland's reputation, as commanding as it is, has never given his name quite the household familiarity of Gershwin's, for instance, or Leonard Bernstein's. Charles Ives was more daring, Roger Sessions and Milton Babbitt are more intellectually challenging, John Cage has been more novel, Henry Cowell more wide-ranging and Carl Ruggles perhaps more profound.

Nevertheless, it is true that no American composer has written more durable, individual, enjoyable or influential music than has Copland, and none has played as dominating a role historically. It was Copland who first made us conscious of the place of the serious composer in the nation's cultural life. He has worked tirelessly all his life to secure and promote that place, not for himself alone, but for all his fellow musicians.

There is, moreover, a real sense in which all the significant currents of the American musical experience intersect in Copland. In such works as the Third Symphony and the Violin Sonata, Copland builds upon the academic, European-oriented, neoclassic side of American tradition, represented by such men as Edward MacDowell or Walter Piston. In pieces like the Piano Variations and "Inscape," he shows his kinship with such "left-wing" experimentalists as Leo Ornstein, John J. Becker, Ives and Ruggles. Jazz informs the Piano Concerto and "Music for the Theater," and 12-tone techniques shape the Fantasy, "Connotations" and "Inscape." And the national mystique of the pioneer and the prairie suffuses his best-known work (the ballets on Western themes, for instance), in which, with the help of a minimum of actual folk material, Copland created a musical atmosphere as American as a 10-gallon hat.

One reason why Copland early assumed a position of leadership among American composers, in the eyes of those both inside and outside the profession, was his aversion to the ivory-tower concept of serious music. From the beginning, making contact with listeners was of paramount importance to him — all kinds of listeners, naive or sophisticated. "The conviction grew inside me," he said during his Norton Lectures at Harvard in 1952, "that the two things that seemed always to have been so separate in America — music and the life about me — must be made to touch. This desire to make the music I wanted to write come out of the life I had lived in America became a preoccupation of mine in the '20s."

The "preoccupation" persisted, and it led to the most remarkable of the many qualities unique to Copland — his ability to shift naturally from an easily accessible, vernacular idiom, as in the ballet "Rodeo," say, to an abstract, stringent one, as in the Piano Sonata or "Connotations."

The same impulse led Copland to reach out to the public, without embarrassment, apology or condescension, through the mass media. In addition to symphonies, concertos and chamber music, his output includes music for radio ("Letter From Home," for instance, in 1944), television ("The World of Nick Adams," in 1957, based on Hemingway stories), Hollywood movies (most notably "Of Mice and Men," "Our Town," "The Red Pony" and

"The Heiress," the score for which he won the 1949 Academy Award for music) and even a puppet show, "From Sorcery to Science," produced for the 1939 World's Fair.

A further index to the breadth of his involvement in the variegated culture of his age can be found in the list of Copland's collaborators and patrons—Edwin Denby and Orson Welles for the school opera, "The Second Hurricane"; choreographers Martha Graham, Eugene Loring, Ruth Page and Agnes de Mille in a landmark series of dance compositions; film directors Pare Lorentz, William Wyler, Lewis Milestone and Sam Wood; lyricist Ira Gershwin, for the film music of "North Star"; bandleader Paul Whiteman, who commissioned "Letter from Home"; Benny Goodman, for whom Copland wrote his Clarinet Concerto; Irwin Shaw, for whom Copland provided incidental music for the Group Theatre production of "Quiet City"; Clifford Odets, who commissioned the Piano Sonata; and his lifelong friend, theater director and critic Harold Clurman, who, among other things, wrote the scenario for Copland's first ballet score, "Grohg." Commissions also came from such diverse sources as Rodgers and Hammerstein, M.I.T., the Juilliard School, the Festival of Two Worlds at Spoleto, and the Dumbarton Oaks Foundation in Washington.

By his own admission, Copland has been "tapering off" as far as composing goes. His most recent work is a modest, euphoric Duo for Flute and Piano, written in 1971, but harking back in style to the insouciance of the '30s. Before that, there was the major "Inscapes" of 1967, commissioned for the 125th anniversary of the New York Philharmonic. He was always a slow, painstaking worker—even in his period of peak activity, he rarely produced more than one large-scale work in a given year—so that no dire conclusions need be drawn from the present lag. He spoke recently of his interest in writing a string quartet ("It seems like a serious and challenging thing to do, to write a proper string quartet"), and England's Bath Festival has been prodding him for a piece to help celebrate the millenium of the Cathedral.

In any case, he's far from inactive. He's still scooting around the country giving talks at colleges and universities, for one thing. "I seem to be attracting crowds everywhere, like never before," he says, "it must be old age." If that's what it is, it doesn't show in the reaction. Last November, he showed up at Johns Hopkins' Shriver Hall, seating well over 1,200, for a lecture and concert of his works. The overflow was so large that the doors to the auditorium had to be locked, while scores of the disappointed milled outside in the cold. Inside, Copland held the throng of mostly youthful listeners in steadfast thrall. His manner is as casual and amiable on stage as off. His discourse is a mixture of horse sense, hard information and wit, and it goes down so easily one doesn't realize until afterwards how much insight was transmitted about very complex issues. It is the same with his prose, which is why such books by Copland as *What to Listen for in Music* and *The New Music* have remained models of their kind.

It is the same, too, with much of his music, which can convey deep and lasting meaning even to the uninitiated listener, using seemingly elementary means as a cover for the expression of subtle musical ideas. In "Appalachian Spring," perhaps his most characteristic opus, Copland made use of an old Shaker hymn tune taken from a collection called "The Gift To Be Simple." It's the Copland watchword in a nutshell.

He particularly enjoys lecturing at colleges. "I never went to a college or a music school, and I guess I have a real nostalgia for it," he reflects. "This is what I missed, the campus life, see. After high school, I devoted all my time to music studies, on my own." He doesn't care for prepared texts, though. "I much prefer a question-answer format to speeches. I know too well what I think. From questions, I feel I can get a sense of the things that really interest audiences."

Harold Clurman once described Copland as a man who "appreciates his own value," and who therefore "achieves modesty without strain." He also remarked that Copland was "the personification of justness." These native traits, clear to all who know him even casually, have put Copland into the rare position of being a great public personage with no visible egomania. Virgil Thomson, another Copland friend and colleague of long standing, has accounted for Copland's marked abilities as a "mobilizer" on this basis. When others would take sides, Copland was always ready to seel all sides, and thus to clear parochial obstacles from the path of mutual understanding.

Clurman, who calls Copland his oldest and closest friend and who is dedicating a new book of reminiscences (*The Ever Present,* to be published in 1974) to him, notes that even when they were both young students in Paris, Copland had a profound moderating effect on his own excesses. "I was a crazy, romantic person," he recalls. "He was a rational, balanced person. He gave me perspective. He cooled me off." Balanced is also the most apt word for Copland's shrewd appraisals of other composers, as recorded in such essays as those collected in *Copland on Music,* for example. A splendid illustration is this little but penetrating observation on Stravinsky:

"One might say that Stravinsky doesn't know how to compose in the sense of Hindemith or Milhaud. He lacks their facility or virtuosity, a kind of facility and virtuosity that allows the notes to run to their predetermined places—almost, one might say, without more than an assist from their composers.

"With Stravinsky one senses that the place of each note in each melody and chord has been found for it only after a process of meticulous elimination, and the place found is usually so unexpected and original that one can

" 'I find I have only varying success, depending on the orchestra.' "

imagine the notes themselves being surprised at finding themselves situated where they are—'out of place,' so to speak."

For all his modesty and selflessness in his dealings with the world, Copland is no plaster saint, and not above relishing his eminence in the right context. Once, during the interview at his Croton residence, he pointed with pride to an edition of his *What to Listen for in Music* (which originally appeared in 1939) translated into Maharati, "a language I can't even read, much less decipher." Then, noting that the book had already been printed in 10 languages, he said with a mischievous chuckle, "I love the idea of explaining how to listen to the Germans."

Currently, Copland spends about half of his time on his conducting activities, from which he takes enormous satisfaction. Copland has been leading orchestras in the United States ever since the Chicago Symphony invited him to appear as a guest at Ravinia in 1956. "I probably would have started much earlier," he now says, "but you know, I was very close to Koussevitzky (the esteemed conductor of the Boston Symphony, 1924-49, and a champion of American music). He was never very encouraging in my direction, despite the hints I gave him about being anxious to take it up. He had a picture in his mind's eye, you see, of what a conductor should look like—and the picture was Lenny Bernstein. It wasn't until he died (in 1951) that I had the courage to try it, though I did manage to practice on some orchestras outside the U.S., mainly in Latin America."

Once Copland got going on the podium, however, he was hooked. "I get a real kick out of it. What could be nicer—it's a group effort for a wonderful end. Besides, it seems to be a very healthy occupation; look at Toscanini, Stokowski. Conductors seem to live quite long—yes, the ones that live."

Copland does a considerable amount of guest conducting in this country, as well as abroad, and particularly in England, where he finds the public especially responsive and where he has made many recordings. (Columbia is in the process of issuing Copland's complete works on discs.) American music .tends to be amply represented on his programs, but he also has a penchant for French repertoire ("Roussel and Faure, not so much Ravel or Debussy," he says) and Stravinsky.

He still finds considerable resistance among orchestral players to difficult 20th-century scores. "A piece like Ruggles' 'Portals,' for instance, in which almost every chord has an abrasive tension—you have to sell it to them by your own attitude and conviction. I find I have only varying success, depending on the orchestra. It's often fun with a university orchestra; the response is often fresher."

145

Only seldom does he conduct all-Copland programs, but he subscribes firmly to the proposition that the composer — given technical competence in conducting — is an authoritative interpreter of his own work. "I wrote it, I should know how it ought to go," he says, smiling with gentle belligerence. But he can also appreciate a divergent slant. He's obviously very fond of the performances by Leonard Bernstein, whom he has known since Bernstein was a teen-age student at Harvard. "From time to time," Copland muses, "I'll say to Lenny something like, 'Oh no, no, you're playing this too slow.' But he has a different view of it. 'It gives it a different meaning, a more expressive cast,' he'll say, 'if you drag it a bit.' And he's right."

Copland sees no need to stick to the beaten track. Only a few weeks ago he slipped into Washington unobtrusively, without the least breath of publicity, to lead the U.S. Air Force Band at Constitution Hall in a program including a new arrangement of his "El Salon Mexico" and "Emblems," his one original work for band.

"There was something about getting a letter from the United States Air Force that did it," he explains. "That doesn't happen every day."

Next winter, Copland is scheduled to appear as guest conductor with the National Symphony on Feb. 5, 6 and 7. In addition to Copland's Clarinet Concerto and First Symphony, the program will include Roussel's Suite in F, a Mozart violin concerto and two of Satie's "Gymnopedies."

Commissions, recordings and guest appearances over the years have given Copland an independence and security rare for the serious composer even today. For the past 20 years, aside from much travel, he has lived in his spacious, secluded country home by the Hudson, where a Belgian couple takes care of his dining and household needs. The house is tastefully but fastidiously furnished in a rather spare, contemporary fashion, its immaculate order reflecting the composer's own work habits and lifestyle. The focus is his studio, with its plentiful daylight and view, its sizable stacks of books, scores and records, and the grand piano where Copland customarily performs his musical chores.

Fate had the good sense to arrange the birth of Aaron Copland in the year 1900, the date being not only a boon to memory, but a symbol of obvious historic pertinence. The family name had originally been Kaplan, but it was transcribed into Copland by a British immigration officer when Aaron's father arrived in England from his native Lithuania, en route to America. By the time Aaron was born, the father had risen far enough up the ladder of immigrant struggle to own a department store. Copland describes his own unpromising beginnings amusingly in an autobiographical sketch in *The New Music:*

"I was born on a street in Brooklyn that can only be described as drab. It had none of the garish color of the ghetto, none of the charm of an old

New England thoroughfare, or even the rawness of a pioneer street. It was simply drab.

"...I mention it because it was there that I spent the first years of my life. Also, because I am filled with mild wonder each time I realize that a musician was born on that street. Music was the last thing anyone would have connected with it."

Nonetheless, music found its way. Driven by an impulse that seemed to come from the air, the young Copland pursued music as the hound the hare, once he came to the realization that this was his calling. He took piano and harmony lessons, studied the scores of the "moderns" — Debussy, Ravel and Scriabin — and began to write pieces of his own.

In the summer of 1921, he left for Paris to enroll in the newly established academy for American music students at Fontainebleau. Clurman, who was to join him as a roommate in the fall, tells the story that on the boat Copland met Marcel Duchamp, the celebrated iconoclast of the art world. Duchamp told him to forget about being an artist, the world had no place for the arts, everything was business these days, he should go into business.

It took much reassurance on Clurman's part to wrench Copland back from the funk Duchamp's counsel had left him in. "I told him," Clurman reports, "that all that anti-art stuff was okay for a Frenchman already over-loaded with culture, but for Americans starting out, it was a different story."

But Paris of the '20s proved to be just the crucible Copland's talent required. He became the first of the "Boulangerie" circle, that troupe of American composers who spread their wings under the tutelage of the remarkable Nadia Boulanger. He attended the concert series of contemporary music led by Serge Koussevitzky, and began to learn at first hand what radical things were transpiring in those pivotal times.

One day during the first of his three years in Paris, Copland was strolling on the Rue St. Honoré when he saw Igor Stravinsky approaching. "It was the first time I had seen him," Copland remembers. "As he passed, I was drawn like a magnet; I turned around and started following him. I had no intention of talking to him, you understand, I just couldn't help myself. I finally gave up when I realized how foolish I must have looked."

Stravinsky was to leave an indelible mark upon Copland's creative production, openly and directly in the case of such earlier work as the Dance Symphony (1925, derived from the unproduced ballet "Grohg"), less specifically but not less tangibly in the rhythmic fabric of many later pieces.

After Copland's return to the U.S. in 1924 came his immersion in jazz and a conscious striving for a recognizably American tone, along with new ventures into a private, abstruse world represented by the extraordinary Piano Variations of 1930. He also began to concern himself increasingly with the problems of status and recognition which affected all American composers during the embattled Depression years. (Copland never involved himself in political issues, but during the McCarthy era a congressman accused him of "questionable affiliations." In a hotly debated move, the

National Symphony Orchestra removed "Lincoln Portrait" from the first Eisenhower inaugural concert as a result of these charges.) Through such activities as the League of Composers, the Copland-Sessions concerts, and the Yaddo Festivals, he put himself in the vanguard of those whose sense of mission went beyond their personal need or aspiration.

All wasn't roses even for Copland in those days. After the premiere of his Piano Concerto in 1927, a critic wrote in the *Boston Post* that "if there exists anywhere in the world a stranger concatenation of meaningless ugly sounds and distorted rhythms than Mr. Copland's Piano Concerto, Boston has been spared it." Nor was this opinion a bilious exception; it was the consensus, at the time.

In the decade following 1935, Copland arrived at his celebrated resolution "to see if I couldn't say what I had to say in the simplest possible terms." The decision was prompted partly by an awareness of the growing new public for radio music and the phonograph, and partly by Copland's temperamental abhorrence for writing in a vacuum. The result was a remarkable series of works which consolidated his standing as the foremost of American composers, starting with "El Salon Mexico" in 1936, including "Lincoln Portrait" and his best known film scores, and culminating in the three great ballets, "Billy the Kid," "Rodeo," and "Appalachian Spring."

During this same interval, in 1940, he began his long and fruitful association with the Berkshire Music Center at Tanglewood, Mass. With his Piano Quarter of 1950, his first excursion into the 12-tone orbit, Copland had in a sense come full circle from his Paris days, once again returning to a European model, but Americanizing and personalizing it in a manner that made it his own. This evolution continued in his major enterprises of the '50s and '60s, the Piano Fantasy, "Connotations" and "Inscape."

Asked to name the three pieces he would select for the proverbial time vault, if he had to restrict himself to that number, Copland replied grimacingly, "that's like asking a mother which are your favorite children." All the same, after some furrowing of brow and some meditative "hmmmm's," he named the Piano Fantasy, "Appalachian Spring" and the Third Symphony, the last in many ways a summing-up of Coplandiana.

That's a magnificent and quite representative triptych, mirroring three separate, principal strands in the composer's makeup. My own list would have to include the Piano Variations, the Copland work singled out by Virgil Thompson as "the most highly personal, the most condensed, and the most clearly indispensable to music."

Thank heaven, though, we don't have to make any such choice. We have all of Copland so far, and perhaps some to come, to peruse and admire. And in that thought, we can only be grateful for the musician whom biographer Julia Smith once called "this simple and great man in our midst."

—April 8, 1973

'I'm a Simple Little Man'

By Jeannette Smyth

Joe Hirshhorn jumped into his chauffeur-driven Valiant for the 10-second ride from the Smithsonian Castle, where there was a dinner last night in his honor, to the opening of the monument named after him.

"Look at the lights!" he cried as his driver pulled up before the Hirshhorn Museum. "I'm getting excited," he sang. "I'm getting delighted. I'm in love!"

He sprang out of the car, marched into the building to the laudatory tune of the Marine Band, ducked behind the courtyard podium on which the assembled eminences awaited his arrival, and went straight to the basement men's room.

Mayor Walter Washington, Lady Bird Johnson, senators and ambassadors alike, and the rest of the black-tie crowd waited.

Joe Hirshhorn, 75, Latvian emigrant, art patron, had arrived, with his clip-on black tie, in Washington. And it wasn't that the town isn't used to characters like him—the halls of Congress swarm with shrewd and colorful politicians. It's just that Washington still can't quite believe that such a man could love Art.

At the pre-opening dinner party, Hirshhorn stood in the gaudy trompe l'oeil marble hall of the Castle, kissing the cheeks or foreheads of one and all. "Have a Schnapps!" he said. "In my language that means whiskey, liquor, beer, anything.

"I'm a simple little man, a simple little man," he beamed.

Filming and recording Hirshhorn's ebullience was the five-man film crew he had hired, for an estimated $30,000, to make a filmed documentary of the occasion. He will donate it, along with a $60,000 one about the development of his collection, to the Smithsonian.

Focus. Hirshhorn embracing David Lloyd Kreeger, art patron, "a charming human being."

Focus. Hirshhorn sitting before melon and prosciutto with the wife of the Smithsonian's director, Mrs. Dillon Ripley. "I'm not excited. This is two years late. But the building is here, and I must confess it looks great."

Focus. Hirshhorn introducing his physician to an ambassador. "He's my surgeon. He's a great surgeon. He took my gall bladder out. Are you still sculpting? You don't love me. You don't get in touch with me."

Focus. Hirshhorn signing an autograph for his daughter. "For my chickie. Love, Daddy Joe."

When he finally got to the ceremonial podium, they played the Star Spangled Banner and he doo-dummed along with it. He leaned forward in his seat to listen to speeches from Ripley and museum officials. When it was his turn to speak they produced a Veuve Ambal champagne carton for the 5-foot-4 art patron to stand on.

His speech was simple and undeviating from the prepared text. "It is an honor to have given my art collection to the people of the United States as a small repayment for what this nation has done for me and others like me who arrived here as immigrants. . . . I am proud to belong to the family of Americans." He went on to thank his mother and to say he hoped she was there "in spirit."

Official Washington quickly fled the cold of the courtyard into the museum itself. Hirshhorn, once convicted of money smuggling and stock manipulation, kissed and signed autographs for ladies in tiaras moderne and sculptured brocade cloches. A hot-combed interviewer sat him in a folding chair by the fountain for NBC's "Today Show." Finally someone pushed his fourth wife, Olga, through the crowd and they crossed the courtyard for a ceremonial dance.

"I want a fox trot. If they don't give me a fox trot I'll take my rent back."

Tossing his head, snapping his fingers, Joe Hirshhorn danced, slightly pigeon-toed, alone with his wife, in the nearly empty courtyard of the Hirshhorn Museum.

—October 2, 1974

Mr. L.G. Broadmoore
and the Way It Was

By Eugene L. Meyer

T IVOLI, N.Y.—Since time immemorial, mankind has striven to achieve new frontiers of knowledge and experience, consigning old theories, technologies and patterns to the junk heap of history.

Not Lawrence Gilbert Broadmoore.

At the age of 23, he is, as much as he can be, the authentic obsolete man, frozen inside a protective pre-World War I time capsule. He says things like "Balderdash!" And, with a restless 3½-year-old visitor pounding his parlor piano, "One mustn't bang too loudly."

His present is an eternal past in which the future is but more of the same, "except I hope to become more skillful in every field of endeavor which requires skill."

In this Hudson River hamlet of 800, he exists by repairing player pianos, gramophones and other outdated machinery, and he lives in an old house with no plumbing or central heating.

Though short of stature, he cuts an imposing figure in his pince-nez spectacles, waxed moustache, hair parted down the middle and high-neck starched collar. He looks like a yellowing photograph in an ancient family album, the young man on the make, the rugged individualist of Main Street.

He learned how to dress from old mail-order catalogs, and how to speak from 19th-century parlor novels. "It sometimes feels as if I'm talking to myself," he says, frustrated by the unwillingness or inability of others to role play with him. "Etiquette is a type of play," he concedes. "One can't expect everyone to play along."

Of course, it is all affected, but it is a sincere affectation, not a put-on, and it goes much deeper than trendy nostalgia. For L. G. Broadmoore has thoroughly thought through his odd lifestyle and deeply believes in it, even if nobody else does.

His is a philosophy born of extreme dissatisfaction with a society that tears down its finest old buildings in the name of renewal, that substitutes quantity for quality, whose science only computers can comprehend. Civilization, he believes, peaked with the Industrial Revolution: Mechanics hold more to marvel at than megatons and modules in atomic weaponry and space. World War I, on the other hand, "marks the end of esthetic civilization in this country, due to new frontiers in immorality opened by the war."

He admits: "I live in a totally insular world, guarded from philosophical relevance by my own vigilance." He is, he knows, eccentric, but not crazy, really. "I've not permitted myself to lose the grip of reason. I try to make myself insane in a certain sense, oblivious to the fact there is anything abnormal about this type of life. When I become sensitive to it, it causes me a certain amount of anxiety."

Anxiety, in a sense, propelled L. G. Broadmoore into the past.

Eight years ago, he was "mostly miserable," living a "significantly mediocre" existence in a middle-class Cincinnati suburb. "I never got along with people my own age," he recalls. But he had two interests to assuage the loneliness: mechanics and history.

After school, he would ride the buses downtown to marvel at the remaining 19th-century buildings. Armed with an 1893 guide, he would look at the magnificent edifice pictured in the book and the decaying ruin behind him, and he would become filled with a sense of poignancy, and outrage. "I refused to accept the idea I had to be a historical pauper."

Suddenly, "this scheme of living in the past struck me—like an inspiration." Lawrence G. Broadmoore, unhappy in the present, would find happiness in the past. He began wearing old-fashioned clothes to school and was threatened with suspension. His parents sent him to a Massachusetts private school and then to offbeat Bard College, a few miles from

"For Broadmoore, it was a rough road to local acceptance, much less stardom."

Tivoli. He dropped out after three years to open the Tivoli Player-Piano Shop.

He picked Tivoli because "it looked as though everyone forgot about it. I thought no one would meddle with it." Now, he worries about the intrusions of developers and speculators — not immediately apparent to a visitor — and takes consolation from reports that there are other still-forgotten towns elsewhere.

"Someday," he says, fatalistically, "I may have to migrate."

Meanwhile, his life is complicated by its very simplicity: "It's very expensive to live simply in a way I consider acceptable. What was simple years ago is now considered complicated."

Thus, "I have some trouble getting non-safety [eyeglass] lenses. I see that they're ground in the 19th-century manner, smaller and flatter."

High-neck collars are also a problem, especially finding anyone to launder them. So he buys them newly starched from Brooks Brothers, at $1.25 each.

Then there is ice. Broadmoore keeps all his perishables in an ice box (but requires an electric refrigerator to keep his week's supply of ice from melting). Until his death two years ago, an 88-year-old local iceman who refused to quit made deliveries. Now Broadmoore drives his 1949 Ford pickup ("as old as I can afford") across the Hudson to Kingston, where he buys a 300-pound block for $3.

"Fortunately, I can still get coal delivered," he says.

His parents, well, they still love him. But they don't understand him.

"I'm a total mystery to them," he says. "They feel I'm making trouble for myself. They consider me to have great potential they see better spent in ecology or working in some great laboratory to reduce noise levels."

Notwithstanding such parental misgivings, his father, a wine merchant, contributed toward the $2,000 purchase of a green frame shop on Tivoli's main street. It is next to the Hotel Morey, a two-story, turn-of-the-century inn whose rooms have not been let for years; only its first-floor tavern is open for business.

On Saturdays, the shop is a gathering place for kids to wonder at mechanics the way children several generations ago must have flocked in fascination to the Wright brothers bicycle shop.

For L. G. Broadmoore, it was a rough road to local acceptance, much less stardom: "I've been the subject of ridicule in many cases. Those youngsters in the shop, when I first knew them, were continually nasty to me and manifested impoliteness to me in many ways. But after a while, I'd get an ally, and he would explain to everyone else there was a great deal of value in what I was doing."

Broadmoore feels no affinity in his work or lifestyle with the craftsperson dropout. "They have a society consciousness that I don't have." But he enjoys talking with "these people." He says it as if it's a cultural exchange program.

"I haven't met anyone with whom I have much in common," he says, a bit sadly. He has one like-minded friend in New York City, "but he has no mechanical inclination, so he has to be involved with people. It's a hopeless task."

The player-piano shop is dimly illuminated by clear, non-frosted bulbs, which look like the old Edison lights. The wiring is '20s vintage porcelain knob and tube. "I've sort of fostered an interest in unsafe wiring over the years," he says.

A framed picture of his hero, Thomas A. Edison, sits on top of a rolltop desk, whose small reference library includes *The How Book: A Standard Guide for the Homeworker, Businessman and Mechanic,* published in 1913.

There is an old Remington typewriter and an inoperative two-piece desk phone. He has no working telephone at the shop or his house, only an answering service number. "I had a phone for a while," he says, "but I found it really disturbed me too much, so I got rid of it."

The shop is an essential part of his lifestyle, because "everything I use I have to be equipped to service myself. The shop, to a large degree, is a maintenance shop for the trappings of my existence, since society refuses to maintain them anymore." And mechanics have made it possible for him to support his simple-complex way of life.

How well he has been supporting himself has been the subject of recent "extensive self-auditing," he says. "I tried to run the business on a 19th-century basis, at 19th-century rates. Sometimes I would work six months for $200. After accumulating a debt over three years, I have had to evaluate time and raise all prices."

Broadmoore rents a former tenant farmer's two-story house, built around 1915 on a back country road three miles from the shop. He pays $85 a month. The only condition is that he not use kerosene lamps. He uses candles mostly, "when I can afford them." Two small electric bulbs droop apologetically from the living room ceiling, flies swarming around them.

He lives alone with a cat. At first, he said, he experienced "a certain amount of trepidation" about living without central heating or indoor plumbing. The transition, however, proved relatively painless. "At this point, obstacles are no longer obstacles." That's not true, however, for all guests. His parents can't deal with the lack of plumbing and stay at motels when visiting.

He has no electrical appliances, save for the ice storage refrigerator hidden under the basement steps — the skeleton in his closet — and a 1910 vacuum cleaner. "I used to use a broom, but now that time has become so valuable, to a certain extent I've had to appease the modern gods of finance," he explains. Such concessions to modern times are few and hidden.

The living room centerpiece is a wood-coal furnace. Stacks of 78 r.p.m. records — none after 1930, most circa 1915 — clutter up two bureaus. There is an upright piano and a Grafanola gramophone, but no radio. "I won't have one," he said. "It wouldn't do me any good because I couldn't get old programs. My grandfather was interested in that kind of modern stuff."

Above the piano is an old photograph of a young woman, his great-grandmother. On one wall is a 1900 painted photo portrait of Josephine Cole, now 90 and a neighbor in Tivoli. Hanging on racks are several boaters and stovepipe hats. There is a stereopticon viewer with a set of Yellowstone slides.

In the kitchen, the sink is filled by water pump. It provides only rain-water, from a 5,000 gallon cistern in the basement that fills with every cloudburst, "like an eternal spring." The water is drinkable, he says, but there is also an outside pump for well water.

He uses a straight-edge razor sharpened on a leather strop. Dishes are dried "in two seconds" on a drying rack placed above the coal stove. There is also a 1904 American Wringer Co. gravity clothes washer. As another recent time-money concession, he has his shop apprentice take his wash to a laundromat.

In the dining room, there is a china closet containing a youthful picture of his grandparents. Upstairs, there are three bedrooms, two with big brass beds. His room contains an upright Edison diamond disc phonograph and a dresser. There is a guest room. Old suits are strewn across the bed in "the library," whose books include several Tom Swifts and *Who's Who in America, 1920-1921*.

In back of the house, in what was once a barn, is the world's most pristine privy and an engineless 1921 Ford.

L. G. Broadmoore is concerned with style, not events, for events mark the passage of time and that is unthinkable in his world. Thus, his walls contain no pictures of the martyred William McKinley or the hero of

Manila Bay, Admiral Dewey; his tables hold no souvenir paperweights from the 1904 St. Louis World's Fair.

Such items were common in many middle-class homes in those turn-of-the-century days of innocence. But then, Lawrence G. Broadmoore is not average, nor common, nor even innocent. He is a wax-museum figure come to life and living on his own terms with the past.

—August 9, 1974

Next: Princess Alice

Alice Roosevelt Longworth. Near the beginning of this interview at age 90 with the closest equivalent Washington has to royalty, "Princess Alice" observes, "I may be an old crone, but I still put on the harness and lumber down the street."

It is a standard line from an outrageously talkative lady who, from her preeminent position, has acutely observed and acutely commented on Washington for as many years as it has been a major world capital. Any interview with Mrs. Longworth would be dominated by those flowing streams of quotations. Just getting it down requires a Sally Quinn-calibre ear and eye. Quinn, you will notice, deliberately begins with Mrs. Longworth talking. But Mrs. Longworth gets in only two words, "I still," before Quinn interrupts to note Mrs. Longworth "rapping her bony hands."

Thus, within the first sentence of a long piece, the author has defined the two main elements of her Longworth portrait—dialogue and supportive detail. The former is used at its most sophisticated in the three final sections (the heart of the story), which are written in extended dialogue and fleshed out as in the best realistic fiction. These three-way conversations over tea, among Mrs. Longworth, her granddaughter and Quinn, are this volume's most ambitious uses of this device.

But if the techniques are bold, the contents of her story are correspondingly bold. It could have been merely a perfectly charming, though predictable, piece resting on material like the "old crone" quote. But Quinn wanted to probe a more challenging side of the subject. As she puts it, "Alice Longworth is a survivor in a town where the word is an anachronism. She has been revered and feared, adored and detested, but there has never been a time when she has not been talked about." In other words, who among those for whom she holds such fascination is right about Alice Longworth?

Quinn gives no definitive answer, but as her article proceeds through witty, biting discussions of sex, marriage, politics, Mrs. Longworth's harsh childhood, Richard Nixon and her self-confessed snobbery, the subject makes it clear that the truth about her personality lies somewhere in between the two extreme viewpoints about it.

There is the cold dismissal of Tricia Nixon ("I wonder what's wrong with her"). But there is pathos in the discussion of her own childhood; after her mother died (Alice was the only child) and, after Roosevelt's remarriage, she was brutalized by her new brothers ("I loved my father, but I was never particularly close to him"). This experience unfolds as a key to her personality. She says, "I decided to defeat it so I became resistant, contrary, and I tried to be conspicuous. That feeling has lasted in some way."

—L.T.

Alice Roosevelt Longworth at 90

By Sally Quinn

"I still," she muses, rapping her bony fingers against her graying head, "more or less have my, what they call, marbles," and she pulls her flowered shawl around her a little closer, throws her head back and laughs gleefully.

Alice Roosevelt Longworth is 90 years old today.

"I may be an old crone but I can still put on the harness and lumber down the street."

When Mrs. Longworth, or Mrs. L. as she prefers to be called by intimates, turned 89 last year she had only a small tea party to celebrate. "I'm saving my energy for a big bash next year," she said " . . . if I'm still kicking around."

This afternoon at 5 she will have her 90th birthday party. "It will be a marvelous and horrible scene," she declares.

She will love every minute of it. "I must say, I'm always on stage. All Roosevelts are exhibitionists," she says. "Am I? Decidedly so. That, my dear, is what becomes of peasants."

And she agrees to an interview a few days before the birthday, set for 5 o'clock tea. "It's irresistible," she admits later. "The delight of pouring out yourself to someone who listens with rapt attention and takes down every precious word."

Her maid, Janie McLaughlin, answers the door and leads the way through the darkened foyer, up the stairs, past the rattiest looking animal skin that you ever saw, hanging on the wall. The Siberian tiger skin belonged to her big-game hunting father, Teddy Roosevelt.

At the top of the stairs, one can hear a cheerful, lively voice on the floor above, chatting away on the phone. Janie picks up a large brass gong and an equally large mallet. The sound reverberates through the house. The telephone conversation upstairs ceases. When Mrs. Longworth appears a few minutes later, she remarks laughingly, "Isn't it funny how things change? I used to sound the gong for my servants. Now they sound it for me."

Her living room is cluttered, cozy, comfortable and dingy, done in pale faded colors, some velvets and flowered prints. The rugs and upholstery are so frayed that in some spots the threads barely hang together. Over the backs and arms of the furniture are pieces of yellowing plastic, a not very earnest attempt at preservation. One suspects that the decay might even be cultivated, a sort of scene-setter, a proper milieu for the venerable inhabitant of the old Dupont Circle mansion that she has occupied for most of her life.

And of course there is The Pillow—the needlepoint pillow that has been so often noticed and to which her detractors point when they deplore her mischievous nature. It, too, is wrapped in plastic and it says, "If you haven't got anything nice to say about anyone, come and sit here by me."

Alice Longworth is a controversial figure in Washington. Those who don't know her—the public, or "the great rancid masses" as she likes to say—see her only as a formidable, amusing, highly entertaining, iconoclastic old lady. But among those in the inner sanctum, those who frequent the Georgetown salons, those who refer to her as "Mrs. L.," there is a sharp division of opinion about her which often causes unpleasant moments.

There are those who think she is cruel, mean and malicious, that she uses other people as the butt of her humor, that she will hurt someone for the sake of a catchy one-liner, that she is essentially cold and insensitive to other people's feelings. She outrages some with her scorn of her cousin Eleanor Roosevelt ("I leave the good deeds to Eleanor") and they readily point out that Mrs. Longworth has never really *done* anything worthwhile in her life.

Alice Longworth has lived in Washington since William McKinley was assassinated and her father became President in 1901. She was 17 years old. She has known every President since Benjamin Harrison, who was in office from 1889 to 1893. Some she liked and some she didn't; over the years she has never hesitated to reveal her exact sentiments about them, or anyone else for that matter.

She has been a favorite of Harry Truman, John Kennedy, Lyndon Johnson and Richard Nixon, but there was no love lost between her and Warren Harding, and Woodrow Wilson. President Eisenhower bored her.

She supported her father when President Roosevelt was running in 1912 on the Progressive ticket and her husband, Cincinnati congressman Nicholas Longworth, whom she married when she was 22 and he was 36, was running for re-election on the Republican ticket. Her father was responsible for her husband's defeat. "It was too horrible, really," she says about that period. "Poor Nick, he stayed out, came back in two years, and then became Speaker, so all was well."

Her total fascination with politics and the people in politics has never waned, though she says now that it's far more interesting when "you've got family in it."

At 41 she had her only child, daughter Pauline, who was widowed at 26 and died at 31. She left an only daughter, Joanna Sturm. Mrs. Longworth's granddaughter is now 27 and lives with her in the Dupont Circle house.

In 1931, Nicholas Longworth, who by then had become the powerful House Speaker, died. Mrs. Longworth never remarried, preferring to remain alone, leading the independent life she seemed always to want, unhindered by the restrictions being the daughter of a President or the wife of a Speaker of the House must have placed upon her.

After spending several hours with Mrs. Longworth it would seem that those who say she is a malicious person are unjustified. To be sure there is a bite to her tongue, but, more often than not, statements that might be thought mean or shocking by some have an edge of truth to them. Mrs. Longworth is honest. "That," she says, "infuriates people."

As for alleged lack of sympathy for others' problems: She never talks about her own sadnesses, "Never, I just don't want to," and she doesn't want to hear about anybody else's.

"I don't think I am insensitive or cruel. I laugh, I have a sense of humor. I like to tease. I must admit a sense of mischief does get hold of me from time to time. I'm a hedonist. I have an appetite for being entertained. Isn't it strange how that upsets people? And I don't mind what I do unless I'm injuring someone in some way.

"I had a pious cousin who used to say she lived in the palace of truth and she would go up to some horrible-looking creature with an ugly red nose and say, 'You have an ugly red nose.'"

Having been a President's daughter and so often in the public eye, Mrs. Longworth has had her share of criticism. But she thinks she is not as sensitive today. "Criticism doesn't bother me. It's so lovely to be able to say that."

"But," pipes up granddaughter Joanna, "you've been old long enough so that people don't criticize you anymore. They're all so overly respectful."

"Isn't it fascinating?" Mrs. Longworth asks. "It's that dreadful desire of human beings to worship."

Her granddaughter, Joanna Sturm, wearing pants and a sweater, has just entered the room and sinks into a chair next to the sofa as Janie brings in the tea tray: a silver kettle over a burner that Mrs. Longworth lights herself, bread and butter, cookies and a tiny fresh chocolate cake.

Joanna is tall with longish, light brown hair, a strong, pretty, intelligent face and an open, easy, likable manner. She is completely at home with her grandmother, who, when she is in the room, relies on her for advice.

Joanna will often come out with an opinion Mrs. Longworth clearly agrees with, and the older woman will gasp with mock horror and disapproval.

"I," says Joanna, with an engaging smile, "am the silent accomplice."

"I'm full of respect for the younger generation," says her grandmother, smiling sanctimoniously at Joanna.

Alice Longworth finds the publicity about her "absolutely fascinating. I view it from a totally detached point of view but I suppose I can sort of see why they want to interview me. I am more amusing than most President's daughters."

One of her most recent interviews was with another President's daughter, Julie Eisenhower, who wrote the story for *The Saturday Evening Post*.

"Totally inane," declares Joanna.

"Oh, Joanna," says Mrs. Longworth, laughing, "it wasn't either. It was lovely."

Later, Janie clears the tea things away and brings in Mrs. Longworth's dinner tray. Mrs. Longworth offers dinner to her guest, then peeks under the plate cover. "Oh good, spareribs, I love spareribs. No one ever serves them. They're fattening, too, and I just can't seem to put on weight. I only weigh 92 pounds."

As soon as she has inspected the meal and begun to dig in, Mrs. Longworth steers the conversation into the beginnings of a gossip session.

"I'll tell you who I think is awfully nice," she says. "Margaret Truman. I've always liked her a great deal.

"I haven't seen the Johnson girls at all. I always get them mixed up but they seem to like to have a good time.

"And Julie Eisenhower has got something. She seems rather smart. Joanna scoffed at her piece about me and I suppose it was rather scoffable, but I did it because I wanted to show that we're friends. I like Julie better than Tricia. I've never been able to get on with Tricia. She seems rather pathetic, doesn't she? I wonder what's wrong with her?"

Mrs. Longworth keeps on munching, venturing opinions, trying out names for reaction.

"I like Jackie very much. But I've always wondered what on earth made her marry Onassis. He's a repulsive character. He reminds me of Mr. Punch . . . Jack was so attractive.

"Ethel," says Mrs. Longworth, "is behaving very badly these days. There's a certain brash quality about her I never liked. I liked Bobby though, a great deal."

Mrs. Longworth cannot stand pomposity or false piety and will go to great lengths to skewer someone guilty of taking himself too seriously. "I'm probably bad about people who have noble, fine and marvelous thoughts. That's so depressing. I never could stand the little pious family things that my sanctimonious cousins used to do. But they're all dead now."

Alice Longworth is a survivor in a town where the word is an anachronism. She has been revered and feared, adored and detested, but there has never been a time when she has not been talked about. Her outrageous ut-

" '...in those days people were always having affairs with their poodles.' "

terances about people and events began when she was a child and she is still adding to the list of quotable quotes.

She would admit that when McKinley was assassinated and her father became President that her feeling was "utter rapture," she was "ecstatic," a line that appalled people in its directness. But she'll just as readily mock herself. When she had her second mastectomy several years ago, she remarked later that she was the "only topless octagenarian" in Georgetown Hospital.

Interviews are always one way of securing information. Mrs. Longworth is as curious and observant as an interviewer, taking the situation in quickly, optimistically prepared to be entertained, amused, informed; but just as braced, graciously, of course, to be bored.

She talks quickly, through her teeth in a rather upper-class way that she will exaggerate for effect from time to time. Often her verbal speed makes it difficult to understand.

Her eyes are very clear. They dart back and forth. Her hands rest in her lap but she twists her fingers as her mind leaps about. Occasionally she will leap up to point out some relic, memento or photograph across the room.

She roars with laughter at the irreverent suggestion that one should prostrate oneself at her feet at the sound of her gong and points her finger admiringly. "Ah," she says, "you've a wicked nature, horrid, I like that."

She is as ready with a topical jab about young people as she is about past generations, and just as much at home with young people as if she were in her 20s. A session with her and Joanna could almost be a women's consciousness-raising session, but for her irreverence about anything taken too seriously. And she once said, "I've never liked people my own age."

Joanna works for the National Women's Political Caucus and, in fact, the treasurer of the NWPC, Lucille Flanigan, lives with them on the top floor. Joanna tells Mrs. Longworth that Lucille will not be there for tea.

"I'm all for the women's cause," says Mrs. Longworth. "I saw too much of the 'silly little womanizing' over the years. But I'm not violent about it. I've never been treated as an inferior by any man."

Mrs. Longworth is reminded of a story of a friend of hers in the old days (the turn of the century) who, after being forbidden by her father to see a young man, dressed in men's clothes and cut her hair. The father remarked, "What an odd revenge."

Mrs. Longworth laughs heartily. "Homosexuality and lesbianism were very fashionable in those days," she says. "And it was quite acceptable. At least as far as I was concerned."

"Tell her about the incident in the White House garden," prompts Joanna.

It seems Margaret Cassini, Igor's mother and the daughter of a South American ambassador, had been a great friend of Alice Longworth's and they had taken a walk one day in the White House garden.

Miss Cassini proceeded to tell young Alice that a mutual friend was saying horrid things about her. Alice asked what, and the friend replied that a certain Miss Alice Barney was claiming to be in love with Alice.

"I don't think that's nasty, why I think that's lovely, so nice. I'm so glad to hear she is," Mrs. Longworth recalls saying with a mischievous smile.

Margaret Cassini apparently snorted with contempt, which pleased young Alice enormously.

"Still," she says, "usually I thought it better to keep away from joking about the lesbian thing since my father was President. But you know in those days people were always having love affairs with their poodles and putting tiny flowers in strange places. But they talked amusingly about their affairs. My family didn't, though. They would have gone absolutely mad with horror. Especially my younger sister Ethel. She would have fainted dead away. But I don't think I have ever been scandalized."

Mrs. Longworth was loving the conversation.

"Not in the sense of moral outrage," says Joanna. "But you're being aesthetically outraged constantly."

"Yes, that's true," says Mrs. Longworth. "By sexual things, by tasteless things. And then some things I think are terribly funny. Like dear old men's things hanging all around them. I think that's terribly funny."

What?

"Men's penises, my dear," she says very deliberately leaning forward, waiting for a reaction.

As soon as she is greeted by a howl of astonished laughter, she leans back and howls delightedly herself and Joanna joins in.

"Oh, I can see it in the paper now," says Mrs. Longworth. "Dear old Mrs. Longworth sitting with her granddaughter talking about men's penises."

The talk moves to marriage versus living together. Would she, if she were Joanna's age today, have married?

"No, I never would marry again. I might live with people. But not for long. I really wouldn't want to do anything pondering or noble or taking a position about someone again. But I might rather just spend a night with them, or an afternoon or something."

She pauses, then reflects for a moment: "Still," she says, "I'm afraid I do believe in marriage."

164

"Why?" asks Joanna. "You hardly reveled in it yourself."

"That's true. I hardly reveled in it."

"You hardly advise it for me," says Joanna.

"I suppose I'm just a neutral person," she muses. "But I followed my father's marriages. He was always so full of guilt. I loved my father but I was never particularly close to him. I enjoyed my stepmother. But it's mean to talk about your parents that way. I don't want to talk about my parents."

The subject is changed.

Well, if Alice Longworth wouldn't have married if she were young today, what would she do?

"I would have run for office. If I were very young I would try to get over the shyness of speaking in public. I still have it. I shuddered with terror when people tried to make me get up and speak. It was just false pride I suppose. But I'm really very shy.

"Every once in a while it hits me. I was like a tenement child, you know, deformed with my legs (she had a disease as a child that was suspected later to have been polio), and I was always very conscious of that. My stepmother used to stretch my legs every night."

Mrs. Longworth also feels shy, she says, because she was the only child of Theodore Roosevelt and his first wife. "My brothers used to tease me about not having the same mother. They were very cruel about it and I was terribly sensitive."

Often accused of being vain, because of her great beauty, Alice Longworth seems unaware of her looks and says she never really thought she was pretty, even when she was young. She jokes now about losing her hair and not having bought a new dress since she was 80.

"I thought I was a rather pathetic creature, terribly homely and that they were just saying I was pretty because I was the President's daughter. Some times I look at pictures of myself then, trying to see what they thought was pretty. But then I determined not to be a pathetic creature. I decided to defeat it so I became resistant, contrary, and I tried to be conspicuous. That feeling has lasted in some way."

The conversation moves to accents, and Mrs. Longworth says she apes whomever she is with. "Except LBJ," she chortles. "And I never aped Pat and Dick," she adds.

"Thank goodness," pipes up Joanna.

"Mean!" chides Mrs. Longworth.

What kind of people does she like, who amuses her, interests her?

"Oh, just the people in this very room, my dear," she coos.

"That's not usually true," says Joanna.

Does she like Gerald Ford?

"Who's Gerald Ford? Oh yes, the Vice President. Do I know Gerald Ford, Joanna?"

"I hope not."

"Oh, Joanna," she says with a grin. "You're so intolerant." She begins to warm up to the game.

What about the Nixons?

She suddenly goes serious and says a bit stiffly, "The Nixons are old friends. I've liked them for years. 'I've known them for a long, long time. I don't talk about them."

A pall comes over the conversation and for a few seconds there is grim silence.

"Well, that certainly put an end to that conversation," jokes Joanna. "Maybe we'd better change the subject."

Mrs. Longworth giggles and agrees and offers tea with honey.

That was not the end of that.

The temptation to get back to Nixon is too much. And later, in the midst of another conversation, Mrs. Longworth leans forward bursting with a less than flattering opinion about how Watergate has been handled by the President — for whom she has always, until now, had only the highest praise. She goes on a bit, then leans back and says, deliberately savoring the pleasure of her remark: "But that my dear, is just between us and not for your story."

As she turns 90, Mrs. Longworth is not thinking about the end. Her phone rings endlessly, she has callers to tea everyday, she still reads till 3 or 4 every morning, and she still goes with friends to dinner parties, which she adores.

She has "plenty of money," as she will tell you, so there are no worries there.

"I have no problems," she will say. "It's easier to grow old if you are able to relax. I relax like mad and I'm interested in everything. Thank heavens I haven't gotten senile. I have good old gusto, that's all."

But in the last year Mrs. Longworth has not been terribly well. Perhaps her two bouts with cancer are taking their toll. She went to her first dinner party in six weeks the other day and was exhausted all the next day.

"I'm crumbling with old age," she says with a wry smile and adds, with just the tiniest trace of concern, "It's just in the last year that I have been getting obviously older."

Mrs. Longworth, for all her impeccable manner, is a snob. "I do believe in privilege," she says resolutely. And part of her snobbism is a kind of nose-thumbing. "*Épater* (titillate) *les bourgeois*," she will say with a nicely turned French accent.

Some people say she has mellowed in her old age. Does she think she has?

"No," she says brightly.

Alice Longworth can still laugh at herself and laughing at herself gives her license to laugh at others.

"When they start comparing you to the Washington Monument," she says, "you just have to open your eyes and take a good look at yourself."

—February 12, 1974

166

A Young Man
Who Went to War

By Myra MacPherson

It seems bizarre and remote, John Sexton's story of death and pain, as
his Thunderbird races in brilliant sunlight down the concrete highways
that seem both soul and sinew of Detroit.

As Sexton drives to his parent's home in nearby Warren—a neat
bungalow with an American eagle decal on the garage door—he talks
simply about the events that literally took him out of the world for two
years.

Captured by the Viet Cong in August 1969, Sexton was chained and
lived in a hole in the ground for 26 months. He is 23, but his once powerful body is old, wasted. A few years ago he lifted weights, got his chin
split with a beer bottle in a fight, ran track, bowled, got in minor car
scrapes, played baseball.

Now there is shrapnel in his face and legs. Bomb fragments tore into his
right eye and left it blind. Most of his right elbow is blown off and his arm
is fused; he can never bend it again. He has a herniated disc, a bad esoph-
agus. Malaria attacks still come in the night; he still gets headaches from
the concussions.

Staff Sgt. Sexton had only two more weeks to go in Vietnam when the
armored personnel carrier he was riding in was ambushed. "I got shot in
the head . . . felt the warm blood pouring down my face. Then a bazooka
round came through. I remember this big white flash and BOWHAM!
and the ringing, my head was ringing. It was like being in a giant bell. My
friend next to me was killed."

Sexton remembers being carried by Viet Cong deep into the jungle, his
blood wetting the canvas stretcher. Today, when he lies in his darkened
bedroom with its deep brown wood paneling and sees a shaft of light
coming through the window, "it reminds me of my bunker and I catch
myself drifting off . . ."

The memories are harsh. For 26 months, Sexton never talked to another
American. He lived in a 4-by-8-foot shelter in the ground where he was unable to stand erect. A half-inch under 6 feet, Sexton once was a thick-
chested 185 pounds. He lost 50 pounds, now is up to 155. At night, when

he was shackled, mice crawled in his hair. He went months without a bath; it was a "constant struggle" not to lose his mind. He thought at times of "just giving up and dying."

On October 8, 1971, Sexton was released by the Viet Cong, the last American prisoner to be freed.

It was Thanksgiving when Sexton returned to Michigan from the Denver hospital. There was a huge parade and Warren proclaimed "John Sexton Week" and for that week named a street after him. The street sign, "Sgt. Sexton," is in his parents' garage. There were floats and marching bands and choirs and banquets and beauty queens kissing Sexton and he cried when he laid a wreath for the dead in Vietnam.

"There were so many things running through my mind riding in that parade. 'Why are they doing this for me?' There are guys still out there and they are the ones that are hurt bad. I really had a complex about this hero thing. I don't claim to be no hero. I didn't do more than no other guys. I know there are mothers saying, 'Here's all this publicity and my son's got his leg blown off.'"

Sexton became a national celebrity. He appeared on national talk shows, went to a Hollywood banquet with Sammy Davis Jr. to raise money for POWs.

He was given a $7,000 Corvette, which he smashed up on New Year's Eve on an icy road, and is sensitive that one newspaper report implied he was drunk. "I only had two drinks. I went out with the intention of getting bombed. I had a quart of gin with me. I was thinking, here it is, the start of the New Year and those guys [POWs] are still over there. But I never took more than two drinks."

Sexton was a stranger to 1971; he wrote 1969 on letters. There was constant cultural shock — four-letter words in movies, unisex clothes. Today, he dresses sharply and immaculately, sometimes takes two baths a day, trying to forget his days of filth and imprisonment.

His friends and family think his feisty stubbornness saved him.

"John was wild; you'd take a bite out of his hamburger and he'd bust you in the nose," said Dennis Wilber, who enlisted with John in 1966. "He isn't no longer a fighter."

Ray Riley, a teacher at the cinderblock Lincoln High School — where "nine out of 10 teachers are for Wallace" — said Sexton was so altered it took him several minutes to adjust when he first saw him. "He's more somber, sober." Riley remembers him as a kid who "liked to go out and raise hell. When he was 17, he'd just as soon tell someone to go to hell as not."

That contentiousness is gone now. He is reflective, soft-spoken, almost gentle. He used to hunt, but no longer — "I don't want to see anything harmed." There is a confused, questioning restlessness about where he's going and what kind of girl he wants to marry, an impatience with the "basic pettiness" of people, and an unshaped desire to break out of the working-class mold that was his youth.

In the old days in Warren, Sexton didn't think much about "life." But in those two lost years, he went to a place in his mind that few go. There were not just hours or days, but months of loneliness and despair. He returned with a special reverence for life, but today it is mixed with a gnawing dissatisfaction. He can't go home to the aimlessness of his youth, although there are bursts of nostalgia for it, and yet he doesn't know how to find a new world.

"It's so different now," Sexton said. He paused. "I always depended on my body. I wasn't that much a studious person. I guess, you know, it's one of those things, you know, I have to overcome, in order to get anywhere. If you can't do manual labor, you have to improve your mind."

He recalls, "The way it was where I lived, you had to fight for respect. You couldn't gain it through conversation. You had to be cool. That was the thing, cool." And Sexton succeeded. In his high school yearbook, with the picture of him, his hair in a wavy pompadour, there are repeated scrawls from friends to "the coolest guy," to "one of the coolest."

Sexton touches the scar on his chin and with a faint smile remembers that fight when he was 17. "We was at a gas station and, see, this guy, his girl wanted to go out with me. He said, 'Give me a beer.' He put his hand through the window. I threw the bottle out the window and as I was coming out, he picked up the bottle and come at me with it."

Sexton's speech is a curious mix of bad grammar and articulateness. A moment later he cuts through the "you knows" he uses to reflect on the "apprehension" he first felt in high school; "that I couldn't possibly obtain the goals I thought I wanted to obtain. I would just sit back in school. If I had someone egging me on, giving me a little enthusiasm, I might have persevered."

Like many of his friends Sexton was easy to overlook. He got average grades, worked half-days in a co-operative retailing program, doing everything from selling clothes to hoisting fertilizer bags for a hardware store. He thought little of the future, "took things as they came," and, like about 70 percent of his class of 300, did not plan on college. He did not try out for sports or the glee club or anything — "the ones who did were the ones going on."

His life was filled with the aimless, restless mobility of Middle America youth that marks "Easy Rider" and "The Last Picture Show"; simply moving is going somewhere. The day Sexton got his driver's license was the day he stopped watching television.

He and his friends still think nothing of driving 80 miles round-trip for a casual date. His favorite relaxation remains a drive "out in the country." He doesn't walk once he gets there, just drives back.

Warren, the third largest city in Michigan with a population of 179,000, is not so much a suburb as an extension of Detroit, 12 miles away. It has no center, and streets of neat homes fan off the main highways glutted with auto plants, gas stations, Burger Chefs. On Sexton's street there are chain link fences and boats in the back yards. The neighbors next door have three tires painted silver with flowers in them. A weathered plastic flag droops over the Sexton mailbox.

The small, brick, three-bedroom home owned by Mildred and John Sexton Sr. is spotless — braid rugs in the kitchen, a well nurtured elephant's-ear plant, an afghan on the couch, a china Pekingese on the TV set. A large golden eagle hovers over a shelf full of bric-a-brac that includes Las Vegas souvenir cups and Sexton's old bowling trophies. A plaque in the kitchen declares: "Never say die, say damn."

Sexton's father is an inspector at the Chevrolet plant; his mother works at Detroit Plastic Products, which stamps out automobile parts. Together they make $22,000 a year. Sexton's grandfather was killed in a Kentucky coal mine and Sexton's father, like so many others, left the South for Michigan's wartime bomber plants and peacetime auto plants.

He was a determined provider for John and his two sisters. "I used to tell John if anything is worth stealing, it's worth buying. If you want it that bad, if I possibly can, I'll get it for you." He says it's important that children know you love them. "And you know your children love you when they fight with you a lot," he says, half jokingly and half meaning that when there is arguing there is communication.

His parents thought John was missing in action most of the time he was captured and now they hover around him with soft looks of pride. "I used to think, 'He's so young, the war can't last that long' — and he growed right into it," said Mr. Sexton. "Why does so many have to suffer for so few who can't get along with each other?"

Everyone in the Sexton family is for George Wallace and John got loud cheers when he appeared with Wallace at Michigan rallies: "Here's a gentleman who for 26 months was a prisoner in a Communist prison camp. He hails from Detroit. Let's give John Sexton a nice big hand." Sexton was supposed to go on to other states before Wallace was shot. John said of the shooting, "It's really a shame — all the people in the United States are 'supposed' to respect one another's viewpoint."

Sexton is for Wallace because "no other man is better for the average man than him. I'm just an average person. I *want* to believe in my country. When I came out for Wallace I knew I would be attacked as a racist, but I'm not. You should have the freedom and choice to choose the people you want to associate with. The government's forcing you to associate with another group of people. The Detroit schools once were the finest—much better than the ones in the rural areas—and they took a fine learning institution and completely destroyed it."

Sexton says, "I can't back the present administration. They promised to end the war and spent four years messing things up—unemployment, inflation, devaluation of the dollar." Sexton is infuriated at George McGovern's stand on amnesty. "He must be making a complete mockery out of me. These are the politicians who got us involved in the damn mess and now they say, 'Man, you shouldn't have been there, you shouldn't listen to me. You shoulda gone to Canada.' Amnesty? They were grown men when they made the decision, let them live with theirs and I'll live with mine. Frank Mankiewicz came to a POW family meeting and said, 'You don't have to worry, most of them aren't coming back anyway,' and I said I don't care. If *one* of them comes back, that one could have been *me.* McGovern says he's going to end the war immediately and then he says he doesn't agree with all of Madam Binh's seven-point peace proposal. Well, I know those people and he couldn't end it without agreeing to all."

Sexton, who went to war "gung ho," was disillusioned early. "You believe in democracy and they don't give a damn. The people steal off you, the ARVNdoesn't want to fight. After awhile the G.I. has contempt and hatred." He doesn't condone but "understands" Mylai. "The VC tortured some of their guys. Some guys are very cold. They can kill somebody and walk up and spit on them. The first people I killed I had to take their weapons. I seen the bodies, and I thought, it's really a shame, just a few minutes ago this guy was alive."

He travels with buddies like Dennis Wilber and Tony Stoppani and Dennis Covis, who share a house. Covis drives a truck, Stoppani "works at machineries at Ford's" at night and takes college courses in the day. Wilber is a "stock man at Chrysler."

Stoppani swaggers like Warren Beatty, shirt opened to the waist and shades on, as he talks on the phone. "Honey, don't cry, I *told* you I was coming to Denver." He slams the phone down and says to Sexton, "What's her face is looking for you. She called here."

They trade cracks about "drinking parties" and all laugh when one says, "We have a buddy, he's famous for wrecking cars." Wilber jokes, "Tony's the only nutball here; he loves Elvis Presley and apple wine." Stoppani tears out, squealing the wheels as he takes off for his job.

Sexton often seems to stay outside the horseplay and laughter. "I fit in because they are my friends." He adds later, "I'm not the joking, laughing type, but I like to be around them. It takes my mind off things."

When Sexton was out of the room, Wilber said, "A lot of guys hate him. They're jealous. They say, 'I'm an ex-G.I. and I don't get no free car.'" Later, Sexton says calmly, "I guess that's just a part of man, his jealousy."

Some of the hundreds of letters he gets are "sarcastic — 'Well look at our big hero in the paper again.'" Three months ago he was bitter about such attacks and said he was "going into seclusion."

"I wrestled with that and finally decided with me out here spearheading things I would remind people about the other POWs. But even that they took and made something of."

Sexton started a fund for, among other things, a neutral team of doctors to attempt to inspect Southeast Asian prison camps. "And some people said not to give money, that it was for myself. The pettiness of people still annoys me. If they only knew what it means to just be alive."

While Sexton was in his jungle hole he thought often about the kind of girl he wanted to marry if he got out: "All I lived for was to have a son." But he is cautious. "I've been through so much, I don't want to have a bad marriage. I date varieties, I tell you. I have to, to find who's best suited for me."

His standards about women and life have changed. "You grow up with certain inhibitions about you, like the morals you grew up with, you know? Before, I believed in those strict morals, but now I'm a life-ist." He doesn't "see anything wrong" about living with a girl before marriage and says, "I want a wife who is just so warm, who loves life so much. I want a girl I can talk with, even when you're angry."

By his own admission, Sexton's future is a big question mark. He says he dropped out of Macomb County Community College last month because he couldn't write after breaking his bad arm when he fell roller skating. He says he wants to go back in the fall, thinks he'll take liberal arts, wants to "work with people," is vague in what capacity. He thought about social work, "but when I think of all those years it takes for a degree." He has $20,000 back pay but feels "useless" because he can't do the demanding manual jobs his friends can. He spends a lot of time giving free speeches to high schools and working on the release of POWs.

To John Sexton, "the one good thing" about his lost years in Vietnam is that it taught him to "really love life. I'm just so happy to be alive."

But this is tempered by an aching sense of loss and impotence: "I want to accomplish *something*," says John Sexton. "I just feel so wasted. I just feel wasted."

— May 21, 1972

Update: John Sexton did return to Macomb Community College and is studying to become a certified public accountant. He plans to marry Linda Livingston, a first grade teacher, in July. Disillusioned at our leaving Vietnam — "Ford just made fools out of all of us who fought" — Sexton is, more than ever, a George Wallace advocate.

May 1975

Next: Ruby Austin

Ruby Folsom Ellis Austin. "15. Do not use dialect unless your ear is good."
— E. B. White, Chapter V, The Elements of Style.

Without Southern-bred Sally Quinn's grasp of the brassy Southern talk of Gov. George Wallace's compulsively indiscreet mother-in-law, this story wouldn't be a candidate for this volume. Told in conventional usage, the quotes would still be good, but the effect would be bland, and the portrait of "a whole lotta woman" would fail. Big Ruby's steady outpouring of raunchy, outrageous utterances on men, booze and politics has to be rendered in language like, "'Y'all come on back here, honey,'" to cite one of the more modest examples, as Big Ruby, striding in white plastic go-go boots, takes Quinn on a tour of her Montgomery home ("ranch-style version of antebellum").

Accurate recreation of dialect serves to define Big Ruby's earthy character as perhaps no other device could. The story ran alongside profiles, also using dialect, of George Wallace (shortly before the assassination attempt on him) and of his prim wife Cornelia, Big Ruby's daughter. Editors normally balk at use of dialect. Writers tend to capture it only piecemeal, or are unable to translate it accurately into type. Also, too often, it establishes a derogatory tone. Quinn avoids all these pitfalls.

Note: Big Ruby said she loved her story.   *— L. T.*

Big Ruby

By Sally Quinn

MONTGOMERY, Ala. — "Ah been lookin' for a husband for two years now, ever since Dr. Austin died," said Ruby Folsom Ellis Austin. "But there's slim pickins in Montgomery. There ain't nothin' here."

"Ah got the only bachelor in Montgomery," said her daughter Cornelia Wallace. "And ah'm scared to death mama's gonna go after George."

"Shoooooooot, honey," said Big Ruby. "He ain't even titty high."

Cornelia had agreed after lunch at the governor's mansion that "Mama" had to be met. "She's really something," she said, "but she has to be seen in her natural habitat."

Cornelia jumps behind the wheel of the state-owned black Lincoln Continental and maneuvers the car out the front gate of the mansion and down the tree-lined streets through the nicer section of town to Ruby's house.

Ruby's house is a modern, ranch-style version of antebellum with enormous ceilings, furniture and mirrors, much of which belongs to Cornelia, who'd rather have it there than in storage. From the kitchen comes the pungent smell of vinegar cooking and Ruby's stentorian welcome.

"Y'all come on back here, honey."

In the center of the kitchen looms Big Ruby, nearly 6 feet tall, short salt-and-pepper hair curled around her heavily made-up face, a black and white suit, white blouse and . . . . . white plastic go-go boots.

Ruby is a king-sized younger Mae West, a whole lotta woman and if you don't like it you know what you can do with it. She takes you to her bosom at once, just like you were kin folks, she bombards you with jokes, then roars with laughter at her own punch lines, she confides her life's woes, then berates, flatters and overwhelms — mostly just overwhelms. Montgomery is not big enough for Big Ruby. She is the sister of James M. (Big Jim or Kissin' Jim) Folsom, a two-term governor of Alabama and she once served as his first lady in the governor's mansion before he was married.

She is twice widowed and dying to try marriage again. And she is not about to settle for being the governor's wife's mother."

Big Ruby was out on the campaign trail with George and Cornelia in Florida. She had a very good time. But Ruby drinks. George and Cornelia don't. She hasn't been out since.

174

" 'Proud of her? You better, by God, believe I'm proud of Cornelia...' "

"Ah get the feeling' some of them people out there on that campaign staff don't like me too much. And Ah'm scared they're gonna tell George Ah was drinkin' too much and showin' my fanny.

"C'mon," she invites, "lemme show you around the house." She leads the way through each room, telling about the furniture while Cornelia putters around her bookshelf. "I came to get my old Rollins College yearbook to look up some friends," says Cornelia, paying little attention to her mother. She picks up a copy of Earl Long's book and a history of the Folsom family. "The Folsom family came over to Boston in 1638," she says proudly. "My uncle used to say that the Folsoms were in Massachusetts 200 years before the Kennedys ever got there." Ruby obviously could care less. She's more interested in showing off the house. "This here's my bedroom," she says. "It's right messy. That there's the library but it's such a mess Ah can't even get in there. It doesn't really matter anyway cause Ah never read. This is some junk jewelry Ah picked up at a thrift for nothing," she continues.

Ruby wanders back past the flower arrangement of cotton balls and points out an antique "as old as the war between the states (weren't nothin' civil about it)."

She shows off Cornelia's silver and china and dining-room furniture which she is keeping for her while Cornelia's in the governor's mansion. "I'm not too good at interior decoratin' but Cornelia's real good. These are her real fancy plates. Ah used 'em one night and she liked to have killed me."

Cornelia is talking on the phone.

"These are pictures of Cornelia in high school, in college, after college. . . ." Life-sized pictures of Cornelia decorate every wall which is not hung with ersatz Louis XV brocades, flocked velvets, satins, gilts.

She plops down on a tiny, spindly legged French chair near the fireplace and sprawls her go-go boots out, ready for a good gossip session. "I'm cookin' up some shrimp for tomorrow night. My boyfriend's givin' a little party. Want to come? He's real nice, a retired Air Force colonel. Ah spend so much time with him Ah hardly have time to do for myself. Ah don't do much anyway. Just mess around."

Aside from men and booze, Ruby loves to talk politics. She's just dying to get in the White House. Would she like to see George Wallace become President of the United States?

"You better believe I would. I sat George down right here in this room and told him he'd have to get himself out of that independent party and run as a Democrat. He didn't have a chance as anything but a Democrat. Then Cornelia kept after him. But he's real smart, he's pretty quick. George don't have flies on his head. Then I gave him advice on poll counts. They were registerin' colored people past midnight, haulin' em in and lettin' em vote when they weren't registered. Ah tole George to get his own poll counters out there."

But when Ruby's had a few drinks she doesn't mind saying (she did in Florida), "Little George could stand to pay a little more attention. He never listens. Always talking. Why, if he'd give me half a chance, Ah could get him elected President. The way things are going now, Ah just don't believe he's going to make it."

Big Ruby's got a lot of politicking behind her and there are several publishing companies who would love to have her write about it. "I'm thinkin' of writin' a book but Ah can't do it unless Ah drink. It loosens up my mind and everything comes back. I'll get around to it someday."

But right now she's interested in having a good time, giving and going to parties. "Cornelia used to have parties all the time before she got married," she said dejectedly. "I guess she needs the rest now though."

But if George got to be President. . . "Wouldn't that be great. Ah just love to entertain. It's always fun when you're in."

Big Ruby walked to the car to say goodbye, "Y'all give us a ring when you come back through Montgomery, heah?" And she really means it.

Some people think Cornelia is just like her mother, others see no resemblance at all. When a reporter asked early in the campaign if she was proud of her daughter, she replied, "Proud of her? You better, by God, believe I'm proud of Cornelia. She's a good girl and a smart girl. Yes, I'm proud of her. Who wouldn't be? Listen, you know what a lot of people used to call her?—I don't know if they still do or not, her being the governor's wife—but you know what they used to call her? . . . They used to call her Little Ruby, that's what."

—May 7, 1972

III. Personal Memoirs

"1. Place yourself in the background. Write in a way that draws the reader's attention to the sense and substance of the writing, rather than to the mood and temper of the author." — Chapter V, The Elements of Style, *E. B. White.*

This first fundamental in White's addendum to William Strunk's classic on prose writing is quite properly his cardinal rule. But it is a rule made to be broken — in those cases where the writer's involvement, either direct or indirect, is so central to the story (just as in first person fiction) that disguising it would distort the perspective. There have always been certain kinds of stories that couldn't be told any other way. So, though the personal narrative is one of the most consciously literary in this volume (Wolfe cites autobiography as one of the roots of the "New Journalism"), it is perhaps the least new or innovative. These 10 stories display varying degrees of personal involvement.

The simplest form is the relatively straight account of something that happened to the author: Paul Hume's account of working his way through the University of Chicago as a church organist for weddings; Tom Donnelly's poignant encounter with an old man who lost his way while on a walk; Henry Mitchell's droll memoir of two interviews he had with elusive, "artless" Elvis Presley.

Sally Quinn's story of her 10th anniversary reunion at Smith College starts out as basically the same genre. But it is broadened, with juxtaposed scenes and contextual detail, into a statement on the generation gap. What emerges is more a story about changed college life than about her experiences.

In Joel Dreyfuss' personal recollections of the late Ted Poston, a pioneering black in white newspapers, the focus is similarly on the subject. And in Nick von Hoffman's warm, emotional eulogy upon the death of Lyndon Johnson — who, as President, Von Hoffman lambasted up one wall and down the other — the author is even more technically apart. He breaks through only in the first person plural and in the second person singular, as Von Hoffman exhorts the late President: "You were always so completely, so absolutely you."

Michael Kernan, in his two affectionate family reminiscences — one of Michael Kernan Sr., his "sunny, remote" politician of a father, and the other of Nicholas Kernan, an uncle permanently banished for misbehavior to an Adirondacks foxfarm — carries further the emphasis on the subject rather than the author. Though both narratives are unswervingly first person singular, Kernan makes the point in both stories that he is employing the first person in a way closer to its common fictional use — these are records of events of Kernan's childhood, written as he has come to remem-

ber them, but not necessarily, he would grant, entirely as they were. Nowhere in this volume are literary devices common to realistic fiction more freely used. And nowhere is more clearly illustrated the vagueness of the line between fiction and nonfiction that Kernan discusses in his reply to Tom Wolfe in this book's first chapter. One suspects that if these pieces were presented as pure fiction, few could tell the difference.

The final refinement in this link between author and subject comes in two intensely personal stories — both about the rites of warfare — that never use the first or second person modes at all. There is Henry Mitchell's moving account of a 30th anniversary reunion of survivors of Tarawa, the bloodiest battle of the Pacific War. Mitchell turns it into an essay on old soldiers recalling their war exploits: "They are stories good men teach to their sons." What is left untold to the reader is that the author himself, telling a war story, is a survivor of the Pacific War (New Guinea). Even though Mitchell does not directly interject himself, Mitchell is very much there in the intensity of tone.

Henry Allen, a Marine veteran, does something similar in his high-powered account of training at Parris Island, S.C., "an initiation that may be the only true rite of passage to manhood that America hasn't yet scoured away as an anthropological anachronism." Allen's syntactical imitation of the "barking and hissing" of the Marine Corps with which the sergeants discipline the "penitents" and his range of religious and anthropological allusions give the reader a taste of the real Parris Island impossible in straight factual exposition. He exposes his personal involvement (through judgment) near the end when he says, "the fear, bleakness and degradation (of the training) can yield a beauty (the trainees will) never be able to explain to anyone who hasn't gone through it and made it."

Note: Just how often the first person singular should intrude into journalism is a subject on which reasonable persons will differ. Tom Kendrick, Style's editor, is a stickler (like White) for keeping it minimal, arguing that in most cases the first person injects a needless barrier between the reader and the story's subject (though he wholly accepts the way the stories in this chapter use it). In addition he feels that it is sometimes gratuitous ego display on the part of the writer and will, when ostentatious, drive up the readers' hackles by reducing their own freedom of judgment.

On the other hand, Tom Donnelly, a Style writer Kendrick admires, believes in relatively unfettered use of the first person, in interviews, reviews, and much else. To him the barrier that bothers Kendrick (namely, the reporter as a selective filter through which the facts pass) is there whether you acknowledge it or not. So why hide it? The two sustain a running debate on the subject, and little hope is held for its resolution.   — L. T.

Passage:
The Way It Is and Was

By Sally Quinn

O vercome by a wave of nostalgia on the last day of my tenth reunion at Smith College, I decided to have just one look at my old house, Talbot. Walking up to the front porch past the bicycles, past the swing and into "Fussers," a sitting room named for the old-fashioned term "fussing" or necking, I was astonished to feel my eyes mist over a bit. I hadn't planned to go up to my old room on the third floor but there I was, knocking on the door, petrified someone would say "come in." Someone said "come in." I gingerly opened the door to find a student sitting cross-legged on the bed filing her nails. "I used to live in this room 10 years ago," I said, not believing I had said it. She smiled patronizingly. "Yes," I went on, trying to recoup, "and when I lived here I had, piled up in that corner, the largest collection of movie magazines on campus."
"Oh, we don't read movie magazines anymore," she replied. "We read love comics now."

It was easy to remember two other times I had driven into Northampton, Mass., past the foreboding black, wrought iron, ivy-covered sign, "Smith College 1871." The first was 14 years ago when I was driven up by my parents on the first day of my freshman year, not knowing a soul, and was deposited on the front steps of Talbot House in tears, wearing the darkest sunglasses I could find to hide my swollen red eyes. The second time was driving back from New York with friends the day before graduation not knowing whether or not I was going to graduate. I did graduate . . . at the very bottom of my class which I figured had to be at least more of a distinction than second from the bottom.

This time I drove back with my old classmate and class president, Toni Krissel Goodale, with whom I would be rooming in Albright House. I wore a beige safari suit, a pullover and chains. Perfect, I thought. Everyone else, it turned out, was wearing little summer cotton dresses, slacks, loafers . . .

Having my suitcase carried upstairs by a freshman who called me ma'am was only the first shock. The second was seeing a sign on the door of the communal bathroom saying, "man inside." That, we later found out, was only in deference to alumnae.

Last weekend was not only reunion weekend for every fifth year (starting with the class of 1903 whose members stayed in the infirmary) but also commencement weekend, the graduation of the largest class (more than 600) in the history of Smith College. One of the first activities was a special panel on where the college was going. It was held in Sage Hall, remembered for endless lecture courses and long naps. The slow hissing sound of steam heat still, after 10 years, produces the same somnolent effect. The hall was packed with earnest, white-haired alumnae, in cable knits, McMullen blouses and pleated skirts, similar, except for the color of their hair, to the students of 14 years ago at the first freshman assembly.

It was in that room that Miss Charlotte Fitch, our class dean, had announced 14 years ago that our class was the first one at Smith which had ever had less than 50 percent private school girls. There was a stunned silence throughout the hall, then a gasp of dismay from the preppies. One classmate, very upset, confided to me that if she liked two girls equally and she found out one was from a private and the other from a public school, she would like the private school girl better.

It was in Sage Hall that same day that Miss Fitch informed us that we had two blacks in our class. There were those who were unhappy with that; and later, at a compulsory assembly with Marian Wright Edelman, a law student from Yale and the first black woman to speak at Smith, some of my Southern classmates sat in the back and snickered, hissed and chanted, "Alabama niggers should be free," on their way out.

We learned rules 14 years ago, too. We had housemothers who helped us obey them. There was to be no drinking, no smoking, no men in the rooms at any time. When a kingsman (campus policeman) or father visited, we were to yell "man on floor" before he appeared. Curfew hours were announced and strictly kept. We were on the honor system. We were to have posture pictures taken, nude, then a semester of required Basic Motor Skills or "BMS" (one learned to walk up and down stairs in high heels carrying a baby).

Miss Fitch told us that day that our class was mostly interested in art history, English, languages and history. We were told about necessary grade averages and the dreaded Registrar's List. "Rege," as I came to know it, was the opposite of Dean's List. I was on Rege the entire time I was at Smith. I lost my scholarship because of it the first year and felt I should inform my father. When I wrote to him I had made the Registrar's List, he misunderstood and thought it was an honor.

Shortly afterward an announcement appeared in my father's home town newspaper to the effect that Miss Sally Quinn has attained the honor of being placed on the Registrar's List at Smith College . . .

We were also told about President Thomas Mendenhall, our new president that year. As a present to our class, which came to Smith the same year he did, Mendenhall gave us a concert—three hours of Ella Fitzgerald. He announced simply, on the stage, "I know you've come to hear her, not me, so I'll get the hell out of here."

Last weekend, on the panel were President Mendenhall, now two years away from retirement, the junior-senior dean and two outstanding seniors.

We learned that much has changed.

An aristocratic, elderly alumna stood up and demanded to know why a course in bartending was now on the curriculum. "Well," explained Mendenhall soberly, "it increases students' chances of getting jobs in the summer, gets them out from behind the waitress tray and into the higher echelons of the labor force.

"Auto mechanics is on the curriculum. We feel that any institution which can turn out someone who can swim, bartend, short-order cook, repair a car and any home appliance is fitting its students to the needs of the times."

Last weekend we were told that the largest major today is psychology, that students are electing, that's right, "electing" a second science course "instead of something sexy like Joyce, Yeats and Eliot," that "junior year abroad" can be spent at Yale or other men's colleges, at Spellman and other black colleges, in Washington, D.C. (for government majors), and abroad. There will be 38 blacks in next year's class. Three years ago they would have elected to live in an all-black house under the Black Student Alliance (B.S.A.), but next fall they will probably prefer to be integrated. Separatism has died down, they say, out of lack of interest. We learned that there are no longer rules. "Twenty-four hour parietals" is the way they say men are allowed to spend the night in the rooms.

Other than that, things are pretty much the same.

Friday night was the class dinner. There were more than 100 classmates and husbands, everyone pinning name tags on at the door—with maiden and married names, of course. Most of the classmates were married, at least those who came back. Most of those who came back seemed to be fairly happy with who they were and what they had become. (Otherwise they might not have come back.) At the head table sat the outgoing and incoming class officers. They got corsages.

There seemed to have been some confusion about what to wear and the class of '63 was in everything from chiffon-and-rhinestone cocktail dresses to crew-neck sweaters and paint-spattered chinos.

There was a lot of screaming, tentative recognitions, comparing of notes . . . "How are you?" "Are you married?" "Do you have children?" "How many?" "Are you divorced?" "Do you work?" "Do you have a beau?"

There was a great deal of heavy and not-very-subtle scrutiny of the state of each other's faces and figures. "Look at all the lines in so-and-so's face" was overheard, and "I can't believe it. She hasn't changed a bit."

There was rather a lot of drinking. Mostly bourbon. Husbands were trying to establish their roles. "I carried someone's suitcase today and just now offered to hang up a coat," complained one. "And both times I've been called a male chauvinist pig."

After dinner (hardly anyone touched the Manischewitz wine), Mendenhall stopped by to chat and give a plug for intercollegiate athletics. (Smith is in the process of raising funds for a new gym). He talked about the increasing number of science majors. "That's because you've got some handsome science teachers," ventured a husband from the end of the table.

Only a few hisses.

"I admire your decision to bring your husbands," said Mendenhall. "I'm sure they'll agree that they came to kind of laugh but they'll take it seriously because they'll begin to understand why you can beat the hell out of them at anything you want."

There were three highlights to the class dinner. The first was an outgoing speech by class president Toni Goodale, who had set up the elections for new officers. (She is married to James C. Goodale, a senior vice president of the *New York Times.)*

There had been complaints of a rigged election. Toni explained the discrepancies in a parody of Nixon's recent statement on the Watergate. In jest she mentioned that only half the class had been sent ballots to save on postage. About half the group didn't get the point and a few outraged classmates approached her afterward with demands of an explanation for such dishonest behavior. Most of the husbands got the point.

Then came the reading of the class questionnaire which evoked no little hilarity.

Finally, as the dinner was breaking up, Sophomore Push, in their white dresses, came to serenade the alumnae. Push is a group of outstanding sophomores. "They used to be all prep school. Now they're nearly all public school," whispered a former Push member. "You can just tell."

Back at the houses, the husbands, who were sharing rooms with their wives, broke out the bottles, and everyone sat up and drank until all hours. The seniors who were still left had men sleeping over and they were having their own parties down the hall. They were borrowing the husbands' bourbon. "Oh yeah," said a young man with no shirt on. "We drink booze now."

———————

It was sophomore year that we were first allowed to smoke in the room. Senior year, we were allowed to have men in the rooms on Sunday afternoons from 3 until 5. Shades up, lights on, doors open and feet on the floor was the idea, if not the rule. Sunday was chosen so we could wash our

"Skirts for dinner apparently went out the same year men in the bedrooms came in."

hair on Saturday. Drinking was always out of the question. Nevertheless, there were always those who would try to ferment apple juice, and a few really daring types who would bring back what was left of the Chianti from Carlo's under their trenchcoats.

The idea that men now stay overnight was unsettling, but something I could live with. The idea of sharing a bathroom with strange men was something I could not. Saturday morning, half awake and groping down the hall in a flimsy nightgown to the communal bathroom (which housed sinks, toilets and bathtubs), toothbrush in hand, I was relieved to see that the "man inside" sign was not on the door. Inside, someone had done the wash the night before and hung it out to dry—two bras, several pairs of underpants and one athletic supporter. I had just begun my morning toilette when the door was flung open and two semiclad young men walked in and said good morning. One walked into a stall and the other began to brush his teeth.

"I'll just ignore them, pretend they are not here," I thought, "and go about my business." I casually took out my special cosmetic beauty grains and began washing my face. "Hey, what's that crap you're putting on your face?" said the one who was brushing his teeth. The other one came out of the stall and a third appeared with his shaving gear, commenting on the bad weather. "Look what she's putting on her face," said the first one to the others, who came over to stare. "It's hard to believe what girls will do to make themselves look good."

I found a private bathroom in the basement. Nonchalantly, I asked some of the students how they dealt with this problem, "not that it bothered me or anything." "Oh," said a very, very casual young woman. "At first you get embarrassed but you just have to get over it." I also asked what you do if you're having a man stay over and you have a roommate. "I got locked out of my room for the first two weeks of school," answered a freshman with little concern. "So I finally told her I didn't want to get locked out anymore. After that the three of us slept in the room. I'd try to find a spare bed on the weekends."

It used to be that we had to wear skirts for dinner. We had grubby rayon skirts we would fold up and put in our mailboxes so when the bell rang we could slip them over our jeans. Skirts for dinner apparently went out the same year men in the bedrooms came in.

The alumnae parade began at 9 a.m. Saturday, everyone in white, with whatever makeshift costume we had thought up. Ours were the worst. The theme was "Diary of a Mad Ms." and we wore black cardboard "Mad Hatter" hats. The person in charge of our costumes felt strongly that the parade should be abolished. They say you get more enthusiastic as you get older. The big argument for keeping the parade is that, overcome with emotion, the alumnae always donate big sums at the meeting afterward. Even one of my classmates cried. Another wore a "Nixon Knew" button on her blouse. I felt like an idiot in my black hat.

Clearly we were all outclassed by the three alumnae from the class of 1903 who didn't march all the way, but sat out the ceremonies in freezing weather. There was the singing of the alma mater. I never did know the words, but it goes something like "Fairest, fairest alma mater/You hold and claim us still . . . " In one part the words were changed from "the red sun where sinks he down to rest" to "sinks she . . . "

The outstanding juniors in hand-me-down pastel evening dresses carried the traditional ivy chain down and formed a circle so the seniors in white, carrying red roses, could weave in and out of it while singing the school song. The only possible way to tell that it wasn't 1932 was the group of black seniors, all with Afros, who banded together during the march.

President Mendenhall was there in his white suit, yellow (Smith's color) vest with senior pins for buttons, and white bucks. "Your bucks are so clean," I said to him. "Who polished them?" "My wife," he replied, without considering his words. "But, but," he quickly stammered, "I know how though."

Mendenhall has always had a rather flexible approach to the problems of being a male president at an all-female school, always the first to head off a crisis by being more open-minded than the instigators. Suggest something wild or radical and he's apt to pooh-pooh it for being old-fashioned. Reverse psychology. Under Mendenhall, probably more changes, both academic and social, have been made than under any other president at Smith. "There is this thing called change," he says. "Posture is a personal matter, something you resist or accept. You have to learn to distinguish between what is fundamental and what is taste and style. People get hung up on superficial changes like hair and clothes. But some of the changes develop essentially to ease the simple problems of human relations, to hold down insensitivities."

Since Mendenhall came there have been the assassinations, the civil rights movement, Vietnam, Cambodia, Kent State, the '68 conventions, Eugene McCarthy, the New Haven Panther trials, and the women's movement. Today he sees the students "working individually within the society, not radicalized but not apathetic, either." One of his main concerns is whether the college, a single-sex bastion, should become coeducational. Two years ago it was 60-40 in favor on campus. Today that has been reversed. He is in favor of Smith remaining single sex. "I think the whole thing is socially conditioned, and until society is equally conditioned, a non-coeducational college gives women the environment to come to identify their full capabilities, and it teaches women to learn how to live and work with other women." *The Sophian*, the school paper, "completely in the hands of the women's movement," demanded Mendenhall's resignation last year in favor of a woman. He didn't resign.

Does he ever get accused of being a male chauvinist pig?" "Nearly every day," he replied with a smile.

My year was the last one of apathy. We loved John Kennedy because he was so sexy and few *really* understood one of our classmates from Rhodesia, who had been declared persona non grata by her own country for speaking out against Rhodesia's racial policies.

Last year when I ran into my old government professor in an elevator, he looked at me and shook his head, "I never thought I'd see the day when you would be writing about politics." (I was a single-minded theater major, intent on becoming a movie star.) But in November of 1963 John Kennedy was slain and that clearly was the beginning of political and social awareness on campuses everywhere, including Smith College.

Today's students apparently are losing interest in movements, marches and major protests, or broad ideological positions, and are, instead, thinking more about what they can do or be themselves.

In several long discussions with different groups of students, most surprising was their apparent lack of interest in the women's movement. There is no large women's rights organization on campus. Although there is a women's center in Northampton, none of the students seemed to know much about it. They were all aware and sensitive to the issues, but not actively involved. "Why should we be," said one student, "we're all women here. There's no one to protest." Did Gloria Steinem's commencement address two years ago have much effect? "Oh, some of the parents were a little shook up when she said 'housework was s--t work.'"

Most of the seniors said they wanted to get married and have children (they figured they had already lived together with men and knew what that was like), but they were also interested in at least preparing for a career. Many of them had no idea what they wanted to do after graduation.

Ten years ago at Smith you wanted to get married and have children. "Ring by spring" was the goal of most seniors. If I couldn't be a movie star, then I wanted no part of any other career, oh maybe a volunteer job on the side. . . .

Saturday night was the second dinner for the class, this one held about a mile away in the Florentine Room of the Blue Bonnet Diner. It was there that the women and their husbands, having taken care of what they did and where they were the night before, began to talk about how they felt about it. There was a surprising number of husbands.

"When she wanted to marry me she suggested we go to the islands on our honeymoon so I could get the rest I needed," said one. "Marriage was the minimal consideration. She did the same thing with the reunion. She said we could do a lot of antiquing up here. Reunion was minimal. She's a smart girl. That's why I married her."

Husband No. 2 said he came because "she's wanted to come for five years. I couldn't refuse her because, after all, she's been living in my world for eight years. I thought it was her turn."

"We came back," said another husband, "because my wife is going through an identity crisis. She has two small children and doesn't work and she wanted to see what her other classmates were doing."

Some came without their husbands because "this is the first time since our marriage that I've been away from him and the children alone. He goes away a lot or we'll go away together. But I just wanted to be on my own for once."

There was little or no talk, except for jesting, about the women's movement. "We aren't active in it, but because of our independence and jobs we're aware of the problems women have," said a single schoolteacher. "It's our married classmates who're going through much more of a crisis. But they don't talk about it because they're stuck and they feel there's nothing they can do."

There were those who were practicing their professions while being married at the same time, but they were few, and even so spent much of the weekend talking about children, schools and birth control. The star mother of the class, who has four children and is very happy with her lifestyle, had her tubes tied. "I believe in zero population growth," she said, smiling a little guiltily.

After we ate, we sang happy birthday to one classmate and happy anniversary to another. Presents were given, a few hugs exchanged, a few tears shed. Just like 10 years ago. Everyone was feeling a bit foolish and sentimental. And there was an air of embarrassment when the Smiffenpoofs, the big college singing group, suddenly appeared to serenade us.

But the Smiffenpoofs looked the same as they had 10 years ago. They had shiny hair and long dresses and they "all looked like virgins," as someone pointed out. They sang the same songs too. In the middle of their concert, after they had asked two of our classmates, former "Smiffs," to sing, and after they had sung "Deep Purple" in honor of their fathers, they gave presents to two departing seniors. There were corsages. Everyone hugged the seniors.

The seniors cried.

—June 3, 1973

No! Not the 'Liebestod'
(and Other Tales)

By Paul Hume

T here I was, taking a shower at about 1:45 on a Saturday afternoon in
the Chicago Theological Seminary. In the shower room, that is. And
the guy who lived in the room next to mine came busting in and shouted,
"Hey, you are supposed to be playing at a wedding!"

"Not according to my schedule I'm not," I hollered back over the roar
of the water.

"Well the (then-current expletive deleted) with *your* schedule. A bridal
party is down in the chapel getting all ready for the 2 o'clock and you had
better get in there fast!"

Obviously that was no time for a man earning his way through the University of Chicago by playing at weddings to argue. I flung on a robe and
roared down the hall, through the narrow doorway that led into the organ
loft of the Thorndyke Hilton Chapel, leaped onto the bench in front of
the little Estey reed organ, switching on its motor as I jumped, and started
playing "Ah! Sweet mystery of life, at last I've found you."

Why just that particular little ditty? Well, I had played it at 12 o'clock,
so it was near the surface. And since I had not expected to play *this*
wedding at all, I thought it was hardly the time for me, the bride, the
groom, or any of their relatives to be choosy.

Ordinarily, brides could be as choosy as they wanted. It worked like
this. You could rent the Hilton Chapel, and thousands did, under Plan A,
B, C, or D. Under Plan A you got the chapel, period. A beautiful stained-
glass-illumined place holding about 54 guests.

Under Plan B you got the chapel and me. (Would you believe the going
rate for the organist under Plan B in those days? I wouldn't. I got a paltry
$2 per wedding. The seminary, which made all the arrangements, got $5
and kept $3. But I was hard up.)

If you got me, you could also send in a list of any music you wanted
played before, during, and after your wedding. Believe me, there is very
little under heaven that I have not played under Plan B.

Sometimes I did not believe the music myself. Like the time one bride's
list came in specifying that I was to play the "Liebestod" from "Tristan

und Isolde." In case your German does not carry you that far, that means the "Love Death." Oh well, who was I to question a bride's motives, much less her choice? So I busted my fingernails over that one. The "Liebestod" simply does not lend itself to the meager sounds of an old, wheezy two-manual Estey reed organ. But I felt eventually that I would triumph.

The morning of that wedding dawned with no hint of what the day would bring. Around 11:30, just after I had finished playing the 11, the phone in the music room of the seminary rang. With the feeling that it might be for me, I answered.

A shaking, not to say emotion-ridden, voice burst out: "Is this the organist for the wedding at 3 o'clock this afternoon?" I hardly had time to admit that I was when her soon-to-be-married voice rose to a mild shriek as she cried, "Well *don't* play the 'Liebestod.' I meant "Liebestraum!" If you make the switch from "Love Death" to "Dream of Love," you've got it.

I sighed into the phone, "okay," and began to think about Liszt's big, splashy showpiece. It had just as many problems for a small reed organ as the Wagner, unfortunately all of them different.

Speaking of playing "Ah! Sweet Mystery of Life" at 2 because it had been all right at noon, reminds me of one of the craziest moments in my entire matrimonial music experience. It happened about 3:55 one afternoon toward the end of a day in which I had played the 10, the 11, the 1, 2 and 3 o'clock jobs. Since the 4 p.m. bride had not sent in any list, I thought, "What was good enough for the 3 p.m. goose will do just fine for the 4 p.m. gander."

So, heading toward the Lohengrin Wedding March, I decided I had just enough time to play the Londonderry Air, which had been requested by the previous pair. (I must admit that I had been surprised to see the 3 p.m. bride, who was 45 if she was a day, because she had asked for the Londonderry Air not under that title but by one of its several alternatives, "Would God I Were A Tender Apple Blossom." However.)

Back to 3:55 p.m. I had hardly played the first four notes of the opening phrase, which immediately identify the piece to anyone who knows it, before a stately woman sitting in the front row, right-hand side (the groom's side at a wedding), stood up, turned around and, looking straight up to the organ loft, said in a loud, clear voice, "Please don't play any more of that!"

Friends, you have never heard an organist move so fast from one piece of music into another. I "went" by no known process of modulation into something safe by Cesar Franck, wondering as I went, "Now what got into her!"

You remember that the organ was up in a loft at the back of the chapel. Otherwise, how could I have played at that 2 p.m. affair while I was dripping wet from the shower? Well, after this 4 p.m. wedding, two elderly ladies who looked just the way Mildred Natwick and Helen Hayes look

"...they wanted Strauss waltzes, and only Strauss waltzes, for three hours."

these days as the Snoop Sisters, crept up from the front of the loft where they had been hiding out. It was the favorite spot for jilted fiancees and uninvited guests to see without being seen.

As they passed me while I was whaling the hell out of Mendelssohn, the Natwick one patted me gently on the shoulder and whispered sympathetically, "Don't mind her. Her husband used to sing 'Danny Boy' and she just can't stand it now." You can figure that one out for yourself; I have never been sure just how she meant it. "Danny Boy" was, of course, another name for the Londonderry Air or "Would God etc."

Plan D was my favorite of the four Hilton Chapel possibilities. While under Plan C they threw in a minister, it was the parties that went for Plan D who got the whole works: chapel, me, a minister, *and* not only decorations but full catering service. This last addition often meant for me the difference between going to bed hungry or eating well.

You see, the caterers knew that I depended on large numbers of weddings in order to survive. True, I got to live at the seminary by virtue of being the chapel organist and secretary to one of its professors. But that only gave me a room at slightly reduced rates. For weddings provided with the full splendors of Plan D, caterers would bring in sandwiches, punch, and gorgeous ice cream shaped like wedding bells, roses, brides, grooms and what have you.

Plan D weddings nearly always came late in the day. This often meant that before one of them, I could slip down to the enclosed garden patio where small receptions were set up, grab a couple of sandwiches and put some of the ice cream into my pockets to eat during the ensuing marriage ceremonies. The reason I could put it *in* my pockets was that dry ice was at that time a commercial novelty. The caterers, not yet being used to it, usually let the stuff get much too hard. Therefore they had to set it out way ahead of time, which made it both easy and safe for me to hide it in a pocket for a while. Of course I forgot once, but that was not fatal.

If June was the biggest month for Thorndyke Hilton weddings, May and October were close behind. I remember one June when I got $86 for my services. At $2 each you can see how many chose plan B, C, or D that month.

Once in a while a bride's mother would decide that they should have someone play the piano at the reception. For these occasions I was on my own about the fee. I got it up as high as $10 for one deal and was happily playing away when a rented butler came by and left a glass of champagne for me on top of the mini upright. Would you believe the bride's mother had no more on her mind than to swoop over and seize that glass, snorting to the rent-a-butler, "The champagne is *not* for the hired help." My mother always told me I should not be a musician.

Then there was the Chinese wedding reception at which they wanted Strauss waltzes, and only Strauss waltzes, for three hours. The fee was $25 and I would please wear a white palm beach coat. So I blew the $25 on a new coat, figuring I could wear it for years. For three hours I sat there and played up and down the Danube and in and out of the Vienna Woods. (I must admit they let the waiters bring me all the champagne I could drink and still play.) When it was over I started to stand up, but something wouldn't let me. It was the green paint from the chair in front of the piano. That was the strangest looking new, white palm beach jacket you ever saw. Maybe mother was right.

—June 2, 1974

On Losing One's Way in the City

By Tom Donnelly

I was headed for a magazine shop on Capitol Hill the other day when an elderly man who had been standing on a corner talking to a woman with a baby carriage called out to me, "Sir, I wonder if you could help me? I seem to be lost." He said, "Thank you for your trouble" to the woman who had been looking around helplessly and pointing in a northeasterly direction. The woman said she was sorry she hadn't been more help and went on her way.

The man smiled and said, "The baby carriage fooled me. It made me think she belongs to these parts but she's a stranger here, just like myself." He explained that he was visiting his nephew, had gone out for a walk, and now couldn't find his way back, though he knew the address, right enough. He said, "All this northeast and southeast business is so confusing."

He told me the address of his nephew's house, and I told him how to get there. For whatever reason, I looked back a few moments later and saw that he was walking in the wrong direction. I called out to him, made gestures indicating he should reverse his course and, when he responded with a bewildered frown, I walked back and told him I'd see him to his nephew's door since it was as easy for me to go that way as another.

The man (I judged him to be in his early 70s) protested that I shouldn't go to so much trouble and then smiled and said yes I should go to so much trouble or he might stay lost for days. He said, "I had the address and directions written down somewhere but now I don't know where. I seem to be forgetting everything these days. As the old saying goes, I'd forget my head if it wasn't fastened on."

As we walked along he told me that his nephew was in the antique business and just recently had the great good luck to come across some genuine Queen Anne chairs that some "old party" had hidden away in an attic. He said, "It's a funny thing the way people always think some ratty old book is a rare first edition worth thousands or some terrible old painting is a Rembrandt. Whereas they wouldn't know a really valuable antique if it rose up and bit 'em."

We spoke of politics and the weather and arrived at the address he had given me. The old man thanked me again but as I started away he said, "Please. Wait a minute. I have to tell you the truth. This isn't my nephew's house. My nephew lives in California. What I said about the furniture— that's all true—that was in a letter I got this week."

He was silent for a longish time. Finally I said, "What was it you wanted to tell me?" He said, "This is so silly. It's so stupid. This isn't my nephew's house, it's *my* house. I've lived in it for 40 years. And for 40 years I've walked around this neighborhood. And today I didn't know how to find my way back here! Isn't that *dumb*? It happened once before. You go out for a walk and suddenly you don't know where you are. It's all strange to you, as if you'd been set down in a street on Mars. *Dumb!* It's just plain dumb!"

I said it wasn't dumb at all. My first impression of the elderly man was that of one who was clear-eyed, erect, something of a personage. He was still all those things. He smiled and said, "Oh well—I'll be all right. As long as I can find somebody who knows where I'm going!" He walked slowly up the steps to his front door, got out a key, opened the door, turned back to nod at me and went inside.

—September 1, 1974

From Tupelo Rocker
to 20th-Century Institution

By Henry Mitchell

E lvis Presley will go on forever, it is understood, somewhat in the manner of Niagara Falls or Sarah Bernhardt — and here he has not even begun his farewell tours.

On the contrary, he is still active as yeast, and his concerts at College Park tonight and Saturday are sold out. All 40,000 tickets were bought in the first four days, and that phenomenon can only make you think.

It is 20 years now since Presley blew into Memphis from Tupelo, Miss., to make a record — he went to Sam Phillips of Sun Records (a noted diskery in country musics of several sorts) to see how much it would cost him to record a song. Phillips listened and the rest is, as you might say, history.

In no time at all, Elvis Presley did not have to pay a dime to record a song. (His first two cost him $4.) Instead, they paid him.

"He is the greatest box office attraction of all time," said a critic of the rocky arts recently.

Phillips released several Presley singles and it was soon clear to all (as it had been to Phillips from the first) that a new popular star was at hand. He has made some 30 motion pictures and sold more than 250 million records, and been a smash in Las Vegas, and had his clothes torn off by friendly fans and has had the rare privilege of infuriating staid persons for some years now, though he is in some danger of becoming an institution.

The first time this reporter ever laid eyes on Presley was about 1955 — the memory blurs a bit — probably shortly before his appearance on the old Ed Sullivan Show on television. He was already more than slightly famous in the country around Memphis, though the rest of the nation was not acutely aware of him.

A respected local newspaper critic, the late Bob Johnson, had been beating the drums for Elvis, whose voice did nothing whatever for me. A flash in the pan if I ever saw or heard one; still, the time came when it was necessary to try to figure out what made Elvis tick, or at least what made his fans scream.

When I got to his pleasant house on Audubon Drive, a brand-new dwelling that in Washington would cost perhaps $120,000, I was greeted by Elvis' mother, a soft, heavy woman whose open friendliness brought to mind the word "sweet." Nobody that I ever heard of could think of anything bad or unkind to say about Mrs. Presley, which was remarkable in a town that had its share of gossips and waspy folk.

The family, she said, had just got in from a family funeral over in Arkansas, over around Bald Knob, I believe, and they were tired.

"Why don't I come back another time?" I said, thinking it might be grim for Mrs. Presley to have a reporter about.

"Oh, no," she said, "we were expecting you." I had the strong feeling that with Mrs. Presley an agreement was an agreement, not lightly to be broken, no matter what you felt like when the time came.

"Elvis is taking a shower," she said. "Go on back."

"Well, I guess he'd like to be able to shower in peace," I said, "so why don't I wait here for him."

Mrs. Presley and I talked a few minutes, about nothing in particular, but enough to impress me with her shining quality, which many others have noted and which made her son's devotion to her more understandable than is sometimes the case.

She hollered back to Elvis and in very little time he appeared, still somewhat damp and informally dressed. The caution most people feel toward strangers did not seem to be part of this singer's nature, despite the fact he does not now permit interviews.

He called me "sir," which was rather upsetting since I was just past 30, but I could see he meant no malice by it. Indeed, he had the same open manner, the same artless eyes and the same natural dignity that you find in hounds of good quality.

He answered questions easily and naturally. Nobody now could possibly remember what was said, but it certainly was nothing very amazing, and I left with a feeling that he was a very clean wholesome youth of the sort that is so common in that part of the South — Mrs. Trollope commented on the attractive men of Tennessee she saw on her early 19th-century voyage up the Mississippi River, though she said we picked our teeth with our knives, which seemed unnecessary to say, and certainly not true now. Elvis was from over the line in Mississippi, but you would not know. His cheeks were pinker than his pictures showed.

It was hard to match this ideal type of rural youth with the abandoned pelvic movements with which he accomplished his songs, but that was part of his naturalness.

The Ed Sullivan Show, after a great storm of outrage from square viewers following his first appearance on that show, arranged for the cameras to show only the top half of him in his 1956 performance on that program.

It is hard to believe it now, but Presley's wiggles upset more people more severely than if the Secretary of State went to church in a fig leaf.

The Supreme Court decision integrating schools was still new, and a strong movement was afoot in the South to repudiate anything black in entertainment. Elvis' gyrations were widely considered jungle-like, primitive, savage, and therefore pro-black. Apart from that, people were more prudish then, more square—not that they behaved any better in those days, but bodily expression in public was more tame back then.

One of the good gray critics of the East uttered a common (for critics) sentiment, that Presley had no discernible singing talent at all in his "whine," and that his chief talent was "the virtuoso of the hootchy-kootchy."

That pretty much did it. Once the subteens discovered that people like critics, preachers and schoolmarms and TV network officials found Elvis lacking in taste, they embraced him with everlasting bonds, of course.

Old George Sokolsky, in a quite typical pontification of the day, demanded to know in his King Features syndicated column what was becoming of the modern generation. How, he wished to know, could Dr. Albert Schweitzer devote himself to "noble deeds" if the likes of Elvis Presley were to be idolized? Why should patriots bleed, why should people lead noble respectable lives (he mentioned the Queen of England, President Eisenhower and other examples) if anybody can just get up there and twang away and become rich and famous?

The whole trouble was that Elvis was reaching nerves that many critics did not have. Sexiness in a country lad is something more likely to strike a few million Americans than to occur to television critics, and the "whine" of Elvis was to the young a liberation cry.

Since columnists buy few records or movie tickets, as it turns out, Elvis' popularity streaked right over their indignant bodies and solemn warnings. Possibly no performer ever owed less to the press, except insofar as its alarms taught kids how to spell his name right.

The only other time I interviewed Presley was in New York when he returned from military duty in 1960. He still called reporters "sir" and still had pink cheeks. He was still very much an entertainment force to reckon with, it seemed to me, though the full collapse of rock and roll was authoritatively predicted by those who ponder trends, as revealed to them in the back of their brains without special regard to the public's rude habits.

His voice was different after Germany, at least to my ears, and his style more polished or artful, but if this was anything but my own imagination, few noticed it.

Some who first swooned for Elvis are grandmothers now. Presley himself is 38 now. And unless you think way ahead, you still find the house sold out.

—September 27, 1974

The Loneliness of Being First

By Joel Dreyfuss

T ed Poston died last week at the age of 67. He was the first black reporter on the *New York Post* and for long periods of time the only black reporter on any major white-owned newspaper in the country.

Being the "first black" at something is one experience many members of my generation have been spared and I was not particularly impressed by the disheveled old man who limped over to my desk in the cramped city room of the *New York Post* to shake my hand the first day I worked there.

I wasn't impressed because some of the young hotshot editors shrugged him off when questioned, and I was ignorant about what he had done and particularly ignorant about what it meant to be "the first."

By the time I got there, Ted wasn't as fast or as productive as he used to be and there were younger people—less talented than Ted in his prime— in the rewrite bank who handled the major stories.

But as time went by I got to know Theodore Roosevelt Augustus Major Poston, and when he wasn't suffering from poor circulation or battling a deadline, we would sit at the only window in the newsroom. We would watch the ships glide down the East River, under the Brooklyn Bridge into New York harbor and he would weave those marvelous stories about his experiences in the South.

He talked about a time any black who went into the Deep South asking questions took his life into his own hands and survived by the speed of his feet and the quickness of his wit. In Ted's case he had the added weapon of humor. Like the time the mayor of a small town introduced Ted to the sheriff as a reporter from "one of them Noo Yawk papers."

"Do you work for a white paper or a colored paper?" the sheriff wanted to know. Ted kind of ruminated for a minute and said:

"Well, Sheriff, down here you all have a law that says if a man has one drop of black blood, he's black. I'm the drop of black blood at the *New York Post* so I guess it's a colored paper." And Ted would throw his head back and laugh that big infectious laugh that reminded one he had a tremendous joy of life and have lived it to the hilt.

But being that drop of black blood was not easy for Ted in an era when a black man had to constantly prove himself not only to the world but to his editors.

Like how Ted got his job at the *New York Post* in 1939. He had been city editor of the *Amsterdam News,* New York's top black newspaper and was fired after he helped organize the Newspaper Guild chapter there.

He went to the *Post* and asked for a job. "If you can bring me a front-page story, I'll hire you," the man said. Ted got on the subway and rode up to Harlem. He had fallen asleep and missed his stop when a noise outside the subway car woke him up. Several black men had surrounded a white in a telephone booth and were threatening him. Ted jumped off the train as a black policeman arrived on the scene. The cop rescued the beleaguered man, who turned out to be a process server who had been trying to hand a summons to Father Divine. The story was on the front page of the paper the next day and Ted was back in journalism.

Most of the readers never knew Ted Poston was black. He was just a big-name reporter who covered everything important. He had exclusive interviews with Huey Long and Wendell Willkie. He covered stories in the South like the Scottsboro rape trial, where they made Ted use the back entrance to the courtroom and had him sit in "nigger's heaven" with the other blacks.

And when afternoon papers lived or died by the strength of their rewrite men, Ted sat at the center of the bank digesting reports from a dozen white reporters and turning out a concise, well-written story.

Ted didn't like to dwell on his own problems at work, his isolation, the racial slurs and the rebuffs that were so commonplace for blacks in the 1930s and '40s. For his generation, such incidents were a "given," a fact of life that we "post-riot" journalists would usually be spared.

My respect for him grew when I was doing research for some articles on blacks in New York. I came across a series done by the *Post* in the late 1950s, after a Southern editor challenged the paper to look at the conditions for blacks in its own city.

Eight white reporters did the legwork and Ted, still the only drop of black blood, wrote the stories, with that flowing graceful prose he also used in the handful of short stories about his childhood in Hopkinsville, Ky., that are scattered about anthologies of black literature. Until late in the 1960s, the usual method of covering black life for most urban papers was for black reporters to do the research and white reporters to do the writing and analysis. Ted Poston's reversal was but another of his casual "firsts."

The walls of Ted's home on quiet, tree-lined Chauncey Street in Brooklyn were covered with plaques and awards and invitations to inaugural dinners from U. S. Presidents.

But when I was learning about journalism few mentioned Ted Poston except other black reporters. He was yet another Invisible Man, who somehow never won the Pulitzer Prize, as no black reporter ever did. And in 33 years at the *New York Post,* he never went beyond the reporters' ranks, a fate that still binds most black journalists.

If we, as young black reporters, grew to respect him, it was because we had to fight some of the same battles all over against many editors, publishers and readers whose racism had been changed more in form than in substance by Ted Poston, Lester Walton at the *New York World,* or Earl Brown at the *Herald Tribune.*

And when we, comforted at least by our token numbers, were in the throes of combat, we wondered at the strength of men like Poston. We wondered whether we would have stuck it out for 33 years. We wondered whether we would have been willing to take the back stairs to the balcony.

And we wondered whether we would have thought it worth the decades of constant pressure and loneliness to eventually see a trickle of blacks penetrate the lily-white newsrooms of America, no longer sitting in the balconies but somehow still virtually excluded when it came time to cover the really big stories such as Attica, Watergate or the peace talks.

And I wondered, had I been Ted Poston, whether I could have avoided being bitter about a newspaper that had taken so much from me without giving me much in return. And I wondered, had I been Ted Poston, whether I would have had the strength, the unselfishness and the grace to walk across the room to an arrogant young black reporter who thought he was going to conquer the world, to thrust out my hand and genuinely say, "Welcome."

—January 19, 1974

A Big, Big Man

By Nicholas von Hoffman

A
h, Lyndon, you're not cold yet and they're calling you great. That's what happens when one politician dies: The rest of them call him great, but, Lyndon, you deserve better than patrotic hagiography. You were better than the eulogistic junk they're saying at the memorial services.

Lyndon, you got your teeth into us and we got our teeth into you. Those five years of you in the White House were a barroom brawl, and, just four years ago almost to the day, when we staggered out of the saloon, dusty and bloody, we didn't hate you anymore. We understood better how you got us into Vietnam than how Nixon got us out and we liked you more, you cussed, cussing, bullheaded, impossible, roaring, wild coot.

You had your credibility gaps and your silent, sullenesses, but we read you. Oh, man, Lyndon, did we know you! You were the best and the worst of ourselves, the personification of our national deliriums. You were always so completely, so absolutely you. Kennedy had Pablo Casals to play for him, Nixon's got Pat Boone to pray for him, but you, Lyndon, you had Country Joe and the Fish singing songs soaked in four-letter words at you.

They're not bringing it up at your funeral, but you had a famous dirty mouth. By most accounts the only man in the history of the White House who could cuss better than you was Andrew Jackson. We on the outside knew how to make obscenity a tool of eloquence, too. We could recognize you, not as a Great American, but as an American man. But you did your own hating and your own cussing, not like these stiffs they've got in there now who import Sinatra and the dregs of Las Vegas to call people filthy names for them.

That wasn't your style, Lyndon. You let it all hang out; but then, man, even when we hated you most, we knew you at least had something. Your dogs had names and you pulled their ears. No official court photograph animal for you to have its picture taken as you asked the mutt's name. Sure, you could be gross. Getting your picture taken in the hospital bed, pulling up your pj's so we could all see the scar on your belly, and they still whisper around Washington that you used to receive ambassadors from foreign countries stepping out of the shower bath nekkid as a jaybird, as they say where you came from.

199

And still you kept your dignity. Maybe because everything you did, good, bad, indifferent or just funny, was so big. You were Andy Jackson's boy. Immoderate and big. No rein on yourself. They say even after the second heart attack you couldn't bring yourself to quit smoking.

Lyndon, you were immoderate, and greedy. You outdid all the rest of us hungry Americans for reaching out and grabbing, fingers always stretched for grasping, but now they're saying after your death that you divided America, left her all split and bleeding. It is true that if ever a man had a reach which exceeded his grasp, it was you, you wicked old devil, but you redeemed this country even while dropping us, plop!, in the middle of the Vietnam Big Muddy.

You fought our Second Civil War and carried out our Second Reconstruction. The credit has gone to John Kennedy but he doesn't deserve it. He had the speechwriters to say fair, promising things, while he and his brother appointed racist judges to the federal bench. Lyndon, it isn't fair to you that Jack Kennedy's picture should be tacked up on the walls of so many poor black homes, Kennedy who regarded blacks as but another pressure group to be tricked or placated.

But some of us remember. Some of us who were in a room in the public housing project across the street from Brown's Chapel in Selma, Ala., that night you talked to a joint session of Congress in your rich, half-Southern accent and we saw you on TV say to them, "We shall overcome." Lyndon, you did your best to overcome. Where Jack Kennedy reacted with official indifference to what happened to black people, you shook and threatened the federal bureaucracy from the FBI to the Department of Agriculture to make them redeem the pledge of equal protection.

Much of what you started is being abandoned, discarded and attacked, and much of it ought to be. You were so impulsive. You tried to solve social problems like a drunken hardware wholesaler trying to snag girls in a Paris nightclub. You drank so much of the social betterment bubbly the nation woke up with a hangover, but God bless you for it. Every right-living nation ought to go on that kind of a drunk every so often, and even if you went about it the wrong way, you got us thinking about what we should be doing. Your Medicare and Medicaid aren't exactly winners, but thanks to you our people will have the health protection.

You were a big 'un, Lyndon. We're going to miss you, you old booger, and we're going to know, regardless of official proclamations, you deserve better than to be saluted, left at half-mast and forgotten.

—January 24, 1973

A Visit to the Adirondacks

By Michael Kernan

When we returned to the East in 1967 after years in California, I decided I should visit my Uncle Nick and bring along my 12-year-old son, partly because it was the thing to do with a namesake and partly because I knew the two Nicholases would get a kick out of each other.

I must have been 9 or 10 myself when my father first took me to the fox farm. The drive was endless: past the aspen meadows of Woodgate, golden and dancing in the failing autumn light, up through the Adirondack foothills to Old Forge, Blue Mountain Lake, Paul Smith's (where we had supper in a tavern that was all antlers and varnished pine and joke placards over the bar that I didn't understand for sure) and steadily north into the cold night, I by now feeling definitely carsick and tired of staring into the underbrush in hopes of seeing a deer, as my father had suggested.

It was after midnight when we stopped at last outside the farmhouse. The roof was the steepest I had ever seen. The walls were stucco, and around the base, supported by a two-foot chickenwire fence, leaves had been packed for insulation. The front door had been nailed shut for years, so we went in by the cheery if faintly lit kitchen.

My uncle must have been about 50 then, a year younger than my father, with the same long Celtic face and fleshy nose and the mildly satirical blue eyes that made him look rather like the writer Nabokov, but less organized. He wore a gray woolen shirt and rough woodsmen's pants and one of those leather bow ties on an elastic.

"Come on in, have some syrup." He led us into the main room where Howard Taylor, Indian-faced and solitary, who owned the farm and had inherited it when foxes still inhabited the runs and pens, stood before the huge stone fireplace.

Dazed by the sudden light and talk, I was seated at the table and given a saucer of pure maple syrup. It was my introduction to the exotic and fascinating eating habits of the Adirondack bachelor.

During the next week I was to taste the great Oneida County cheese that curled your teeth and that I wasn't allowed at home, black tea with lumps of cream from great mugs, milk, honey and dense homemade bread all mushed around in a bowl and slurped with a spoon, the beautiful steak that my father had brought and that was fried to leather, and slumgullion containing chunks of what Nick called, gravely, "our special lamb," or out-of-season deer. Slumgullion was a sort of permanent stew, kept on the stove in a large iron pot and augmented with leftovers day by day, week by week, its character changing with each meal, but always good except when you got a piece of something that had been there for two months.

While I sipped syrup and chomped an immense thick slice of bread, I listened, as I was to listen all week, to the anecdotes that came in sausage-strings, unendingly, often cryptic or half-heard, about the local people who gradually became to me mythic, larger than life, antic figures in a mural:

Fisherman esthete Harry Candee, who for some reason I saw as a big man with a great curving belly and the back-tilted head of an asthmatic, driving his friends mad with boredom as he recounted his trout sagas complete with roster of flies used.

Old, bearded, stocking-capped Albert Debar, whose ancestors named Debar Mountain (3,306 feet) and who sat forever on his cabin porch to be pointed out by passersby.

Even Howard Taylor himself, the prototype American tinkerer who had built the farm's electrical system himself from powerdam to generator to wiring, who could if required take advice politely though not gracefully (iron-gray hair falling over slitted eyes, lean jaw munching with slow, absent circular motions the cheese on which he subsisted) but who would infinitely rather find out for himself.

(Once, to remove a boulder for his new dam, he designed a derrick, had it welded onto a pickup truck and drove the thing up from Utica. Forgot about the railroad underpass at Remsen, had to detour 200 miles, burned out a bearing, and when at last he completed the dam — seven years later — he found his new lake was flooding state land, causing a lot of angry letters from Albany.)

Aside from Howard, the only one of these storied figures I actually met was Charlie Briggs, a part-time hermit who lived at the foot of the mountain by Debar Pond in the Castle. We walked there one morning, down the three-mile driveway almost lost among the alders, aspens and birches, past the nearly obliterated racetrack built by the original owner, a turn-of-the-century Bavarian sportsman. The rambling structure itself, four stories high, with turrets, bay windows, widow's walks and 11 chimneys, was falling apart. Most of the windows were broken. Paper sagged in curving swatches from the walls, and the floors were covered with crumbled plaster from the discolored ceilings.

We called, got no answer. Charlie's flat-bottomed boat was beached. On the warped, paintless porch steps stood four fishing rods, dried worms baked onto the hooks. A hunting knife was stuck into the top step beside a smear of blood and fish scales. We went inside, stepping over piles of plaster, past the 12-foot-thick concrete firewall, up the back stairs to a tiny room.

"I had wanted to keep Uncle Nick to myself, preserved in my memory..."

"Come in, come in, come in." Charlie consisted of bright squirrel eyes above ragged gray whiskers that grew up out of his red wool shirt, buttoned against the 95-degree heat. He wore a greasy red toque.

"Thought you only wore the beard in the winter to keep warm," Nick said.

Charlie ran his hand up his jaw. "Naw. Summer too. Keeps the flies off."

He shaved about every four years.

At the foot of his cot detective magazines were piled waist-high. A fine Hallicrafters battery radio stood on a shelf. By the bed was a bucket of kitchen matches. Cans were stacked on a table by the Coleman stove.

The men talked; I listened. Every time someone held up a match or cigarette butt to be disposed of, Charlie said, "Throw it out the winda." Finally I sidled around to the single window that overlooked a large interior courtyard. Directly below was an unbelievable heap, an empire of boxes, bedsteads, chairs, planks, magazines, curtains, rugs, bathtubs, old tires, fresh garbage and thousands and thousands of tin cans. The stack came almost to the window. It must have been 30 feet high. It sprawled in its miscellaneous grandeur across the entire courtyard.

I beckoned my father over to see, and later he nudged Nick to take a look. On the way home they chortled, "Throw it out the winda." It became a family byword.

My uncle always distanced himself from the people he lived among, and they sensed it and called him mister, many of them. He had been a promising law student once, I was told, but was such a mean, aggressive, falling-down, fighting, impossible drunk, even for a drinking family, that the rest of them brushed him under the rug, banished him for life to be the foxfarm caretaker for Howard Taylor, who worked at the family law offices.

To me the only thing more appalling than the family's ruthless Victorian shame was his apparently meek acceptance of the life they had decreed for him. But perhaps I never knew the whole story.

There were no women in that life, aside from an upholstered mother-hen neighbor, a Mrs. Gale, who fried the steaks and brought homemade bread and great white soft, floury sugar cookies. With Howard and my father, who had married late, and Rob, a walleyed troglodyte Taylor cousin who collected lawnmowers, we made a bachelor household whose serenity was seriously disturbed only once in my memory.

That was the summer we brought a 7-year-old cousin up from New York to tag after my disdainful 15-year-old self. The night before we returned it was decided that Frankie needed a bath. Desperately.

The three men (Rob had disappeared as usual) sat on three separate lumpy sofas avoiding each other's eyes.

"You're the married man," Nick told my father.

"It's your house," my father told Howard.

"You took him through that swamp," Howard told Nick.

"No," said Frankie, who wore what has been called the deadpan expression of the born heller.

"Well —" Nick pushed himself erect at last " — let's all do it, then. Come on upstairs."

"No," said Frankie.

An hour later they got him into the bathroom, and I heard the water running into the lion-footed bathtub beneath whose faucet the porcelain had been stained brown by a 70-year trickle of icy iron-tasting water. Scrabblings, thumpings, mutterings and the clear high voice of Frankie.

"Here, get that leg," Nick shouted.

"It's too hot," said my father.

"Watch it! The soap!"

That was Howard.

"No," said Frankie.

"You wouldn't want your mother to see you all dirty, would you?" asked Nick. "She'll whale you."

"And you couldn't come back here," my father said.

That did some good, for I heard no more voices, only occasional puffings and gruntings and the musical squeak of heels in the tub. The four of them came down together around midnight. They all looked pretty clean.

So many things had changed by the time I moved East: the Castle had long since burned down, and the foxfarm too, and Charlie Briggs had died, and Howard Taylor, and I gathered that Nick lived in a trailer on the house site overlooking the drained pond where once I had launched my sailboat with a crew of panicky grasshoppers and had shot frogs with my BB gun and had caught a 14-inch rainbow to my speechless excitement.

I was planning to take my son there in the spring. Then it was the following fall. I didn't relish the drive all the way up from Washington, but I also hated to spend the money on flying to Plattsburgh and renting a car.

A year passed, and another. We got it all organized one June, and I wrote Nick to expect us. He wrote back from a nursing home in Malone: he was in his 80s, after all, and trailer life had proved too rugged. He signed the letter, penciled on lined yellow paper, as he had always signed his polite, formal replies to my childhood Christmas cards. Affectionately, Nicholas E. Kernan.

We didn't go that time. I forget why. My son went off to visit friends somewhere. And the next summer we all went to California.

One day, fishing north of San Francisco in a murmurous, leaf-flecked forest stream, I spotted a squirrel, very close, watching us. By instinct I moved out one hand slowly, fingers together, palm down, toward the boy to get his attention without startling him into sudden movement. Then I indicated the squirrel with my glance.

I wondered where I had got that gentle gesture, and all at once it came to me: my uncle and I had been fishing from Charlie's boat on Debar Pond years before, dozing away the afternoon while half-dead bullheads flopped at our feet. My uncle's hand softly poked my knee just that same way, so I wouldn't start, and I followed his gaze without moving. There on the shore stood a gigantic black bear, rarely seen in the Adirondacks, paws up, sniffing, not 20 feet away. An instant later it whirled and crashed off through the brush.

In the vivid flash of that recollection I made up my mind. We had to visit Nick. I was determined. This fall for sure, I said. Even if I had to take the kid out of school. Even if I had to get a leave. It was 1971.

I fixed a date, a weekend in September, looked up plane schedules and priced rental cars. All I needed now was the address and, if possible, the phone number so I could make sure he would be ready to see us.

By chance I ran into a cousin (yet another cousin) who was passing through town and, knowing that she kept better tabs on the family than I, told her of my planned visit and asked if perhaps she knew the name of Nick's nursing home in Malone.

"Oh heavens," the cousin said. "Why, Nick died almost a year ago. You mean to say nobody contacted you?"

It was as though, I decided later, I hadn't really wanted to go. It was as though I had wanted to keep my Uncle Nick to myself, preserved in my memory just as the family had hidden him away so long ago. I should have remembered that the past doesn't need any help from me, that the past is invulnerable and changeless, and that it is the present that is fragile.

—September 17, 1972

Father and Sundays Past

By Michael Kernan

I can tell a show-biz joke about Dean Martin's liver or Howard Hughes' money as well as the next guy (though I do tend to laugh along with my audience), but there is a certain family anecdote that—hilarious as it seems to me, even after 30 years—I never can seem to put across. Is it just a matter of technique? Of filling in the background? I don't know.

W e lived on a farm in upstate New York. We were not farmers. I never did know exactly why we bought the place with its 40 acres and soaring elms, its orchards and pastures, its grand porch and halls and huge bedrooms, but I understand that it was one of those old estates people were always picking up in the '30s for a few thousand. Also my father, defeated for a second term in the New York State Senate and suffering from lung trouble, found it convenient to retire just then.

That first year we, or rather the couple who ran the farm for us, did everything: made cider and wine, which we drew from spigoted barrels in the cellar; made maple syrup and butter and preserves, raised all our vegetables and reaped eggs and broilers from the henhouse where I was later to preside over my 4-H project: a brood of 500 chickens, every single one of whom I despised from chickhood for their filthy way of life, their obstinacy and their incredible, infuriating stupidity. In the years that followed, our ambition waned and we sold the land gradually to a Midas-like truck farmer who was building an empire all around us.

My father always retained the sunny, remote placidity of a tenth child in a formal, urban Victorian family, remembered by his older sisters as a small, round-eyed boy swinging on the front gate in silent absorption or plugging snowballs at the iron deer on the lawn next door, hurling for hours with steady ferocity, wrists raw from the snow bangles on his mittens, while his mother called him for supper and night turned the lawn into a blue pock-marked battlefield.

His great gift as a politician had been an ability to converse instantly and easily with absolutely anyone: bus conductors, scrofulous blind pencil sellers, jowly men with veined noses in city hall who disposed of me with a professional smile, the grinning man at the cigar counter of his club who sometimes gave me a gold net bag of chocolate coins while I waited for my father to come out of the bar, the Italians on Bleecker Street, many of whom could speak hardly a word of English and to whom my father made a celebrated campaign speech (it was on a street corner, and from the beapostered truck in which the party chieftains had arrived as in a tumbrel, my father reached down for a hand to help him to the pavement, addressing the nearest face with an innocent, fervent and utterly trusting appeal: "Hey Buster. . . ." whereupon the man grinned and helped him down), which was to sing "O Sole Mio" in his quavering vibrato and a conductor-like waving of both arms when he came to the third bar, for he knew no more words. The crowd laughed and miraculously took up the song. I realize that this sounds like a slightly repulsive gesture, like an ethnic joke, but for some reason people almost always accepted the man (he had hunted for jobs in an era when factories still put out signs saying No Irish Need Apply, after all) in his sophomoric innocence.

At the farm he dealt with carpenters, plumbers, icemen, the Midas neighbor and his succession of blue-jawed tenant farmers, the state highway crew he inveigled into plowing our long driveway one winter morning, the parish priest, the professors at the local college and their wives and my mother's friends, who tended toward bead necklaces and those baroque silk scarves one brought back from Venice.

One summer day when my father was defeathering a chicken in the yard, the milk truck (we had long since got rid of our cow and used as a playhouse the windowed stall that my mother had decreed for her the instant she saw a stanchion up close) pulled into the drive and I heard my father call the milkman: "Hey Buster . . ." and ask his advice about chicken plucking, and the next time I looked the milkman was demonstrating while my father watched. Then he spotted me. "Come on over here, Buster," he said, "and see how he does this," so I came over and suddenly I was the one plucking the chicken. Under my father's tutelage I also became an expert scyther, lawn cutter and ice cream cranker.

When we lived in California briefly, we had a blind Skye terrier whom my father used to walk among the tall, bearded palms of La Jolla, and apparently the dog's clouded eyes attracted attention, that and my father's gentle affability, for gradually he built up a stable of bridge-playing dog lovers: retired courtesans, movie producers, tycoons recovering from heart attacks, deaf lady distance swimmers and petered-out womanizers, not the kind with pencil mustaches and undulant creamy white hair, but seamy-cheeked, sad-eyed wanderers who once had been loved too forgivingly.

They all, all of them, called him Mike. It was one of the crosses my mother had to bear, though she at least no longer had to sit on platforms

"The giant stopped, planted his staff in the road and gazed at us."

with him at rallies (there to be reminded of the time she had said, upon being introduced to the senior Senator Wagner of New York: How do you do, Senator Vahgner) or attempt to chat with city hall's veined noses.

After our return from California, my father and I spent a lot of time on the porch listening to the Dodger games and smoking his oval cigarettes. This is how I still see him, arms regally resting on the arms of a rustling rattan chair, the everlasting cigarette between his fingers, his fedora well down over his high Celtic forehead as he stared out across the valley with that radio-listener gaze.

We had read about the Russian monastery in the papers and thought to break through February Sunday afternoon ennui by driving the 20 miles to the place, founded by refugee Georgian monks on the bare rolling hills above the Mohawk River. Folding the map, we drove along a soggy ridge, into a valley and onto a mud track that threatened to disappear and leave us marooned in a slushy field of corn stubble. Let's turn around, my mother said. No, we'll ask somebody, my father said. A depressing prospect, for we had not seen a living creature since we had left West Winfield.

Amazingly, however, when we reached the end of the valley, we saw the top of a brilliant gold onion dome, an eerie sight on the steppes of upstate New York. And a moment later we noticed a man walking toward us. He wore black robes that reached to the ground and that were fringed with mud. A huge pectoral cross dangled to his belly. His curly black beard came all the way down to the cross and all the way up to his great dark Byzantine eyes. With his kamelaukion, a black structure jutting fantastically up and out from his temples a foot into the air, he seemed nine feet tall. Striding ponderously with staff in hand, he approached us as though about to impart some thunderous cosmic news. I later realized that the mud was making him walk in that slow, apocalyptic fashion, but at the time his high-held head and the supernatural dignity of his stare shocked us into reverent silence.

We drew nearer. My father rolled down the window. The giant stopped, planted his staff in the road and gazed awesomely at us. I waited for his mouth to open, wondering madly if actual sounds would come out, recognizable words though of course not in any language we would understand, or if, as seemed more likely, an unearthly gonging or the bray of a shofar or simply a cloud of silvery flakes would issue from the blackness of that unbelievable, phantasmagoric jungle of hair, to float sparkling and glittering to the ground.

208

My father stopped the car and learned out the window.

"Hey Buster . . ." he said.

The rest of us froze in horror.

But the beard broke open in a radiant, spade-toothed grin of welcome, camaraderie and instinctive recognition. "You are lost?" he roared. "I can help?"

Well, there it is, and now that I see it in black and white it doesn't look so funny to me, either. Still, as I recall that lost Sunday afternoon, an afternoon that exists now only in the minds of myself and my sisters (unless the monk is alive somewhere, his beard white, his face sunken, his mind as gentle and clear as a summer day even though dimmed now and then by a succession of clouds driven on fierce stratospheric winds unfelt by the watcher), I can conjure up that antic encounter, and I suppose I must resign myself to the realization that it can never be transmitted to anybody else and that in a few more years it will have disappeared utterly, without a trace, like a shout.

—January 24, 1972

Recalling a Pacific Hell

By Henry Mitchell

You know your places: God be with you all.
— Henry V to his troops at Agincourt (Act IV, Sc. 3)

O ld men forget, but once each year on a certain day they feast their neighbors and tell great thumping lovely lies about their battles.

It was always that way: The men at Salamis or the ones at Shiloh used to twist ears and wheeze out memories, and some of them were true. They are stories good men teach their sons.

So last night the Marines of Tarawa got together, some of them, at the Center House of the old Marine Barracks. That's where you go after ceremonial parades to bend elbows if your doctor still lets you.

Last night there was no parade, unless you count the men who couldn't come, but there was some elbow-bending still and some fellowship that even strangers shared.

Tarawa, with its island beach of Betio (you call it TAIR-uh-wuh, and Betio rhymes with ratio), is half a mile square in the Central Pacific, or 18 times the size of the White House lot. On it, 30 years ago yesterday, men fought and some of them, some last night, have lived to see old age.

Lt. Gen. Julian Smith is 88, if you can believe it, and Gen. David Shoup, who commanded the Second Marines there and later was commandant of the Marine Corps, is now retired and not so young as formerly. "There are more damned stories about Tarawa," Shoup said. "Every man there has a different one."

Those with a taste for figures can compute how the 6,000 corpses filled up the 320 acres, more or less, and those fond of pictures can still dig up old stills and movies of the 75 hours and 42 minutes that began that November morning in 1943.

But the plain truth is, one blasted palm tree is much like another and broken men look much alike. Pictures don't tell you much. Men do:

"It was just this time of day," said Gen. Smith, gazing at the burning logs from his leather armchair, "that I was getting the bad news. Every regiment was reporting 100 dead: I had to ask for reinforcements, 'The is-

210

sue is in doubt.' But ultimately — well, I never had any doubt how it would at last turn out. But talk to David Shoup — more than any other man the credit of Tarawa is his." Smith was division commander working from his ship offshore. Shoup was unit commander on the island.

"The significance of Tarawa, I would say," Gen. Shoup said after stretching himself before the fire a minute, "is that there they [the Japanese] learned we could kick the s--t out of them."

"It was the first time," said Lt. Gen. William K. Jones, who had brought in the reinforcing Sixth Marines, "we had a big landing in rubber boats. I well remember saying to myself as we landed with the bullets flying, 'Jones, what the hell are you doing here?'"

"It was the first time we were tested," Shoup had said, against a powerfully dug-in Japanese fortress with the whole force of the enemy within a few yards of the landers.

Most of the 30 men last night had had some command position at Tarawa, but some hadn't. Bob Sherrod was there, who rode the boat on the first day as a reporter for *Life*. Earlier in the day he had been in New York with Frank McGee on the "Today Show," but made it back in time for the reunion. He didn't say on television what he'll say if you ask him, or what he tells you in his book, *Tarawa,* for that matter — that he was so scared at first, he didn't even feel the emotion of fear, yet his bones trembled.

His bones understood things better than his brains.

Six million pounds of explosives were dropped by air on the tiny island (killing virtually no Japanese, as it turned out).

Nothing went quite as planned. Life and death rarely do, and God knows wars don't. The tides didn't work right and the landing boats didn't clear the barrier reefs blocking the beach. They had to use amphibious tanks, alligators, which were not so plentiful and slowed things down. Also, they made great targets in their fewness. Men got out in belly-deep or neck-deep water, some of them trudging 700 yards through the waves as the 5,000 Japanese who were secure in their concrete emplacements tried out their machine guns.

"I figured our gear weighed 112 pounds," said retired Col. Roy Elrod.

"So if you stumbled into an underwater bomb hole," said former Col. Elery Poppe, "you went on down unless somebody could pull you out. Even if you weren't wounded."

For all that, more than half the 685 marines who died in a few hours, died on land, jumping inside enemy emplacements to fight.

The first man Sherrod saw die, died in a ludicrous accident on ship, not the way a warrior would want to go: His plane fell off the catapult and he drowned. They didn't have to bury him at sea, it was already tended to by fate, but they said for him the psalm, "Out of the depths have I cried," and they sang him a rest to the paradise of God because that was his particular faith.

But others died easier, in the sense that even in their bad time they could easier see that the lives of their companions hung on their arms, and on their deaths.

Still others, it was learned, even now have no stars or crosses to mark their faith, or anything else, except the big sea that men sail on or the air a republic breathes. So these were remembered well in flowing cups last night, and in some guarded allusions, and in a minute where everybody bowed his head, a reunion custom.

When all the men, most of them with their wives, had eaten a good supper and laughed at each other's jokes, then they thought, each one alone, of his old companions.

So when they had got some kind of comfort from each other's yarns and bull, they then went home and were soon (God willing) sound asleep.

—November 21, 1973

The Corps

By Henry Allen

PARRIS ISLAND, S.C. — He is seething, he is rabid, he is wound up
tight as a golf ball, with more adrenalin surging through his hypothalamus than a cornered slum rat, he is everything these Marine recruits with
their heads shaved to dirty nubs have ever feared or even hoped a drill
instructor might be.

He is Staff Sgt. Douglas Berry and he is rushing down the squad bay of
Receiving Barracks to leap onto a table and brace at parade rest in which
none of the recruits, daring glances from the position of attention, can see
any more of him under the rake of his campaign hat than his lipless mouth
chopping at them like a disaster teletype: WHEN I GIVE YOU THE
WORD YOU WILL WALK YOU WILL NOT RUN DOWN THESE
STEPS WHERE YOU WILL RUN YOU WILL NOT WALK TO THE
YELLOW FOOTMARKS. . . .

Outside, Berry's two junior drill instructors, in raincoats over dress
greens, sweat in a muggy February drizzle which shrinks the view down to
this wooden World War II barracks, to the galvanized Butler hut across

Photo by Frank Johnston

213

We don't promise you a rose garden

the company street, the overground steam pipes, a couple of palmetto trees, the raindrops beading on spitshined black shoes.

Sgt. Hudson mans the steps, Sgt. Burley the footmarks. They pace with a mannered strut, like men wearing white tie and tails, their hands folded behind their backs, their jaw muscles flexing. One senses there's none of the wisecracking "See Here, Private Hargrove," or "Sgt. Bilko" Army routine here, no hotshot recruits outsmarting dumb sarge for passes to town.

In fact, during his 63 days of training at Parris Island, unless a member of his immediate family dies, a recruit will get no liberty at all. He will also get no talking, no phone calls, no books or magazines, no television, radio or record players, no candy or gum, one movie, one newspaper a week, and three cigarettes a day. Unless he fouls up, gets sent to the brig or to motivation platoon, and loses the cigarettes.

WHEN I GIVE YOU THE WORD TO MOVE OUT YOU WILL MOVE OUT DO YOU UNDERSTAND ME?

Hudson meets the first one at the steps like a rotary mower ripping into a toad, so psyched he's actually dancing on tiptoe, with his face a choleric three-quarters of an inch from the private FASTER PRIVATE FASTER JUST TAKE YOUR DUMB TIME SWEETHEART MOVE! MOVE! as this hog, as recruits are colloquially known, piles out of the barracks in a stumble of new boots, poncho, laundry bag and the worst trouble his young ass has ever been in, no doubt about it when Burley meets him just like Hudson, in an astonishment of rage that roars him all the way down to the right front set of yellow footprints YOU LOCK YOUR BODY AT ATTENTION YOU LOCK YOUR BODY. . . .

Or maybe Burley writhes up around this private to hiss in his ear — and Burley is very good at this — *you hate me, don't you, you hate me, private, you'd better hate me because I hate you,* or any of the other litanies drill instructors have been barking and hissing at their charges ever since the first of more than one million Parris Island graduates arrived on this flea-ridden sand barren in 1911.

Until there are 60 of them out there in the drizzle with the drill instructors shouting themselves hoarse, 60 volunteers who had heard from countless older brothers and street corner buddies and roommates that it would be exactly like this but they volunteered anyhow, to be Marines.

Right now, with lips trembling, eyes shuttling YOU BETTER STOP THAT EYEBALLING, PRIVATE!! fat and forlorn, they look like 60 sex perverts trapped by a lynch mob. They are scared. They are scared as fraternity pledges during a cleverly staged hell week, shaking like boys about to abandon their virginity.

It's a primal dread that drill instructors invoke and exploit in eight weeks (soon to revert to the pre-Vietnam 11 weeks) of folk theater, a spectacle staged on the scale of the Passion Play at Oberammergau, an initiation that may be the only true rite of passage to manhood that America hasn't yet scoured away as an anthropological anachronism.

Fifteen minutes after that first recruit panicked out of receiving barracks, Berry, Burley and Hudson have stampeded all of them into their new squad bay. While 1st Lt. Roger McElrath lectures them on the vast variety of crimes and punishments on display in the Uniform Code of Military Justice, the D.I.s are hidden in a room called the drill instructor's house, changing their uniforms. Squared-away drill instructors change uniforms up to six times a day. It is no more possible for a drill instructor to appear sweatstained, soiled or wrinkled than a Vatican priest.

"Goddam, goddam, goddam," Hudson is saying, over and over. Fresh sweat blisters his brow. All of them are flushed and breathing hard, swearing and fumbling for cigarettes like a roller derby team at half time.

"They look good," Berry says. He's baby-faced, actually, earnest with a flair of cynicism, like a professional athlete. "We got 15 brothers (blacks). They'll pick up drill right away. The others can get the rhythm off them. Not too many fatbodies, not too many belligerents. This'll be a good platoon."

The problem for D.I.s picking up platoons isn't exhaustion, though, or even getting psyched to that glitter of madness, but "getting too psyched up, so psyched you might grab a kid to straighten him out and BAM, that's it, it's your stripes," says Gunnery Sgt. Ronald Burns, a drill field veteran who now meets the late night buses hauling recruits in from the Charleston and Savannah airports.

Brutality to the Marines is like usury to Jews—a nightmare that threatens their very existence. It is also the leading figment of the Marine mystique and the stock brag of any Parris Island graduate. It is a legend like that of the "Old Corps," which always seems to have ended about three years ago. In the Old Corps, Marines tell each other, there was none of this Standard Operating Procedure (SOP) for recruit training, none of these maltreatment questionnaires and "swoop teams" of inspectors to hamstring the drill instructors.

Nothing to keep a D.I. from working over recruits during nightly "thump call," from slamming the whole platoon into "Chinese thinking position," an excruciating calisthenic in which you prop yourself solely on elbows and toes, and not to be confused with other outlawed old favorites such as six-point kneeling, steam engines, dry shaving, blanket parties, smoking under a blanket, the game of Flood and Air Raid, ethnic taunts, profanity, and allowing a recruit to eat all two pounds of the divinity fudge his girlfriend mailed him, eat it in three minutes flat, lover boy, every goddam crumb.

All outlawed now and outlawed too back in 1956, when rumors of Trumans' plans to merge the Corps into the Army still haunted Marines, and Staff Sgt. Matthew McKeon made every front page in America by leading

" 'They join because they want their girl to be proud of them. . .' "

an unauthorized night march into Ribbon Creek, out behind the rifle range, and six recruits drowned in a mass panic.

Since then, enforcement of the SOP has been screwed down tighter every year at both Parris Island and San Diego, a more recent recruit training base that trains enlistees from the western half of the country.

The SOP orders drill instructors to instill "instant obedience to orders." It also forbids them on pain of court-martial from touching a recruit, except to adjust a military position.

It prescribes 63 days of training which will include: 89 hours on firing the M-14 rifle, 60 hours of drill, 57 hours of physical training (PT), 23 hours of inspections and testing, 12 hours on clothing and equipment, 10 hours on history of the Marine Corps, and 114 hours of "commander's time," to include one hour each night of "free time" for writing and reading letters and doing anything else that does not involve talking, smoking, eating or leaving the squad bay. There are also endless hours of rifle cleaning, shoe shining, and singing of the Marine Corps hymn:

From the halls of Montezuma
To the shores of Tripoli . . .

"Parris Island is a game. If you can play by the rules, you do very well," says Lt. Scott Shaffer, a Navy psychologist (the Marines get medical and religious services from the Navy) who interviews a daily parade of bedwetters, attempted suicides, weepers, catatonics and others suspected mentally unfit for the Marine Corps.

"It's very behaviorally oriented, like a big Skinner box. You do well, you get rewarded. You do badly and you're punished. Positive and negative reinforcement. Personally, I'd like to see more positive reinforcement (reward)."

This doesn't explain, though, why anybody joins in the first place, especially in an age of beer machines in Navy barracks, and Army boot camps that promise you don't have to lose your dignity to get your training.

"They join because they want their girl to be proud of them, or their parents, or the gang on the block. Or they want to be proud of themselves. They want to be somebody, want to be able to go home a big, bad-ass Marine," says Gunnery Sgt. Mike "Big Mac" McCormick, who is all of that at 6-feet-4½ and 212 pounds, with five years on Parris Island drilling recruits and training drill instructors. "That's the best lever you've got on that recruit—pride. Next comes fear."

But neither pride, fear nor game theory can explain to anyone who has been through Parris Island why he endured those long, dusty, staggering exhaustions of runs, or the standing at attention in chow lines, thumbs locked to trouser seams while sand fleas put on a flying circus in his ears.

Or the incessant, insane, "Catch-22" paradoxes—a recruit pumping out jumping jacks, sweating his T-shirt translucent while his D.I. yells "DO YOU WANT TO DO MORE?" and the private, of course, answers "NO, SIR," until he realizes the correct answer is "YES, SIR," and the drill instructor tells him to stop doing any more, of course.

Given the fact that there are choices, such as the Air Force, which at least offers job-skill training, it would seem the only reason any human being puts up with Marine boot camp is that he wants to—a horrendous thought, if you're an enlightened believer in the basic rationality and pleasure drives of modern, educated man.

Think about it: drill instructors might as well be Pueblo shamans scaring candidates for tribal membership and manhood with nothing but masks and chants. (That wry ferocity drill instructors cultivate, the squinted eyes and the mouth about as generous as a snapping turtle's, and the jutjawed arrogance of their back-of-the-throat voices.)

And recruits, swaddled in their new uniforms and shorn of hair, are no more civilized, perhaps, than Australian aborigine boys who are circumcised and wrapped in blankets to be purified and symbolically reborn.

In *Man and His Symbols,* Joseph Henderson, a disciple of Carl Jung, states that the archetypal initiation that has pervaded all primitive cultures involves submission (enlistment), symbolic death by ordeal (degradation and physical demands far beyond what the recruit believes possible), and symbolic rebirth as a member of the collective consciousness (the Marine Corps).

It all fits, even the fact that the lessons taught at Parris Island involve stress or ceremony but few combat skills, except "instant obedience." The Marines leave the grenade throwing and small unit tactics and camouflage to Camp Lejeune, in North Carolina, where, for the first time, recruits are greeted as "Marine." Rifle firing is strictly on a formal bull's-eye target range, in the official National Rifle Association positions.

In fact, drill instructors may gain their extraordinary power from invoking all the archetypal terrors of initiation while never actually threatening the life of the recruit—a threat that would break the bond of trust between recruit and D.I., a bond so strong after only a few weeks that some drill instructors have been able to thump hell out of recruits with no fear they'll turn him in.

Like a score of fellow recruits, Pvt. John Hedrick, 19, of Lynchburg, Va., answers only "Yessir my drill instructors treat me well, Nossir, there's no maltreatment, Yessir, I'd enlist again if I had it to do over."

"The Ditch is Parris Island's last-chance purgatory, 480 meters of sand, mud, barbed wire..."

Of course, there is bound to be some falling away from the faith, apostasies that drill instructors watch for with those quick glares, stalking up and down a row of recruits in a mess hall, say, making sure the hogs or ladies or maggots are popping those heels and squaring those corners.

The drill instructors watch because once a recruit sees the whole ritual is just a magic show, he loses both his fear of the D.I., and his motivation. And motivation is what Parris Island is all about. It not only makes you a Marine, not only makes you like it, but also makes you believe in it.

("The worst thumping I ever got was when the D.I. called the retreat from the Chosin reservoir an 'advance to the rear,' and I snickered," says Mike Jerace, who went through Parris Island in 1963.)

So secret doubters who stop shouting those yessirs at peak bellow, who stop trembling and panting like a dog in a thunderstorm to crank out one more pull-up, are apt to spend one to 10 days at motivation platoon: Last year, 3,384 of 28,153 Parris Island initiates did time at motivation platoon, and 557 were later discharged from the Marines "for reasons of defective attitude," said Capt. John Woggon, who directs Special Training Branch. (Which, besides motivating recruits who aren't putting out 100 percent, also takes a pound a day off "fatbodies," reconditions hospital discharges, and punishes legal offenders in its Correctional Custody Platoon.)

Motivation platoon is a ferocious speed-up of the carrot-and-stick routine, starting with eight to 20 maddening, grueling miles of speed march broken only by patriotic lectures and movies about epic Marine heroisms at Tarawa, Iwo Jima, Khe Sanh . . . Then fighting with padded "pugil sticks" between recruits who may never have been in a fight in their lives. And finally, lining up sweating and gritty, muscles shrill with fatigue, for The Ditch.

What happens to most recruits in eight weeks happens to most of motivation platoon in 30 minutes in The Ditch. The Ditch is Parris Island's last-chance purgatory, 480 meters of sand, mud, barbed wire and corrugated storm pipe all half-flooded with tidewater that these recruits will crawl through on their knees and bellies with metal rifle frames YOU WILL JUMP INTO THIS FIRST WATER OBSTACLE YOU WILL COMPLETELY IMMERSE YOURSELF YOU WILL THEN CRAWL ON YOUR KNEES DOWN THAT DITCH YELLING MARINE CORPS WITH EVERY BREATH YOU BREATHE. . . .

Baptism in a waist-deep mud puddle and the crawl begins. Shaved heads stream mud and water, mouths yaw wide as anatomy displays gasping MARINE CORPS, MARINE CORPS as they grind their way down that ditch like nothing so much as Mexican *penitentes* struggling on their knees for miles to win salvation at the Shrine of Our Lady, the ultimate prostration, the last plea . . .

Under the frantic frustration of the barbed wire, through the drainpipes that deliver them into a mock-up of an Indochinese village where they form up shivering and chanting MARINE CORPS while Staff Sgt. Sam Michaux pounds time with his boot. Then Michaux delivers the last speech before the penitents are sent back filthy and exhausted to their platoons.

"This is the world, sweeties, and your drill instructor wants to help you BUT BY GOD YOU BETTER HELP YOURSELVES because when the going gets rough, you can't say anymore I'M GONNA TAKE MY LITTLE RED WAGON AND GO HOME. The next time you think you can slack off you'd best remember that a HARD HEAD MAKES A SOFT ASS and yours is GONNA GET KICKED."

Meanwhile, Platoon 220, like another platoon yesterday, and another tomorrow, is just beginning its long initiation back in its barracks, or "barn," as the drill instructors call it, with its paint-flaked bunks lined up like stanchions, its bathroom of cement floors and naked squads of gleaming seatless toilets.

Cardboard placards advertise the Eleven General Orders like religious mottoes in the bare-bulb glare of this drizzly afternoon indoors. Decades of sweat and pivoting boots have worn the floors to a shine. Platoon 220's home is shabby but immaculate, like the tin-roof shack of a "good nigger," like Parris Island itself, in fact, a grim, mundane 3,300 habitable acres on which neatness and thrift are the only aesthetics, instant obedience the only ethic.

In the next eight weeks, Berry, Burley and Hudson will whipsaw these 60 recruits with reward and punishment. As former Marine commandant Gen. David M. Shoup once said, they will "receive, degrade, sanitize, immunize, clothe, equip, train, pain, scold, mold, sand and polish."

They will condition this stampede of adolescence until it understands a great paradox called military fear, a first law of survival that states the only thing you have to fear is not being scared enough to put up with the insult and hassle that are any military existence, with the chronic disaster of war.

Platoon 220 will discover the ease and convenience of this tautology just as they will discover that this fear, bleakness and degradation can yield a beauty they'll never be able to explain to anyone who hasn't gone through it and made it.

Eight weeks later, for instance, in the lambency of a Southern twilight in spring, Platoon 220 may fall out on the grinder for close order drill,

"... the only thing you have to fear is not being scared enough..."

which they'll be very good at by then, and they'll feel the cool flutter of their new tropical uniforms against their legs, and their rifles will flip from shoulder arms to port arms with one, crisp crash, and they'll lean back in a limber strut to the singsong of the D.I.'s cadence—a voice burnished by years of too much fatigue, coffee and cigarettes—the whole platoon floating across the quiet parade field like a ship at sea.

—March 5, 1972

IV. New Perceptions

The five articles in this chapter are grouped separately because they represent conscious efforts for Style writers to explore conventional subject matter in unconventional ways.

They are not being different merely for the sake of being different. The writer's aim is to look at old subjects from new angles. Formula journalistic stereotypes — the bland, unfocused feature and the pyramid news story — are jettisoned for literary patterns that are more flexible, and complex, vehicles for bringing fresh insights to the subjects — in these cases, Washington dinner parties, Washington hosts, teenage cheerleaders, the Mardi Gras and the Kentucky Derby. — *L.T.*

Next: At Dinner

As Henry Mitchell points out here, Washington dinner parties like the one he describes "go on nightly in the capital" and are regularly covered as news because, instead of being warm occasions where friends gather, they are frequently intrinsic parts of the power process, where the powerful gather for business with other powerful.

Since the parties are regarded as news, the stereotype has been to write about them in conventional pyramid news structure, treating trivial, though perhaps fascinating, tidbits as news. Certainly that is the right way to write such a story when something of major impact is learned, as when the Post's *Dorothy McCardle scored a beat on all the city's political reporters several years ago when she learned over cocktails of Speaker John McCormack's decision to resign the next day.*

More often, the hard news formula produces, at best, a mock news story. That way, this story might have begun: "Justice Potter Stewart said last night that Castro's notion of cooping up air hijackers in 4-foot boxes appeals to him. It was at a party honoring the departing Greek ambassador that . . ." With all apologies to Justice Stewart, who cares? Hijacking is not a major concern of the Supreme Court; thus such a story is at best marginally news (maybe best used as an anecdote in a "talk around town" column).

This, in effect, is the point of Henry Mitchell's story. His assignment was to explore the dinner party as an institution, focusing on a single typical example. He actually attended four before reflecting their common elements through this one. Using scene-on-scene structure, extended dialogue, specific detail, both ironic understatement and overstatement, and loads of other literary devices, he relates a true picture of the Sidney Zlotnicks' dinner party for the departing Greek ambassador, as he saw it. Most important of all, he breaks the cliche that such events are necessarily high-key and glittering. This one comes through here as an event that, like most, is rather bland and ritual.

Note: Since Mitchell attends a seated dinner, he considers pulling out a notepad at the table improper. Instead he memorizes, not just quotes, but dialogue. He stops at the end of exchanges that strike him, and three times silently repeats them to himself. Capote, too, successfully rested on his memory for In Cold Blood. *It's a formidable device, if you're up to it.*

—L.T.

The Dinner Party

By Henry Mitchell

"**A**n ambassador is like a centaur," said departing Greek Ambassador Basil George Vitsaxis at a farewell dinner, somewhat alarming all nonambassadorial males whose wives were dispersed about the table. But he quickly added, "That is, half man and half wife."

This produced enthusiastic drumming on the table by Mrs. Egidio Ortona, the better half of Italy. If she had been English she certainly would have cried, "Hear! Hear!"

As the ambassador added a few well-chosen compliments to the women who assist, sustain and put up with diplomat husbands he pleased the ladies of Luxembourg and Switzerland as well.

In an adieu to America in the carnation-laden and elegant dining room of his hosts, wealthy Washington attorney Sidney Zlotnick and his wife, Vitsaxis concluded:

"People say we are collectors, but I say we collect chiefly memories — memories of good things. Some hear, when they hear music, only the dissonances; and in laughter they see only a grimace. But we try to see, even in tears, the happiness that lies beneath."

"Well said — beautifully said," broke in Supreme Court Justice Potter Stewart, clapping. And the whole table of 20 guests rose in a toast to friendship's memories before adjourning all together (no sexism here) for coffee and brandy in the drawing room of the Zlotnicks' Massachusetts Avenue home.

It was the sort of evening, not rare in the capital, at which people of note in public life meet one another, often for the first time; and hosts are valued who manage to get interesting people together, especially if the food and the appointments in general are polished and civilized.

Arthur Burns, chairman of the Federal Reserve Board, had to leave early to meet his wife at the airport. In her absence a reporter was invited, and never mind if it made too many men.

The women were dressed to kill and the men were modestly penguined. There is no great standing on ceremony — you join right in and once you're under the roof a guest is a guest, after all, and nobody is beastly, even to the press.

On the contrary, everyone talks at a great rate to everybody in sight, thus differing from large receptions and daily life. The leper's spots fall off, as it were.

––––––––––

The Greek theme had been sounded earlier at dinner, a really beautiful affair including a remarkable chocolate mousse the likes of which you don't find on every corner nowadays. J. Edward Day, Postmaster General under President Kennedy, was telling Nancy Beall, wife of Maryland Republican Sen. J. Glenn Beall Jr., how impressed he was with two gold cups in the Athens museum.

"The Vaphio cups," volunteered Vitsaxis.

"I liked the bulls on them," Day said. "I raise Devons on my farm."

Asked if his bulls were specially lively (the Vaphio cups show bulls tossing topless girls over their horns), Day said no they weren't, actually, and their placidity was what was so nice about them.

"You don't have to keep after them every day. They're like solid red Herefords, but so calm — not at all like an Angus which is always looking for a hole in the fence. The Pilgrims used Devons for oxen in the 1600s."

"They must be an excellent breed, they doubtless give Devonshire cream," somebody observed and the talk changed to that ancient butt of jokes — the Washington bureaucracy.

"But private industry is just as bad or worse," said Justice Stewart, and Day said indeed it was. Once when he worked at an insurance company, he said, there were five levels of dining rooms and God help you if you ate above your station.

And once, he said, he asked a subordinate to cash a check for him and heard him ask another man, "Is Day entitled to new money?" Above a certain corporate rank, you got clean, fresh dollars. This made everyone smile, and raised a general discontent with beaten-up old bills such as one still occasionally sees, in common places like restaurants.

The lobsters at dinner were certainly not like restaurant lobsters, but were the size of dolphins and artfully stuffed, avoiding the labor, the mess and the frequent mishaps of cracking.

Mary Frances Smoak, wife of Acting Chief of Protocol Marion H. Smoak, swept one off the serving platter with such practiced grace that disaster nearly resulted when the creature's claws proved entangled with another lobster. It landed safely on the plate, however — she's never lost one yet, she said.

She is one who has learned the wisdom of skipping courses — you don't have to eat the tenderloin of beef just because it's served, after all, and too much rich food is bad for the figure, some say.

Guests arrived at 8. It certainly doesn't do to be early, but even in Washington it is thought rude to be late. The small ground-floor entrance hall contained nothing but a vase of carnations and a seating chart to prevent confusion and peering about at the place cards at dinner.

It disappoints butlers if you don't have a coat but the night was mild and some of us risked his disapproval. To the left, the Zlotnicks received their guests in a room with a strolling guitarist — at least he strolled till the room promptly filled. Evelyn Zlotnick wore an Italian dress with a sort of apron — not entirely practical for the kitchen since it was embroidered heavily with gold, turquoise, and slivers of red coral.

She is one of many in Washington who do not drink at all parties — never two days in a row. This spares the liver a terrible fate and besides, she said, the mornings are so much nicer.

Parties like hers, which go on nightly in the capital though often secluded from public gaze, answer a human as well as a political need. Often a public figure blows in from the West knowing few of his rank; and ambassadors of course have special needs to meet people.

Besides all that, there is the normal human desire to meet people pleasantly — the city can be a shock to a man from Portland who has no close friends here and who cannot go banging on doors adjacent to his rented house.

Many friendships originate at just such dinners where the rule of survival — as well as the claims of civility — require a certain tact in accepting people of all sorts of backgrounds. These rarely replace old friendships back home, but they're better than nothing and besides it's nice to know a man if you someday have to deal with him.

The men made more effort than usual not to stand about in a herd, but there was a little knot discussing the general state of Maryland politics.

Justice Stewart remarked that Maryland had always had religious freedom and was surprised to hear Sen. Beall say the state is only about 20 percent Catholic now, though it was alone among Catholic colonies in America.

Religious intolerance was roundly condemned by everybody — Day, who is a Methodist, said he'd run into a man who was horrified at George McGovern and when all else failed him in expressing his indignation at the Democratic candidate, blurted out, "He's a Methodist."

Hijacking, also predictably, found no advocates. Justice Stewart said he's like everybody else. It disgusts him but he has no idea how to stop it.

"Anything you do is wrong if it doesn't work," he said. If you shoot, it can be wrong; and if you just sit there, it can be equally wrong.

He said Castro's notion of cooping up hijackers in 4-foot boxes the rest of their lives had a certain appeal to it on the surface, but then the law is a longtime — not a surface — matter.

"I like that picture," said a woman motioning to one of the Zlotnick's paintings. She confessed that her taste ran to 18th-century hunting scenes and that "I think that's just awful over there."

"You don't like the Roualt?" her astounded companion asked. The woman, who said she'd be ruined if her taste in pictures were ever identified publicly, asked her host for a remedial course and tour of his art collection. When last seen, she was dutifully admiring a Vlaminck near the stairway.

"Good night," people said on the stroke of 11, having learned from dozens of other Washington dinner parties that it doesn't do to stay forever.

Cinderella didn't turn into a pumpkin, one guest reflected, till the stroke of 12.   — November 17, 1972

Next: The Host

This story caused, and continues to cause, more of a stir than any other in the volume. The reason: if the preceding profile of a typical formal Washington dinner would never have been handled that way *under the strictures of the old social coverage, this hard, cold study of how one moves up in social Washington would never have been written* at all.

Its point of departure is a portrait of Steve Martindale, an ambitious, aggressive young host, an unabashed collector of celebrities who knows most of them will never reciprocate his hospitality. A recent claim in the Washingtonian *magazine that the publication of this story "will stand as an historic day in the annals of the mediacracy" and that it "ended the romanticism of social reporting" may go too far (regrettably, the latter is demonstrably alive), but the story* is *a kind of turning point.*

Earlier generations of Washington party-givers (mostly women) who opened their affairs to the press never received this kind of hard-nosed journalistic scrutiny; in fact, one of those earlier grande dames was a newspaper publisher herself, Cissy Patterson (who owned the Times-Herald, *which was acquired by the* Post *after her death). Indeed, though one wouldn't want to press the point too far, the only remotely obvious parallel to Martindale and to the more important point at which Quinn is driving here (in focus, if not in scope) is Jay Gatsby in Scott Fitzgerald's* The Great Gatsby, *a brilliant example of the kind of realistic fiction to which the best work in this anthology owes a debt.*

But the real meat of Quinn's story is development of a thesis — an exacting, sobering examination of "how to make it" as a host or hostess. (Note, for example, the reference in this respect to the Sidney Zlotnicks, the hosts in Henry Mitchell's dinner party profile.) The thesis links the Martindale portrait to the atypically formalized format (for Quinn) of a lexicon of 12 precise rules of procedure; she calls them the "Law of Twelve." They constitute an authoritative, sometimes wry, exegesis that delineates the odds of success, humiliation, neglect, abuse and survival on the way up in the Washington party circuit. One suspects that no one who is a part of that world has gone totally unscathed.

The lexicon structure, mixed with generous scene and background digressions, is complicated. The conversational tone ("Persistence. Without persistence, forget it") provides the necessary irony that checks the story's somber implications.

Note: Though the basic idea of this story is a kind of benchmark of how such subjects might be approached, its structure is frankly idiosyncratic, and in that sense is very much like the "New Journalism," though being a "New Journalist" was hardly one of Quinn's major goals here. The "Law of Twelve" represents something, she acknowledges, that "had been building up in me for years," long before she heard of Steve Martindale. Like much of the best writing, it may be one of those odd pieces that only she could have written.

— L. T.

The Law of Twelve,

Which Makes Washington Whirl,

and the Boy From Pocatello

By Sally Quinn

T his is a story about a young man from Pocatello, Idaho. But more than
that, this is a story about how to make it in the Washington social
whirl.

Before we talk about the young man, we should begin by discussing what
is meant exactly by "the Washington social whirl."

Everyone has his or her own idea of what this city is all about, but there
is one aphorism with which most will agree. Washington is a company
town. It has one industry: government. What happens socially in Washington revolves around the administration, the Congress, the courts, and
those who report and comment on them.

Social prominence in Washington has little to do with traditional social
credentials or wealth.

It has to do with power. If you have power, you are in. If you haven't,
you are out.

If you have power, you don't need to try to make it. You already have.

All is not lost, however, for those who have no power but still long to be
a part of it. There is an alternative role. The powerful have egos. They need
them fed. They have appetites. They need them fed, too.

This is where our story begins.

———————

Two years ago John Lennon and Yoko Ono were trying to establish resi-
dency in the United States and were being denied it because the ex-Beatle
had been busted for possession of marijuana. They were especially anxious
to stay in this country because Yoko Ono was searching for her daughter
who had been taken away by her former husband. They were desperate.
They had appealed for help to every powerful person in New York they
could meet, including John Lindsay.

Then one night they met a nice young man named Steve Martindale at a
party. "He told us that he lived in Washington, that he used to work on the
Hill for Sen. Charles Goodell and that he could introduce us to a lot of im-

portant people who might be able to help," John Lennon said later. "If we came down to Washington he said he'd have a party for us to meet them and invite the press so we'd get publicity for our cause."

Martindale, then 28, did just that. The Lennons came and everybody else who was invited came to meet the Lennons. Sen. and Mrs. Charles Percy (R-Ill.) were there, Sen. and Mrs. Alan Cranston (D-Calif.) came, the Javitses couldn't get there at the last minute but had accepted, Margot and Gilbert Hahn (former City Council chairman) were there, Joan and Tom Braden (the columnist) were there, and the press was there.

"That," says Martindale's friend and colleague, Liz Carpenter, former press secretary to Mrs. Lyndon B. Johnson, "put him on the map. Before that nobody had ever heard of him. But after that they all sat up and said, 'Who is this?' "

Then there was the party for Daniel Ellsberg, the party for Adlai Stevenson, the party for former North Carolina Gov. Terry Sanford, the party for Arnold C. Weissberger, the photographer, the mammoth party for the cast of "Jumpers"—then playing at the Kennedy Center—the party for dancer Martha Graham and the intimate party for Joan Braden's birthday. Those who are really in the know say it was that one that really put him on the proverbial map. Alice Longworth came. Henry Kissinger came. Evangeline and David Bruce came. Joe Alsop came. Art and Ann Buchwald came.

It was what you might call a Royal Flush. There were hostesses in this town who would have scratched Steve Martindale's eyes out for that guest list. Telephones buzzed all over town for days. "Who is this 30-year-old kid who can draw that kind of a crowd? What does he do? Where does he come from? Does he have money?" they asked. It was just too much.

"I'm from Pocatello, Idaho," Martindale will tell you right off. "And I don't hide it."

But Steve Martindale wasn't your ordinary kid from Pocatello. He had ambitions, aspirations beyond those of his schoolteacher parents and his disc jockey brother. That's why he was head of the Idaho Teen-age Republicans, why he went to Stanford University and graduated with honors, why he spent his first summer in college working in Washington for his congressman, and his second summer at Stanford's extension in Italy.

Because he wanted to be a success, he worked for the House Republican leadership and became close to "Charlie" Goodell, "Jerry" Ford and "Mel" Laird. That's why he became a Rockefeller fellow at Harvard in preparation to be a divinity student. And that's why he didn't become a divinity student. It is why he quit his first year of law school at the University of Idaho to work on Nelson Rockefeller's presidential campaign.

Focusing on his future, he came to Washington to work for Sen. Goodell as his executive assistant, then later became his deputy campaign manager. When Goodell lost his re-election bid, Martindale enrolled in night law school, and while working days for the Drug Abuse Council, he graduated.

Martindale understands that meeting people and making contacts come from a variety of experiences and ventures. This is why he is a member of the Governor's Club of New York, active in the Ripon Society, a member of the Board of Washington's Choral Arts Society and head of the Men's Committee for Wolf Trap Farm's Charity Ball, why he is vice chairman of the Board of Trustees of the New York Studio of Drawing, Painting, and Sculpture, on the board of the Martha Graham Foundation and works closely with Roger Stevens at the Kennedy Center.

And just to keep his hand in, he'll help out at a fund-raiser for Rep. Wayne Owens from Utah at the Averell Harrimans' starring Robert Redford—even though Wayne Owens is a Democrat. He shrugs and smiles about paying $150 to go to an event like that and wonders if it "will ruin my Republican credentials."

The reason Martindale didn't go to divinity school, (he's a Mormon dropout and feels that he is "very religious, a good Christian person, but not tied to any religion") was because he had made a decision. "I decided what you do in life is pick an institution that has the greatest and most lasting impact on society and work there." The Church, he felt, was not that institution.

So when Steve Martindale graduated from night law school in 1973, he went to work for Hill and Knowlton, the oldest, and one of the most prestigious, public relations firms in America. After one year, he has become a registered lobbyist and has just been promoted to vice president.

A good cross section of social Washington recently showed up at Steve Martindale's for a seated dinner for 24. There were people from the press, Capitol Hill and the administration. The dinner was catered. There were four round skirted tables set up in the library. The food was simple and good. The flower arrangements were daisies. Candles burned on the tables, and the wine and champagne flowed. The atmosphere was relaxed, and after dinner the guests toasted their host, he toasted them and they toasted each other. Everybody seemed to have a good time. Most of them were pleased to have gotten a rare chance to see people from different circles. Steve had done it again. He had put together another party that was a success.

Never mind that many of the people he had invited, some for the fifth or sixth time, had turned down the invitation. Never mind that some of those who were present apologized to others for being there or made excuses. Never mind that Martindale hadn't ever been invited to many of his guests' houses himself, nor probably ever would be. From his point of view he had achieved what he wanted that evening.

Steve Martindale is getting to be a controversial figure in Washington among those who make things move. To some he has emerged as the leading host in town. To others he is, well, a social climber.

Martindale is aware of this. It embarrasses him a little to talk about it, but he will. And he did recently at a luncheon interview at his Wesley Heights house.

He lives in a rich neighborhood — large houses with big shady trees — in a house that would seem unattainable to most anyone of his age and financial situation. But he shares it with three other bachelors. That way he can live and entertain in the style to which his acquaintances are accustomed, and he and his housemates can afford to have a full-time, live-in housekeeper who cleans and cooks for them.

Still, the house is furnished bachelor style, with pieces of unmatched furniture, no attempt at decoration, a toilet seat cover with a peace symbol on it, a hodgepodge of china and silver, and a door handle that keeps falling off.

He greets you at the door and leads the way to the sun-filled study, offering a glass of white wine. He seems nervous, and has a difficult time relaxing for a photographer.

Steve Martindale is handsome in a clean-cut way. He looks like a young Republican. Only his sculptured haircut, a perpetual tan and a rather flashy manner of dressing keep him from looking like all those nice young men in the White House. He has an open, friendly manner. Likable, you might say. He seems bright but not brilliant, pleasant but not a wit, interested which makes him seem interesting, and, above all, attentive. He has the manners of an older man, more gentlemanly than anything else. He also has an eye for detail, a knack for remembering names, a sharp instinct for who and what are important, topical, trendy, relevant. He is most agreeable, and he creates an atmosphere of sympathy — harmony almost — in which, if he were to disagree, which he seldom does, he would make it seem only that he was wondering out loud.

He turns red when the subject of social climbing comes up in relation to entertaining. He goes on the defensive a bit. "In this town if you give parties you're always open to accusations of being a social climber or a power grabber," he says. "I don't think that I am but a lot of people will tell you I am. I could give you a whole list of them I'm sure. But I don't think about it. I've repressed it. I do know, though, that I have gotten some negative feedback. I think it relates back to the question of, 'Is he a serious person or isn't he?' But I'm comfortable with it. I've decided that the pros of meeting interesting and powerful people, and growing and learning the way you can only in Washington far outweigh the cons of worrying about what people call you."

Martindale doesn't like to be called a successful host. "I don't want to be, nor can I afford to be, the great host of Washington," he says. On the other hand, "I don't think anyone comes to this town to be a recluse."

The powerful react to him in various ways. Some people feel he is using them. Others feel they are using him. A lot of people like him and think what he's doing is fine, that he livens up an otherwise uneventful social scene. Other people are angered, embarrassed, annoyed, even revolted by his methods. Some of the people he says are his friends are embarrassed to say anything either nice or unkind about him for the record, yet they don't

want him to feel that they refuse to talk about him, especially if they regularly go to his parties.

Martindale lists among his two closest friends in Washington Joan Braden and Margot Hahn. He met Joan Braden while he was working for Goodell in New York and she was working for Nelson Rockefeller's gubernatorial campaign. When Martindale came back to Washington, the Bradens entertained him often at their Sunday night salons where people like Alice Longworth and Henry Kissinger are regulars. As Martindale will tell you, "I met Joanie and Henry through Nelson."

Having met most of Washington through Joan Braden, Martindale began to entertain, himself, inviting those he had met at their house. Because he was a friend of hers, they went. Joan Braden is what one would call a *recherché* hostess. She never permits her parties to be covered, so she gets only the most desirable kind of publicity—little mentions here and there in columns when the word leaks out. It was Joan Braden who had the first party for Henry Kissinger and his bride Nancy when they got back from their honeymoon and she lunches often at the Sans Souci.

Margot Hahn, the wife of former city council chairman Gilbert Hahn, is a better known party-giver. Her evenings are casual and fun, but she distinguishes herself by her cooking, which some say is the best in town. She also has a flair for entertaining in amusing and different ways, where Joan Braden is more conventional in her approach. Margot met Steve through Joan.

Both women helped Martindale out in the beginning, Joan Braden giving him tips on caterers and Margot Hahn giving him ideas on how to enter-

Drawings by Garry Trudeau

tain inexpensively and cleverly. "My family never did any entertaining at all," says Martindale, "so I didn't know how to do anything. Margot and Joanie pretty much taught me everything I know. They're both terrific teachers. It's quite an art to learn to entertain well and it takes a long time to gradually pick it up. But one thing they've taught me is that the best way to have a successful party is to have people who know how to go to parties. Margot and Joanie are fantastic. They both know how to make a conversation work, how to make it interesting and bright."

When asked about Martindale, "Joanie" at first said, "I don't think I have anything to say." Asked how she met him, she offered this: "He was working for Goodell and I was working for Rockefeller. When he first came he was nice to my kids and I played tennis with him occasionally. He once had a birthday party for me and, to tell you the truth, I almost didn't even go. I don't go to his parties anymore. I haven't been for a year and a half. To tell you the truth, I'm not very interested and I don't know much about him."

Margot Hahn, on the other hand, finds that Martindale's interest in meeting the people that make things happen in Washington "is so blatant that it's disarming. People say he uses them but I can't see it. Being my friend is getting him zero. You know, the social life in Washington is sort of dreary these days. I always have fun there and where else can you go to meet people from a whole cross section of town. I look upon Steve's success as a host as a funny phenomenon of Washington. Sort of the way I felt about Gwen Cafritz. But if he can do it and do it well, more power to him."

Do it well. That's the key. The remains of many a would-be host or hostess lie dwindling on the bottom lines of endless dull party stories, buried on back pages of old feature sections.

They didn't do it well. All right, then, who did do it well? Gwen Cafritz did it. Perle Mesta did it. But since then there has been a vacuum. An entertainment gap. People have tried and failed over the past few years, dropping along the way from lack of interest, lack of money, lack of time, or lack of the proper instinct for how to make it work. The few who have succeeded have many attributes in common, readily identifiable by the top Washington social observers, those who are really "in," and who have watched this town over a long period of time.

It must be pointed out that this is a comparatively small group of people in Washington's power structure who like to work behind the scenes to make this town move. They are important and powerful people, often people you also read about on the front pages of the paper every day. Occasionally you will read about them attending social events too, but at these times they are working, *really* working—like the scores of other well-known names who make up the daily fare of this city's newspapers' regular coverage of receptions and benefits.

"Washington is about the only town where the word 'nouveau' is laudatory..."

When people are *really* working socially they are doing one of several things. They are involved in a testimonial, they are helping to raise money for a charity, they are helping to raise money for a political campaign, they are helping to publicize a cause they consider important, they are attending or giving political or diplomatic receptions.

In all of these cases it is not only proper and accepted, but *de rigueur* to invite the press to cover. These are the "social" events in Washington that one reads about in the papers. But they are not the "social" events where most people truly socialize.

There has been heavy media coverage, for example, of such recent "social" (read "political") events as the Averell Harriman testimonial dinner which was a fund-raiser for the Democratic Study Group. Jackie Onassis came. Then there was a reception for Rep. John Rhodes at the home of the Clark MacGregors; Ethel Kennedy's annual Hickory Hill pet show; the Saudi Arabian Embassy buffet for Fahad Ibn Abdul Aziz; the barbecue at Polly and Jack Logan's to raise money for the Hearing and Speech Clinic; the reception at the British Embassy for the Leukemia Society of America attended by Joseph Alsop; Kennedy Center Director Roger Stevens' party after the opening of "Jumpers" attended by 2,000; "intimate" Golden Circle parties on other opening nights at the Kennedy Center. This is not to mention White House dinners, invitations to which not so long ago produced intense passion and enthusiasm.

So who we are dealing with, then, are those people who don't pop up regularly in "social" news accounts.

Washington is about the only town in the world where the word "nouveau" is laudatory, where the least known people often have the greatest chance of making it. And it all depends on what crowd you want to make it with. If it's the inner sanctum, the behind-the-scenes circle, it is a treacherous venture at the least. And one must meet the necessary requirements and requisites. That includes Steve Martindale.

Martindale and others must subscribe to what might be called an unwritten "Law of Twelve":

I To begin with there must be a social hole to fill, a host or hostess role to be filled.

"My theory," says NBC newsman Doug Kiker, a favorite on the party circuit, "is that people who entertain go through a cycle in this town. An age passes. Perle Mesta and Gwen Cafritz are out of power and so are the limousines chauffeured to mansions. Then a lot of people who start out being host or hostess get tired of it. So periodically there's an entertainment vacuum. That's what's happening now."

A famous columnist, who preferred not to be quoted, put it this way: "Every town has one of these people. You just have to put up with the Steve Martindales in Washington. It's the kind of thing where everybody shows up and says, 'Why am I here?'"

"I'm glad to open up my home whenever I can be useful," Martindale will tell you. "If someone comes to town with a book or a play, if I can help them I will."

"Gwen could do it, Perle could do it," says another columnist. "Then the Arabs took over. Now there's a vacuum. The average person just wants to see his friends, he doesn't want to give a party. This town is really ripe for a guy like that. And you always feel in Washington that you better go or you'll miss out on something. But you've got to lay it on the system, not the guy. You can always get people to come out for a free meal, even if at the end you kind of say, 'Gosh why was I there?'"

What baffles a lot of people around town is that nearly all the contenders for the vacated position of "hostess with the mostest" are men. True Davis, former Ambassador to Switzerland, Peter Malatesta, former aide to former Vice President Agnew, Alejandro Orfila, ambassador from Argentina, and Ardeshir Zahedi, the Iranian ambassador, are all giving Martindale a run for his money.

Martindale isn't particularly interested in them. "I've never been to True's and I've only been to Peter's once or twice. I don't know what their trip is but it's not mine. I'd like to get to know Ardeshir better though. He succeeds. How do you account for that? I hope he'll come here."

Martindale is very curious about Perle Mesta and Gwen Cafritz. "I don't know Gwen and I never met Perle. But did anyone really go to their parties? I mean did they really get the good people like the Alice Longworths, the Alsops, the Polly Wisners? I can't believe it."

II Once one has established that there is a need, it must be filled. To do that one needs a sponsor. In Steve Martindale's case, it was Joan Braden.

"Joan was the key," says Liz Stevens, wife of American Film Institute Director George Stevens. "Certainly we and most people we know met him through her."

But there are bad vibes these days. A well-known columnist who is a frequent guest of the Bradens says, "Joan launched him. But I think she's turned a little sour on him. I think she feels she's been used. Or maybe," he added, "she thinks he's stealing her act." No matter. Steve Martindale has been launched.

236

" 'I'll say one thing for him... 'he knows the difference between Holy Trinity and St. Matthew's.' "

III The third thing one must have to succeed is an innate understanding of who's in and who's out, who to cultivate and who to stay away from. To have a finger in every pie. To make a point of knowing and meeting people in different circles. Being totally *au courant*. Reading the paper.

"He's got taste and nothing but guts," says a well-known newspaperman. "How he contrives to get Martha Graham there I don't know, but I don't get that many whacks at meeting Martha Graham so I go."

Another well-known columnist says, "You go, maybe with misgivings, but you go because maybe there'll be someone you will meet that you need to know for your work. That's the technique."

"People in Washington have a high level of responsibility," says former New York Sen. Charles Goodell. "They don't shed it at night and they like to be with others who don't shed it. Some really important political and business contacts are made at affairs like that."

"Steve understands that this is the most democratic town there is," says Liz Carpenter. "He knows somebody can pick his teeth but if he's a Supreme Court Justice people will want to see him."

"When I gave the birthday party for Joanie," says Martindale, "the first thing I had to figure out was who liked her and who would come. And of course, for Joanie, they would all come."

And Martindale makes a point of knowing who to ask. "I know practically everybody in this town. I get around. There's hardly a night that I don't go out somewhere. Oh, I'm sure there are people I don't know that I should, but I've been very lucky. It's a small town.

"The fact that the Nixons don't entertain makes a big difference in Washington. There is Kissinger, though. He does go. But he's the only one. The Saxbes go out a lot and I knew them in the Senate. I see a good deal of them. I haven't even met the rest of the Cabinet. Who the hell are they? Oh well, I'm sure when Jerry Ford gets to be President that will all change. I know them fairly well. They are not great friends but she's fun to dance with. I like the Percys a lot. If Chuck Percy were President things would really be different. Sharon and Jay Rockefeller are friends. I knew Sharon at Stanford, have known her for a long, long time."

The Kennedys present more of a problem. "I know Ethel. I see her once in a while but I don't know them well. I've been to Teddy's for dinner. But I think you have to be a Buchwald or something. You have to have grown up with them to be in with them. They don't seem to like to make new friends. I've gotten to know Ethel but I don't think she'd count me as one of her closest friends."

But that doesn't mean he'll give up. Though a Mormon, Steve is often seen at early mass at Holy Trinity Church in Georgetown, otherwise known as the "Kennedy Church" or the "celebrity church."

"I'll say one thing for him," says a frequent invitee. "He knows the difference between Holy Trinity and St. Matthew's."

And of course he knows who his guests don't want to see. "When I suggested an attractive couple I knew to him," said the wife of a television personality, "he said he thought they were awfully nice but he didn't have room for them." Everyone knows what that means.

"I never have anybody because I think I ought to," says Martindale. "And I never go to somebody's house if I don't want to have them back. I've never had the diplomatic types. I'm not on many embassy lists and I really don't want to be."

IV One must have grasped the technique. Once you've established who you want, the problem is getting them there. This is where the "pyramid theory" comes in. What this means is that you get a big name and use it as a building block. As in, "I'm having Henry Kissinger to dinner, won't you come?" Then you build on it. Say you've called Alice Longworth and tell her you're having Kissinger or vice versa.

Then you've got them both to build on and nobody will refuse. There is also the "guts ball pyramid theory." That is to have no name to build on, call Alice Longworth and lie and say you're having Kissinger. Then when she says yes you call him and say you have got her. Or vice versa.

"I've heard terrible stories about Gwen and Perle," says Martindale, "calling the Secretary of Transportation and saying they're having the Secretary of the Treasury, then calling the Treasury and saying they're having Transportation."

"When Steve calls and says he's having a birthday party for Joanie," says a prominent hostess, "then ticks off five or six names like Henry and Mrs. L., it just sounds like too much fun to miss."

"Steve's a notorious name-dropper," says a columnist. "He'll call and say, he's got the so and so's and 10 other good people and you just can't stay away."

V Persistence. Without persistence forget it. "Steve has a persistence that's unreal," says a partygoer. "And gall. He'll call five and six times and then I go and then I say I'll never go again and then he keeps calling and I go."

"Most people," says one columnist, "are sort of cowards. If a guy's persistent enough and asks you nine times, you get the guilties. I used to dread coming home from work at night because I knew there would be an invitation from Steve Martindale. So you begin to feel awful and then you finally accept and go."

"He drives us crazy with invitations," says the wife of a senator. "He calls or sends notes and says he's having all these interesting people and you keep saying 'no' but finally you just give up and go."

"If I meet someone at a dinner then I'll feel free to invite them to my house," says Martindale. "But only if I feel we have a particular rapport or that we've connected. I have to have the feeling, though, that they know who I am."

VI A very thick skin is an essential in this game. "I know instances where I know he's not been invited to something and then when I show up, there is is," says a Martindale observer. "Whether he manages to get himself invited or just crashes, I don't know, but there he is."

"He has no sense of pride," says a newspaperman. "He's not sensitive about being turned down."

"People are using him as much as he's using them," says the wife of a columnist. "But he seems to understand that."

"People like Steve understand that they may not get invited back and they may get turned down a lot but that's part of the territory," says a prominent columnist. "People save their faces for going by laughing at him behind his back."

"Who?" asks Alice Longworth when asked about Martindale. "I don't know who he is, I can't remember ever going to his house but perhaps I did. I haven't the least recognition." When told he was a leading host in town, she replied, "My Lord, is that still going on?"

"I wouldn't want to hurt his feelings," says Mrs. Longworth, "I don't want to be rude, but I just don't know who he is. He probably thinks he's very recognizable."

VII One must have the ability to mix the right people, the flair for giving a good party, the instinct for knowing how to see that people have a good time.

"I must admit," says one television personality, "that we end up having a really good time. All our friends are there so we enjoy ourselves. He's very smart that way."

"When Steve first called and asked me to a party I couldn't remember who the hell he was," says Doug Kiker. "But I figured what the hell and I went. Since then I've always had a good time. The parties are pleasant, there's good food and plenty of wine, a pleasant host and here are all your friends."

"The food is awful good and we always have terrific fun," says Liz Stevens.

"Everybody always has a good time and everybody gets something out of it," says a political wife. "Rose Mary Woods goes and she gets a lot of publicity out of it and all our crowd gets to meet Rose Mary Woods, which we would never ordinarily get to do."

"Why do I like to go?" asks Liz Carpenter. "Talk is a feast in Washington and anybody who can serve it up will be a success. Conversation is the major course. You miss a great deal if you don't go around town and see things through different glasses. Washington is a smorgasbord and Steve feasts on it. There's no reason for living in this town if you're not going to pick its heart and soul. Steve does it with a very easy manner. I think Perle used to work at it."

Martindale says his secret is this: "I always put two press people with two politicians and you can't lose. I generally seat my dinners. Eighteen to 24 works well in this house at tables for six. I always have people that I like. That way I find nobody is ever a disaster. I have a good cook that I use and a good caterer. Unfortunately, the way things are now, politically, you can't mix people the way you used to be able to. You do it at some risk. One can't be quite as comfortable mixing people of divergent political persuasions these days."

VIII Styles of entertaining change in Washington but they change subtly and gradually, so one day you may give the best parties in town and the next, for seemingly no reason, you can't get a soul to come. For those who want to succeed, an instinct for, and a sense of what people want is vital.

"I wonder if the party circuit and party-giving isn't a perishable attraction," says Bob Gray, Martindale's boss, head of Hill and Knowlton's Washington office. (His constant companion is Rose Mary Woods. Liz Carpenter is also a vice president at Hiil and Knowlton.)

"It used to be that everybody went out every night. That's gotten to be a real bore. Times have changed. The social side of Washington is so much more business oriented now, but it has to be done by cutting down the barriers in terms of formality. So when I receive an invitation I think two things: Is it going to be fun and interesting and is it going to be productive? Steve manages to make his parties both."

"I think with the party thing that there is more attention to seriousness today," says Martindale. "I don't think you can really give a party for party's sake. If I just had a lot of money and nothing else, nobody would come. It's important to get people who will create an interesting or serious discussion. I want to be taken seriously in this town. I don't want to give big cocktail parties. All my friends are horrified by that sort of thing."

What Martindale has figured out is that the lavish parties of yesteryear are out out out. Chauffeurs are basically out; lots of servants are out; black tie is out; elegant crystal and china are out; 10-course dinners are out; finger bowls are out; huge parties are out; decorations are out; mansions are out. Informal is in. Casseroles and salads are in.

"...those who have succumbed to the lure of publicity haven't made it."

"In the old days, hostesses like Nancy Dickerson would have elegant dinners and coordinate the color of the borscht with her dark red peonies," says one partygoer. "Nobody does that anymore. The choicest thing you can do now is have carry-out Chinese."

The more informal, the more relaxed the guests are, then the more successful the party is. But the most important change is this: Having your party covered by the press is out. When those in the inner sanctum arrive at a party and see a reporter and photographer it is the kiss of death for any would-be host or hostess. "It simply is not done," said a leader of Washington's social whirl.

"I gave a big cocktail party for the photographer Arnold Weissberger," explains Martindale. "The point of the party was to get attention for his book. Mary Martin, Celeste Holm, Anita Loos and Rose Mary Woods were there. I invited the press. A lot of people came and took me aside and asked me, 'What's going on?' I explained to them, but it was different. I could tell. They stayed for me because they were my friends, but I knew I was pushing them and I couldn't do it again. It's the kind of image they don't want to be associated with and, frankly, neither do I.

"Betty Beale calls me all the time and bawls me out for not inviting her to my parties," he admits. The reason, as Martindale sees it, is that "the New Frontier set a bad tone by pushing people in the pool and it had bad repercussions for politicians back home.

"Now people are much more guarded about their private lives. And social reporters are much more sophisticated. They ask tougher questions. One doesn't have dinners and have them covered because then your guests don't have the freedom to know they can say something and not have to read about it the next day.

"Joanie Braden," says Martindale, "is particularly sensitive to press write-ups, maybe because this is such a public town and it doesn't look too good to read about how we're all raising hell while a lot of Americans are standing in unemployment lines."

Still, Martindale thinks this whole sensitivity to publicity has gone a little far. "Everybody was appalled, for instance, that Henry Catto wanted to be Chief of Protocol because you have to go to all those horrible public parties. The taint is that pervasive.

"I think this anti-publicity thing has swung too far. I think we need a little balance. They say people who go after publicity are on the make, but I think it's a question of style and how you do it. If you're on the society pages you become well known and it's an entree into Washington life. I want to be taken seriously in this town but you have to be careful about getting a reputation of not being a substantive person, of being just a party boy."

Apparently, however, regardless of "style" or "how you do it," those who have succumbed to the lure of publicity haven't made it. Over the last 10 years or so, the treacherous climb to the social pinnacle has been attempted by many. They all have failed. One answer is clear: too much publicity.

Mr. and Mrs. Sidney Zlotnick have opened their home for years to the great and powerful. They specialize in Embassy Row. But the Zlotnicks are often not asked back and their involvement is mostly one-sided. Allison LaLand, the public relations representative from the Hilton Hotel, has had small *soirées* as well, with senators, ambassadors, and members of the administration. But one rarely sees Mrs. LaLand at the intimate little dinners that are given in return. In both cases, the Zlotnicks and Mrs. LaLand have overexposed their guests.

This is not to say that no one else in Washington entertains. Nor is it to say that those who do entertain are necessarily socially ambitious. Several of Georgetown's most sought-after salons are the never-publicized evenings of socialite Mrs. Frank (Polly) Wisner, Gov. and Mrs. Averell Harriman, columnist Joseph Alsop, and *Washington Post* publisher Katharine Graham.

These people, and indeed, most of those who attend Steve Martindale's parties, entertain only sporadically, and for pleasure. Their wariness of publicity may stem from the fact that many of those in the "in" crowd are members of the press themselves: columnists, editors, and television personalities. And they don't want to be covered by their own.

IX Party-giving is a lot of planning and work. One must be willing to put in the time and effort and thought. Martindale is.

"Washington is one big PR con game applied to power and politics," says the wife of a columnist. "Somebody with no qualifications at all except a great drive to do it can make it."

"Steve is willing and able to make a commitment to the time involved and that's what it takes," says Charles Goodell.

"One of the qualities Steve has," says Bob Gray, "and the primary requirement, is energy and willingness to do it. I don't know how to say this without being demeaning. But I remember Perle once telling me that the way to become a successful hostess was just to hang a lamb chop in the window. That's literally true. You just have to make the effort and Steve has a voracious appetite for being a host."

How often does Martindale entertain?

"I knew you'd ask that question," he says, hurriedly pulling a list out of his pocket. "So I wrote it all down. I think I average about two a month. Not very often really, when you think about it."

X The emotional need and the gratification from party-giving is as uplifting to some as professional success. It must be there for one to have the drive to do it.

"Steve is a guy who obviously starts with the basic attributes," says Charles Goodell. "He's attractive and intelligent but he enjoys the entertaining, the toasting and the details that go with it, the association with interesting people acting in roles on higher levels is very stimulating to him."

"I guess," says Greg Mendenhall, one of Martindale's housemates, "you're dealing with the personal needs of Steven as a person and his basic drives. Party-giving fulfills him."

"When I get really depressed," says Martindale, "I give a party. I know having great people will cheer me up."

XI Parties cost money. How do you do it on no money? Martindale has inherited no money at all. He probably makes a good salary, though he won't discuss it. There are two ways he can entertain the way he does.

"Don't forget, he's in public relations and it helps his business so he can write it all off," says Mendenhall.

Both Martindale and his boss Bob Gray insist that he gets no expense account of any kind for entertaining. "If he takes a client for lunch," says Gray, "of course he can get it back. But we don't foot the bill for his parties."

It is the style and manner of entertaining today which make it possible to do it on little money.

"I do the cooking myself quite often," says Martindale. "I try to have good food and good cheap wine. There's no good crystal or china. People can't expect to come to a bachelor's house and be impressed with that kind of thing. Nobody's awed by their surroundings here. They can be comfortable. But Joanie and Margot have taught me how to do it inexpensively. When I gave that birthday party for Joanie it cost me $1,000 for 32 people. Knowing what I know now, I could do it for $400 or $500. But I thought I had to have a good wine for David and Evangeline Bruce. But the hell with that. David Bruce can just drink good old Almaden like everybody else. He probably wouldn't know the difference anyway."

XII Finally, there is an intangible element — a characteristic which cannot be acquired just because someone aspires to being a successful host or hostess. That is, having the right kind of personality. A pleasant personality. Not being offensive in any way. Being attentive. Flattering people but not fawning. Putting yourself out for people in little ways. Helping with favorite charities or political campaigns. Befriending the wives of powerful men so that the wives will make their husbands go. For example, acting as an escort when the husband is out of town. But the most important part of this personality characteristic is this: The successful host or hostess must never be a threat to his or her guests. For the men, this means that the host must not be too powerful or famous, must not be a potential block for the guest in any way. For the women, this means that a hostess must not be too beautiful or too sexy. Neither one may be a professional or sexual threat to any of his or her guests. One should have no fear about offending the host or hostess. One should feel secure in the knowledge that the host or hostess is lucky you are there.

"I like Steve," says a frequent guest. "He's such a baby. He really has nothing to offer, but in my stomach I feel sorry for him and I hate hurting people. I feel quite duped by him and yet I like him."

"He's so sweet," says another. "He's everything my husband can't stand about this town but I just hate turning him down."

"I think he's the head of the CIA," says Art Buchwald.

"He's a mystery to everybody," says another columnist. "He's not cruel, he doesn't hurt anybody but he's on the make and he makes people nervous because he's so nice."

"When I first met him I thought, who's this?" says Doug Kiker. "But I like him. He's a sweet, open, friendly guy. And what the hell. All he's doing is inviting people to his parties. What's wrong with that."

"He's so darn nice and friendly," says Liz Stevens. "You can't help but like him."

"Somehow he puts you in the position of feeling guilty and defensive because he's so nice," says the wife of an official.

"A lot of people say he's a social climber," says Teresa Heinz, wife of Congressman John Heinz. "But if he is, he's the nicest one I know. He canceled his plans for the weekend to help my husband with his campaign and when I had a baby he stopped by the house and brought me a present. He writes notes and sends little arrangements at Christmas time. He always treats me very kindly and I have a nice time at his house."

"I'm not a great power in this town that's going to make or break you," admits Martindale readily. "That's why people feel comfortable here. They can let themselves go and not worry."

There is one small problem, however. The problem of being a lobbyist and being in public relations and the possible conflict.

"I was nervous at first," says Steve, "that my friends in the Senate wouldn't want to see me. But I find that they're always glad to see you if you've got hard information about your subject and I always do."

Martindale's clients are Weyerhauser Lumber, The Wine Institute, Miles Laboratories and the Loral Corporation. He says that he does not entertain his clients at his parties, unless, of course, they happen to be in town.

"When I have an evening at home," he says, "I don't ever think of it as a business evening. If the chairman of the board of one of my companies were in town I would include him the same way I might include an out of town houseguest of one of my dinner guests. But let's not kid ourselves. I was in part hired because I do know people. I can represent their interests better that way. But I think parties that are strictly for business usually aren't fun anyway."

Martindale says he deducts some, but not much, on his expense account. "Maybe I'm an idiot. I guess I could deduct more but I just haven't done it."

He says he thinks the company feels his entertaining is good. "They've never objected to it, but then they've never raised my salary to pay for it or sent over a case of wine, either."

Bob Gray, his boss, puts it this way: "We did not hire Steve because he has a yearning for social publicity. We hired him because he's a liberal Republican and we needed one. I have others here who are higher ranking than Steve who've never given a party."

Steve does make up for excluding a lot of clients from his parties by taking them to lunch at Sans Souci. Nearly every day he can be seen sitting at a key table in Washington's most exclusive restaurant . . . with a telephone on the table.

"His entertaining is a mixed blessing for us and him at Hill and Knowlton," says Bob Gray. "It's fine for him to mix and be on a social basis with people who can help us. But there's a tremendous danger that he may be labeled as a male entertainer, a playboy, or that he may acquire a Perle Mesta image. That gives people the impression that he's less substantive. Then maybe people won't take him seriously or won't see him in their offices as readily. Then, too, there is the delicate problem for him of asking himself when is he imposing on a friend on behalf of a client."

There is hardly a person in Washington with any power or cachet who has not been invited to Steve Martindale's. Some go, some don't. But Martindale knows who to invite.

"It's too early yet to see what he wants out of it or what he's going to get out of all this entertaining," says an observer.

"By God," says Martindale, "I am a serious person and I intend to make a professional impact on this town one day."

Like how? "Well, I plan to go into politics."

Doesn't that mean going back to live in Pocatello?

He pauses, takes a deep breath and then he finally says it.

"Then maybe I'll do something which is related to politics. I guess once you've lived in Washington you can never go back to Pocatello."

—June 23, 1974

Next: Cheerleaders

This may be the most complex story ever written on what many would regard as the mundane subject of cheerleading, but the idea behind it is quite simple. Assignment to your dance critic: go out and bring to the cheerleaders of the Maryland State playoffs for Class A high school football the same insight and expertise used for Balanchine or Graham.

Sometimes such way-out gambles to pierce stereotypes work, and sometimes they fail. This one works.

In his essay on the genuine mystique of what he calls "the pop art choreography of the competitive drive," Mike Kriegsman demonstrates that dance and cheerleading derive from the same anthropological origins, sexist as they may be. As in ancient dance, "cheerleaders are not only prompters (of destiny for the opponent), they also serve (with their eroticism) as surrogates for the victor's spoils." A little rough for wholesome, prosperous Montgomery County, Md., you wonder? But then Kriegsman carries the ritual fertility, harvest and combat parallels forward, getting gradually more specific, pinning down his thesis and finally ending with specific examples of cross-influences in this century between cheerleading and the dance.

The structure and tone are straight, hard, logical exposition. It's the idea that breaks the cliche. The piece is fun, but more important, it unexpectedly probes the commonly accepted image of "wholesomeness" in our hallowed rites of youth. —L. T.

Roots in Dance, Rites of Fall

By Alan M. Kriegsman

"Whadya want? Victory! Whadya want? Victory!"
"Front, center, tackle, guard — hit 'em again, hit 'em hard!"
"First 'n ten, do it again!"
"Mighty tough te-am! Ya can beat anybody, but ya can't beat Us!"
"H-H-H, u, s . . . . . . T-T-T, l, e . . . Hustle!"

Fresh young faces, flushed with cold and excitement. Flaring miniskirts, flashing, slender legs, splayed in the air in symmetrical formation. Shouts and yells, screeched to the crowd in forceful unisons, answered by thunderous roars. It's the cheerleaders, doing their stuff for the big game, the culmination of the season, the ultimate prize.

The occasion was the Maryland state playoffs for the Class A high school championship, at Gaithersburg, Saturday, between the victorious Friendly "Patriots" and their valiant underdog opponents, the Northwood "Indians." But in many respects, it could have been anywhere along the feverish gridiron circuit, heated to a platinum glow by a football mania that has a whole nation in its grasp.

What was also plain to see was that there's more to cheerleading than leading cheers. It's a communal ceremony, a rite. It's the pop-art choreography of the competitive drive, performed against one of the greatest machismo spectacles ever devoured by an avid public.

Actually, cheerleading connects with the most ancient roots of dance art, dance as a sacred invocation of divine powers. Among prehistoric peoples, and in primitive societies even today, men and women dance to accelerate the rains, to hasten the return of the sun, to bring forth crops and children. But dance also, from time immemorial, has been a sacramental adjunct to war, a bodily hymn designed to influence the gods toward the certitude of triumph. The cheerleaders do the same thing, in a manner of speaking. They whip the combatants up to the necessary level of ferocity, they inspire fear and trembling in the opposition camp, they call upon destiny to look with favor upon the exertions of their champions.

There's also something ineradicably erotic about cheerleading, however much it is presented as entirely wholesome and innocent. The author of *Dancers Through the Ages* writes that "to throw up the leg, the ethnographers tell us, is an antique figure of a fertility rite, executed by the women and practiced by many peoples and races." Cheerleaders are not only prompters, they also serve as surrogates for the victor's spoils—they're tempters as well, goading the male players on to visions of conquest, on the battlefield and off, and enticing the fans to partake in the common fantasy.

This aspect may explain why active supporters of women's liberation view the cheerleader as a traditional and exploited female role that should be discarded.

In recent years, the erotic connotations have been outlandishly exploited, in the wake of a pervasive contemporary license in all sexual matters. Cheerleaders, as the titles of pulp pornography clearly indicate, have shared the ignominious fate, dictated by rampant male chauvinism, of stewardesses, cocktail waitresses and others whose function is to "serve" males.

The girls of the Northwood and Friendly squads seemed either indifferent or amusedly resentful toward the sex-object stereotype.

Aside from the obvious cachet of popularity, what is it that lures them into cheerleading? "We really want to support the team, we think they're just great," was one response, with a lot of nodding of heads. What about the advantages to one's social life? "Well, sure, it helps, but that's not why we do it," said one. Another piped up, "We want to make 'em yell, that's why," and that appeared to provoke general assent.

The whole scene of the game, the field and the rooters has the aspect of a symbolic ritual of combat. The bobbing throngs in the stands, the streamers of colored paper tossed like flares, confetti bursting from extended arms like paper shrapnel, the noise, the waves of elation and despair, the occasional eruption of fisticuffs on the sidelines, not to mention the teams themselves, with their ceremonial formations, the huddles, the charges, the speeding collision of hurtling bodies, the multicolored "armor" of the uniforms.

Most of this movement, en masse, is random in form, the result of innumerable surgings and ebbings. But the cheerleaders' routines are literally choreographic, precise patterns of movement and gesture, to fixed rhythms, and highly specific in expressive content.

A dancer might analyze the actual steps and movements in the fancy French lingo of the classical balletic art—the split as a "grand ecart," the jump as a "saut" or "jeté," the turnabouts as "pirouettes," and so forth. The basis is the same, however, and so are the overall principles which govern the design of steps and patterns. The leap is the inevitable punctuation of almost every cheer, for instance, because it is the ideal analogy of exultation, and the ultimate paradigm of victory over an opposing force, i.e., gravity.

There are any number of conspicuous differences, of course, between cheerleading and dance. For one thing, there are no "pas de deux" in

"Sports of various kinds have always permeated the dance vocabulary…"

cheerleading, which knows an occasional solo twist or two but is mainly an ensemble activity in which all the participants do roughly the same thing at the same time. That's because the whole force of the movement has to be amplified toward the single goal of exciting enthusiasm. For a similar reason, there are no adagios. The movements are strictly up-tempo, since their overriding purpose is to stir up partisan frenzy in an unbroken crescendo.

Cheerleading does require diligent training and rehearsal, though, almost to the degree of dance. The squads at Northwood and Friendly devote a minimum of six hours weekly, after classes, learning the routines and honing them to a fine edge.

What's more, division of labor obtains in football spectacle as much as anywhere else in modern life. In addition to the cheerleaders, there are also the majorettes and the pompons, separate and distinct corps of girls, each with their own dress, function and style of movement. The majorettes and the pompons take over during the half-time break, turning the field into a giant musical and visual pageant. But during the game too, they're in the stands, leading the audience response to the cheerleaders, and instigating cheers of their own.

Older editions of the *Encyclopaedia Britannica* discuss the evolution of cheerleading under the entry "Cheering" (there's no such entry in recent editions; presumably it's too "frivolous" a subject). The Eleventh Edition (1911), for instance, notes that "rhythmical cheering has been developed to its greatest extent in America in the college yells, which may be regarded as a development of the primitive war-cry . . . this cheering and singing forms one of the distinctive features of intercollegiate and scholastic athletic contests in America."

If, along the way, cheerleading has lifted a few leaves from the book of dance, it has worked the other way around as well. Sports of various kinds have always permeated the dance vocabulary, because they are such naturally rich sources of vital and characteristic movement. In modern times, the dance stage has seen a host of works like Balanchine's "A La Francaix," which is based on tennis; Ashton's "Les Patineurs," on ice-skating; William Dollar's "Combat," on horsemanship and dueling; and Gerald Arpino's "Sea Shadow," which owes much to the movement of swimming. And then there's Merce Cunningham's "How to Pass, Kick, Fall and Run," which brings us full circle back to the pigskin.

— November 28, 1974

Next: The Mardi Gras and the Derby

Sally Quinn wrote in her "Martindale and the Law of Twelve" story that "Washington is about the only town in the world where the word 'nouveau' is laudatory." In this pair of stories, she profiles two outposts of privileged, formal aristocracy—New Orleans, La., and Lexington, Ky.—where the opposite is the case.

Routine coverage of these communities during Mardi Gras or the Kentucky Derby usually focuses on glittering externals—the balls, the Mardi Gras parades, the race at Churchill Downs. Generally, these are all you read about, for either or both of two reasons: (1) force of journalistic habit; (2) inaccessibility of the socialites' private functions to the reporter. By knowing, or getting to know, the right people Quinn overcame the second handicap and got behind the scenes to give detailed dissections of who is "in" and who is "out," and why.

In New Orleans, she focuses on the complex, discriminatory mechanics by which Mardi Gras is ruled through the few. And among the rich horse-breeders of Lexington, "one's social standing is more or less defined by one's horse situation" and she goes on to profile the hierarchy.

Strikingly, numerous themes recur in both stories—snobbery (disregard for "tackies"), all-out pursuit of fun for fun's sake (no Washington partying for business purposes here), anti-Semitism, racial discrimination and provincialism. Once again the Quinn ear for the apt quote and eye for the telling detail give the stories added authority. And the Lexington story is a tour de force *in another way: she dictated it by phone on deadline off the top of her head with nothing but notes to back her up.*

Note: As with several of the best stories in this anthology, Quinn spices the accounts by picking up the language of her subjects (one gets "a 'buzz' on" at the Mardi Gras balls instead of getting "drunk"). She wryly backs into the race problem in New Orleans ("There's this awkward thing about discrimination"), and backs into a scandalous article about Princess Margaret, published just before she was to arrive in Lexington ("Just about everybody in Lexington had three magazines on their coffee tables this week").
—L. T.

Mardi Gras: Playing a Game of Kings, Queens and Peasants

By Sally Quinn

NEW ORLEANS — A well-placed young man in New Orleans society was telephoned by a reporter who asked for guidance to the Mardi Gras celebration. He graciously agreed to act as escort and entree to various exclusive events. Then he paused, "I just want to ask you one question, honey," he said hesitantly. "Are you white?"

A city councilman, a native of New Orleans and a member of a prominent and well-to-do Jewish family, also offered to help. He suggested the Boston Club, an exclusive WASP men's club, as the perfect place to watch the big Mardi Gras Day Parade. "Call my best friend and tell him I sent you," he said. "He'll be glad to take you." The councilman, of course, could not go.

"I'll tell you something honestly," said a wealthy restaurateur involved in a middle-rung and relatively democratic Mardi Gras organization. "We have many, many, many Jews. But every time I suggest taking in a Negro the other members balk. They keep saying to wait a while and let's not rock the boat for a couple of years."

"New Orleans is a city of aristocrats and peasants," said an artist from a socially undistinguished background. "The middle class finds it very uncomfortable here. Maybe the big society Mardi Gras balls discriminate but the middle-rung ones don't. They'll take Jews but the upper-class Jews don't want to join them because they're just as snobby as everyone else. But it's the snobbery, politics and intrigue that make Mardi Gras great."

In 1950 the Duke and Duchess of Windsor wrote a dear old friend in New Orleans — a proud member of the local Jewish aristocracy — and invited themselves down for Mardi Gras. She wrote back instructing her royal friends that she personally could not have them as she was not included in the festivities. They should try some other friend. They did. The Windsors are considered in New Orleans to be the most truly elegant out-

251

of-town guests to come to Mardi Gras since Grand Duke Alexis Romanov appeared in 1872 and inspired the idea for "Rex, King of Carnival."

"They were Comus' most popular guests," said a local admirer. "They got right into the spirit beautifully of the 'court,' bowed to the king and queen and everything and let's face it, they have class. No one's interested in having some tacky little celebrity who wants to be treated like a queen."

When Lynda Bird Johnson came to New Orleans and got herself invited to Comus, the most social ball, there were some grumbles from the insiders. "She's just country people, even if her father was President," said one of them. What was worse, Lynda Bird added insult to injury by bringing movie star George Hamilton along with her. At least she got in. Bess and Harry Truman, and Joan and Teddy Kennedy never made Comus.

"These are private parties," said a member of one of the best krewes (Mardi Gras social clubs). "If any nice dignified person wants to come and is invited by a member, that's fine. But no one is dying to have them and we don't go looking for those people. If President Nixon came, for instance, that wouldn't be considered a coup. Nobody would get excited." Nobody got excited about Gen. John J. Pershing, Gen. George Marshall or Gary Cooper, other past Comus guests.

Mardi Gras means "Fat Tuesday" in French and is the last day before Lent begins. It signifies the end of Carnival (Latin for "farewell to the flesh"). It begins on the twelfth night (Jan. 6) and ends at midnight before Ash Wednesday (March 7).

It actually began in 1699 when French-Canadian explorer Pierre Le-Moyne, Sieur d'Iberville, named a spot 30 miles up the Mississippi "Point du Mardi Gras," after his national holiday. Spontaneous celebrating was conducted after that by the largely Catholic Creoles, the original inhabitants of New Orleans, until 1857. That year a group of Anglo-Saxon Protestants from Mobile, Ala., started a secret organization called "the Mystik Krewe of Comus," and had a torch-light parade without, of course, calling attention to themselves. Their theme was "The Demon Actors in Milton's Paradise Lost." They were considered *arrivistes*.

In fact, anyone whose family hasn't lived in New Orleans for decades is considered a newcomer, and that's not a compliment. "Hell," said one would-be social young man, "my family has been here for over 50 years and *we're* considered newcomers."

WHAT IT IS: One thing newcomers will never understand is what Mardi Gras is all about. Not that those who've been here any length of time understand. The main difference is in attitude. For New Orleaneans Mardi Gras is a *serious* affair. It is serious for those whose families have controlled the city for two centuries, serious for blacks who have their own

" 'The masking lets you live out an alternative lifestyle.' "

important place in the Mardi Gras, serious to the Jews who originally were part of the celebration and are now excluded, serious to those who in recent years have started their own krewes, marching groups and truck floats, and serious to those newcomers who are social or political climbers.

No one in New Orleans doesn't care one way or the other about Mardi Gras and what it should be. They will describe themselves as impassioned, vehement, crazed, frenzied or freaked-out. They might also say, as one socialite kept insisting coolly, "It's all nothing but a lot of foolishness and nonsense." Just ask him though how he feels about outside criticism and he flares, "It's none of their goddamned business. Why don't they stay away and leave us alone and let us have our Mardi Gras to ourselves."

Whether they are "in" or "out" most New Orleaneans, while proudly explaining that tourism is the town's second largest industry, hate tourists who come for Mardi Gras. They're either dirty or pranksters or maybe just curious bystanders but they don't seem to fit in. Tourists and "hippies" are not that distinguishable from one another to the locals. They're all outsiders. "The whole point of Mardi Gras is group participation," says George Schmidt, a local artist and carnival buff.

"It's a derived aesthetic; responses are ingrained since childhood like sights, sounds and smells. It transcends all classes. The masking lets you live out an alternative lifestyle. It's hypnotic, fantasy and enchantment, violence, chaos, mystery. Tourists and itinerants can't possibly get involved so they try and destroy it."

A local socialite says the carnival is like "an enormous encounter group, a huge emotional orgy, a catharsis where you act out your feelings only because you are masked. The last thing in the world you want around," he says, "is someone who's not with you all the way."

Leon Irwin III, a national Democratic committeeman whose family members for generations have been leaders in all the best krewes, a member of the exclusive Boston Club, and an outstanding civic leader and businessman, feels out-of-towners don't fully understand Mardi Gras. "This is a local tribal festival; it's expressly for fun," he says, "and enjoyed by most members of the community in different ways. When it ceases to become this, it should itself cease."

"New Orleans is not part of America, it's a colony, part of the third world. Americans can't understand this," says George Schmidt.

"My momma says," said a lawyer, "Mardi Gras is so important that even if all of New Orleans had chicken pox, we'd still have it. And maybe it would be a good thing too. Keep the tourists away."

There have been rumors about the possibility of Mardi Gras violence stemming from the Howard Johnson's sniping incident in January. One rumor is that Rex will be assassinated at Canal Street. "Maybe it would be a good thing," pondered an old-time reveler. "That might just be what we need to scare the tourists away."

HOW IT'S DONE: New Orleans is the only city in America where social status is determined by men. All of the social organizations for Mardi Gras are called krewes and are men's clubs. (Not to be confused with the exclusive and restricted Boston and Pickwick Men's Clubs.)

The krewes are responsible for organizing the Mardi Gras balls and the parades.

Anyone can belong to as many krewes as he likes. Dues range from $250 to $300 per year and all the krewes are shrouded in secrecy. There are only four krewes one really needs to know about: Momus, Comus, Proteus and Rex. "We kind of feel it has the sound of a law firm," said a stodgy member of M,C,P&R.

Each krewe has The Captain and he has his lieutenants, or The Committee. There is almost no internal organization and some members of some krewes don't even know who's on The Committee. A strange laxity, considering it's The Committee that has absolute power and decides who will be asked to join, which women will be invited as special ("call-out") guests, who will be banished to the balcony merely to watch and most important, whose daughters will be chosen as queen and maids of the court. This is equivalent to a debut and the only deadly serious aspect of Mardi Gras.

Balls begin sometime around Christmas and lead up to Mardi Gras day when the Comus and Rex balls take place. Invitations are as coveted as those to Buckingham Palace. Krewe members must fill out forms with information explaining who their guests are, and include two references. Krewe members are the only ones allowed to wear masks and costumes. Invitations to guests come in two forms. Well-placed ladies — wives, mothers, friends, debutantes — get "call-outs." These allow the invitees to sit in a special section so as to be easily called out to dance. Nonmember male guests (always in white-tie and tails) may be invited as floor committeemen and are instructed by the master-members to call out the ladies. Floor committeemen may never, never dance themselves.

Gentlemen are allowed to drink only between certain "call-outs" and women are not allowed to drink officially at all. Hence the custom of getting drunk beforehand, bringing one's own flask and sipping in the parking lot, or slipping off to the ladies' room. "If you don't have a little 'buzz' on, you'd never make it through all this," a socially-prominent participant pointed out. Some of the men probably would have gotten a "buzz" on riding to the ball on floats. Even some of the more aristocratic floats are notorious for having so much booze on the floor that the riders can't stand up and have to be tied to the floats. Two men have died in the last several years from falling off floats with "a little 'buzz' on."

"Fantastic," said a krewe member of one of the deceased. "What a terrific way to go."

THE PROBLEMS: There's this awkward thing about discrimination. No Jews, Italians or newcomers have much to do with the real carnival. Of the top four krewes, only Rex, which is more civic than social, accepts Jews and then only as members, not in the inner circle. It seems odd, since the first ruler of Rex, in 1872, was a Jew named Louis Salomon. Some Jews were even partly responsible for keeping Carnival alive financially during the Depression. But somewhere along the line things didn't work out too well socially for the Jews. No one is quite sure why.

Members of the exclusive krewes feel the Jewish problem is overstated. "This whole thing is just for fun and very democratic," said one. "The Jews could start their own krewe if they wanted to. Everybody else has. (There are now more than 50 krewes, including Italian krewes, black krewes and women's krewes.) Anybody from a bank president to a garbage collector can have his own club. And besides, it's a religious holiday."

However, Leon Irwin III feels strongly that "a sense of exclusiveness that the Jewish community feels about Mardi Gras is unfortunate and regrettable. I think that this situation is unacceptable to growing numbers of members of some of the traditional Mardi Gras organizations, particularly young people. I think this question, like so many others, is progressively and slowly changing."

Rumor has it that Rex might even be a Jew in the next four or five years. However, this could create problems. Rex is traditionally a member of the restricted Boston Club; at midnight of Mardi Gras, Rex traditionally goes over to the restricted Comus ball and bows to the king of Comus.

City councilman for New Orleans' silk stocking district, Peter Beer, is a Jew who has lived here all his life. His father belonged to Rex and was one of those who helped during the Depression. Beer has spoken out publicly against Mardi Gras for its waste of public funds (more than a million dollars for maintenance, police, fire protection and cleanup) and its discriminatory aspect.

"The discrimination drains away good will," he said. "A large percentage of the leaders of the community are Jewish. So you have a guy, who, but for Mardi Gras, would be in a position of complete acceptability. He can't help but feel hurt or react less responsively in the community if his best friends and business associates 360 days a year can't associate with him the other five."

With all the talk about no tourists, there is one group which goes all-out to attract as many people to New Orleans for Mardi Gras as possible. They have even started their own krewe, Bacchus. "Dedicated to wine and good times. It's most apropos of our group and we do stand up for that," says one of its founders, restaurateur Owen Brennan Jr.

"We started this group because a lot of tourists who come to New Orleans couldn't parade or dance because everything was private. The whole purpose is to promote New Orleans and Mardi Gras. We even have a celebrity king flown in from out of town."

"A celebrity king from out of town!" shrieks a Bacchus detractor. "Do you *realize* how that is the antithesis of everything Mardi Gras stands for? This is our celebration. Even the local peasants don't want a celebrity king from out of town." Brennan knows he is criticized. He is a member of Hermes, a less elegant, more democratic krewe, "for business reasons."

Those against Mardi Gras say big business opportunities suffer here because companies won't send big executives who aren't able to make it socially as newcomers. "Come 1975," says Brennan, "when the Super Dome opens, we're going to package Mardi Gras for tourists. We'll have a continuing parade inside the Dome for 75,000 people while simultaneously, in the four adjoining halls, we'll have four supper dances going on with four name bands. Terrific publicity!" Brennan plans to donate the proceeds to the police and fire departments.

This year's big celebrity king of Bacchus is Bob Hope, who is doing an NBC special on Mardi Gras. (Comus has allowed itself to be filmed only for network news shows and one story goes that they mistakenly allowed a Walt Disney film crew to film the ball and discovered later that the film was to be spliced with shots of Annette Funicello. The idea was killed.)

Of all the problems concerning Mardi Gras, the one that is rarely mentioned is the black problem. It is still not much of an issue in New Orleans. The blacks have their own krewes in various degrees of social acceptability and they traditionally carry the flambeaux in the parade. "The Jewish problem is far more serious here," said a white krewe member. "There's been very little pressure to integrate the balls." He dismisses the subject with, "We're just not ready for that yet."

There are those who feel Mardi Gras is on its way out, that with all the financial problems, violence, itinerants and discrimination it cannot possibly continue. But if what one Momus, Comus, Proteus, Rex member says is true, it will probably never cease to exist. "It is a game of kings and queens. You can do or see whatever your fantasy is for a day. And if a guy is not very successful at the office, if his father is president of a bank and he sits and reads the paper all day, it gives him a sense of power and importance to be on a committee of a good krewe. What the hell, he can dress up like a king and ride a float to the stadium and have millions of people clamoring for a wave or a favor from him. Everybody loves a king."

—March 3, 1973

'Bluebloods,' 'Tackies'
Midst the Bluegrass

By Sally Quinn

L EXINGTON, Ky. — Just about everybody in Lexington had three
magazines on their coffee tables this week: a copy of last month's
Town and Country with a Derby society layout, a copy of the latest issue
of this month's *Antiques* magazine with a layout of old Lexington houses
and a copy of April's *McCall's* magazine with a cover layout of Princess
Margaret and Antony Armstrong-Jones titled "The Curious Marriage of
Princess Margaret" and quoting Margaret on the cover saying, "We're
a scandal."

Some people were outraged by the piece, which portrayed Margaret as a
bored and bitchy woman whose marriage was a farce, and others were
amused, but one thing was for sure. Everybody was curious. "She can't
be all that bad," said one of Lexington's leading hosts, "but then," and he
said it almost hopefully, "maybe she will be. And boy I'd sure like to see
her refuse to shake *my* hand."

So there were, to be sure, mixed emotions about Princess Margaret
coming to the hundredth annual Kentucky Derby, the only time British
royalty had been to the Derby in Louisville since the Duke and Duchess of
Windsor came in 1951, and the only time royalty had *ever* hit Lexington,
which is 75 miles east of Louisville.

Princess Margaret's first public outing into Lexington's society was
yesterday to visit Spendthrift Farm, owned by "po' ole cousin Leslie
Combs," the best horse hustler in the world.

Arriving at the stable with her husband, Lord Snowdon, and her hosts,
Mr. and Mrs. Cornelius Vanderbilt (Sonny) Whitney, Princess Margaret
was shown several of the horses, then posed for pictures for the scores of
local, national and international press, then disappeared back into the
rented limousine to go "up to the house."

The press was led away and Margaret and her party arrived at "cousin"
Leslie's for a mint julep. With her was "cousin" Leslie (a widower),
"cousin" Leslie's daughter, Juliet, and her husband, David Trapp, Leslie's
son and wife, Mr. and Mrs. Brownell Combs, and several houseguests.

David Trapp was dressed in a shocking blue Arnel jacket, red, white and blue dacron pants and blue suede shoes. "My, don't you look dashing," said Mary Lou Whitney, whose husband was in dark country tweeds, looking him over disapprovingly from head to toe. "So do you, kid," said David right back.

Princess Margaret, in a conservative white dress and coat, smiled a big smile at the tall, good-looking David. Later at "cousin" Leslie's she said to him, "I'd like to take you back to London with me."

"Damn," said David later, "how do you like that? She's not so bad after all. In fact, she's real nice."

Princess Margaret did stand up the whole time at cousin Leslie's, so no one else could sit down, but that was okay with everybody and, though her lady in waiting grimaced and asked, "What *are* we drinking?," Margaret drank her mint julep.

She shook hands with everybody. She responded when people said "Hi" and she did not seem disapproving when nobody curtsied or called her Ma'am.

But "cousin" Leslie, a millionaire horse breeder now in his 70s, and who still has an eye for the ladies, as everyone will tell you, got in the last word. In fact, people are still talking about how when "cousin" Leslie met Queen Elizabeth he called her honey and pinched her. But Juliet says that's not exactly true. She says he never pinched her and he only called her honey after he'd talked to her for an hour about horses.

"Honey," said Leslie, taking Margaret by the arm, "y'all come over to my place on Sunday and get you sump'n to eat and drink. The cats'll be there and the kids'll be playing."

"I beg your pardon," said Margaret.

"It's just an old coal-town expression. That's where the colored people live," Leslie explained later. "It means we're going to have some fun."

If you want to have fun when you come to the Kentucky Derby, then Lexington is where you should come. And, even though the actual Derby at Churchill Downs is in Louisville, most anybody who is anybody spends his time in Lexington. As one social observer points out, "Most people in Lexington wouldn't be caught dead in Louisville until post time."

What most people don't seem to understand is that Lexington is an elegant, if somewhat provincial, very Southern town. Louisville, in the eyes of Lexingtonians, is nothing but an overgrown, tacky Midwestern town and, what's more, Louisville does not have horses to speak of, which is, of course, what the whole thing is all about. "Louisville is about as noted for its horses as Chicago is," said a local Lexingtonian disdainfully.

Anybody who's been down to the horse country knows that even though the Derby is held at Churchill Downs, the whole thing is really a rather vulgar and commercial scene attended by Lexingtonians mainly because of

258

"...one's social situation is more or less defined by one's horse situation."

tradition and because it's their life's blood. But ask anybody in Lexington where the really elegant racing takes place and they'll tell you Keenland Racecourse in Lexington, a very small, very family sort of racecourse. The only one in the country that faces the sun, which encourages children, and where there are no loud speakers. In other words, a real gentleman's racecourse compared to Churchill Downs.

Socially, Louisville tends to be more Midwestern. There is, for example, very little discrimination against Jews. In fact, many of the town's most socially prominent citizens are Jewish. But that is not the case in Lexington where one will, occasionally, at a friendly, informal gathering, hear an anti-Semitic joke or two.

Neither town, however, has come so far as to include blacks in its social life, and both seem very Southern when one looks at their "help" — blacks in liveried chauffeur outfits, or butlers in stiff white starched jackets, or, as in Lexington, maids in crisp uniforms, who really do call you "Missy" and "Massa" and say "sho nuff."

Since Lexington is where the beautiful farms are, the endless rolling green hills and white fences (although many Lexingtonians are beginning to paint their fences black because it's more economical), and where the horses are, one's social standing is more or less defined by one's horse situation: i.e., whether you've got 'em or you don't.

There is a very strict line drawn between the horse people and the non-horse people, though they do mingle with each other. They know who they are. Then, of course, the horse people are divided into two very distinct groups. The "blue bloods" and the "tackies." Now, most blue blood Lexingtonians won't come right out and tell you who they think is a tacky and who isn't. But what they will tell you is the way it can be determined. "Simply," said a member of a very distinguished local family, "those who like publicity and those who don't."

"Not necessarily," said another blue. "One of the most well-bred couples in Lexington has their own publicity agent."

"But it really doesn't matter what your family background is," said the former. "The nice thing about Lexington is that it doesn't really matter who you are as long as people like you. If you are from the best family and they don't like you you've had it, but if you are nice and fun you've got it made. Lexington is the easiest Southern society to break into."

Derby time for Lexingtonians is play time. The real work time is in July when millionaires from all over the world come to buy from the breeders and owners who make their names and their fortunes off producing Derby winners. In the old days the blue blood farm owners were reluctant to get into the selling business because they found the commercial aspect of it so distasteful. Putting strangers up in your own house, bowing and scraping to people you've never seen before, flattering people you didn't like just went against the grain of those who had been used to the genteel life.

But now, the money is getting to be so fantastic (this year for the first time a yearling was sold for $600,000) that even the staunchest blues are giving in to the green. Even so, you still have to have a substantial fortune to get involved in horse-breeding. As one knowledgeable person said, "To buy one mare would cost at least $50,000, and then it has to be $50,000 you don't mind losing."

Because more and more Lexingtonians are getting serious about horses and money (all these Rolls Royces with telephones, gargantuan diamond rings, manor houses, dinner dances and fancy trips cost money), most of the celebrities who come in for the Derby prefer to stay in Lexington and drive the hour and a half to Louisville on Derby Day.

Those who stay in Louisville the whole time are the hard-core horse business people, the journalists, the trainers, owners, jockeys and those who are involved in the serious business of Derby Day. Each morning between 7 and 9 the owners, trainers and jockeys head out to Churchill Downs to visit their horses, watch them work out and "smell the manure," as one of the more colorful owners remarked.

Last Wednesday night the annual trainers' dinner was held in Louisville and was attended by most of the horse heavies who had come to work rather than play. The annual award, which usually goes to a person who has most helped racing, went this year to Triple Crown winner Secretariat, a final capitulation to the importance of The Horse.

Among the guests was Secretariat's owner, Penny Tweedy, referred to disdainfully by Lexingtonians as "Greedy Tweedy." Penny Tweedy has outraged men and women in the horse world by what they regard as a strident and aggressive attitude toward racing.

Penny Tweedy's behavior toward her husband reportedly disgusted Mary Lou Whitney. Mrs. Tweedy apparently got so involved with her horses that she lost Mr. Tweedy and they are now in the process of filing for divorce.

Mary Lou Whitney wasn't the only one who was upset by Mrs. Tweedy's approach. The hands around the stable at 7:30 in the morning find it highly unattractive, and stable talk often turns to the burgeoning role women are playing at the track. "Did you ever think what the attraction these women have for horses is?" said one of the men.

The men's attraction for racing, they will explain when pressed, is the old macho bit. "These guys have a need to prove their masculinity and they know they can't be a Johnny Unitas snaking his way down the field for a

" '...if a filly can beat colt, she's too masculine to be a good mother.' "

touchdown, but if they've owned a horse or trained a horse or ridden a horse that wins then, in a sense, they've won too."

This male chauvinist piggery at the track extends to the genteel environment of the rolling hills of the Lexington bluegrass and even to the distinctions made between horses. Wednesday, Mr. and Mrs. Cornelius Vanderbilt Whitney extended their hospitality to the press by a guided tour around the 500-acre Whitney farm. Whitney, after showing off his World War II medals, family trophies, his Yale crew team pictures, a letter he once received from Queen Elizabeth and other memorabilia, read a short story he had written about first coming to the Kentucky Derby when he was 17, then gave a tour of his farm.

On the tour he pointed out the grave of his father's mare, "Regrets," the only mare ever to win the Kentucky Derby in 99 years. " 'Regrets' gave birth to 11 foals," said Whitney, "and none of them ever won a race. Among horses, female horses who beat other female horses have produced winning foals, but the girls who beat the boys never can. I guess if a filly can beat colt, she's just too masculine to be a good mother."

Later Mrs. Whitney appeared on the tour to introduce two mares, one of which was called Silver Spoon, and explained what a beautiful lady Silver Spoon was. Turning to the press as if she had just had a conversation with the horse, Mrs. Whitney remarked, "She says I'm such an elegant lady because I love classical music and when I went to California I was much more glamorous than all the movie stars," and then turning to the horse she said, "Isn't that right, darling?" Silver Spoon said nothing but throughout this repartee Silver Spoon was relieving herself unperturbed by Mrs. Whitney or the crowd of photographers who were taking her picture.

The press conference at the Whitney's was part of the preparation for the arrival of Princess Margaret.

There are several versions of how Princess Margaret came to be invited to the Derby, depending on who's telling it. The bitchiest one is this: The board of directors of Churchill Downs decided that for the hundredth anniversary of the Kentucky Derby a member of the British Royal family should be invited. The reason for this was that the Kentucky Derby was named after a famous British horseman named Lord Derby (pronounced Darby by the British and also by some affected Kentuckians). Lord Derby tossed a coin with Lord Bunbury to see which of them should give his name to the race. If Lord Bunbury had won we would be talking about the Kentucky Bunbury today. At any rate, it was decided a member of the British royalty should be present and an invitation was dispatched, through United States Ambassador to Great Britain Walter Annenberg, to the queen. Well, the queen apparently wanted to come, but the problem was that the queen is planning to come to the Bicentennial in 1976.

So if the queen came to the Kentucky Derby it wouldn't be such a big deal to come to the other celebration. And anyway, she couldn't go to the Derby without making it a state visit rather than just an official visit, the way Princess Margaret's is, and she would have to be received by the head of state, i.e. President Nixon, and it was just all too complicated.

So she offered the queen mother. That apparently sent everybody into a state of hysteria, because Kentuckians are upset anyway that the Derby doesn't appeal to as many young people as they would like, and they didn't want to set a septuagenarian tone to the event.

There was a lot of diplomatic back and forth, politely trying to dissuade the queen from sending the queen mother without insulting anybody, and politely trying to suggest that Princess Margaret come instead to liven things up a bit. It finally all worked out, but there were several prominent Kentucky socialites who had to retire with the vapours after such a trying ordeal.

Once Margaret's visit was set, Churchill Downs hired a Lexington PR firm to handle the press. Never having handled a member of royalty before, the press setup was an almost hilarious example of overkill.

For instance, the arrival of Princess Margaret at the local private airport Thursday was treated as the White House would treat the arrival of the head of a major state. Countless numbers and colors and shapes and sizes of press and security badges were passed out to members of the press who had to be cleared by local, state and national police as well as Scotland Yard. Buses. The press was escorted in buses by motorcycle police with "sireens" going full-blast down the nearly deserted road to the airport.

Once inside the airport, over an hour before the arrival of the princess, the press was cordoned off on one side of the hangar and a red carpet and podium were set up directly facing the press. There the mayor and his wife and son (who was to present a bouquet to the princess), a major-general, the Whitneys and other officials gathered in a line facing the press and waited, and waited, and waited. . . .

When the plane arrived the princess and her husband were escorted to the podium, where she was presented with flowers and the major-general made a short speech. Mary Lou Whitney curtsied and Princess Margaret smiled and they all piled into limousines along with her equerry, her group captain, her personal secretary, her lady-in-waiting, her personal bodyguard, her personal dresser, her personal lady's maid and Rene, her personal hairdresser and her 38 pieces of luggage, and off they went to the Whitneys'. And that was it.

262

"Who are all these people and what are all these badges?" asked one of the members of the police department of a Secret Service man after the princess had left. "How the hell should I know?" said the Secret Service man. "I haven't got any idea what any of them mean."

The security was extraordinarily tight (there were as many Secret Service men as President Nixon has, according to the PR firm) and became even tighter after a Thursday evening threat on Princess Margaret's life. The local police received an anonymous phone call saying, "This is the voice of the IRA, a disenchanted branch. We ask you to watch Princess Margaret this week, and you will see an unusual sight." Princess Margaret apparently was not told of this threat but those who were entertaining her were.

Those who were entertaining her were also told earlier in the week of some of the princess' likes and dislikes, including the fact that she likes Scotch whisky, Chesterfield cigarettes and Coca-Colas; that she likes to have with her at all times a glass of drinking water; and, to the surprise of some, that she likes to do the can-can. While Princess Margaret was drinking juleps at Spendthrift Farm yesterday morning, a call went out to a motorcycle policeman behind the gate that someone should go to the Whitney farm and fetch her sunglasses and her cigarette holder.

A word about juleps. Hardly anybody in Kentucky drinks them. They are just for show. The reason people don't drink them is that they are too complicated to make for a number of people, they're much too sweet for those who like good bourbon and they're much too strong for those who care anything at all about remaining coherent. Most people in Kentucky during Derby time drink gin, vodka and Scotch.

If one were to guess, one would have to say that this will be a successful visit for both the princess and her host city. Her trip to Spendthrift Farm yesterday morning seemed to please her enormously and was a great coup for the charming "cousin" Leslie and his daughter, Juliet, who is one of the most distinguished hostesses in the bluegrass region. The afternoon events were equally successful as Princess Margaret went to Darby Dan Farm to visit the queen's mare, Daisy Chain, which has been sent over here to be bred. Everyone was surprisingly charmed by Margaret's accessibility and her unexpected warmth.

"I guess Princess Margaret just figured what the hell, what's the point in being rude to us. We can't help her or hurt her and we're not going to use her and we're never going to see her again, and we're all just here to have a good time anyway," said David Trapp.

"You know Lexington gets so many big shots coming in and out of here to buy and sell horses, like Presidents and Vice Presidents and all, that it just doesn't impress us one way or the other. Hell, Hubert Humphrey once told me that he likes to come to Lexington more than any place he could think of, 'cause it was the only place he could relax and be himself, and people just left him alone."
                                                              — May 4, 1974

V. Humor

Art Buchwald, whose superb satirical column appears in Style, along with many other newspapers, is one of the most amiable of beings. Once, however, he called us upset, by his easygoing standards, with a justified complaint. The headline on one of his columns, he noted, had given away the punch line toward which the whole piece was built.

That kind of botch is what you risk anytime you start tinkering with, or analyzing in detail, humorous essays. You give away the surprises and ruin the effect for the reader; one might just as well lead a review of the latest Agatha Christie with the solution to the case.

Without exposing fine points about the following humorous essays, two generalizations might be made: (1) each, instead of being mere rambling collections of disassociated punch lines, is sharply directed at a central point; (2) the technique is invariably to begin with a simple and vulnerable assumption, and then by repeated complications that undercut the assumption's vulnerable side, to reduce it to tatters.

Of the five examples, two are fantasy (both by Tom Donnelly, the latter of them a searing prophecy 9 months beforehand of the resignation of President Nixon and of the funereal mood that would envelope that event) and three are fact. However, it must be clear to the reader that, in the final story about a hunt with basset hounds, the author's pro-basset bias is so obsessive no one could ever rest secure that Mr. Mitchell, the author, hard as he may have tried, was capable of recording "objectively" for posterity the facts of that historic day.
—L. T.

Gone With the Wind, Part II

By Tom Donnelly

Writer-director Francis Ford Coppola has come up with a different sort of sequel in "The Godfather, Part II." It has been customary for Hollywood's sequel-makers to simply concoct new adventures for assorted heroes and heroines: Billy Jack, Al Jolson, Fanny Brice, Mrs. Miniver, etc. In "The Godfather, Part II," Coppola not only shows us Michael Corleone (Al Pacino) going from bad to worse as the head of America's most famous gangster family, he has taken chapters from Mario Puzo's novel that weren't used in the original "Godfather" film and given us the early history of Michael's father, Vito, who used to be Marlon Brando and now is Robert De Niro.

I don't see why the approach dreamed up by Coppola for his second go at the Corleone saga shouldn't be applied to other massively popular literary properties. Take "Gone With the Wind," for example. The early lives of Scarlett O'Hara's parents were barely touched on in David O. Selznick's film edition of the Margaret Mitchell classic. And over the years millions of folks have tossed and turned at night wondering if Scarlett got Rhett back or not. No doubt about it, "Gone With the Wind, Part II" is a movie that cries aloud to be made . . .

That is, after Hollywood has launched the greatest talent hunt in its history to find a new Rhett Butler, a new Scarlett O'Hara, a new Mammy . . .

The movie opens with an enormous close-up of a sobbing Scarlett O'Hara. Rhett Butler's voice reverberates on the sound track: "My dear, I don't give a damn." After a moment Scarlett dries her tears. "I won't think about it now," she says, apparently to the world at large. "I'll think of it all tomorrow at Tara. I can stand it then. Tomorrow, I'll think of some way to get him back. After all, tomorrow is another day."

At Tara, we fade in on Scarlett sitting on the veranda, finishing a mint julep. "Fetch me another, Mammy," she says. Mammy shakes her head in disapproval. "Ain' right foh a lady to drink so many juleps, Miss Scarlett," she says. "Even yoh poh Daddy, de late Mistah Gerald O'Hara, called it quits wid nine." But Scarlett insists, and as Mammy goes off to make an-

GONE WITH THE WIND
PART II
STARRING...

JACKIE GLEASON
as RHETT BUTLER

MIA FARROW
as SCARLETT O'HARA

TELLY SAVALAS
as ASHLEY WILKES

...with **BOB HOPE** as **GEN. WILLIAM TECUMSEH SHERMAN**

Thrill again to the burning of Atlanta.
Blanch at outrageous profanities.
Wince at Scarlett's alcoholism.
Marvel at Rhett's business acumen.
Watch the Bank foreclose on Scarlett's mortgage.

other drink, Scarlett murmurs, "Oh, Pa! How I wish you were here to tell me again those dashing stories of your early life!"

As Scarlett stares into the remains of her tenth julep the mint turns into a bank of shamrocks and we are back in old Ireland. The shamrocks are suddenly stained with blood: Young Gerald O'Hara has just fatally shot an English absentee landlord's rent agent. Gerald's mother pops out from behind a tree. "Well done, me fine broth of a boy!" she cries. "Sure and after you've buried the body under the pigsty you'd better be off to America to join your brothers in Savannah, though the dear God alone knows where that may be!"

Montage of Gerald O'Hara setting sail for America (steerage, of course) and arriving in Savannah where he goes to work in his brothers' store, becomes proficient at poker and drinking, and wins both a valet and a plantation at the gaming tables. We see Gerald being married to the lovely Miss Ellen Robillard, of the proud-as-Lucifer Robillards, and as Ellen's wedding veil seems to rise like a curtain so the camera can show us her very thoughts, we learn that Ellen is marrying Gerald because her true love was shot to death in a barroom brawl.

Back to Tara, in the present. Mammy comes in with another julep. Scarlett snatches it from her. "Great balls of fire, but I need this drink," she cries. "Those flashbacks make me furiously thirsty!"

"Those juleps makin' you look positively tacky," cries Mammy. "You got yoh shawl all tangled up in yoh hayuh and yoh hoop skirt is up around yoh neck. When ah thinks of the hours Miss Ellen and ah spent tryin' to teach yoh ta ack lak a lil lady!"

Yet another flashback shows Mammy and Miss Ellen teaching Scarlett how to smile so her dimples leap, how to walk pigeon-toed so that her wide hoop skirts sway entrancingly, and how to flutter her eyelids in a manner calculated to make any beau quiver with desire.

The past fades out and we are back in the present. A bitter and somewhat sodden Scarlett cries, "All those airs and graces didn't help me hold on to Rhett Butler! Didn't keep him from runnin' to Belle Watling whenever my back was turned, and even when it wasn't!"

Scarlett is well launched on a soliloquy devoted to her loathing of Belle Watling when it suddenly occurs to her that what Belle did, she can do. "I'll open a pleasure palace!" cries Scarlett, "and if I know Rhett Butler, sooner or later he'll come calling! I'll have him tied up in knots before he knows what's hit him. I'll change my name so he won't suspect a thing. . . ."

Six months later Scarlett is sitting moodily in the front parlor of her pleasure place when Prissy, her maid of all work, ushers in a tall, handsome man with much fussing and fanfare. "Mah lan, Miss Scarlett, yoh evah think you see this big tall hansome gempmum again?" Scarlett rises with a wildly beating heart, but almost immediately sinks back on her crimson velvet settee with a small groan.

Illustration by John Twohey

The caller is Ashley Wilkes, once the great love of Scarlett's life but now the drag of drags.

Ashley can't make head or tail of the ledgers kept by his accountant and he wants Scarlett to explain them to him; after all, she promised Ashley's late wife, Melanie, that she would always look after Ashley, his sawmill, and his son, Beau. "My accountant does something he calls triple entry," Ashley murmurs wanly. "He says that's better than double entry. But why doesn't the business ever show a profit and how is he able to live like a prince on the salary I pay him?"

Scarlett and Ashley have their heads together when the door opens and a tall, swarthy, handsome, dissipated man stands there, none too steadily. "Rhett!" cries Scarlett. "Rhett Butler! You've come at last! Oh darling, I knew you would!"

But Rhett says, "So, you're still drooling over hapless Ashley, are you?" Scarlett frantically explains that she and Ashley are just talking business and Rhett is the one she loves madly. But Rhett says, "My dear, I don't give a damn," and lurches out into the night.

"Fiddle-dee-dee!" cries an exasperated Scarlett. Prissy trips into the room to announce that a railroad magnate has just arrived and is looking for a fast game of cards and an equally speedy brunette. In double exposure we see Scarlett's father winning Tara at poker while Scarlett cries, "What Pa can do, I can do!"

Scarlett gambles and wins the dining car on the Atlanta Special. She figures that sooner or later Rhett Butler will be taking this train; everybody does.

Ashley Wilkes does, for one. He has heard that Scarlett is acting as hostess on this diner and he wants her to advise him about his son Beau, who has just been expelled from the University of Virginia for setting fire to the mathematics department, mathematics being his worst subject and Beau hoping the fire would lead to a cancellation of exams.

We see a reenactment of the fire. Suddenly a looming dark shape blots out the flames. We have switched to the present again. Rhett Butler stands in the dining car doorway, staring at Scarlett and Ashley. "Still besotted about that milksop," says Rhett, "this really is the end of the line." Scarlett frantically explains that she was only advising Ashley on what to do about his pyromaniacal son. Rhett says, "My dear, I don't give a damn" and gets off at the next stop.

In the final scene of "Gone With the Wind, Part II," Scarlett is making a deal with a bounty hunter and a taxidermist. She wants two heads mounted on either side of the great fireplace at Tara. "I can't decide whether to hang Rhett on the left side and Ashley on the right," she says, "or vice versa." She shrugs, and as she goes to work on a mint julep she says, "but I don't have to think about that today. I'll think about that tomorrow. It's going to be **FUN** to think about. The most fun I've ever had."

—January 7, 1975

The Panda Watch:
at Home at the Zoo

By Judith Martin

T he pandas (pandas? what pandas?) will be at home to the public at their new palace at the National Zoo on Thursday at about midday, after Mrs. Richard Nixon officially welcomes them to Washington in a morning ceremony.

In preparation for this event, which the White House describes as casual and which the Smithsonian has had several people working on for two weeks, Dr. Theodore Reed, director of the National Zoological Park, held another of his peerless press conferences yesterday. Dr. Reed has just returned from Peking, where he delivered two musk oxen to the zoo and picked up the pandas which Chou En-lai promised President Nixon.

Not only does he now pronounce Peking "Peying," but he can—and did—write the names of the 18-month-old pandas, Hsing - Hsing (male, 74 pounds) and Ling-Ling (female, 136 pounds), in Chinese characters on the blackboard.

Dr. Reed also had the following scientific information to offer:

. . ."They're so sweet and cuddly and lovable that you just want to pick them up and hug them and squeeze them, and they'll beat the hell out of you."

. . ."Anything that dribbles down their chests, they lick off all the drippings. Very nice, very neat, very proper eaters."

. . .The exchange musk oxen, Milton and Matilda, now in Peking, are losing hair "because it's their shedding season," and their coughs are better. But at best, "I just don't think musk oxen have got the sex appeal of pandas. You like musk oxen, but pandas will steal your heart away."

. . ."The Chinese have, like us a panda cult." To prove this, Dr. Reed exhibited panda brand cigarettes, tobacco cans, wall hangings, glasses and cut-outs from the Friendship Store in Peking, but admitted he hadn't gotten to the zoo gift shop. "Holy mackerel, when you've got Roxellanae to look at, you don't go to gift shops." (Roxellanae, he explained, are golden-haired monkeys with snub noses, named after a snub-nosed girl named Roxella or Roxanne who was a friend of King Solomon's. You don't learn at 500 White House briefings what you learn at one of Dr. Reed's.)

Someone came up with the information that pandas don't mate instinctively, but have to have live demonstrations before they got the picture, and asked whether Hsing-Hsing and Ling-Ling (who have never met) patronized such displays. "If they had such a course, they're a bunch of nuts," Dr. Reed said. He also cast doubt on the information, but admitted that was one thing he hadn't asked in China.

Meanwhile, the delegation of Chinese zoologists and officials, including the director of the Bureau of Public Service, who is described as being in charge of "public parks, zoos, streets, repairing, forestry, public housing, electricity, gas, water and sewerage" in Peking ("What does Mao do?" asked a reporter), were plowing through a 10-course meal at the Yenching Palace.

For some of them, it was the first decent meal they had seen in days. "We fed them a roast beef platter in Guam, and they just looked at that big hunk of raw meat," said Reed. "They were too polite to say anything, but we noticed they didn't lick their plates as we did."

One of the things they were putting away at lunch yesterday, in between the toasts to peace, Nixon, Mao and pandas, was bamboo shoots, which is also what pandas eat. "Yes, but the pandas get fresh ones, and we can only get canned," said one of the restaurant owners. The zoo grows its own fresh bamboo, "but they don't market it to us," she said.

And how did Dr. Reed eat in China?

"Oh, man. Oh, boy. Oh, wow," he said.

—April 18, 1972

'Aladdin':
'Histrionic' Tour de Force

By Henry Mitchell

Belly dancers in the British Embassy under the patronage of Lady Ramsbotham have danced right sweetly all week long. One is glad one went.

One would not have dreamed, for that matter, of missing it.

And yet, like so many things that seem at first to lie before us like a land of dreams, it was not quite what one had thought it would be.

Lady Ramsbotham, wife of the British ambassador, provided the patronage, the aegis, the blessing, the imprimatur, as you might say. But she is not—in case anyone was so vicious as to think—turning the embassy into a harem or a center for general orgy or even one of those "conference centers" where the Lord only knows what goes on.

All that has happened, once the fantasies are cleared away, is a children's show called "Aladdin and His Wonderful Lamp," and the belly dancers or slave girls are merely incidental, however welcome, in this vaudeville holiday treat.

A major production of the British Embassy Players, the cast is drawn largely from the embassy staff with some Americans. It is what the English call a "pantomime," and its interminable length (not that the children wearied) and rustic humor in which everybody on stage falls at least once per scene and is burned or scalded at least once per act, is said to derive from the old Italian commedia dell'arte.

Now we all know the story of Aladdin. We all know the storied romance of Basra, Bagdad and Isfahan.

In the British version, however, the setting is Peking and, this reviewer thinks, either Liverpool or Hull. It is all geographically unsettling, if one may say so, and this reviewer cannot find anything in the original "Aladdin" about the Widow Twankey operating a laundry, or a giant panda, or two British cops on scooters—in a word, substantial liberties appear to have been taken with the text.

The dancing girls (provided by Adrianna's Mecca of Middle-Eastern Dance on Wisconsin Avenue) seemed fully authentic, however, and one would willingly have assigned them greater roles in the interests of historicity.

Nevertheless, such is the magic of the stage, the magic of a small orchestra, the magic of stage lighting, the magic of living breathing pratfalling actors, that one is soon enchanted. Of course, one's childhood was only several years ago. The fellow working the bass viol, the girl dimly flirting with the piano keys by a 15-watt light, the actress in quilted satin on the gorgeous stage — well, one cannot resist it long.

From time to time the children screamed warnings to the stage that theft or other wickedness was afoot. Investigative reporters all.

Forthcoming productions (needless to say, this Aladdin is totally sold out, so don't apply for tickets) are a Noel Coward play and a summertime music hall.

Last year Sir Peter Ramsbotham sang "She's Only a Bird in a Gilded Cage," which may give you the idea.

There is no inherent reason the Embassy Players could not put on "Diocletian's Revels" next January, under the patronage of the Bishop of Ely, with the dancing girls and firecrackers and much else, though this has not been announced or even planned; and there is no real reason, some have said, why the tots have to get all the tickets.

—January 11, 1975

Dickk's Last Tape (With Apologies to Samuel Beckett)

By Tom Donnelly

It has been suggested that there may be in existence a tape of President Nixon "listening to his own tapes," or as one journalist put it, "eavesdropping on his own eavesdropping." When I first heard of this peculiar possibility I at once thought of Samuel Beckett's haunting playlet, "Krapp's Last Tape," wherein a man "meditatively eats a banana" and plays back an autobiographical recording he had made many years earlier. It's not, of course, the specifics of Beckett that fit the present case: It's the mood.

Are you ready for "Dickk's Last Tape"?

A late evening in the future.

Dickk's den.

A small table occupies a front and center position on the stage; two drawers in the table open toward the audience. On the table there are a tape recorder with a microphone, a number of cardboard boxes containing reels of recorded tapes and a telephone.

Seated at the table is a man with a prominent nose (a ski-jump nose, some might call it), a strangely nervous smile and eyes with a glitter of defiance in them. Though he is not a movie star or pro football player, the man's face is hauntingly familiar. And no wonder, that face has been shown thousands of times on television and in the newspapers, two media the man devoutly detests. It is a President of the United States who confronts us. Or would confront us, if he didn't have this habit of averting his gaze and staring suspiciously into the shadows.

Dickk remains a moment motionless, heaves a great sigh, looks at his watch, fumbles in his pockets, takes out a small bunch of keys, raises it to his eyes, selects a key, gets up and moves to the front of the table. He stoops, unlocks the first drawer and takes out an opened carton of cottage cheese. He sniffs it, studies it and then drops it on the floor. He unlocks the other drawer, takes out another opened carton of cottage cheese, sniffs it, apparently finds it good, places it on the table, rummages around in the drawer and produces a ketchup bottle. He upends the ketchup bottle, aims it at the carton on the table, misses, unwittingly puts his left foot in the carton of cottage cheese on the floor, nearly falls but rights himself and this time manages to cover the cheese in the carton on the table with ketchup.

There is a feeling that he is going through a once vital ritual, that once upon a time he sat at his desk, ordering the affairs of a nation and even of a world while fueling himself with the most modest of victuals. It was for lesser men to dine on beef and red wine . . .

Dickk peers into one of the cardboard boxes on the table and takes out a spool.

Dickk: "Ah! Box . . . three . . . spool five! Spool! (He smiles happily.) "Spooool! Love that word!" (He loads the spool on the tape-recorder, takes a fork out of his vest pocket, flicks a switch and prepares to listen to a tape as he digs into his cottage cheese and ketchup.)

The first voice we hear is that of a very much younger Dickk.

Young Dickk: "I come before you as a man whose honesty and integrity have been questioned . . . I am sure that you have read the charge and you've heard it that I, a United States senator, took $18,000 from a group of my supporters. Now, was that wrong?" Dickk switches off the machine and talks to himself for a bit. "No, no, no, that wasn't. Every penny of that $18,000 went to help me get elected. How could that be wrong? How? How? How?" (He sits there, brooding.) "Those days were so long ago and far away. How young I was! Eighteen thousand! You couldn't landscape a half-way decent petunia bed for that! Why, you couldn't buy . . ." (He is silent as he aimlessly stirs the ketchup into his cottage cheese.)

Dickk tries another tape; since it is old and frayed and full of jumps the effect is somewhat surrealistic.

Dickk's voice: "Now . . . what I am going to do — and incidentally this is unprecedented in the history of American politics — I am going to give this television and radio audience a complete financial history. . . . I was born in 1913 . . . and I should say this — that Pat doesn't have a mink coat but she does have a respectable Republican cloth coat . . . I probably should tell you, because if I don't they'll probably be saying this about me, too — we did get something — a gift . . . You know what it was? . . . It was a little cocker spaniel dog . . . all the way from Texas. Black and white spotted . . . And our little girl — Tricia, the 6-year-old — named it Checkers . . . and I just want to say this right now, that regardless of what they say about it, we're going to keep it . . ."

(He turns off the tape and sits there vacuously repeating the dog's name.) "Checkers! Checkers! Checkers!"

Dickk removes this tape and puts on another. A woman's voice is heard saying, "And wait'll you see the new draperies! To anybody else — like Aristotle Onassis — the cost would be $1,000 a yard but if you like them you'll be getting them for $850. Or I guess I should say the taxpayers will! Oh, believe me, San Clemente is going to be a byword. It's a name that will live in the annals of interior decoration. Now I was thinking of solid gold . . ."

Dickk sighs, puts more ketchup on his cottage cheese and tries another tape.

A male voice, one of conspiratorial timbre, says: "All right, Mr. President, now here's our plan . . ."

With a snarl Dickk flicks off the tape recorder. He makes several grossly unflattering remarks about certain personnel, ending rather mildly with "Couldn't have pulled off operation Broom Closet . . ."

Dickk tries still another spool, and this one he seems to find soothing: "Fourteen million from them, and 20 million from *them* and they'll do it in money orders, traveler's checks, bonds or cash tucked into a few dozen brown paper bags . . ." Dickk plays this tape over and over, smiling the while.

Dickk's smile is even broader when he plays the next tape. "Yes, indeed, Reverend Billy, as I have said before, serenity in battle is a product of faith. And faith, apart from that which stems from religious heritage and moral training, comes to an individual after he has gone through a necessary period of indecision, of doubt and soul-searching, and resolves that his cause is right and determines that he must fight the battle to the finish."

Dickk opens another box, rummages about in it, grows increasingly agitated and begins to mutter, "Tape X! Where is Tape X! The prize of my whole collection!Somebody's been getting into my tapes! That's the one where I made my big announcement! The one where I resigned!" After he says this he stands a moment, bemused. "Or, did I? Did I say I wouldn't resign? Did I tough it out? Isn't that strange? I don't remember! Oh where, oh where can it be?" In his extreme agitation Dickk is throwing tapes this way and that way, and cottage cheese and ketchup the other way . . .

There is no tape on the machine, but Dickk has inadvertently flicked the switch and the spools are revolving in silence.

— November 9, 1973

'Woof,' He Said, 'Where's the Hare?'

By Henry Mitchell

Up rose the sun, and up rose 100 of the nation's most energetic basset hounds to streak through the woods of Loudoun County, Va., in search of their quarry at 6:30 yesterday morning.

The rabbit was seen many times in the ensuing hours, though not often by the bassets.

"You would not expect a basset to catch a rabbit," said Ralph Bushee of Carbondale, Ill., who had flown in for these national field trials for basset packs. "Oh, if the rabbit were very old or sick — but it is not the expected thing. It's thought perfectly successful if the bassets chase him down his hole." It is almost as good if the hounds just sound off.

The National Basset Club trials are sponsored by the National Beagle Club — a tender point for the basset people who tend to think beagles are bassets that didn't quite make it in breadth of paw, magnificence of ear and dewlap, amplitude of face (wrinkles) and so on.

"Why, there's Sovereign," Bushee went on, viewing the brilliant day in a little clearing in the woods, perched on one of those sticks people sit on at race tracks. "They've put him back in the pack four times already this morning."

Sovereign, for his part, thought a woodland stream was more interesting than some dumb rabbit and was drinking contentedly, wagging his tail.

"The thing the judges are severe on," Bushee added, "is leaving the pack. That, and not working."

Sovereign sniffed about a black walnut tree, gazed steadily at a dogwood laden with scarlet fruit, sauntered under a huge possum-grape vine without noticing the berries, and ignored the distant music of the hounds who had picked up the scent about a quarter-mile distant.

Bushee, retired curator of the rare book collection at the University of Southern Illinois, walks slowly and often rests.

"Basseting is a gentle pastime," he said, not like golf or gardening or strenuous things like that.

276

"What more could you want?" he demanded, still surveying the world from his stool which becomes his stick when he decides to walk on a bit. "Here we have already had two sightings of the rabbit, without moving."

"That's true," said a woman. "We have seen more rabbits than hounds."

A cottontail appeared from nowhere and sped within 10 feet of Bushee, who notified the huntsman, who blew his horn, and the whips (who whip the ground in an effort to keep the hounds more or less together) came alive, and the hounds were greatly encouraged to pick up the trail, and in due time the word got through to them.

Sovereign was the first to flash past (he had either rejoined the pack or else was strolling in the neighborhood when the rabbit hopped by) and headed up hill after the rabbit.

The other bassets, arriving somewhat later, had a grand conference on which way to go. They saw Sovereign heading up the hill, so after much sniffing and thought, they headed down the hill, roughly 180 degrees off course.

Eric George, in the bright livery of the Strathalbyn Club of St. Louis, hove into view, on foot like everybody else except the two judges who were on horses in order to see better.

"Yes, they're lovely," he agreed when a woman said the hounds looked just great. Accompanying him was Jane Luce of the Tantivy Club of Kansas City, who had the distinction of having a rabbit run between her legs earlier in the day.

"Beowulf and Elizabeth have been pulled," said Bushee when the others courteously asked how his Southern Illinois Club hounds were doing. That is, they had been eliminated from the trials, as judges weeded down to the winner (who was Calliope of the Flint Hill Club of Long Island).

"Elizabeth is too independent," Bushee said.

"Well, sometimes you need some independence in a basset hound," said Miss Luce.

But not, apparently, as much as you find in Elizabeth.

Sovereign was wandering about. He too was pulled and sent back to the kennels, at the center of the National Beagle Club's headquarters, which is a 500-acre farm devoted to raising wild rabbits so the dogs can find one to chase, eventually. The beagle trials are next weekend, but yesterday ended the three days devoted entirely to bassets.

"One theory of the basset's origin is that they descend from St. Hubert hounds, those great medieval French hounds, bred on down [that is, lower to the earth]. There are English bassets," Bushee said, "which are faster on their feet, deriving from an outcross to harriers."

Then there are show bassets, which may not be worth a ham hock when it comes to hunting.

"Listen to them, isn't that beautiful," said Bushee as an excited yowping floated gently over the next hill where the bassets were hot after the rabbit or thought they were. "You can tape them, you know, and reconstruct the whole event that way." You, of course, recognize what each hound sounds like. Some have voices like flutes, some like the bell at Notre Dame, and some like a 1942 tractor. Bushee's hounds, it was learned, have beautiful voices. So do George's and Luce's.

"As I see it," Bushee said, "the great thing is to listen to their music, and from time to time see them race past. They should come almost in single file, gaily feathering [that is, briskly wagging their tails held straight up]. No need to chase after them. The rabbit runs in a circle, and the hounds follow, so you can't miss them even if you stay still in one place."

Sure enough, the hounds reappeared, not in single file, but muddling about like a compass in the Hall of Magnets. Their tails were certainly wagging, however.

Sometimes a hound disgraced his colors by stopping, when he got a cluster of humans, going from one to another to see if he was the rabbit.

Your good basset hound does not have a mean, brittle, narrow sort of intelligence, like those dogs that can be taught tricks, but rather has that profounder cast of mind that some, who do not know the basset well, might call stupidity.

Luncheon was served back at the headquarters, two and a half hours late—bassets are excessively hard to hurry along—with Joseph B. Wiley Jr. of Bedminster, N.Y., and Mrs. Walter L. Moore of St. Louis presiding as joint chairmen of the trials.

"Beauregard, is that you. BEAURE-GARD," hollered John E. Campbell of Barrington, Ill., making a quick check of the kennels before lunch. Yes, it was Beauregard. He did not win as your common victors do. He was dewlapped like a Thessalian bull, however, and could sing at heaven's gate as well as any lark. He was tired.

He greeted Campbell courteously (though he is not even in Campbell's pack) and spread his great paws against the wire and sang briefly, then headed for some nice straw for a nap. If you are going to be a great beauty, you need your rest.

The huntsmen were all at lunch by this time, but the hounds in their kennels were dozing, occasionally wagging a tail in their dreams, though none, so far as could be analyzed, was chasing rabbits.

—November 4, 1974

Contributors

HENRY ALLEN was born in 1941 in New Jersey and was graduated from Hamilton College, in Clinton, N.Y., with a major in English literature in 1967, after a three-year enlistment in the Marine Corps.

Allen took a copyediting job at the *New Haven Register,* then became a trainee at the *New York News,* where he did financial writing. He then traveled to India, returning in April 1969 to support himself at two more journalism jobs in New York while he devoted his energies to poetry, "new consciousness" and radical politics. Soon after, he hired on at the *Post.*

Allen is writing a book on the arrival of the concept of religious enlightenment in America, titled *The Flash,* for the Viking Press.

JUDY BACHRACH, born in 1947 in New York City, is a graduate of Chatham College in Pittsburgh, Pa., and holds an M.S. from the Columbia University Graduate School of Journalism. For two and a half years, she was television critic at the *Baltimore Sun.* In January 1973, she became the New York correspondent for the *Philadelphia Inquirer;* five months later she got a call from the *Washington Post,* came on down, and stayed.

PHIL CASEY is an old newspaperman and glad of it. He is 54. has been in the newspaper business for 28 years, most of those with the *Washington Post,* and he's glad of that, too.

He was born in Portland, Maine, was graduated from Colby College in Waterville, Maine, and attended the U.S. Army during World War II. It was a lousy job, he says. This is better.

TOM DONNELLY was born in Syracuse, N.Y., in 1918 and was graduated from Syracuse University in 1940 but has not received his diploma to this day because his receiving it was made contingent upon his paying dues to some honorary society he belonged to. For five years or so he wrote obituaries and movie reviews for the *Syracuse Herald-Journal.* From approximately 1945 to 1972 he worked for the *Washington Daily News.* Upon the expiration of that journal, he joined the staff of the *Washington Post's* Style section to write a very general column titled Donnelly's Revue.

JOEL DREYFUSS, who writes here of Ted Poston and the *New York Post,* had been a reporter for that paper, as well as for the Associated Press, before joining the *Washington Post* Style section in 1973. Born in Haiti in 1945, he was reared in Monrovia, Liberia, and New York City, and he holds a bachelor of science degree in sociology from the City College of New York.

PAUL HUME, born in Chicago, where he grew up to study piano, organ, voice and the theoretical side of music, has been music editor of the *Washington Post* since 1947. During 25 of those years, he has also been a professor of music at Georgetown University, as well as director of its choral groups. The author of *Catholic Church Music,* he has also collaborated with his wife, writer Ruth Fox Hume, on the biographies of pianist Paderewski and tenor John McCormack.

MICHAEL KERNAN, a Washington Post staff member since 1967, was one of the original crew of the Style section. Before coming to Washington by way of a self-granted fellowship for six months of freelance writing in London, Kernan worked for 13 years at the *Redwood City* (Calif.) *Tribune.* Earlier, he worked four years at the *Watertown* (N.Y.) *Daily Times,* editing and writing. Kernan, born in 1927, is a 1949 graduate of Harvard College, with honors in English.

ALAN M. KRIEGSMAN, came to the *Washington Post* as music critic in 1966 from the position of assistant to the president of the Juilliard School of Music. Before that he was drama and music critic of the *San Diego* (Calif.) *Union* and from 1954-60 lectured and taught at Barnard and Columbia Colleges and Columbia University. He holds bachelor's and master's degrees in music from Columbia University and studied at the University of Vienna on a Fulbright Scholarship. Kriegsman is now dance critic of the *Post.*

MYRA MacPHERSON was born in Marquette, Mich., and began her newspaper career in Detroit, first on the *Free Press* and then the *Times.* In 1960, she joined the *Washington Star* as a general assignment reporter. At one point she wrote a city-side feature column, and from 1966 to 1968 covered Washington for the women's pages of the *New York Times.*

MacPherson came to the *Washington Post* in the fall of 1968 and wrote for Style from its inception in January 1969 until the fall of 1973, when she took a leave of absence to write a book on the effect of politics on political families. Called *The Power Lovers,* it is scheduled for publication in 1975 by G. P. Putnam's Sons.

JUDITH MARTIN, 36, is a native Washingtonian, not in the usual Washington usage of the term to mean someone who has lived in Washington for more than 12 years, but because she was born there. She came to the *Washington Post* directly from Wellesley College. For 10 years, she covered diplomatic parties for the women's section; when that section was incorporated into Style, Martin got to sit down and write cultural and feature stories. A collection of her *Post* columns has been published under the title of *The Name on the White House Floor* (Coward, McCann & Geoghegan, 1972).

EUGENE L. MEYER, a native New Yorker, got his start in journalism with the *New York Herald-Tribune* and then the *Philadelphia Evening Bulletin,* after graduating from Columbia College (N.Y.) in 1964. An occasional contributor to Style, Meyer, 32, joined the *Washington Post* in 1970 as a member of the metropolitan staff and won a Newspaper Guild Front Page citation for a series on the politics of inner city redevelopment.

HENRY MITCHELL was born Nov. 24, 1923, in Washington as his parents were passing through but grew up in Memphis, his family's home. He was educated, as the term goes, at the University of Virginia over a period of seven years and left law school without a degree. His employment resume lists his first job as copy boy at the *Evening Star* in Washington; then to the *Commercial Appeal* at Memphis for 15 years; then editor for four years of *The Delta Review,* then to the *Washington Post* in 1970, first as a desk man then as a writer. He lives in the city with his wife, son and daughter.

In 1975, Mitchell was awarded a Special Citation by the judges of the Washington-Baltimore Newspaper Guild Front Page Awards "for bringing elegant writing, wit and knowledge to subjects too often dealt with in pedestrian style."

SALLY QUINN, an Army Brat, was born July 1, 1941, in Savannah, Ga.

Before her father retired, she moved 22 times, lived in the United States, Japan, Greece, Germany, Switzerland, Spain, Mexico and France, and she attended 22 schools. After graduating from Smith College in Northampton, Mass., with an A.B. in theater arts, she went to Europe for several years, then returned to the U.S.

Until she was 27 years old, Quinn had never held down a job longer than six months. She'd also had no previous journalistic experience when she joined the Style section for a trial period in June 1969. But she has been with the *Post* ever since, except for a six-month sabbatical as the first network anchorwoman for the CBS Morning News. She is the author of *We're Going to Make You a Star,* published by Simon and Schuster in 1975.

TOM SHALES was born in the Midwest (Elgin, Ill.) but left it to attend The American University in Washington, D.C., then stayed on to become entertainment editor of the perpetually faltering weekly *D.C. Examiner.* After two and a half years of that, the paper folding under him, he began writing freelance pieces for the *Washingtonian* magazine, a local arts paper called *Woodwind* and the *Washington Post,* which finally hired him.

Now a general assignment reporter in the Style section, Shales, 30, has also written for *Oui* magazine, *After Dark* and National Public Radio, which distributes his weekly film reviews and occasional interviews on tape to 150 noncommercial FM radio stations.

JEANNETTE SMYTH was named "copyboy" at the *Washington Post* in August 1969. A year and a half later, when she was named after her husband, the Style section hired her as a reporter.

Born in 1948 in Roanoke, Va., she was educated in the Caribbean, Africa and South America, where her father worked as a fisheries biologist. She went to school, however, at Ithaca College, graduating in 1969 with an A.B. in comparative literature, minors in philosophy and sociology.

NICHOLAS VON HOFFMAN, who now writes a syndicated column which appears in Style, was born in New York City but really began his career in Chicago. From 1954 to 1963 he worked with Saul Alinsky on the Industrial Areas Foundation. He then spent three years with the *Chicago Daily News* as a race relations reporter, and it was that experience that he drew upon to write his first book, *Mississippi Notebook.* In 1966 he joined the *Washington Post's* national staff and in 1969 moved over to Style. Until recently he appeared as a regular commentator with James J. Kilpatrick on CBS' "60 Minutes."

HOLLIE I. WEST, unlike many of his relatives, has never lived in Boley, Okla., the subject of his contribution to this volume. He was born in the nearby town of Wewoka, in Oklahoma's once oil-rich Seminole County.

West studied journalism at Ohio State University and was graduated in 1959. He worked for the *Oakland* (Calif.) *Tribune* and the Associated Press between 1963 and 1967, covering the free speech movement in Berkeley, race riots in Chicago and municipal politics in New York City. West came to the *Washington Post* in 1967, and in 1973-74 he was a Nieman Fellow at Harvard University.

282

JEAN M. WHITE, as a high school junior, started working for *Grit,* which is not a household cleanser but a national weekly, published in her home town of Williamsport, Pa. Her newspaper career was interrupted by studies at Bucknell University and a job as a chemist, but she eventually decided to try newspaper work again.

White went to the Columbia Graduate School of Journalism, where she was graduated in 1953 with a Pulitzer Traveling Scholarship, which took her to Lapland. She had begun work on the *Washington Post* two months before leaving for Lapland, then returned as a general assignment reporter with a specialty in arts coverage. She moved to the National Desk to cover urban problems and the civil rights scene. White came to Style as cultural editor and two years later returned to reporting.

WILLIAM CRAWFORD WOODS was born in Philadelphia in 1944 and educated at Chapel Hill, George Washington (A.B. philosophy) and Johns Hopkins (A.M. writing). He served in the Army as a broadcast journalist stationed in Tokyo in the late '60s and did a little college teaching after.

In 1968, he walked in off the street to convince the editors of Style to establish the position of "rock critic," which he filled until succumbing to the lure of Hollywood, where he spent an abortive summer as a screenwriter for Otto Preminger in 1970. On his return, he became a staff reporter and television critic for the *Post,* but fled that job within six months to freelance.

Woods' first novel, *The Killing Zone,* was mentioned in the *New York Times'* Best Fiction list in 1970, and his short fiction, which has appeared in slicks and quarterlies, in the *Best American Short Stories* annual of the same year.

TOM ZITO, born on a hundred-degree day in September 1948, was reared in the quaint oil refining town of Bayonne, N.J. In 1970, Zito was graduated from Georgetown University, the nation's oldest Catholic college magna cum laude, Phi Beta Kappa, with an A.B. in philosophy. While at the university, Zito and (now) *Common Cause* regional manager Bob O'Leary created a radically oriented features magazine—*The Courier*—that infuriated the Jesuits and caught the eye of a *Washington Post* editor. After an interview Zito applied for a job as a photographer and eventually was hired as a writer.

In addition to his staff work at the *Post,* his writing has appeared in *Gleanings In Bee Culture, The Audio Engineering Journal of Mexico, Playboy, Commonweal, Esquire* and *Rolling Stone.*

THOMAS R. KENDRICK and **LON TUCK,** editor and managing editor of Style respectively, both began their *Washington Post* careers as copy aides.

Born in Brunswick, Maine, Kendrick, 41, received his A.B. from Amherst College, where he studied under Robert Frost and Benjamin DeMott, and later earned an A.M. in international communications from Indiana University. After working for a short time as a copy aide for the *Post,* he left to obtain his master's and serve three years in the Air Force. He returned to the *Post* in 1960 as a reporter (first covering the police beat and, ultimately, national civil rights stories in Mississippi and Alabama). In 1970, he left his position as deputy metropolitan editor to become managing editor of Style. He became editor in 1972.

Tuck, 37, is a Texan, born in Sherman, in the vicinity of which both sides of his family have lived for more than a century. He was one of the first of his family to leave—to attend Princeton—and not come back to stay. After returning to study law at the University of Texas, Tuck headed east again and eventually applied for a position with what was then his favorite newspaper, the *New York Herald-Tribune.* An editor there pointed him in the direction of Washington and the *Post,* which he joined in 1961. He has served as a copy aide, metropolitan reporter, Virginia editor, cultural editor and now managing editor of Style.

Suggested Readings

These lists include books and articles related to specific authors or articles in this volume, as well as other readings about "New," literary and personal journalism.

Books

Bernstein, Burton, *Thurber,* Dodd, Mead, 1975.

Dennis, Everette E. and William L. Rivers, *Other Voices: The New Journalism in America,* Canfield Press, 1974.

Flippen, Charles C., *Liberating the Media: The New Journalism,* Acropolis Books, 1974.

Gill, Brendan, *Here at The New Yorker,* Random House, 1975.

Hayes, Harold, ed., *Smiling Through the Apocalypse: Esquire's History of the Sixties,* Dell, 1971.

Johnson, Michael L., *New Journalism: The Underground Press, the Artists of Non-Fiction and Changes in the Established Media,* University Press of Kansas, 1971.

Kesey, Ken, *Ken Kesey's Garage Sale,* Viking Press, 1973.

Kesey, Ken, *One Flew Over the Cuckoo's Nest,* Viking Press, 1962.

Kesey, Ken, *Sometimes a Great Notion,* Viking Press, 1971.

MacPherson, Myra, *The Power Lovers,* G. P. Putnam's Sons, 1975.

Martin, Judith, *The Name on the White House Floor,* Coward, McCann & Geoghegan, 1972.

Mills, Nicolaus, *The New Journalism: An Historical Anthology,* McGraw-Hill, 1973.

Mitchell, Joseph, *Old Mr. Flood,* Duell, 1948.

Pirsig, Robert, *Zen and the Art of Motorcycle Maintenance: An Inquiry Into Values,* William Morrow, 1974.

Quinn, Sally, *We're Going to Make You a Star,* Simon and Schuster, 1975.

Solotaroff, Theodore, ed., *Writers and Issues,* New American Library, 1969.

Thurber, James, *The Years With Ross,* Little, Brown, 1959.

Weber, Ronald, *The Reporter as Artist: A Look at the New Journalism Controversy,* Hastings House, 1974.

Welty, Eudora, *Losing Battles,* Random House, 1970.

Welty, Eudora, *The Curtain of Green and Other Stories,* Harcourt Brace Jovanovich, 1941.

Welty, Eudora, *The Optimist's Daughter,* Random House, 1972.

Wolfe, Tom, *The Electric Kool-Aid Acid Test,* Farrar, Straus & Giroux, 1968.

Wolfe, Tom, *The Kandy-Kolored Tangerine-Flake Streamline Baby,* Farrar, Straus & Giroux, 1965.

Wolfe, Tom, *The New Journalism,* Harper & Row, 1973.

Wolfe, Tom, *Radical Chic & Mau-Mauing the Flak Catchers,* Farrar, Straus & Giroux, 1970.

Woods, William Crawford, *The Killing Zone,* Harper's Magazine Press, 1970.

Articles

Arlen, Michael J., "Notes on the New Journalism," *The Atlantic,* May 1972.

Balz, Daniel J., "Bad Writing and New Journalism," *Columbia Journalism Review,* September/October 1971.

Dennis, Everette E. and William L. Rivers, "What Is the New Journalism?" *Communication,* Fall 1973.

Gordon, John, "Tom Wolfe: Reactionary Chic," *Ramparts,* January 1972.

Halberstam, David, "Eustace Tilly Revisited," *(more),* April 1975.

Hentoff, Nat, "Behold the New Journalism — It's Coming After You!" *Evergreen Review,* July 1968.

Macdonald, Dwight, "Parajournalism, or Tom Wolfe and His Magic Writing Machine," *The New York Review of Books,* August 26, 1965.

Macdonald, Dwight, "Parajournalism II: Wolfe and *The New Yorker,*" *The New York Review of Books,* February 3, 1966.

Markel, Lester, "Lester Markel: So What's New?" *The Bulletin* of the American Society of Newspaper Editors, January 1972.

McHam, David, "Old Ain't Necessarily Good, Either!" *The Bulletin* of the American Society of Newspaper Editors, January 1972.

McHam, David, "The Authentic New Journalists," *The Quill,* September 1971.

Murphy, James E., "The New Journalism: A Critical Perspective," *Journalism Monographs,* May 1974.

Newfield, Jack, "Is there a 'new journalism'?" *Columbia Journalism Review,* July/August 1972.

Newfield, Jack, "Journalism, Old, New and Corporate," *The Dutton Review* ed. by Susan Sterns, E. P. Dutton, 1970.

Podhoretz, Norman, "The Article as Art," *Doings and Undoings* by Norman Podhoretz, Farrar, Straus & Giroux, 1964.

Talese, Gay, "Joe Louis: The King as a Middle-aged Man," *Esquire,* June 1962.

Tebble, John, "The Old New Journalism," *Saturday Review,* March 13, 1971.

Van Gelder, Lindsy, "You Can't Make News Out of a Silk Purse," MS., November 1974.

Wakefield, Dan, "The Personal Voice and the Impersonal Eye," *The Atlantic,* June 1966.

Wolfe, Tom, "The New Journalism," *The Bulletin* of the American Society of Newspaper Editors, September 1970.

Wolfe, Tom, "Why They Aren't Writing the Great American Novel Anymore," *Esquire,* December 1972.